Theatres of Human Sacrifice

SUNY series in Psychoanalysis and Culture

Henry Sussman, editor

THEATRES OF
HUMAN SACRIFICE

*From Ancient Ritual
to Screen Violence*

MARK PIZZATO

STATE UNIVERSITY OF NEW YORK PRESS

Published by
STATE UNIVERSITY OF NEW YORK PRESS
ALBANY

For information, contact State University of New York Press, Albany, NY
www.sunypress.edu

Production, Laurie Searl
Marketing, Susan Petrie

Library of Congress Cataloging-in-Publication Data

Pizzato, Mark, 1960–
    Theatres of human sacrifice : from ancient ritual to screen violence / Mark Pizzato.
        p. cm. — (SUNY series in psychoanalysis and culture)
    Includes bibliographical references and index.
    ISBN 0-7914-6259-5 (alk. paper) — ISBN 0-7914-6260-9 (pbk. : alk. paper)
        1. Violence in motion pictures. 2. Violence in popular culture. I. Title. II. Series.

PN1995.9.V5P59 2004
791.43'6552—dc22
                                                                                2003070444

10   9   8   7   6   5   4   3   2   1

to my father

John Frank (Gianfranco) Pizzato

and my uncle

Anthony J. Catalano

who taught me the meaning

of making choices

in sacrifice

and

to my friend

Tullio Maranhão

who helped me find insight

in the crossing of cultures

may his crossing to the other world also be

enlightening

Contents

Acknowledgments

Parts of chapters 1, 3, and 4 were previously published in *Ethnologie und Inszenierung: Ansätze zur Theaterethnologie*, ed. Bettina E. Schmidt and Mark Münzel (Marburg: Förderverein Völkerkunde, 1998); in *Spectator* 16.2 (Spring/Summer 1996); and in the *Journal of Popular Film and Television* 26.2 (Summer 1998).

Special thanks to my colleagues who read (or heard) various parts of this book and gave their advice: Harvey Greenberg, Dale Grote, Jane Hoehner, Tony Jackson, Gary Maciag, Tullio Maranhão, Angelo Restivo, Catherine Rice, Teresa Scheid, and Judith Sebesta. Thanks also to the editors and readers at SUNY Press, especially James Peltz and Laurie Searl. Although Herbert Blau did not advise me on this book, I continue to be influenced by his generous advice on my work as a graduate student a decade ago.

I must also thank my sons, Luke and Peter, for their indulgence as I spent many hours at the computer screen, working on this opus rather than playing with them. Such sacrifices were not easy; I hope they value the result. Writing this book certainly helped me to work through the legacy of sacrifice in my own childhood, so as not to repeat it unaware.

Prologos

Why do humans perform acts of violence for a watching audience? This book explores the performance of violence in various cultures, from ancient human and animal sacrifices to modern sports and cinema, through psychoanalytic theories and theatrical paradigms. How is the sublimation of human sacrifice today, on sports fields and movie screens, like and unlike actual bloodshed in prior cultures? Does it create a current community of ritual belief in the divine powers of mythic heroes and demons? What effects might melodramatic violence have on a mass audience—with purely good and evil forces battling apocalyptically onscreen—especially after September 11, 2001, and the subsequent "war on terrorism" in our new millennium? Is a fundamental catharsis of fear and desire, of terrorist paranoia and capitalist greed, still possible today, through complex characters and tragic violence, involving our mass-media warriors and godlike stars?

Life sacrifices each of us. In a biological sense, we are offerings of evolution, required to die, whether we reproduce or not, so that our species will advance to new generations beyond us.[1] Theologically, we might believe in another, metaphysical plan for our lives. But each of us must bear the sacrificial legacy and repetition temptation of specific traumas in our given fate of family, class, and race—casting us as offerings. Through such social and internal pressures, we make further sacrifices, consciously or not, scripting the drama of our lives as a performance for others, including the audience that will outlive us. For we know we are going to die someday, with each second moving us closer to that endpoint. Each moment of life bears a movement toward death, threatening our hopes of immortality with the inevitable violence of decay. We may avoid thinking about our own deaths, yet we are attracted to the performance of violence by others, involving life-threatening fears or glimpses of death, onstage and onscreen. (The popularity of *America's Most Wanted*, *Cops*, *Fear Factor*, and *Survivor* as "reality TV," plus an overdose of that with the World Trade Center and Pentagon plane

1

crashes, are recent examples.) Through such spectatorship we experience the fear, suffering, and death of others vicariously. We identify with the struggle of the human offering or feel superior to the doomed victim. We explore the potential meanings of our own mortality, our being towards death, through the sacrifice of others onscreen.[2]

The performance of violence, from ancient ritual to screen sacrifices today, gives context and sense to the losses of life, gradual or sudden, in each spectator's particular death drive.[3] But such sense-making, through surrogate bloodshed and dramatic fictions, may cause a repetition of violence (by inspiring vengeful imitation) or a curative awareness of its disastrous consequences, depending on the melodramatic or tragic modes of performance. In the pages that follow, I will explore this thesis through many historical examples and theoretical details. Those readers who become frustrated with the denser passages may skip to the end, to the "Exodos," to consider my conclusions, then return to the prior comparisons for further insights.

Pleasurable entertainment—making money through the melodramatic thrill ride—has become the dominant aim of screen violence today, rather than a more complex catharsis through tragic insights. The danger of a Manichean or fascist worldview, with simplistic projections of good and evil, has vastly increased with melodrama's success as a violent pleasure from nineteenth-century (and prior) stages to current multimedia screens. Consider how many more dramas of death are watched in movies and television today, by all classes of society, compared with earlier periods of theatre. Like the best drama of ancient Greece, challenging the Dionysian audience with a new rite, to question myth, fate, and gods, cinema and television sometimes involve the mass audience in a communal working through of specific, personal and social traumas—when complex characters and tragic plots are presented onscreen. More often, though, we get a superficial expression and temporary purging of current fears and desires through normative, melodramatic violence (addictively masking deeper traumas): a purely good hero saves or avenges innocent victims by almost losing to, yet triumphing over clearly evil villains.[4] We are at a critical point now in the long history of violent entertainment from ancient theatre to today's cinema and television, especially with the current melodramatic characters and justifications for violence in the "war against terrorism." Shall we accept and enjoy simple violence in movie and TV fiction? Or will we seek more complex engagements with the Real, beyond imaginary stereotypes and symbolic polarities of good and evil,[5] so as not to repeat the violence of prior sacrifices?

For one hundred years, psychoanalysis has helped individual patients cathartically work through the repressed memories, wild fantasies, cryptic dreams, and repetition compulsions of sacrificial traumas. For thousands of years, theatre has experimented with replaying traumatic dramas as collective dreams, fictional and real, to entertain and instruct, so as not to repeat actual sacrifices of blood and pain offstage. This book will focus on specific edges of the conventional theatre history narrative, finding in those margins the traces of ritual sacrifice that theatre today often masks, especially in the melodramatic modes of mainstream cinema and TV sports. The repetition of violence onstage or onscreen, in its fictional safety as "just play," might appear quite distinct from actual human or animal bloodshed in religious sacrifice. ("No animals were harmed in the making of this movie," the screen sometimes professes.) Yet theatre's sublimation of ritual bloodshed towards fictional violence still involves the investment of emotion and time by actors, directors, designers, technicians, and spectators. With cinema there is a lapse in time between the film artists' sacrifices and the audience's ritual participation. But bodies and minds also submit to the rite on both sides of the screen. What is gained in the sublimation from ritual bloodshed to fictional, stage and screen violence is a further degree of repetition and creativity. Actors can offer their lives again and again on the live stage, rising from death at the curtain call. Or they can be shown many more times as ghosts of themselves onscreen. But the reality of the investment as a sacrifice, for good or ill, for both players and watchers, is often lost. Its mortal wounds are overlooked or justified through the offering's transcendent theatricality and pleasurable entertainment—unless a more tragic awareness of trauma, involving particular repressions and repetitions, is evoked.

TRAGEDY IN MELODRAMA

Displays of violence have become quite commonplace on our film and TV screens. Usually, the violence onscreen is portrayed melodramatically, with clear-cut villains who deserve the pain and heroes who ultimately triumph over fear, suffering, and conflict. But I would argue that today, like in ancient Greece, the best in theatre and popular entertainment touches upon the tragic wound of mortality in each of us, through specific sacrificial imperatives played out on the stage or screen, providing a potential catharsis of spectators' sympathies and fears. This book seeks to redefine Aristotle's notion of catharsis in relation to modern stage and screen violence—as well as ancient ritual sacrifice—through current psychoanalytic and theatrical theories. I will revise a doctrine at the heart of Euro-American theatre's initial emergence in ancient Greece, by applying it to various types of violent performances at the edges of that tradition. This exploration will shed new light on theatre's aesthetic and historical boundaries. But it will also address the problematic effects of dramatic violence, as shown on millions of cinema screens today.

My goal is not to attack melodrama itself as a villain, nor to promote live theatre and ancient ritual as generically superior to screen media. Indeed, I will argue that the melodramatic mode provides a foundation for tragedy—in theatre's emergence from prior rites in ancient Greece and in parallel rites and contests of other cultures. Although the term *melodrama* is only a few hundred years old, its polar, good and evil characters, its innocent victims, its violent conflicts, its revenge plots, and its triumphant endings can be found in the mythic and communal context of ancient sacrifices: with warring gods, human or animal scapegoats, cosmic cycles of destruction, and promises of transcendence. Christianity also provides the melodramatic villainy of Satan and his devils, along with the Jews in their crucifixion of Jesus, as shown in many medieval plays with their violent plots and spectacles, or in the recent film *The Passion of the Christ*. (But the triumph of Christ on the cross also bears a tragic dimension of sacrifice, as considered in chapter 5 here.) American film and TV melodramas—from westerns to war movies and sci-fi, from film noir's gangsters and spies to cop, lawyer, rescue, and hospital shows, from horror movies to slasher and serial killer dramas—reveal the expansion of this culture's heroic ego, in the past century, with a manifest superego destiny to save certain victims and the world's order from enemies, criminals, and aliens.

Despite its escapist adventures and emotional manipulations, melodrama may have some positive effects: promoting communal strength and individual courage. Yet it typically does this by evoking paranoid terrors and projecting pure evil upon certain vilified types, focusing the abject mourning of loss into blame against others and violent action in revenge. Some melodramas, especially since the Vietnam War, have involved a more tragic questioning of formerly good and evil characterizations and ostensibly moral violence. But the usual formula in most Hollywood action movies perpetuates conventional American stereotypes of good and evil, with righteous justifications for violence, in the sacrificial rites of millions of movie spectators, in theatre seats worldwide—extending the missionary reach of global capitalism and its secular religion of entertainment. Even the terrorist counterattacks of September 11, 2001, making real the violent scenes from numerous disaster movies and alien-invader films, while producing thousands of tragic victims in the "holy war" of Muslim martyrs against the virtual reality of Western materialism, created new figures of melodramatic villainy for TV news shows and subsequent cinematic fictions.

Thus, the reemergence and media expansion of spectacular, sacrificial bloodshed, from ancient rites to modern stages and screens, conveys the terror of potential chaos, while rehearsing an ultimate submission to providential authority—with melodrama's seductive formula of the good being threatened by evil, yet triumphing in the end. Melodrama's reassertion of metaphysical righteousness, through individual heroism, becomes even more tempting, and perhaps addictive, with the postmodern collapse of universal values, fragmentation of the Self, and millennial dangers of Y2K catastrophes or apocalyptic terrorism. Spectators all over the world are buying Hollywood melodrama—though some may reverse its casting of stereotypes.

Ironically, the erotic display of and justification for violence in American action movies may encourage some extremists to become martyrs, to sacrifice their lives *against* the West as evil empire—while at the same time consoling Westerners (insecure in their virtual reality wealth) that "the good" is still on their side.

Psychologically, the purely good and bad objects of melodrama appeal to the paranoid-schizoid fantasies and fears forming the basis of the mind in early infancy, as well as later in life. With maturity, such identifications can become complex, depressive, yet integrative projections and introjections (in Kleinian terms).[6] But I would argue that this requires a tragic engagement with the Real, through a more ethical "sacrifice of the sacrifice," a crossing of fundamental, melodramatic fantasies, according to Lacanian theory and its cathartic cure for individual patients. In his *Poetics* (chapters 10–11) Aristotle criticized dramas that have simple plots, with little or no Discovery in the Peripety—as we see today in the superficial twists of violent action in many film melodramas. Instead, Aristotle advocated complex tragic dramas, where plot twists coincide with insightful recognition scenes, so that spectators' fearful sympathies with the flawed hero and his impending catastrophe might involve a more complete exploration of the sources and effects of violence, through the sacrificial offering onstage—a crossing of conventional expectations, especially in fantasies of revenge. Such complex drama is even more crucial today, with the multiplex screens and interactive media of our global marketplace shaping millions of minds, reinforcing or challenging fundamental fantasies of Self and Other.

The clear-cut morality of melodrama, with good victorious over evil in the end, can backfire with its justification for stereotypical projections, paranoid fears, and preemptive strikes against villainy in real life. Melodramatic politics have recently produced tragic results for innocent victims, with fundamentalist warfare against the evil Other, as the TV audience witnessed on 9/11, and in further acts of vengeance on both sides of the "Axis of Evil" since then. For several decades now, there have also been specific acts of copycat violence directly inspired by certain films in Europe and America, such as *A Clockwork Orange* and *Taxi Driver* in the 1970s and *Natural Born Killers* in the 1990s. (The latter two films and their copycat crimes will be considered in chapters 3 and 5.) When Stanley Kubrick learned that real-life gang members were imitating the violence of his characters in *A Clockwork Orange*, he took that film out of distribution in Britain and kept it out for a quarter of a century, until his death in 1999. Kubrick's film does offer a Brechtian critique of society, shifting sympathies and challenging viewers to rethink judicial punishment, through the explicit violence of Alex's gang and the hypocritical politics of his rehabilitation. The imprisoned Alex is tied up and forced to watch violent movies in a behavioral modification treatment that supposedly reassociates such actions with pain, instead of pleasure. This torture fails to cure him, however, and suggests a problem with the film's own cathartic potential. Kubrick never explores the specific sources and consequences of Alex's brutality, beyond his dull-witted, indulgent parents and purely vengeful victims. This encouraged some spectators to perceive the cruel acts as pleasurable entertainment, ripe for imitation—somewhat like the backfire in Alex's therapeutic overdose of screen violence. Perhaps the gang members even felt challenged by the film to repeat the violence, making it real, as a kind of "wickedness competition" (Seneca 2).

And yet, the popularity of melodrama onscreen today also sets up the vast potential for tragic insight, when heroes, villains, and victims are presented more fully, as flawed characters, bearing good and evil on both sides of the conflict and showing the self-destructiveness of revenge. Thus, a complex ethics of sacrifice will be theorized here: encouraging artists and audiences to create and watch fictional violence more critically, by sacrificing the normative ideals of melodramatic sacrifice—onstage, onscreen, and beyond. This critical, tragic catharsis, working against the easy violence and moral triumphs of popular melodramatic entertainment, may also bring some degree of cure against the repetition compulsions of vengeance and mimetic sacrifice in individuals, families, and communities.[7]

The theatre theories of Bertolt Brecht and Antonin Artaud, which will be used often in this study, have had some influence in film studies in recent decades.[8] But remarkably few film or TV scholars today consider the parallels and precedents with theatre. This may be due to the predominantly narrative approaches in the development of film studies through English and foreign language departments,[9] while the study of television has been "housed in schools of journalism and communication, which [have] relied heavily on social-science methodologies of the quantifying and positivist type" (Kaplan, "Feminist" 211). Film scholarship was greatly influenced by psychoanalytic theory in the 1970s and 1980s, especially through Christian Metz and various feminist appropriations of Lacan, and also in the 1990s through Slavoj Žižek. Cognitive science has provided strong competition recently, however, particularly through the work of David Bordwell, reconnecting film theory with the social-science approach of TV studies.[10] And yet, I would argue that both film and TV studies would benefit from a reconsideration of psychoanalytic theory through ritual and theatrical paradigms. My psychotheatrical approach suggests that the "image schemata" theorized by cognitive science, as organizational metaphors for thought, perception, and behavior, could be viewed more insightfully through the theatre of Jacques Lacan's imaginary, symbolic, and Real dimensions.

Today's theatre scholars do not often venture to discuss film and television either.[11] I hope that the current study will help to bridge these divides, if it is accepted in its interdisciplinary spirit, especially regarding the issues of performative violence, sacrifice, and catharsis. I am not attempting to trace direct historical influences between media, nor to find universal paradigms. But I will compare key examples between various cultures and periods—opening views upon our own performance media, sacrificial identities, and possibilities for catharsis (or its backfire of mimetic violence), through similar yet different events and structures in the past.

The term *catharsis* is sometimes used by film theorists, but usually in the simplistic sense of "purging" emotion, whether the argument is made for or against its validity as an effect of screen violence.[12] Through various performance examples in this book, I will argue for a reconsideration of Aristotelian catharsis—not only as a simple, melodramatic purging, but also as the complex, tragic purification or clarification of sympathy and terror, desire and fear.[13] I will also demonstrate how other paradigms of theatre (mask, costume, and setting, plus performance, audience, and choral spaces, as well as mimesis and script) relate to both ritual and screen violence.

There is no easy cure or quick remedy for ingrained patterns of repetitive violence in minds and societies. Stage or screen melodramas, at their worst, may reflect and confirm these fundamental fantasies, but do not cause violent acts without prior motives or mental illnesses in spectators. The appeal of violent action movies worldwide, crossing language barriers like nineteenth-century American stage melodrama, makes tragic drama rare onscreen and its potential remedy for social ills at best incremental. However, there is also a yearning in the mass audience today for more than just commercial entertainment, vicarious thrills, and illusory justice (as the recent popularity of Shakespeare as a screenwriter shows). There is always the possibility for a more ethical community of screen viewers and artists—engaging the Real through tragic complexity. This can be built, gradually, with increased media literacy: with spectators seeking the tragic edges of the Real in films and demanding better drama onscreen, through the votes of each cinema ticket and video rental. The pages ahead attempt to theorize the potential of a more complex catharsis for movie audiences in the future—by comparing ancient rites and contests with significant examples of tragedy within melodrama today. And yet, the actual effects of such cracks in the dominant melodramatic fabric of our virtual reality still depend a great deal on who is watching and how, as well as what is onscreen.

Several decades ago, literary theorist Peter Brooks argued that melodramatic characters symbolize the Freudian superego, ego, and id—making the effects of the genre akin to psychoanalytic catharsis: "cure and resolution in both cases come as the result of articulation which is clarification" (*Melodramatic* 202).[14] He also made a brief reference to the dominance of melodrama on television, as a way that "psychology has been externalized" (204). Brooks's view of melodrama (along with Thomas Elsaesser's) has greatly influenced film studies, with the recent valorizing of excessive emotion in "women's melodramas." Such films of the 1940s have been praised for their "exploration of woman's desires, wishes, conflicts" (Kaplan, *Motherhood* 64, 115), for involving perverse, bisexual viewing positions (Williams, "Film Bodies" 150), and for showing how "the hysteric *makes herself the limit* of the world she brings into being" (Copjec 265).[15] These views apply to what I would call tragic moments in melodrama—or in less violent, sentimental drama (and romance), from eighteenth-century theatre to twentieth-century film. Thus, I will address melodrama not as an exclusive genre, for women or men, but as a mode of fictional violence across various periods and media.[16]

Brooks distinguishes melodramatic from tragic catharsis, by stating that tragedy's mythic orders of meaning, invested with "holy" communal power, are irreversibly lost (*Melodramatic* 205–206).[17] He rejects "spurious appeals to synthetic mythologies," which might make tragedy possible again, and instead values the "purgation, purification, recognition . . . [and] clarification" of melodrama, which "substitutes for the rite of sacrifice an urging toward combat in life, an active, lucid confrontation with evil." I am taking precisely the opposite approach, because I disagree that the psychomythic orders of tragedy have been completely surpassed today and I find a continuing danger in the sacrificial simplicity of melodramatic victories over evil. This is not to deny melodrama's popular power and emotional expressiveness, especially for immigrant or international audiences, through visual and musical languages, from nineteenth-century theatre to twentieth-century film and TV. But my focus is on the spectrum of cathartic possibilities for sacrificial violence onstage and onscreen, between the opposing ideals of melodrama and tragedy—as a dialectic that appears within works of either genre.[18] (Comedy and farce as violent genres will not be considered here, although tragicomedy will be, as characteristic of postmodern catharsis, with shocking switches of tone and open-ended plots.) As Elsaesser puts it, regarding classic films: "the best American melodramas of the fifties [are] not only critical social documents but genuine tragedies, despite or rather because of the happy ending" ("Tales" 378). However, to fully understand the potential for tragedy within melodrama, onstage and onscreen, we need to look at the beginnings of Western theatre in ancient rites of violence.

THEATRE'S MATERIAL GHOSTS AND GODS

Two specific goals of ritual sacrifice continued in ancient theatre, despite its historical birth as distinct from such rites: (1) the oblatory, efficacious goal of giving up something valuable to the gods, in order to gain something in return,[19] and (2) the communal goal of confirming a collective identity through shared and repeated actions.[20] Theatre changed the oblatory orientation and communal significance. The giving up still involved the physical sacrifice of time, energy, and emotion onstage, yet not of blood or life, except as stage blood and fictional death. The ritual audience of gods and ancestral

ghosts, for whom the sacrifice was made, changed to involve the materially
present, human audience as Other,[21] although in ancient Greece the statue of
Dionysus was also part of the theatre audience (as were statues of other gods
in Roman times). The actor gave entertainment instead of his life's blood and
gained appreciation from the communal Other. The spectators also sacrificed
their individual presence (submitting to the communal act of watching
together) and received both personal pleasure and social instruction. Thus,
the two goals of ritual sacrifice became more integrally bound in theatre: the
actor's sacrifice, albeit fictional, was offered to the human audience, as well
as to the divine, and that also confirmed the collective identity of the audience as it watched the actor's individuality onstage.

However, this dialectic of individual and communal, human and divine,
mortal and transcendent, must have been crucial to ritual even prior to theatre's invention. Both ritual goals, of offering and communion, were fueled by
their opposite—some degree of disbelief and dissent, which made the collective act meaningful.[22] That dissenting voice, within the repeated actions of
ritual sacrifice, shows the inspiration for theatre's legendary emergence in
ancient Greece. But it also shows a Möbius strip of theatre within ritual and
ritual within theatre,[23] in the performance of individuality and community—
before and after theatre's "birth" as a distinct art form. Through that distinction, however, theatre emerged as a mode of performance with greater individual creativity—reacting against, yet fueled by ritual conformity and the
Other's demand for blood sacrifice.

Theatre was born, according to the ancient Greek tradition, in the sixth
century BCE when Thespis became an individual actor, stepping out of the ritual chorus, as it offered a dithyrambic song and dance for the god Dionysus.
Thespis (and others) invented theatre by impersonating a mythic character
and wearing a mask, creating dialogue in conflict with the choral voices.[24] But
the ritual chorus continued to play a crucial role in Greek theatre (in the
sixth and fifth centuries).[25] There was a separate contest for dithyrambic cho-
ruses at the festivals of Dionysus, along with the dramatic contests for
tragedies, satyr plays, and comedies. All three types of drama included a chorus of characters, singing and dancing their odes collectively in the orchestra
circle—a ritual body representing the Greek spectators. (The first and last
odes of the drama, for the entry and exit of the chorus, were called the *parodos* and *exodos*. The first episode, prior to the *parodos*, was the *prologos*.) The
Greek audience watched and reacted emotionally to the individual characters onstage, through the chorus performing in the orchestra, between the
stage and seats.[26] Dramatically, too, the actors performed their episodes
between the ritual odes of the chorus, and in dialogue with the chorus (or
choral leader) during some odes and episodes—as can be seen in the extant
scripts.[27] Certain ritual moments also appear during the episodes in various
plays. Orestes and Electra leave offerings at their dead father's tomb at the

beginning of *The Libation Bearers.* Jocasta enters holding garlands and incense to "visit the altars of the gods" in *Oedipus the King* (Sophocles 45). And Antigone insists, throughout the play titled after her, that her dead brother receive the proper, chthonic, burial rites. There are details of human sacrifice in Euripides' *Hecuba, Iphegenia Among the Taurians,* and *The Bacchae,* as well as murders "envisaged as sacrifice" in various other plays (Seaford 340, 372, 380, 386–387).

Theatre emerged from ritual through creative improvisation, according to Aristotle's *Poetics*[28] as well as the legend of Thespis. But theatre continued to reengage with and reemerge from ritual in each performance of a Greek play.[29] The festivals of Dionysus, where theatre was performed, also continued to involve ritual sacrifice in the shedding of animal blood (as I will discuss in chapter 1). The offering onstage of a human body did not involve actual bloodshed, but it did show the actor's psychological and physical alienation from the communal womb of the ritual chorus. (I will apply Nietzsche's theory of this to modern cinema, via Bazin and Kristeva, in chapter 3.) Thus, the latent dissent within ritual became manifest in theatre, through the distinct persona of character impersonation. The actor as character showed the symptomatic, tragic flaw (*hamartia* or "missed aim") of his identity, struggling against the collective voice of the chorus.

This dialectic of Thespian ego[30] versus the communal womb continued in later periods of European theatre history, even though the ritual chorus appeared in other ways. In the Middle Ages theatre reemerged when monks took on individual roles to act out the Biblical scenes of choral chants, improvising upon the ritual prayers. In the Renaissance, secular humanism's return to ancient Greek patterns, after the religious theatre of the Middle Ages, involved the elimination of the chorus in the neoclassical ideals for drama. And yet, opera was invented in the Renaissance, as a different return to ancient theatre, emphasizing the role of choral songs—while intermezzi, ballet, and masques developed the dance. Such experimental returns to ritual or extensions of theatre away from ritual, in these earlier periods, relate to the contradictory, modern theories of Artaud and Brecht, who are major influences on the postmodern as well. Artaud desired a return to primal, ritual cruelty in theatre, for sacrificial communion and catharsis, even at the risk of melodramatic gnosticism and emotional excess.[31] Brecht advocated anti-Aristotelian, tragicomic twists that would involve spectators emotionally but then distance them from the stage, moving them through personal alienation toward social awareness. Thus, a particular kind of sacrifice is evident in these, apparently opposed, spiritual and materialist theories of modern theatre: stressing ritual community and Thespian ego in different ways. In the pages ahead, I will use both theorists to delineate the edges of ritual sacrifice in theatre's past and present media.

As Euro-American theatre moves, in its history and performance structures, from various ancient rituals into the postmodern media of film and television, there might appear to be more freedom for individual creativity and spectator choices, with special-effects violence, multiplex screens, and remote controls. But film and television, as descendents of theatre, involve a covert submission of the actor's body to screen idealism and of the spectator to the pseudocommunion of a mass audience. Of course, the screen actor and spectator are not present together in time and space as in theatre. At the rare moments when fans do find a star's body actually near them, their ecstasy shows the sacrifice that each side makes, as materials for the creation of gods onscreen.[32] The fans do not see the real person of the actor, while sacrificing themselves to his or her divine presence. As they devour the superstar's apparent aura, in a bacchic frenzy of flashing cameras, screaming voices, and demands for autographs, the human actor is also sacrificed to their communion, crushed behind the mask of stardom. Like theatre's separation of a Thespian ego from the communal chorus, film and TV seem to give greater freedom, power, and pleasure, through ego idealization beyond the mortal body. But cinema and television return their audiences and actors to a ritual of im-mortal sacrifice (of mortal submission to the immortal illusion). This submission, especially with the melodramatic formula of an individual hero triumphing over evil, reorders social bodies to conform ideologically to certain plot and character patterns. However, more complex heroes, whose tragic violence shows the potential for evil, even within the good, may involve the ritual, screen audience in eye-opening contradictions.[33]

   In part II of this book, I will explore possible positive or negative effects of screen violence, applying the paradigms of ritual and theatrical sacrifice discovered in part I, to specific works of film. Like Artaud, who valued a return to ritual cruelty in theatre, I see a beneficial, cathartic effect for many in the mass audience, when screen violence is structured tragically. Yet I also see a grave, mimetic risk in the screen's usual rites of melodramatic violence. Like Brecht, who theorized a tragicomic distancing of the spectator from the lure of communal oneness, I value depictions of violence in cinema that remind us of our materiality and mortality, of the social and personal sources of evil, rather than giving us the simpler escape route of transcendent identifications. (I reject the neoclassical separation of tragedy and comedy as purely distinct genres, and the parallel argument, by some modern theorists, of the "death of tragedy" in the twentieth century.)[34] Unlike Artaud and Brecht, I find the most insight in a combination of their theories of ritual cruelty and theatrical alienation with current psychoanalytic notions of self and other. For the lure of ritual within theatre—from ancient dances and songs of the chorus to today's screen spectacles, sound tracks, and mass audiences— evokes a tempting regression to psychic origins, to preverbal movements and sounds, along with the overcoming of alienation in choral communion.[35] Both the extension of theatricality and the return to ritual in today's various dramatic media involve the dialectic of a Thespian ego and choral (m)Other within each artist and spectator[36]—especially regarding the legacy of melodramatic good and evil in ancient rites or the potential for tragic catharsis.

ETHICAL EDGES

How does a theatre of human sacrifice take place within the mind, from early life to life-long dreams, as well as in external performances? Psychoanalyst Jacques Lacan describes a "mirror stage" in human infancy illustrative of the mimetic structuring of identity throughout life: one's desire is the desire of the Other (*Écrits* 1–7).[37] At the age of 6 to 18 months, the infant expresses joy at its image in a mirror (or in the mother's eyes, says Lacan). But the apparent wholeness of that mirror-image Gestalt belies the infant's experience of physical discoordination and fantasies of a fragmented body (also expressed in later dreams and art works). The performance of an ideal, whole ego (as imago) contradicts the violence within the performer's body, as the infant sees its individuality in the mirror and in others' watchful desires. This early theatre becomes internalized in each of us from childhood onward, as we imagine how we appear to others and then continually reshape that self-image, through external modifications and internal fantasies, while also perceiving the horrors of fragmentation and nonexistence at the mirror's edges.

According to Lacan, the infant already experiences an alienation from its body as it applauds the ideal actor in the mirror (*Écrits* 6). Its sense of self, as desiring ego, is also dependent upon other spectators' desires and approvals (or disapprovals). So the child develops its individuality as a mask, or as various masks of character that are performed throughout life in different situations. Its imaginary ego becomes framed more and more by the patriarchal, symbolic order (by the Father's Name and No) as the child separates from its former, symbiotic, preverbal identification with the mother, yet continues to perform for the (m)Other's desires. Competition for ego attention in the imaginary order or for name recognition in the symbolic can produce aggression and violence—in stage, screen, and life mirrors. But theatre space and its sacrifices involve Lacan's third order as well, which is inaccessible to, yet fundamentally affects the imaginary order of perception/fantasy and the symbolic order of language/law: the Real of abject loss and lacking being. At this Real edge of the symbolic frame and imaginary mirror, like the navel or myceleum of the dream (in Freud's terms), an ethics of sacrifice can be found, even as meaning itself vanishes. For the Real is not simply an abyss of indiscernability beyond the stage or screen edge; it is also the void within the spectator, reflected at the tragic edges and creases of the spectacle and its drama. An ethics of the Real would realize this tragic void within oneself, rather than projecting it upon the evil villain, melodramatically.

Lacanian theorist Alenka Zupančič explains this sacrificial sense of ethics beyond conventional morality: "the Real happens to us (we encounter it) *as impossible*, as 'the impossible thing' that turns our symbolic universe upside down and leads to the reconfiguration of this universe. Hence the impossibility of the Real does not prevent it from having effect in the realm of the possible. This is when ethics comes into play, in the question forced upon us by an encounter with the Real: will I . . . reformulate what has hitherto been the foundation of my existence?" (235). Her colleague Slavoj Žižek calls this "a fourth ethical attitude," beyond hysterical desire, obsessional demand, and perverse enjoyment—in the sacrificial drive that encircles the Real: "the ethical compulsion which compels us to mark repeatedly the memory of a lost Cause" (*For They* 272). As Marek Wieczorek summarizes, "Žižek has expanded this psychoanalytic insight into the realm of politics. The drive is the compulsion to revisit, to encircle again and again, those sites of lost causes, of shattered and perverted dreams and hopes, not out of nostalgic longing for something that was believed to be good and only contingently corrupted (Communism), nor as a cautioning against the recurrence of gruesome or traumatic events (Nazism), but because the marking of all lost causes signals the impossibility of all totalizing ethics and morals" (xii). The pages ahead will explore the tragic edges of the stage and screen as such a site: as a marking of the Real beyond the symbolic and imaginary mirrors of dramatic fiction and reality, as a threshold of lost origins or causes, as a tracing of the sacrificial drive and its ethical, cathartic possibilities.[38]

This effort is not just a nostalgic longing to recover the dream of lost ritual power (as in Nietzsche's vision of the Dionysian chorus). Nor is it simply a defensive fear against trauma's recurrence (as in the good-versus-evil battles of today's screen melodramas). But I am attempting here an engagement with the impossible, with something in the Real of history and of certain stage and screen works that disturbs our current conceptions of stage blood or mass-mediated violence as merely fictional. The reader is invited into this ethics of reconsidering violence onstage and onscreen through the psychological and cultural heritage of human sacrifice, even if the symbolic universe of theatre, film, and TV is not turned totally upside-down. Thus, there will be extended passages in the chapters ahead that focus on certain details of blood rites as theatrical edges, with theoretical passages framing those historical reconstructions and cross-cultural comparisons, allowing the impossible Real, or its special effects in the possible, to be glimpsed at various edges and intersections of the symbolic and imaginary. This approach might seem to contradict the conventional academic investment in distinct disciplines and period differences. Yet, the desire here is not to show essential ties or origins, but to discover (by encircling specific lost causes) a Real sacrificial drive in the present—and thus to enable the cathartic restructuring of current symbolic ideals and imaginary projections.

Furthermore, it is the argument of this book that the showings of violence in ritual, theatre, and mass media today can be evaluated as positive or
negative, ethical or not, in their potential effects on the audience—even
though a nearly infinite variety of shows actually occurs in different spectators' minds as they watch the same performance together, with each viewer's
personal associations, distinctive fantasies, and conscious or unconscious
transferences. Although the precise psychological effects of violent works on
particular spectators may be impossible to determine, the power of specific
identifications becomes apparent—in ancient rites and today's screen
media—through the theatrical aspects of sacrifice. A calculus can be made of
the modes of catharsis in a certain stage or screen work: the tendency toward
a melodramatic purging of fearful sympathies (producing ritual conformity
and the possible mimetic backfire of copycat violence in real life) or a tragic
clarification of sacrificial drives—although such poles might only be
approached asymptotically by numerous different theatres in the minds of an
audience. In part II of this book, examples of Real monsters at the edges of
the film screen will be explored, with their imaginary and symbolic manifestations shaping audience effects in melodramatic or tragic directions. In part
I, explicit violence in ritual sacrifice and gladiatorial sports will be investigated for uncanny reflections of today's melodramatic and tragic modes of
performance, at the edges of Euro-American theatre history.

Theatre and cinema relate not only to the theory but also to the practice
of psychoanalysis and its spaces of dream interpretation. As Klaus Theweleit
has recently suggested, Freud developed a kind of theatre in his office, setting
up the therapeutic convention of the analyst sitting in a chair behind the
patient on a couch, as they both reimagine the play of dreams within the latter's mind. I would add that the analyst and patient together create a drama
of imaginary and symbolic transference between them, while re-viewing the
play of dreams and fantasies within their minds, at the edges of an impossible
Real that they, to some degree, share. Through such plays within a play, they
are both spectators and actors, as if onstage themselves (for an absent audience as Other), yet also projecting and viewing projections in the spaces and
walls around them. Thus, the edges of performance and perception become
crucial to the therapeutic catharsis—as in Freud's theory of the dream's navel.
For it is there that interpretation ends and analysis becomes "interminable,"
or true change begins.

Initially, Freud used the term *catharsis* to mean the curing of patients by
the expression and purging of repressed Oedipal desires. This hope parallels
that of many American theatre experiments in the 1960s and 1970s (starting
with Julian Beck and Judith Malina's Living Theatre in the 1950s). They
attempted to cure social and sexual repression by changing the stage edge:
breaking through the proscenium frame and its conventional fourth wall to
include audience participation as a radical, liberating politics of physical

touch and communal action (as with the Living Theatre's "group grope"). But Freud discovered, as did many in the theatre, that such a simple, cathartic goal becomes illusory when it meets the stage edge within the mind:[39] the aporia of traumatic violence at certain points of indiscernibility in dreams and memories (the navel as mycelium).[40] Lacan's revision of Freud redefines catharsis in a more complex, tragic sense as purifying desires and clarifying drives at that edge of the Real. Yet, current American ego psychology, along with recovered memory therapy (Whitfield), often aims at a purging of surface symptoms through stronger ego identifications, whether using talk or drug treatment: a triumph of the heroic ego over traumatic pain and past villains, as in stage and screen melodramas. A more Lacanian therapy and theatre would focus instead on a greater cathartic awareness of the "missed aim" (Aristotle's *hamartia*) of repeated tragic symptoms and fantasies—as being produced by a fundamental, structural symptom (the Lacanian *sinthome*), and eventually leading to sacrificial catastrophes for the heroic actor and dreamer. This focus on the tragic *sinthome* offers a different kind of cure: a sacrifice of the melodramatic sacrifice. Rather than repeating violence by blaming and punishing certain villains for the victim's trauma, and thus boosting the hero's ego, a truly cathartic sacrifice reveals tragic errors of judgment and painful consequences for all involved in such righteous vengeance.

A SACRIFICIAL IMPERATIVE

How is fictional violence today related to actual, ritual sacrifice in the past? This book will investigate the personal and social psychology of sacrifice by looking at performance types and works in the margins of theatre's conventional, Euro-American history: from Greek, Roman, and Aztec rites to recent examples of sports and film violence.[41] When I apply current psychoanalytic theories to these marginal sites, it is not with the presumption that all minds work the same way in all cultures. Indeed, the various premodern examples presented here (showing a dialectic between ritual and theatre at the edges of its history, as well as in theatrical space) involve cultures with a greater emphasis on communal identity, unlike the modern independent ego. But the ritual/theatre dialectic extends, I believe, to the postmodern fragmentation of ego and the current split-subjectivity of screen media in our new millennium.[42] We are both more individualistic and more widely communal than prior generations, in our theatrical and ritual illusions of star personas and mass audiences. This creates greater competition between ego masks, induces further submission by ritualized spectators, and leads to the sacrifice of actors and audiences, yearning for transcendence or community, in the simulacrum (and hypertheatre) of fluid identities.[43] Thus, in our new century, the danger increases of melodramatic justifications for violence, moving mimetically from stage and screen to real-life sacrifice (more subtly than the use of radio and TV propaganda to stir ethnic hatred in Rwanda and the former Yugoslavia). But we also have a greater opportunity for tragic awareness and the questioning of mimetic sacrifice,[44] through personal and social catharsis, if we regard media violence today in relation to various theatrical precedents—and become more critical consumers as the mass audience.

Popular and scholarly debates today about mass-media violence often have a short memory, forgetting the long history of staged aggression in the theatres and rituals of many cultures. To counter this amnesia, the current volume will relate the appeal and possible effects of screen violence—in sports, movies, and TV drama—to specific sacrificial rites and performance conventions in earlier cultures. Using Lacanian psychoanalytic theories and Kristeva's idea of the *chora*,[45] this book finds a sacrificial imperative within the human mind, as structured by various patriarchal cultures and manifested in distinctive rites and dramas. By comparing different performance practices, from ancient human and animal sacrifices to fictional violence onstage and onscreen (in relation to real violence offstage and offscreen), this study will provide insights as to the current ritual lures and effects of mass-media spectatorship—especially regarding the pleasures, risks, and purposes of violent display.

In part I, Aristotle's idea of dramatic catharsis will be reinterpreted through postmodern psychoanalytic theories of subjectivity, Oedipal sacrifice (symbolic castration), and therapeutic catharsis. The purging of fear and sympathy thus becomes redefined as the purification of desire and drive, relating the communal experience of ritual theatre to specific goals in the Lacanian treatment of individual minds.[46] This provides a new theory of the potential cathartic purpose of violence in performance, drawing also on the diametrically opposed ideologies of Artaudian cruelty and Brechtian alienation in modern theatre's challenges to its audiences.[47] But it also highlights the more common, melodramatic and capitalist (rather than tragic and cathartic) values in film and TV violence—and the risk of a negative effect on the mass-media consumer, with the mimetic repetition of violence in real life. The first and second chapters move outside the dominant narrative of Western theatre history to explicit acts of violence at its edges: in the animal sacrifices that formed part of the Greek festivals where theatre became a distinct art form, in the Roman games of death, and in the Aztec rituals of human sacrifice and gladiatorial sport. However, certain theatrical elements are examined in all of these rites, offering comparative insights upon the hidden sacrifices of real bodies, behind the fictional and sportive violence of today's ritual screens, including NFL football on TV.

Part II focuses on specific examples of screen violence, at the choral edges of cinema ("choral" in the sense of Kristeva's theory of the *chora* and the ritual chorus of theatre's sacrificial origins). Certain characters and scenes are investigated as monsters and acts screening—presenting, yet masking—

the real violence in society and in the mass audience. James Whale's classic film about Frankenstein's monster, Kenneth Branagh's recent remake, and Oliver Stone's surreal presentation of romantic serial killers are all examined in chapter 3, regarding the theatre frames and spaces that haunt the cinema screen. Female monsters onscreen will also be considered, as distinctive figures for the sacrificial drive in individuals and subcultures.[48] In the fourth chapter, a certain historical drama about violence in Chicano culture, translated from stage to screen by writer/director Luis Valdez, reveals connections to both Brechtian theatre and Aztec ritual sacrifice, through the monstrous yet heroic figure of El Pachuco. The final chapter offers examples from more mainstream films, though again by ethnic directors, the Italian-Americans Martin Scorsese and Francis Ford Coppola, exploring the self and other sacrifices of martyrs and scapegoats onscreen—and of the filmmakers themselves—with ties to Catholicism and ancient Rome.

Thus, the cathartic logic of various ritual sacrifices investigated in part I, from ancient Greece, Rome, and Mesoamerica—expressing and purifying communal violence, while communicating with ghosts and gods—offers insights even for the secular audiences and radically different technologies of the postmodern.[49] In fact, the alien parallels between cultures compared here magnify the critical view of the present, as in Brecht's sense of historification, and amplify the homeopathic resonance, like Artaudian cruelty. The ancient rites might then become another kind of theatre to the reader of this book, as mirror stages reflecting the uncanny violence in postmodern media. This will hopefully illuminate not just the spectacle of brutality on numerous screens today, but also the edges of a sacrificial drive within the homes and minds of the mass audience: in ourselves, in the others we fear, and in the Other we desire.

PART I

Catharsis between
Sacrificial Cultures

ONE

Blood Sacrifice in Ancient Greece and Aztec America

THEATRE WAS BORN from ritual in ancient Greece, or so the old story goes, fixing that mirror in a particular choral frame.[1] But theatre—as the embodiment of the Other while others watch—was also part of ritual before it became a distinct art form.[2] Ritual sacrifice shows this theatrical side in the presentation of an oblatory agent, whether animal or human, to incarnate the desire of the Other, as impersonator of the god and/or as the god's food, for the sake of audience communion. In Richard Boothby's Lacanian view, sacrifice "recapitulates on the level of ritual practices the original sacrifice of every human being—that of separating from the mother by renouncing the security, comfort, and satisfaction of her body" ("Altar-Egos" 59). But I would argue that such ego separation, sacrificing maternal symbiosis (in the Lacanian "mirror stage"), is precisely the theatrical impulse within ritual: the separating of a distinct Thespian "actor" from choral performers and spectators, which defines the historical emergence of theatre as distinct from Dionysian ritual.

Theatre seems to be born out of ritual, yet continues to bear the potential return to a communal womb—because theatrical phylogeny extends the recapitulation of psychological ontogeny in ritual sacrifice. Like the infant separating from its mother's body in order to become an individual ego, yet carrying that primordial experience and Oedipal temptation within the mind throughout childhood and into adulthood, theatre reimagines its historical birth in each performance: acting out the return to ritual or the distancing of character and audience. (The theories of Antonin Artaud and Bertold Brecht exemplify these contradictory directions in modern theatre, pushing beyond the normative morals of communal rites and ego freedoms to an ethics of further sacrifice either way.) A

21

look at the theatre within ritual, not just the ritual within theatre, illuminates the persistent temptation of sacrificial desire and the potential for its
cathartic clarification, in theatre's progressive separation from, yet cyclical
return to its (m)Other. The rites of blood sacrifice behind Western theatre's beginnings in Greece, and beside its colonial edges in Mexico, can
reveal something of the Real today: the sacrificial *chora* (space of becoming) in stage and screen illusions of a "mass audience" and the hero's transcendent individualism.

THEATRE WITHIN RITUAL

In ancient Greece the move from ritual sacrifice to more theatrical forms of
performance involved a shift in the focus of collective aggression.[3] Instead of
an animal as sole "scapegoat," sacrificed to please the divine audience,[4] to
interpret life plots (with a priest reading its open entrails), and to stimulate
primal emotions in earthly spectators (with a bloody display and communal
meal), the human body became the focus of sacrifice in theatre.[5] However,
the festival of Dionysus, as primary setting for the development of theatre,
continued to involve rites of animal sacrifice. In fact, the sacrificial altar was
located approximately forty yards behind the *skene* (stage house) doors of the
Theatre of Dionysus in Athens, on the hillside of the Acropolis (Wiles,
Tragedy 57). "Here on the altar many bulls would have been slaughtered and
their innards roasted whilst the dithyrambs were danced. The performance
[onstage and in the orchestra] is physically located between the god [the
statue of Dionysus in the theatre auditorium] and the sacrifice in his honour . . ." (58). By staging violence through the human drama onstage, as well
as the animal bloodshed behind it, the Greeks also returned to the cannibal
origins of animal sacrifice in the myths and cults of Dionysus: figuratively
tearing apart and eating the character represented by the actor onstage.[6]
While human sacrifice within the theatre took place as a fiction, behind the
doors of the *skene* or in some other offstage space, a Dionysian chorus evoked
the primal emotions of *sparagmos*[7] through their song and dance, between the
audience and the hidden drama, stimulating the play of violence in spectators' imaginations. Thus, like a movie sound track today, the choral music
mediated the eventual display of violated bodies through an *ekkuklema*
(wagon bearing a corpse) or bloody mask (as with Oedipus' blinded eyes).[8]

Prior to and during the invention of theatre as a distinct art form, Greek
animal sacrifice involved many theatrical elements. Typically, the human
participants wore symbolic costumes and ornamentation. Travel to the place
of violence was staged as a choral procession with flute accompaniment[9] (as
in the theatre orchestra). The sacrificial animal participated in the costumed,
choral procession, "likewise decorated and transformed—bound with fillets,
its horns covered with gold" (Burkert, *Homo Necans* 3). In fact, the perfor-

FIGURE 1.1. An ancient sacrificial altar, probably showing the garlanded bull offered at the festival of Dionysus. This altar is currently placed in the ruins of the Greek theatre at Corinth, but did not originally reside there. The photo, courtesy of Clifford Ashby, also appears in his book *Classical Greek Theatre* (University of Iowa Press, 1999).

mance of the animal en route to the sacrifice bore special significance. Apparent willingness or compliance to be sacrificed evidenced the participation of a divine director as well, "of a higher will that commands assent" (4).

At the destined site, the major set piece was, of course, the sacrificial altar. But the sacred space of performance included the spectator-participants, through special gestures and props: "the sacrificial basket and water jug . . . [were] carried around the assembly, thus marking off the sacred realm from the profane" (Burkert, *Homo Necans* 4). The spectators' direct involvement as collaborative actors in the rite (more than in Greek theatre) was also expressed by a ritual washing of hands. The lead actor, the sacrificial animal, was sprinkled with water, too. Its response of a bowed head signified its agreement to take on the primary role in the life and death drama about to be played out. The heroic animal, its human chorus, and the sacred setting were more aggressively joined through the next communal gesture: "unground barley grains" were taken from the basket and thrown at the scapegoat, at the altar, and at the earth. Another prelude to the violent climax came then as the choral leader cut a lock of hair from the animal's forehead and threw it into the sacrificial fire (5).

Each of these scenes increased the binding of human and animal in the fate that awaited the latter. At the ultimate moment of surrogate martyrdom, the women in the sacrificial chorus underscored the plot's climax (and the stage edge *chora*) with "a piercing scream" (Burkert, *Homo Necans* 5). The final acts then involved certain vital props produced from the dying body, further dramatizing the mortal/immortal cycle: the blood was caught in a bowl and sprinkled on the altar stone; the heart, "sometimes still beating," was placed upon the altar as well; lobes of the liver were used for prophecy; and the rest of the flesh was turned into a communal meal, after roasting on the sacrificial fire (6). The bones were put on the altar, along with certain pieces of flesh, to be consumed by fire and the gods. The skull, however, was "preserved in the sacred place as permanent evidence of the act of consecration." The skin was sold to purchase another victim or other votive offerings (of wine and cakes) for the next performance (7).

These details of a typical sacrifice of a goat, ox, or bull illustrate a specific sense of theatricality, of playing with individual and social identity, life and death, violence and consumption—in Greek rituals of Homeric times and at festivals later on, including the City Dionysia, where European theatre emerged as an art form. Recently, William Morgan and Per Brask have argued that theatre evolves out of ritual practices in various societies like a superior biological species, "temporarily coexist[ing] with the ancestral species from which it has evolved" (190).[10] They even find a Machiavellian aim behind such a plot: theatre supplanted ritual in ancient Greece and Aztec Mexico (their prime examples): "as a preferred non-physically coercive means of exercising social control, through thought control" (194). This new device of theatre, in their view, emerged "from a need perceived by authorities in state societies, to address potentially socially disruptive issues in such a manner as to render their subjects passive" (190–191).

However, there are many dimensions to the theatricality of sacrifice in ritual and in art. Theatre did not begin as a new, superior species, evolving beyond former ritual performances (a theory that suggests the hubris of European imperialism as well as social Darwinism). While theatre often functions as a safety valve for mimetic violence, it is not merely a form of societal control, rendering the scapegoat, chorus, and spectators as passive victims.[11] Instead, theatre extends the perverse elements already present in ritual orthodoxy, entertaining a dynamic struggle of diverse desires and questions, about politics and metaphysics, through varying degrees of active submission and violent rebellion.[12] The development of theatre in ancient Greece thus signifies a more individualistic sense of identity, against the communal womb, culminating (two millennia later) in modern egoism and postmodern split-subjectivity, with new rites of submission and rebellion involving the film and TV screens.

Multiple characteristics of theatre within ritual can be revealed by comparing Greek and Aztec practices as to: (1) the offering of a sacrificial animal or human as lead actor, as divine food incarnating the mortal and immortal character of the god; (2) the staging of violent desires and fears through certain settings, costumes, props, and actions; and (3) the collective focus of political and sacred energy in the fetishized victim, at the stage edge between this world and others. In both ancient Greece and preconquest Mexico, unlike modern Euro-American society, the other worlds of the supernatural and the afterlife, of gods and ghosts, were not far offstage from the ordinary and the mortal. In fact, sacred and secular performance practices were often intermixed. But this also helps to show the significance of a theatrical view in many kinds of rituals, sacred and secular, from ancient to modern, from stage to screen violence today. While it may be easier to condemn Aztec human sacrifice as inhumane and completely different from fictional violence, it is far more insightful to perceive certain parallels to our own time, through the Greek mirrors of theatre and ritual.

TRANSCENDENTAL SAVAGERY

The conquering Spanish were shocked to learn that the civilization of the Aztecs, with its monumental architecture, complex artwork, and imperial organization, practiced regular human sacrifices on a mass scale along with ritual cannibalism. The Dominican priest Diego Durán wrote an extensive study of Aztec festivals. He wanted to warn fellow missionaries that pagan practices and beliefs, as works of the Devil, were continuing covertly in their own time, a half-century after the Spanish Conquest.[13] Durán, though born in Spain, grew up in the New World and learned Nahuatl (the Aztec language) at an early age. He did not witness the Aztec rituals he describes, but interviewed Amerindians who had been firsthand spectators. Durán's study was not published in his lifetime,[14] but it offers a valuable view for us today (along with the similar work of Bernardino de Sahagún)[15] to see through the European abhorrence of human sacrifice and cannibalism, into the repression, yet expression of such desires in Euro-American theatre as well as Aztec rites.[16]

Cannibalism was also a horror to the ancient Greeks. They considered it to be the practice of mythic monsters and primitive gods—or of barbarians and savages far outside Greek civilization. "For although Greek society rejected cannibalism utterly, yet, by virtue of what it did have to say about it, it compelled dissident individuals and groups to express their rejection of society in terms of this very form of illicit consumption" (Detienne, "Between" 217).[17] Dismemberment (sparagmos), eating raw flesh (omophagia), and cannibalism were central themes in the myth of Dionysus, in Dionysian cult practices, and in related political rebellions against the Greek state at the time of theatre's emergence.[18] Dionysian cannibalism was, in current theoretical terms, the abject chora (Kristeva), the carnivalesque (Bakhtin), the extimate Other (Lacan)—perversely outside, yet central to the institution of theatre as social control: "the Dionysiac movement, while maintaining 'transcendence through savagery' as an ideal, remained an essential part of the religion of the polis. It was always opposed, but always inside" (Detienne, "Between" 225).

Prior to the arrival of Europeans, the Aztecs had transformed the practice of human sacrifice, dismemberment, and cannibalism into ceremonial expressions of their civilization, displaying that inside element of transcendence through regular theatrical rites.[19] Although the Aztecs performed various types of poetic drama, farce, and acrobatic entertainment,[20] their ritual use of the bodies, hearts, and skins of war captives and slaves—as sacrificial actors, props, and costumes incarnating various gods—shows even more about the Other within the theatre of the Old World and the New.[21] During monthly festivals throughout the Aztec calendar,[22] the tragic drama of human sacrifice was displayed, in ritual performances centered in temple courtyards,[23] but also moving throughout the city (like medieval European theatre). Though not bound within a single festival or stage space, the theatre of Aztec ritual was nevertheless highly structured: in casting, rehearsals, preludes, props, costumes, settings, performance spaces, symbolic gestures, and the positioning of certain members of the audience as a chorus.

For example, the slave actor who was disguised as the god Tezcatlipoca (Smoking Mirror)[24] received careful training and stage direction for a full year prior to the ultimate sacrifice. He was costumed, according to Durán,[25] "in the complete attire and insignia of the deity," given that divine character's name, and worshipped by the highest levels of society for months (126). "The man to be sacrificed dwelt in the most sacred chamber of the temple; there he ate and drank; there the lords and the principal men came to revere and serve him." This actor as god walked throughout the city, creating a sacred parade—comparable to that attending the Greek sacrificial animal, but over an extended period of time. Aztec lords and dignitaries accompanied the god-actor *(teotl ixiptla)*[26] like a Greek theatre chorus, surrounding its sacrificial hero, with the entire city as orchestra and stage, although in preconquest Mexico it was the divine character himself who played a flute, drawing spectators of all classes, genders, and ages. "Women with children in their arms came out, placing the little ones before him, greeting him like a deity, and this was done by most of the people" (126–127).

The god-actor was caged at night, says Durán, "to prevent his escape" (127). On the fatal day, at the climax of the ritual drama, with spectators gathered in the temple courtyard, four priests grasped the hands and feet of the god-actor, holding him across the sacrificial stone, while a fifth priest "opened his chest and extracted his heart, raising it with his hand as high as he could, offering its steam to the sun" (106–107). The extracted heart (perhaps still beating)[27] was then thrown into the face of "the idol"[28] and the rest of the body was rolled down the temple steps. Thus, a slave, from the lowest class in Aztec society, was raised to the highest level, worshipped as a god by priests and nobles, and ultimately transformed into immortal food, performing his final role literally "from the heart."

In his contemporaneous study, the Franciscan missionary Bernardino de Sahagún gives further details on the casting and performance of the divine actor. Certain captive warriors (probably taken during ritual battles with neighboring city-states)[29] were selected and trained as "slaves" to eventually impersonate the god Tezcatlipoca (64).[30] Sahagún reports many specific casting priorities, as remembered by his indigenous witnesses. Intelligence and physical ability were important for the dance and flute training, but most important of all was beauty.[31] To play a god the actor had to be "slender like a reed; long and thin like a stout cane; well-built; not of overfed body, and neither very small nor exceedingly tall." Sahagún continues more poetically: "[He was] like something smoothed, like a tomato, or like a pebble, as if hewn of wood." The ideal actor's teeth "were like seashells, well arrayed in order" (65). But Sahagún also gives a long list of disqualifying defects: specific imperfections of hair, skin, head, forehead, eyelids, eyes, cheeks, nose, lips, tongue, manner of speech, teeth, neck, chin, ears, back, hands, stomach, navel, buttocks, and thighs (64–65). Like today's mass-media stars, the Aztec *ixiptla* had to keep the right shape while playing the god, or else take a crash diet: "if they noted that his body became even a little fat, they made him drink brine, so that he became thin; the salt water thinned him, so that he became lean; he became hard; his flesh became firm" (66).

FIGURE 1.2. The Aztec heart sacrifice, as illustrated in Sahagún's sixteenth-century *Florentine Codex*. Courtesy of the University of Utah Press.

How did the Aztecs compel their star actors to play the ultimate sacrificial role[32]—like the ancient Greek animal nodding its assent to be slaughtered? There were certain rewards for the Aztec actor, as he gave his yearlong
performance of a lifetime. He lost his human character (before losing his life),
but gained an immortal identity—through costuming, performance gestures,
and the desires of his audience.[33] The emperor Moctezuma, according to
Sahagún, adorned the *ixiptla* "in great pomp with all costly articles, which he
caused to be placed upon him; for verily he took him to be his beloved god"
(66). Black makeup "anointed" him. The "soft down of eagles" was put in his
hair, "which fell to his loins." And he was given a crown of "sweet-smelling
flowers" that flowed down over his shoulders. He wore gold pendants and
bracelets, turquoise "ear plugs," a snail shell "lip plug," and a breast ornament
of white seashells (67). The golden bells placed on his legs jingled as he
walked in sandals made of "ocelot skin ears."

However, after fasting and walking around publicly in this divine costume for some time, the actor performed a transitional gesture, a prelude to
his own dismemberment, scattering the costume pieces "in various places"
(Sahagún 67). Then, twenty days prior to his final performance, he was given
four women to enjoy as his wives,[34] the hair cut of a warrior captain, and a
new "heron feather ornament." On his last day as god and human being, the
actor playing Tezcatlipoca, with his wives "consoling him," traveled by canoe
to a certain beach and temple (68). There "he ascended by himself" the temple steps, "of his free will, to the place where he was to die," shattering on the
first step his flute and other tragic props—showing the drama of life's beauty
and death's victory.

After his death, the actor's body parts functioned as further ritual props,
expressing the tragicomic paradox of death in life and life in death. His heart,
the "precious eagle-cactus fruit,"[35] and his blood, "most precious water," were
vital resources to Aztec society. They nourished the sun on its dangerous journey through the land of the dead (in the bowels of the earth), enabling its
otherwise uncertain resurrection each morning.[36] The actor's severed head
also gained further symbolic life. Pierced at the temples, it was strung with
others on the Aztec skull rack,[37] so that, as Sahagún puts it, "he ended in the
adornment in which he died" (68).

This viewpoint of a sixteenth-century Franciscan ethnologist, collating
the memories of Amerindian spectators,[38] reveals an uncanny connection to
the postmodern sense of character (and gender) as social construction. One
is more and more aware, in the hypertheatre of postmodern life, that identity develops through the desire of the Other. "You are what others see in
you," rather than "I think, therefore I am." In Aztec society, the son of a
nobleman could lose his high status if he failed to perform on the battlefield
(Clendinnen, "Cost" 50);[39] people of various classes could slip into slavery if
their debts became too great (Durán 281). Yet, a slave or a captive warrior

30

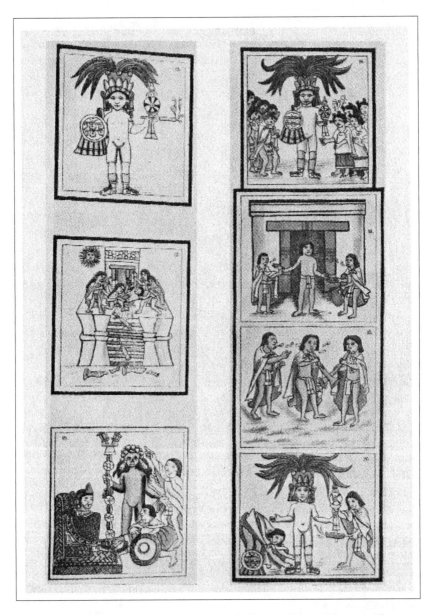

FIGURE 1.3. Illustrations of the Aztec festival of Toxcatl from Sahagún's *Florentine Codex*. On the left (from top to bottom): the god-actor portraying Tezcatlipoca, the heart sacrifice at the temple after the god-actor has broken his flute on its steps, and the god-actor appearing before the emperor. On the right: the people as audience around the god-actor, the god-actor in training as singer and flute player, and the god-actor being worshipped. Courtesy of the University of Utah Press.

could transcend all social classes, his body parts becoming immortal relics, by acting a certain role for the sacred entertainment of others watching.

Ancient Greek theatre sublimated its cannibal impulses in the fictional sacrifice of a tragic hero, dismembered plotwise through fatal pressure applied to a flaw in character. This metaphorical bloodshed of the hero's mask, in its tragic fall through the emotions of choral communion, was thus related to the political as well as religious shedding of actual human blood. The Aztecs more directly sacrificed warriors taken in battle, after costuming and rehearsing[40] them as god-actors. But the Greeks used their own warriors in training, young adult males (beardless *ephebes*), who performed their marching orders as the choral actors of tragic drama. These "billy goat singers" (*tragoidoi*), whether portraying male or female characters, young or old, according to different scripts, exemplified the political containment of Dionysian ambiguity in their rectangular, rank and file dancing in the orchestra circle.[41] And yet, they also show the ritual release of sacrificial energy and potential human bloodshed—especially when compared with the warriors in Aztec rites. Both cultures, despite many differences in performance tastes, focused their theatrical rituals on the interplay of mortal identity and social aggression, on the human body in violent, transformative display.

ALTAR-EGOS AND BODY PARTS

Despite the popular belief today in Euro-American individualism and social mobility, our personal characters and life plots are fated to a great degree by circumstances of birth,[42] formative events, and the desires of others that we absorb—through immediate contact and through the mass media. A special few of us, with the right looks and talents, are cast as celebrities. They are given godlike status for a time, yet are inevitably sacrificed as their mortal lives depart too much from their immortal images onscreen. This shows us, in extremis, our own fatal masks, although the screens of film and TV also help us to forget our fates and masks.

Striking parallels can be found between today's media stars, reflecting ego ideals in the mass audience, and the sacrificial actors of ancient Greece or preconquest Mexico, incarnating the fate of spectators' mortal bodies and immortal desires. Not only the Greek actors playing out the original Oedipal triangle or other family tragedies, but also the young warriors in training who acted as their chorus—both performed a rite of sacrifice expressing personal dramas and social duties through the sufferings of mythic characters. Aztec warriors also became actors, performing as gods, after being captured and before being sacrificed. While today's onscreen egos appear to declare an

I borrow the pun in the title of this section from the title of Richard Boothby's essay, where he gives a very useful application of Lacan toward a general theory of sacrifice.

independence from this stage history of ritual submission, communal sacrifice, and tragic fate, a look at that heritage behind the screen shows parallel structures in the mirror stage theatrics of prior civilizations.

In both ancient Greece and preconquest Mexico, ritual theatre functioned like a collective mirror stage, replaying the "drama" that Lacan describes of the infant before the mirror and (m)Other's eyes (*Écrits* 4). Like the child's ideal image in the mirror, contradicting its experience of a "fragmented body" and of "dehiscence at the heart of the organism" (2),[43] mythic imagos of Greek and Aztec performers appeared to transcend the fictional *sparagmos* onstage or actual dismemberment at the altar by fully acting out the Other's desire. The living actor's masked and costumed form—plus, in the Aztec case, the dead performer's heart, skull, and skin—became immortal images and symbolic props reflecting, surviving, and sustaining the Real violence within the viewers and their societies.[44] Paradoxically, the actor framed and cut in the mirror of Greek or Aztec ritual theatre became both a whole and broken icon, imaging the transcendent, godlike ego and its *corps morcelé*.

The Real fragmentation behind the mirrors of ritual performance took place not only at the edges of stage and altar, but also in the "mass audience." The yearly festival to the Greek god Dionysus (through which the art of theatre emerged) and the monthly festivals to various Aztec gods (all of which involved human sacrifice) were major civic events in ancient Athens and preconquest Tenochtitlan, attended by most, if not all the citizenry. Like today's daily ritual of TV news crime scenes, or weekly dramas displaying graphic violence, these performances expressed the destructive fears and desires of the social body—the carnivalesque passions of a collective *chora*—while also confirming the images and symbols, faces and props, of the Other's moral authority.

There are certainly great differences between the Greek or Aztec mass audience and today's, not only in relation to technology, but also regarding the Euro-American ideal of ego independence, mirrored onscreen. Greek and Aztec characters (or ritual actors) showed their audiences a conditional sense of identity responding to a predetermined plot. As Sophocles' *Oedipus, the King* demonstrates, a Greek hero could not escape the rule of fate that was embedded in his character by his parents' desires, even if he and they were forewarned through oracles. In the more oracular and apocalyptic culture of the Aztecs, the past always repeated in the future and all males of the nobility were destined for war. Thus, their well maintained verbal history (with no written language) was itself an oracle and the ideal fate for each newborn son of the ruling class was to die in battle or as a captured warrior sacrificed by another city-state.[45] The Aztecs even developed a ritual form of warfare, the "flower wars," in which the purpose was to capture enemy bodies, alive and unscathed, for future sacrifice.

At the birth of a male, the Aztec midwife greeted this little "captive" with war cries. Then the mother, who was considered a "warrior" in her battle to give birth, would hear the midwife say to the infant:

> thy home is not here . . . here is only the place of thy nest, thy cradle, thy cradle blanket, the resting place of thy head . . . Thou belongest out there . . . Thou hast been sent into warfare. War is thy desert, thy task. Thou shalt give drink, nourishment, food to the sun, the lord of the earth. (Quoted in Clendinnen, *Aztecs* 175)

The Aztec ego, male and female, was strictly shaped by social and cosmic law: the child was merely on loan to his mother until the social drama of the sun's desire climaxed in each warrior's death on the battlefield—or dismemberment at the sacrificial altar. "Perhaps thou wilt receive the gift, perhaps thou wilt merit death by the obsidian knife."

This fatalism might seem very foreign to today's mass-media spectator, who is given the illusion of being directly addressed in his or her own home by the luminous figures on the TV screen—and of having a godlike (remote) control over their presence, while choosing from many other egos on numerous channels to mirror the viewer's power and freedom. But the TV (and computer) screen has become the primary baby-sitter and myth-conveying midwife to millions of children in America and around the world, saying to each child: your identity "belongest out there" in the media marketplace. A century ago Freud found the key to the modern ego in the ancient Greek drama of Oedipus. Similarly, we might glimpse an uncanny, extimate truth[46] about our postmodern subjectivity in the alien mirrors of Mesoamerican sacrificial identity.

FROM SOLAR TO PROSCENIUM MIRRORS

Even when an Aztec warrior was victorious—bringing home a live prisoner to be sacrificed at the temple—the captor's family mourned his future death. After the prisoner was sacrificed at the temple altar, his flesh was sent to the captor's home, cooked in a maize stew, and ritually eaten by the captor's family. Then they pasted feathers on the captor, "because he had not died there in war, but was yet to die, and would pay his debt. Hence his blood relations greeted him with tears and encouraged him" (Sahagún 48).[47] The still living, victorious warrior was identified with the dismembered and consumed captive, who had been likewise pasted with feathers before the sacrifice. The victor himself did not eat the captive's flesh, expressing instead his identification with the enemy warrior as sacrificial food: "Shall I, then, eat my own flesh?" (52).

He did, however, wear the flayed skin of the captive (thus impersonating the specific god the victim had played) as did other victorious warriors at the festival of Tlacaxipeualiztli.[48] "Each one of the captors came forth from his house, and appeared in and went wearing the [captive's] skin. . . . So [foul] did they smell [that verily] the stench wounded the head" (Sahagún 56).[49] The victor also displayed his captive's thighbone on a pole in the courtyard of his home. He costumed the thighbone with a "sleeveless knotted cord jacket and a small spray of heron feathers"—creating, in effect, a puppet actor of immortality out of his victim's remains. "And he wrapped the thigh bone with paper, and provided it a mask. And this was called the god-captive" (57).[50]

What drama was being performed by these ritual practices—at birth, at the sacrificial altar, and at the captor's family home?[51] As is generally known today, the main rationale for Aztec human sacrifice was to feed the sun, lest it fail to rise again each morning. But certain Aztec origin myths reveal further mirror-stage meanings behind this rationale. Whether a god-actor or a child was being sacrificed,[52] whether a mass execution of hundreds of captured warriors or the individual identification of live captor and dead captive was being performed, these rituals mirrored the primal myth of the gods' own sacrifices to energize the sun. (Each rite also mirrored specific characteristics of the god honored by it). The Real death and dismemberment of human bodies became the imaginary restaging of divine sacrifice at the creation of the Aztec sun, reconfirming the fragile symbolic orders of both nature and culture.

According to various Aztec myths, the gods sacrificed themselves—after the creation and destruction of four previous suns and races of humans—in order for the fifth, the current sun, to rise over the Aztec empire.[53] In the myth, two gods sacrificed themselves by diving into the creative fire. Thus, the fifth sun was born, but it would not move. Other gods then agreed to offer their lives, too, giving the fifth sun movement. One of the primary Aztec divinities, Quetzalcoatl,[54] cut out the hearts of these gods with a sacrificial knife—just as the human priest does to each captured warrior playing the role of a god. According to the myth, the dead gods' clothes were then gathered in sacred bundles, to be worshipped by the new race of humans under the new sun (Taube 44). This mythical detail also relates to the ritual use of a divine costume in the god-actor's various performances, from temple rehearsals to musical processions in the city streets, to his final act on the sacrificial altar, as well as the postmortem performance of his skin (worn by his captor) and of his costumed and masked thigh bone, in the home and neighborhood theatres.

From our own theoretical seats today, the mirror of the Aztec stage and its solar orientation offers a new view of the Euro-American tradition of proscenium theatre (and its relation to cinema and television). The imaginary sacrifice of the gods, reincarnated by real human actors, fuels the symbolic order of the sun's rising and setting over the Aztec empire. This solar, cosmological framework of Aztec ritual theatre provides a stark contrast to the secular, proscenium frame of early modern, European theatre—which was eventually imposed upon the Aztecs, along with medieval stagings of religious dramas and open-air mock battles, by the Spanish conquerors (Harris, *Aztecs*). Prior to the Conquest, Aztec society clung to the symbolic order of the "fifth sun," believing that the current solar frame was doomed to die like the four before it, yet continuing to maintain it anyway, on the life-support system of human sacrifice. Meanwhile, Europeans moved toward a human-centered, scientific theatre, onstage and in politics—though that also meant mass sacrifices (especially with the Spanish Inquisition). The symbolic order of a more humanist, sixteenth-century theatre was seen in the Cartesian coordinates of the proscenium frame and wings, producing a central vanishing point through perspective painting techniques. This new technology of performance exhibited the self-confidence of Renaissance science to conquer space by framing illusions of infinite distance and by using *trompe l'oeil* scenery to create a moving picture onstage. First, there was Torelli's chariot and pole system, which could simultaneously change one series of flats for another, magically transforming the view. Then, there was the Bibienas' baroque technique of *scena per angolo*, with multiple vanishing points painted in the perspective scenery, drawing the spectator's eyes towards various directions of infinity. Thus, our modern, cinematic illusions of ego power—with the spectator's view moving through space and cutting between camera angles—began to take shape in the proscenium mirrors of seventeenth- and eighteenth-century European theatre. The beginnings of a cinematic imagination can also be found in Shakespeare's poetics on a bare stage with spoken décor (Lehmann). But it becomes even more apparent, as a new illusion of godlike transcendence through human sacrifice, from ancient and medieval to Renaissance staging devices.

While Renaissance theatre architecture, like neoclassical drama, ostensibly imitated classical Greek and Roman models, distinctive structures emerged in new symbolic directions. Ancient Greek theatre had been performed in the open air. Its *theatron* (the "seeing place") was cut into a hillside. Its orchestra (the place of the chorus) was a flat circle of earth with an altar at the center. And its *skene* (the scene house) was initially a temporary shelter in which actors could change costumes and masks before emerging for a new scene. Eventually, the Hellenistic Greeks developed a raised stage, separating the actors from the chorus in the orchestra. The framework of Greek performance shifted away from the orchestra, as former ritual threshing floor, and away from the chorus, as bearing the heritage of Dionysian and mother/earth goddess cults. Scenic effects increased onstage as the *skene* became more elaborate—with facades on two levels (the *episkenion* and *proskenion*) and various other spectacular devices. The chorus may even have joined the actors onstage, rather than singing and dancing around the sacrificial altar in the orchestra (Brockett 42–43). And yet, the Greeks still placed their theatre under the sun, performing each tetralogy (the series of three

FIGURE 1.4. Baroque opera scene with multiple vanishing points (*scena per angolo*) designed by Giuseppe Galli Bibiena, 1719. Courtesy of the Metropolitan Museum of Art, the Elisha Whittelsey Collection, the Elisha Whittelsey Fund, 1951. (51.501.2731)

tragedies and a satyr play) from morning till late afternoon (Ashby 118–123), so that the sun's path in the sky formed a natural frame to the stage, along with the earth below it.

The Romans reduced the orchestra to a semicircle in their freestanding, permanent theatres. But they still left an opening to the sky, with an awning to protect spectators from the sun. Medieval theatre also exposed itself to the elements—except when played in the cosmological space of a cathedral. Whether indoors or out, medieval drama staged heaven, earth, and hell, with their respective residents, as intimately associated. However, in the Renaissance (especially in seventeenth-century Italy and France), European theatre changed its relation to natural and supernatural forces, harnessing such perceptual and conceptual energy through new modes of representation. Mythic beings would still appear in intermezzi or masques as decorative entertainments, but they came to reflect human rulers as primary signifiers and social imagos. The sun's frame was replaced by the Cartesian proscenium. The fated tragic hero was supplanted by a Machiavellian *cogito*, then by the Enlightenment man of sentiment, and then by the modern freethinker. These historical steps eventually produced the twentieth-century theatres of cinema and television with their distinctive proscenium frames: focusing the view of a mass audience through illusions of infinity onscreen, as if controlled by the mind's eye. Today, movies and TV offer the spectator a godlike vision, flying through various subjective and objective spaces. But they also fix the viewer's body in a seat at the screen's edge, demanding attention at the vicarious sacrifice, by catching the eye and ear, for the sake of ticket money and commercial offerings.

THE BOTTOM OF THE FRAME

The comparison here with the Aztec ritual stage and its solar order requires a further consideration of the underside of that frame as well. Whereas European theatre, from Greek to Roman to medieval to Renaissance, gradually displaced the forces of myth and nature in favor of human scenic controls, Aztec sacrifice found its raison d'être in the sun and the earth. As the logic of another Aztec origin myth shows, ritual sacrifice not only nourished the sun's daily life (and the empire's expanding shadow), but also the earth. In order for water and food to arise from the earth and sustain Aztec life, the earth, like the sun, had to be fed with human blood and hearts. For the earth goddess herself had been dismembered by the gods Tezcatlipoca and Quetzalcoatl; they tore her in half to form the earth and the sky. Then the other gods created trees from her hair, grass from her skin, springs and caverns from her eyes, rivers and large caves from her mouth, mountains from her shoulders, and mountain valleys from her nose. Thus piecemeal, the earth monster would continue to cry out each night—as she swallowed the sun and passed it as sacred excrement in the morning. She would refuse to produce food for humans, the Aztecs believed, unless she was continually fed by human flesh and blood. "It is she who is obsessively represented on the underside of the ritual vessels designed to receive human blood and hearts. Whatever the icons they bear on their upper surfaces, whatever great forces they invoke, underneath she is there, her insatiable maw wide open, great claws at elbows and knees, in the squatting position Aztec women adopted to give birth" (Clendinnen, "Cost" 78).[55]

This monstrous earth mother formed the underside of the Aztec's solar performance frame, regarding the temple stage as sacred mountain and the prop bowl for human blood. Here the Aztec frame directly shows the sacrificial *corps morcelé* (fragmented body) usually hidden under the proscenium illusions of ego power in Euro-American theatre, film, and television. The Aztec earth monster, Tlaltecuhtli (Earth Lord), is both male and female. From a psychoanalytic view, this points to the infant's fantasy of a phallic mother, who threatens to re-engulf the child (like the earth does to the sun) although giving it birth and sustaining its life.[56] The phallic mother also seems to dismember the child, when the child develops a separate sense of itself and loses her as an extension of its own body, whether through breast weaning and toilet training (Klein) or through symbolic castration and linguistic alienation (Lacan).[57] Aztec society acted out this fundamental fantasy with the sacrifice of real human bodies, dismembered at the altar and rolled down the temple steps, and with the offering of human blood in a sacred bowl bearing the earth mother's image.[58]

Preconquest Aztec theatre bears insights, especially in its mythological frame, for our secularized tradition, which has tended, since the European Renaissance, to bury its ritual heritage beneath the illusions of a Thespian ego and Cartesian proscenium. Lacan's statement, "the gods belong to the field of the real" (*Four* 45), relates in this case to the intimacy of Real sacrifice, mythic dismemberment, and human mortality in the imaginary and symbolic dimensions of Aztec performance—or to the extimacy of that Real at the heart of our own proscenium media. The Aztecs used the imaginary roles of their gods to justify mass sacrifice and thereby expand the symbolic order of their warring, imperialistic culture.[59] Euro-American mass-media capitalism uses the glamorous roles of film and TV stars to justify, yet hide, the sacrifices of many bodies behind and beyond the screen, as its symbolic order expands through the nearly worldwide popularity of violent dramas and seductive commercials. But that sun will lose its force, too, someday. In the meantime, we may become more wary of our submission to its demands—and find pleasure in the sacrificial roles we inevitably play— through further comparisons of our ritual theatre to that of the Aztecs and ancient Greeks, regarding the postmodern subject, split and multiplied by the mass media.

ANIMISTIC PSYCHOLOGY, PUPPETRY,
AND DANCING HEARTS

C. Fred Alford has recently used Kleinian object relations theory along with Lacanian psychoanalysis to describe parallels between postmodern subjectivity (as split by the Other's desires, beyond the wholeness of the modern ego) and the sense of self in Greek tragedy. Despite historical distance and cultural differences, Greek drama shows what postmodern theory postulates: the lack of autonomous being, as the desire of the Other (of the gods) acts upon and within character,[60] so that "man is the object, but not the subject, of his own desires" (23). Alford sees this sense of *psyche* within Greek tragedy emerging historically from prior sacrificial blood rites, through a progressive "Dionysian crisis" akin to the healthy shift in human infancy from a paranoid-schizoid stage to that of depressive integration of good and evil object relations (11–12, 50–58, 72–76).[61] These Kleinian stages also relate, in my view, to the melodramatic and tragic paradigms of ritual sacrifice and theatre, from ancient to postmodern. Melodrama onstage and onscreen, like ritual sacrifice, displays a paranoid fear of the monstrous villain (or angry god), a schizoid splitting of good versus evil characters, and a justification for violence in the victim's and hero's sacrifices—the former as abject, the latter as ultimately triumphant. Tragedy, however, when it appears in ancient Greece, in modern theatre, and in postmodern (tragicomic) media screens, shows a more complex, mature stage of depressive integration of good and evil forces in each character, involving its audience in the cathartic clarification, not just purgation, of violent fears and desires. Thus, in Lacanian terms, the spectator may experience, along with the tragic hero, a sacrifice of the sacrifice: a crossing of sacrificial, mimetic repetitions of melodramatic violence and vengeance. This Lacanian sense of tragic sacrifice as cathartic rite of passage offers the ancient and postmodern insight that Alford relates—that one is the object, not the subject of one's desires. But tragic sacrifice also subjectifies the lost cause (of the Other's desire) in the ethics of the Real, so that a change in destructive, symptomatic repetitions can occur. A tragicomic reintegration of postmodern split-subjectivity may be possible, through a reconstruction of fundamental fantasies, not just a (Kleinian) bolstering of the depressive-integrative ego as a mask covering the lack of being and the impossible Real.

This theory will be fully elaborated in the chapters ahead, through dramatic examples from the stage and screen. But a tragic edge can also be found in the melodrama of Aztec human sacrifice, disclosing a rhythmic *chora* of multiple souls in various body parts as properties of the ritual dance, tied to animistic forces in nature and culture.[62] Such a sense of Aztec "psychology" illuminates further parallels between Greek, Mesoamerican, and postmodern theatres of the mind and society—disturbing the conventional distinctions between such cultures (or the good and evil oppositions of melodrama), which may mask the Real violence they share.[63]

In retrospect, the ancient Greeks demonstrated the beginnings of modern ego individualism with their theatrical and democratic experiments. Yet they also show the contrasting edges of postmodern subjectivity—not only with the tragic hero subjected to (objectified by) the Other's desire, as Alford points out, but also with the schizoid subjectivity of multiple souls in each person's character. In fact, the belief in multiple souls was common in ancient Greece and among the early Christian theologians. Even Aristotle, who argued for the soul's unity, defined the vegetative, sensitive, and rational parts of the soul—the first two of which humans shared with plants and animals.[64] The belief in a single, whole, unfragmented soul, independent of the material body and natural world, and original to each person, only developed gradually in Christian Europe, from the Roman Augustine to the medieval Aquinas to the Renaissance's Fifth Lateran Council (Furst 6–7).

At a time when the modern, whole soul—and secular ego—reached a crucial codification during the European Renaissance, the Aztecs continued to display a premodern sense of multiple souls in the body and in the body parts of the sacrificial god-actor. These pieces of the Aztec body and soul relate in uncanny ways to today's dispersion of identity in the very different, virtual realities of postmodern media theatres. We experience a piecemeal sacrifice of body and soul at the film and TV screens, with closeup cuts of stars' body parts as fetish objects and with the audience's psychic investment split between numerous images within the drama and through the juxtaposed commercials of TV. Current brain research has also discovered that there is no single center to the mind, no physical seat for the Cartesian ego, but a chorus of various areas working in some degree of harmony (Dennett and Damasio). Such choral harmony (or dissonance) within the brain, according to cognitive science and neurology, along with the postmodern experience of schizoid spectatorship, finds uncanny echoes in Aztec, premodern psychology—through a very different view of cosmic forces tied to other body parts beyond the brain, which were crucial to that culture's sacrificial theatre.

The Aztecs believed that all social and natural objects shared certain energies. The sun needed the nourishment of *teyolia* to rise each morning after passing through the bowels of the earth and the land of the dead. *Teyolia* was a psychic and cosmic power within the human heart, the force of movement shaping one's sensibilities and thought patterns.[65] A god-actor was infused with an "extraordinary amount" of *teyolia* through his or her theatrical performance (Carrasco, *Religions* 69). The extraction of the god-actor's heart then released *teyolia* to the sun, empowering its morning rise. The earth also cried out at night for nourishment; the earth goddess needed the energy of human and animal blood to produce in return the fruits that nourished man.[66]

But the human head, hair, and blood carried a different animistic power, *tonalli*, which shaped individual temperament and destiny.[67] These body parts and fluids also became props in the performance of ritual warfare and human sacrifice, increasing the *tonalli* of victorious warriors, of their city, and of the hungry gods (Carrasco, *Religions* 68).[68] The hair of captured warriors was kept by their captors. The skulls of sacrificed god-actors were strung together on the temple "skull rack." And their blood was offered to the lips of stone icons. Thus, Aztec sacrificial actors were not just mimetic victims. They became holy objects, before and after death, sacred puppets who absorbed a particular god's power and personality through symbolic costumes and props.[69] "It was not men who died, but gods—gods within a corporeal covering that made possible their ritual death on earth. If the gods did not die, their force would diminish in a progressively aging process. Men destined for sacrifice were temporarily converted into receptacles of divine fire" (López Austin 376–377). They then gave the ultimate, cathartic performance. The divine power in these god-actors rejuvenated the sun and earth and all of Aztec culture.[70] Without that theatre, the Aztecs believed their world would end.

The Aztecs' sacrificial theatre shows the collective power of performance when it is invested with cosmic and natural, as well as social and psychological meanings—unlike the secular rites of technological magic in film and TV watching today. At their various monthly festivals (each dedicated to a different god), the Aztecs not only cast captured warriors as god-actors, they also created divine puppets out of nonhuman materials. These *ixiptlas*, primarily made out of maize dough, were costumed in the god's symbolic attire, paraded through the streets, then sacrificed and dismembered at the appropriate temple, like the human *ixiptlas*—with blood from the god-actor sprinkled on the vegetable icon and both at certain points consumed.[71] This view of Aztec ritual reveals, to the postmodern spectator, a revolutionary *chora* of human and material interrelatedness, prior to mirror-stage individualism and Cartesian humanism, but persisting at the premodern heart of those modern illusions. The multiple animistic souls of Aztec psychology, connecting individual minds, social powers, and natural orders, show that the postmodern, schizoid subject is not an entirely new phenomenon. The sensibilities, thought patterns, temperaments, and destinies of our desires (i.e., our teyolia and tonalli) are channeled today by mass-media consumerism. Thus, like the *chora* of ancient Greek ritual sacrifice, repressed by, yet sometimes erupting through theatre's Thespian ego, mimetic mirrors, and eventual proscenium frame, Aztec sacrificial god-acting can speak in an uncanny way across the edges of Cartesian frames and screens, from the pre- to the postmodern.[72]

As Artaud pointed out, early in the history of film: "The human skin of things, the derm of reality—this is the cinema's first toy" (*Collected* 21). Though he later became disillusioned with film and turned fully toward the ritual element of theatre, Artaud at this point (1927) also found his hope in cinema: "It does not separate itself from life but returns to the primitive order of things." If Artaud was right, then cinema and television today bear an even greater potential to reveal the "human skin of things," like the Aztecs wearing human skins to portray their gods. (Artaud not only read Sahagún, but also traveled to Mexico to commune with the native Tarahumara in 1936.) Usually, however, film and TV idealize actors as godlike puppets without materiality, separating them from real life and encouraging the substitution of such images for life, in the minds of the mass audience. One way to perceive "the derm of reality," onscreen and off, might be through a return to the "primitive order of things," by comparing how today's actors offer their skins for the illusion of transcendence, apparently becoming what the Other desires on millions of screens.[73] The Aztec *ixiptla* gave his or her skin as a post-mortem epidermis; current performers give theirs through another technology, while still alive. Yet they also suffer the loss of their ideal, youthful skins, immortalized by the screen media, as their real bodies age—despite the best efforts of plastic surgery. They are thus sacrificed, like the Aztec *ixiptla*, to produce an immortal imago of face and body, in the half-life of the media limelight, for millions of fans to absorb and mimic, with a similar, fatal futility. But the awareness of such collective mirror-stage theatrics, in mass-mediated life today, also relates to the primal perception of hearts and blood, in Greek as well as Aztec performance.

In ancient Greece, as Marcel Detienne describes, the Dionysian maenad's dance was a "dance of the heart," a leaping *(pedesis)*, "when Terror rose ready to scream and the heart began to leap, to dance to an accompaniment of clacking crotala. The heart stamped its feet on the diaphragm, dancing a wild round on the body's entrails" (*Dionysos* 57). Dionysian dance, in ancient theatre and cult rites, was a return to the infant's primal energy. "A newborn is a frenzied little animal, crying and gesticulating without rhyme or reason and imbued with an instinct to jump (*to kata phusin pedan*), always ready to jump or leap. Without this instinct neither rhythm nor harmony would exist" (58). Even today, in the *chora* of stage and screen sacrifice, the spirit of Dionysus recalls the mimetic drama of the mirror stage, between six and eighteen months, when each of us experienced an early climax in the theatre of human lack: caught between the fragmented, leaping, infantile body and the ideal mask of ego reflected in the (m)Other's eyes. As Detienne puts it: "In Dionysian anthropology, the heart muscle is like an internal maenad in the body of the possessed, constantly leaping within" (59).

Aztec ritual performance removed that dancing heart from its corporeal theatre to show it leaping beyond death, as immortal food for the sun. The heart thus became im-mortal, an object of desire (or Lacanian *objet a*) surviving beyond the death of the body—yet bearing the interdependency of divine, human, and natural worlds. The extracted Aztec heart, like the leaping Greek dancer, expressed the heart within the bodies of the audience as well: the inaccessible, yet Real beating of life and death together. With such a tragic (or tragicomic) awareness, today's spectators might also realize the mortal, cathartic leaps of their own hearts in the action and music of the drama—rather than simply escaping from life through the pervasive, melodramatic mirrors of stage and screen violence.

CATHARTIC ENCOUNTERS WITH THE REAL

Various Aztec and Greek props exemplify Real elements that might touch us cathartically today, disrupting the imaginary and symbolic simulacrum of media violence and revealing its mimetic, sacrificial pressures. Blood was used by both cultures; it was collected sacrificially from the dying human or animal, then sprinkled upon the altar and specific icons to show the movement of desire between Real bodies (of actors and spectators), imaginary gods, and symbolic demands.[74] This circulation of blood and desire within the social body also related to the wearing of human or animal skins, in Aztec and Greek performance. (Greek vases show the significance of animal skins in the costuming of satyr and maenad figures, from the mythic Dionysian chorus to its theatrical correlative.) The skin upon the body was a surface form put into play between certain actors, showing the submission of both performers and spectators to the transience of character. The Aztec use of human skulls as ritual props, like the Greek use of sacrificial animal skulls and theatrical masks,[75] showed the hidden structure of identity transformed into an exoskeleton. The Real of death (as Lacanian *das Ding*) was represented in the skull, which would outlive the living faces onstage and in the audience, becoming an immortal, yet material face—like the mask of mythic character in Greek drama. Unlike the virtual perfection of the made-up or surgically remodeled face of today's movie and TV stars (especially in closeup), the Greek mask and Aztec skull offer a more ethical reminder of the Real of the actor's body decomposing behind it.

This encounter with Real mortality, displayed in the ritual theatres of the Greeks and Aztecs, is the most significant way in which their collective mirror stages can illuminate the transcendent deceptions and symbolic demands of our own. Our culture displays plenty of sacrificial violence onscreen, but usually in order to purge our fears and sympathies, allowing the audience an illusion of transcendence over the suffering of screen characters. We can vicariously participate in the dangerous adventure, yet leave the movie theatre or change the TV channel unscathed. Such simple catharsis may have intoxicated and relieved the ancient Greek audience, too, as a purgative interpretation of Aristotle would attest. Perhaps the Aztec audience also felt a thrill and release of sympathetic fears at the sacrifice of the *ixiptla*.[76] The scapegoat in each case, whether a Greek tragic hero (with warrior chorus) or a captured Aztec warrior, could be seen as a safety valve, siphoning off the desire for violence within the community, as René Girard's modern theory insists.[77] And yet, the mythic, ritual, and familial framework of sacrifice in these cultures points to another possibility, related to our own times as well. The performance of violence may not only function as a cathartic fetish to purge and thereby control rebellious impulses in the social body. It may also present a cathartic purification of desire and clarification of lacking being: a collective mirror-stage experience that reveals the Real losses behind idealized imagos, shaped by certain symbolic pressures.[78] Each of us today, like the Greek victim/hero or Aztec *ixiptla*, is fated to play out a mortal role—to fight for a meaningful identity in a limited lifetime. If we cling to screen illusions as fashionable identifications, we miss the Real drama of our own heart, blood, skin, and skull.

Of course, there remains a great difference between the Aztec and ancient Greek world views—as between theirs and our own. Theatre history has conventionally mapped its Western lineage through Greek drama's original distinction from ritual, especially in the tragic hero's defiance of the gods, yet ultimate submission to fate. The admiration, by neoclassical rule-makers, for that humanist struggle helped to solidify the metanarrative of theatre's separation from the womb of ritual. However, theatre's umbilical cord to ritual's bloody show has often been resurrected, in theory and practice, in various anticlassical experiments throughout the Renaissance, Romantic, and modern periods. It may be time now, in the postmodern, as we realize a new sense of multiple, schizoid subjectivity, split by the Other's desire, to discover our uncanny kinship not only to the Greek hero's fate as ritual *pharmakos* (scapegoat), but also to the Aztec *ixiptla*.

The Aztec world view involved a sacrificial anxiety like, yet unlike the imperialist culture of their Greco-Roman, Judeo-Christian conquerors. Although the Aztecs, like the conquistadors, imposed their beliefs and rituals on other cultures, the Aztecs captured human bodies, precious objects, and territory in order to feed and extend a solar order that would inevitably fail. Whereas the Spanish brought Franciscan missionaries to the New World who believed their conversion of the natives to Christianity would lead to a millennial kingdom and the Second Coming of Christ (Carrasco, *Religions* 5), the Aztecs captured souls to feed a dying sun. According to the oracle of the Aztecs' mythic calendar, their theatre of human sacrifice displayed a tragic defiance of, yet submission to fate—on a much broader scale than the Greek hero's. Their world would end, they believed, along with the current sun, at a certain point in time—as it did with the conquistadors' arrival.

Such fatalism may seem a self-fulfilling prophecy; but all cultures transform over time, as did that of the Spanish invaders as they merged with the Aztec (Mexica) to form the Mexican and Mexican-American heritage. Now, in a new millennium, our postmodern, capitalist culture appears to be the opposite of the Aztec sun: an immortal, high-tech amoeba, spreading worldwide forever. Aztec animism involved the life and death forces of the natural world; ours finds its spirits through electric circuitry, digital codes, broadcast waves, and Internet webs in various virtual worlds.[79] But our "$un" is also dying through its thriving—through its environmental, economic, and cultural transformations. In each of our lives, we sacrifice time and emotion to feed it, as we watch its mass-media mirrors and stages, trying to make sense (as the apparatus makes money) out of the desire for violence. Yet we often forget, while participating as spectators in that simulacrum, how our blood and bodies also feed the earth and sun of the mass-media *agora*,[80] through the fetishizing of certain god-actors whom we then imitate commercially, buying the props that the stars make sacred onscreen. A new triangulation of theatre's ritual history is needed, from Greek and Aztec to postmodern,[81] to get a better view of this curse of mimetic sacrifice inherited, but vastly expanded from the days of Aristotle, which today's ordinary, mass-media theatres perpetuate, especially in the repetition compulsion of violence, onscreen and off. The next chapter will consider further parallels between ancient European, Amerindian, and postmodern sacrifices—to discover not only ritual submission and mimetic repetitions of violence in sublimated forms, but also the potential catharsis of that curse, from melodramatic to tragic stage edges.

TWO

Roman, Aztec, and NFL "Gladiators"

IT IS TEMPTING TO VIEW ancient Roman theatre, especially in contrast to the Greek golden age, as revealing the worst tendencies of our own times. Oscar Brockett declares that Roman theatre was "dominated by variety enter tainment," which he compares to "American television programming" (49). Brockett extends this parallel as a critique of the mass audience, then and now. "The Roman public was as fickle as our own: like channel-switchers, they frequently left one event for another and demanded diversions capable of withstanding all competition." Brockett's parallel reflects a common fear of artists and historians that the competition with film and television draws spectators away from the art of theatre today—like the mass entertainments of ancient Rome, in the complaints of Terence and Horace.[1] This tendency increased from the Roman Republic into the Empire, with greater displays of real violence in gladiatorial contests, wild animal hunts, and public execu tions. What can be learned from this migration of the Roman audience away from classical theatre toward explicitly violent contests and shows? How does it reflect the lure of violence in sports contests today, which gather a much greater audience, both live and onscreen, than any theatre agon(y)? Instead of marking an ideological separation between violent entertainment and artistic drama, or criticizing Roman spectators for being fickle and vulgar like our own mass audience, this chapter will look for elements of theatre that continued into the Roman amphitheatre—manifesting common interests and theatrical desires that persist in other ways today.

Obviously, there are great differences between the technological abilities and cultural tastes of our TV age and the violent excesses of ancient Roman performance. Violence on film and television appeals to us today not only because it seems real beyond our wildest dreams, but also because we know it

47

is an illusion created through camera work, stunts, and postproduction machinery. However, the increasing popularity of cinema violence and pseudodocumentary horror films like *The Blair Witch Project*; of TV's "reality-based" crime, accident, and game shows; of fist fights on talk shows; of news broadcasts showing high-speed police chases, riots, natural disasters, terrorist attacks, and "live" warfare; as well as of interactive video and computer games that directly involve viewers in simulated bloodshed, demonstrates a shift in mass audience desires across the indefinite threshold between the appearance and reality of violence onscreen. Brockett's channel-changer analogy thus hinges on the appetite for violence, not just variety, in ancient and post-modern spectatorship: the desire to experience the limits of one's own identity through depictions of the real fragmentation and death of others, onstage or onscreen.

A direct look at the Roman gladiator fight *as* theatre illuminates symptomatic fears and desires shared by audiences of theatre and popular entertainment, of drama and sports today[2]—especially when this view is triangulated through performance paradigms (and uncanny excesses) in another premodern civilization that is usually left out of the theatre history textbooks.[3] The ritual sacrifice of Aztec "gladiators," as recorded by Spanish conquistadors, shows a link between theatrical desires and imperial orders in various Euro-American civilizations: ancient Rome, Mesoamerica,[4] and Renaissance Spain.[5] This yields further insights about the desiring machinery and empirical expansion of mass-media capitalism at our own millennial turning point—displayed in the sublimated civil war of professional, televised sports.

Five aspects of theatre in Roman and Aztec gladiator contests are of particular interest regarding today's spectator sports and the mass audiences they draw: (1) the persistent context of ritual sacrifice, involving an encounter with death at the stage edge; (2) the interplay of corporality and metaphysics in the scripting of rules and scores; (3) the political and spiritual significance of certain dances, costumes, and props; (4) the star athlete as sacred actor, as both hero and scapegoat; and (5) the communal, yet competitive participation of spectators, owners, and rulers in the power play. Roman examples will be drawn primarily from gladiator contests, with some references also to wild animal hunts and public executions. For Aztec comparisons I will consider the sacrificial performance of "gladiator" contests in the ethnographic writings of Spanish missionaries and reports of the Aztecs' sacred "hip-ball game" (*ulamaliztli*).[6] As to potential insights for the theatre of sports today, I will suggest various parallels with the most violent of the major American team genres, professional football, although other sports (including hockey and soccer, which dominate in other countries) would offer appropriate examples as well. The growing popularity of televised professional wrestling demonstrates a more obvious theatricalization of sports, with its prearranged scripts, choreographed moves, and melodramatic characters. But football bears more potential for postmodern, tragicomic catharsis, with audience sympathy and fear for players on both sides as more complex figures (in more ambiguous dramas) than wrestling's heroes and villains. The violence of football also involves a seasonal sense of death and rebirth, as a traditional American rite of fall and winter passage, tied to the Thanksgiving, Christmas, and New Year's holidays, as well as to each weekend's Sabbath.

In February 2001, the World Wrestling Federation started its own professional football league, the XFL, offering more "extreme" physical contact for the rest of the winter and into spring, with nationally televised games on Saturdays and Sundays. Although the XFL died after just a few months of performance, it played up the parallels between American football and Roman sacrifice (in the same year that *Gladiator* won the Oscar for Best Film). An XFL player for the New York Hitmen used the word "Gladiator" as his name on the back of his uniform. On March 4, 2001, a player for the Memphis Maniacs injured the quarterback of the Orlando Rage so badly that he had to be taken off the field on a stretcher. While the game was delayed for this, the crushing sack was replayed many times in slow-motion onscreen. When asked if the unfortunate incident would affect how he played the rest of the game, the sacker told the interviewer that they were all "gladiators" and that it was "live or die out there." Likewise, in Oliver Stone's recent film about professional football, *Any Given Sunday*, a team doctor calls the players "gladiators" and one player literally loses an eyeball on the field. Yet, the film shows the traditional ideal of self-sacrifice for the team in conflict with the current mass-media drive toward individual stardom, on the field and beyond. While such sacrifice and stardom for today's gladiators is very different from that in other cultures and centuries, the apparent transcendence of certain players finds uncanny parallels in the theatres of Roman and Aztec rites, especially regarding the appeal of violence for many spectators.

SACRIFICIAL SHADES

Roman gladiator contests emerged first as funeral games to honor the dead. This suggests that a fight to the death, as spectator sport, served as the dramatic focus and potential catharsis for mortal fear, mournful sympathy, and vengeful rage—at the death of a military leader or wealthy aristocrat.[7] Like the Greek theatre's origins in Dionysian ritual dance, the gladiator show arose as a ritual communication with the Other beyond human life: "an offering or duty paid to the *manes*, or shades, of dead Roman chieftains" (Barton, *Sorrows* 13). The Romans believed that unsatisfied spirits could create catastrophes, or return from the dead to drag the living into the underworld, or be made to speak through a blood offering.[8] Thus, the gladiatorial sacrifice, as entertainment after the initial funeral rites, continued to play upon the stage edge between life and death—to make the dead character speak as if immortal, through the violent action and flow of blood.[9]

The Roman relation to the departed soul at the funeral game offers an uncanny parallel to the ritual of weekend football, enjoyed by so many Americans (mostly male, but a growing population of females as well), whether in the stadium or around the TV set at home, from late summer and fall toward the death of the year in winter. Through the display of "violence every Sunday"[10] and newspaper lists of the wounded each week, the best contests go into "sudden death" overtime or show an intense *agon* down to the last ticks of the clock. (The aim of each contest may not be the literal death of the opponent; yet defensive players often try to injure a key player on the other team, such as the quarterback, in order to take him out of the game.) Ultimately, certain players and their teams survive into the playoffs, but only one team becomes immortalized as the winner of the "Super Bowl" in the new year. Its star players speak through today's mass media like gladiatorial ghosts, reviving the heroic spirits of past American leaders, who won their wars in various theatres, but ultimately lost to death. With the yearly rite of the NFL (National Football League) season and Super Bowl, Americans may not think they are attending a funeral for lost leaders—or celebrating American immortality and manifest destiny. Yet they participate in a ritual theatre that confirms collective culture and ancestry, through an exorcism of community rivalries, by focusing current violence into the surrogate combat of athletes and the performance text of their scores.

Charles Laughlin has delineated the general characteristics of modern sports as ritual, via cognitive psychology, phenomenology, and anthropology. According to Laughlin the genetic "wiring" of the human species for play produces the phenomenon of ritual as a revelation of hidden social and cosmic forces. Professional teams represent specific communities and team names often declare totemic associations with forces of nature.[11] The players and cheerleaders enact archetypal characters (hero, enemy, and princess). They perform in "virtually sacred spaces," evoking a sense of festivity, along with the chants and rhythmic activity of the audience (97). "The epiphanic dimension of games and sports is quite real for both players and spectators, yet the interpretive frame for relating the epiphanic dimension of play to a dynamic cosmos has been lost" (99).

Here is another sense in which the theatre of sports becomes an inverse funeral. Rather than mourning the loss of a collective cosmic frame, Americans celebrate a common enthusiasm for the athletic contest, through particular team and player identifications. For many NFL football fans, this secular worship follows immediately upon the trip to church on Sunday morning. In contrast to Laughlin, I would argue that the epiphanic dimension of sports today, viewed through prior historical paradigms of sacrificial sports as ritual theatre, does reveal a performance frame that interprets the cosmic relation of mortal fear and immortal desire.

The lack of being that characterized the *manes*—for whom the Roman gladiators initially performed via the desires of a living funeral audience— offers an uncanny parallel to the postmodern subject watching the sports performance onscreen. Unlike the home crowd around the football field, the TV audience (at home or elsewhere) cannot directly contribute its visual or vocal presence to influence the contest. Yet the athletes are performing for the cheers and jeers of both the present crowd and the mass-mediated audience. The two audiences, in effect, ghost each other.[12] The TV audience shadows (and numerically overshadows) the live fans in the stadium; but those present spectators, while participating more directly in the violent passions of the athletic contest, also become shadows of mass-audience desire on the TV screen. Then again, so do the athletes, especially as each slow-motion replay doubles the live broadcast, improving the fantasmic, immortal view.[13]

THE METAPHYSICS OF SCRIPT AND SCORE

The Romans may not have viewed living athletes and spectators as lacking being like the dead. But the growing desire of the Roman audience to see gladiators face death and to watch the experience of dying, from early funeral games to grander public spectacles (over hundreds of years), shows a fascination with the shade and script in each living being.[14] Even the vilest criminal, sentenced to die in the amphitheatre, became noble in Roman eyes—if he displayed the courage to transcend his fate. Various Roman philosophers valued the mass carnage of sacrificial entertainment for that very reason. Public execution not only demonstrated the power of Roman justice and served as a deterrent to potential criminals in the audience; it also offered a redemptive moment for the guilty victim. Although gladiator shows and wild animal hunts appealed to the basest carnal desires in the mass audience, they still demonstrated the virtue of suicidal fearlessness.[15] Arena performers were both despised and idolized, as sacrificial victims and as sacred objects. They acted out a script linking them to the common fate and fear of death in every spectator. However, by putting on the mask of death, as killer or victim, gladiators also showed a kind of immortality.[16] Whether through victory over another mortal body or through noble indifference to one's own death (even when losing the contest), the gladiatorial actor gave the illusion of transcending his fatal script.

The postmodern players of televised sports do not fight to the death as Roman gladiators did. But they do become sacrificial victims and sacred objects in their violent struggle to achieve victorious scores, noble statistics, and immortal identities. Symbolically, the miracle-play martyrdom of football onscreen bears some of the cruel drama of mortal wounding in the Roman games. Those football players who are cut from the team roster are simply discarded and forgotten. Other athletes whose careers end prematurely through the frequent injuries of professional football also fade quickly from public memory after being carried off the field and screen. Violent plays are often memorialized by TV highlights, yet the perversity of audience pleasure at the performer's pain becomes subsumed into the virtue of the score—especially when it's an opposing player who suffers a great "hit" in the eyes of the fans, through the choral voices of the TV announcers.

In Lacanian terms, the sports fan finds *jouissance* (ecstatic joy as partial substitute for lost, symbiotic bliss with the mother) through identification with the ideal ego of a victorious athlete or team.[17] Like the mirror-stage infant, the fan rises out of his or her lacking, fragmented body through an imaginary merging with the wholeness of the Other's successful desire—when one's favorite team or player wins. But that share of illusory immortality rests upon and remains vulnerable to the Real mortality within athletes and spectators, which is also put in play between them. The creative and destructive *chora* in this play space of athletic, mortal conflict often produces aggressive *jouissance* in the game's violent excesses, threatening the symbolic order of stars and rules. A choral breath of death resounds in the rhythms and rhetoric of the fans' cheers (e.g., "Kill 'em!"), as well as in the rage for victory on the field.[18] But the symbolic score creates a consensual climax—as both teams fight against the clock—that restrains and gives meaning to the ecstatic violence of the game's bodies, despite their imaginary ego competition and Real pain. The ritual of shaking hands with opponents at the end of a football game also shows the exorcism of ego conflict through good sportsmanship. However, today's players and teams also fight for mass-media fame, a stardom to outlive their mortal careers, like the Roman gladiators battling for a public, entertaining, and honorable death. Both games, although in very different cultural contexts, offer a ritual communication with dead heroes of the past, through current, youthful athlete-warriors, who act out immortal desires in mortal bodies—their own and those of the spectators.

Sports appear to be unlike theatre in that they are unscripted; the final score is unknown until the game is played out. And yet, any performance of a dramatic script also involves improvisation, no matter how much it has been previously rehearsed. A sports conflict follows the script of the game's rules—and of the dramatic meanings set by tradition, by team rivalries, by the season's standings, etc.[19] In team sports, certain plays have been rehearsed by the offense and the defense; these settings and scripts are then performed when called by the coach or leading player. The score of the game develops as a newly written script (and dialogue), defining the present drama and violence of athletic action, through the rules, practices, and game plans scripted in the past.[20] But the sacrificial dimension of these scripts becomes more apparent when compared with the metaphysical scoring of Aztec as well as Roman rites of violence.

The Aztec festival of Tlacaxipeualiztli was briefly mentioned in the previous chapter, but deserves further consideration here.[21] At this spring festival, captive warriors' hearts were removed; then their skins were flayed and worn by others, in a fertility rite representing the renewal of life through vegetation, especially maize with its flayed husks. Both the sacrificial victim and the wearers of his skin were god-actors, impersonating the god Xipe Totec (the Flayed One or Flayer), through specific insignia of props and costume. (Women were also sacrificed and flayed during another festival, Ochpanitztli, in the roles of the mother goddess Toci and other goddesses.) The young Aztec warriors who played the role of *xipeme* by wearing the flayed skins, along with other props and costume elements of the god, walked through the neighborhoods collecting food offerings (tortillas, maize cobs, and fruit) from each home in exchange for the blessings of the god. They also engaged in a mock battle with other Aztec youths, who snatched at their navels, grabbing at the skins they wore and bringing out their anger.

If comparisons are made to current American culture, these rites may seem more like Halloween than NFL football. But the props and costumes of professional football do bear a sacred, sacrificial aura. A star player's jersey garners supernatural respect, especially after the player has retired or died. This "skin" is encased in the Hall of Fame, along with other relics of the player. (The Aztecs kept their flayed skins in a sacred cave after they had been worn.) In rare cases a famous player's jersey number will be retired with him. But if it is not, then other players on his team gain the aura of the previous godlike athlete when they wear his number. Fans also buy and wear team jerseys with the number and name of their favorite player. Team names and insignia on helmets and uniforms, like the animal skins and feathers worn by Aztec jaguar and eagle warriors in gladiatorial battle, provide a metaphysical aura as symbolic communal costume, bearing a specific totemic spirit. Helmets, shoulder pads, and other football equipment are not only practical, protective devices; they also idealize the figure of muscular, macho masculinity. Regarding such gender dynamics, one might analyze as well the flashy, skin-tight pants showing off the powerful legs that penetrate the other team's territory, or the pigskin as fetish prop (and ejaculatory object carried by the player's body as sacred phallus) that will ultimately reach into the erogenous end zone, producing the climactic *jouissance* of a score. Like the Aztec sacrifice of flayed skins and hearts, today's football games are seasonal fertility rites of patriarchal, homosocial bonding and territorial struggle (with female cheerleaders rooting on the sidelines)—although the vegetation connection may lie only in the manicured grass or artificial turf.[22]

Tlacaxipeualiztli also involved certain warriors selected for the "gladiatorial sacrifice," as the Spaniard Sahagún termed it (48–49). These warriors were captured in ritual "flower wars" between city-states, as were the warriors sacrificed in other rites. Aztec gladiators thus represented—like Roman captives

FIGURE 2.1. Illustrations of Tlacaxipeualiztli from Sahagún. Notice the flayed human skins being worn by god-actors portraying Xipe Totec (with extra hands and feet dangling from wrists and ankles). Courtesy of the University of Utah Press.

used as gladiators—the conquered territory from which they came. Here a parallel appears with the significance of home and visiting teams in professional football.[23] Although an NFL city does not engage in ritual warfare to capture opposing players, the visiting team is certainly treated as the enemy by the home crowd and local TV fans. Today, less than a century and a half since the American Civil War, professional sports teams provide a much safer outlet for intercity and interregional hostility.[24] As the Aztec example also shows, the athletic event can even evoke respect for the enemy and his homeland, if he meets his fate with courage and skill, as the Roman audience likewise desired. Thus, a more complex appreciation of the enemy warrior—as Roman, Aztec, or NFL gladiator—might evoke tragic sympathy and fear, not just melodramatic derision and revenge.

The Aztec enemy gladiator, unlike his Roman counterpart, had a definite, prescripted end. Immediately after the contest, his heart was removed as an offering to the sun. There was no chance for him to live and fight again—as the Roman gladiator could in defeating his opponent or in fighting well enough (even if he lost) to please the crowd and get the emperor's approving signal. Yet, the captured Aztec still performed with athletic skill and a warrior's courage for the present audience—and for those in his home city who would hear about his performance later. In the final moments of his sacrificial script, a strong performer would say (according to Sahagún): "You will speak of me there in my home land!" (47).[25]

IM-MORTAL DANCES, COSTUMES, AND PROPS

Prior to this sacrificial climax, and prior to the gladiatorial combat, the selected captives would dance in a procession—somewhat like today's pregame parade of players and the half-time ritual of marching bands. According to various accounts, captive Aztec warriors wore white feathers pasted to their heads, arms, and legs (Broda 210). Their entire bodies were painted white, except for their eyelids and lips, which were red. They wore a sleeveless paper jacket and the cone-shaped hat emblematic of the god Xipe Totec. The musicians in the temple square, who played and sang hymns with the priests as the warriors danced, also wore the Xipe headdress (*yopitzontli*). The processional dance displayed the symbolic costumes, makeup, and markings of the players—though with more direct ties to divinity than today's football helmets and uniforms, the black makeup under athletes' eyes, and the costumes of cheerleaders, marching bands, and cartoonish mascots.

The Aztec home team was also elaborately costumed, as they displayed the art of sport and war. The elite eagle and ocelot warriors appeared in the skins of those animals—as they did in battle—with quilted cotton armor underneath (Broda 211). They raised their shields and war clubs to the sun, showing in the dance their fighting gestures. The procession also included god-actors (*ixiptlas*), costumed as various Aztec divinities. These gods became spectators of the sport, taking their seats according to rank around the playing area. The highest-ranking god-actor was the chief priest, richly costumed as Xipe Totec. As he watched the gladiators, he held a broad knife for the heart sacrifice that he would perform after the fight upon the bodies of captive warriors, who had also been dressed as Xipe before the fight. The Aztec priests and warriors, costumed as gods or sacred animals, performed as dancers, actors, and spectators, as well as athletes and surgeons, in the ritual theatre of the sport and sacrifice.

But the god-actors as spectators also masked the presence of foreign rulers who were secretly brought to the temple square to watch the fight from hidden boxes, made of branches and covered with flowers. These box seats were called *tzapocalli*, as were the gods' seating area. Why were the rulers of the home and visiting teams' cities watching the sport in secret, while priests watched (and then performed the subsequent sacrifice) so publicly in the guise of gods? This scene of doubled spectatorship shows the overlapping of metaphysical and political scripts for the scoring of Aztec gladiator fights— with the metaphysical as a public performance frame and the political as a backstage structure (a hidden area of the auditorium). In other words, the priests and populace could watch and perform a cosmic drama of im-mortal struggle, while the rulers played a private game that also plotted the fates of warriors' lives.[26]

This may show something of the hidden Real in the imaginary/symbolic theatre of professional, televised sports today. Although NFL players do not have their hearts sacrificed after a game, fans of the home and visiting teams do offer their hearts, at least metaphorically, by identifying intensely with the players' passionate, physical struggle. Some fans use costume and makeup to express that team identification in quite fantastic ways—playing also to the TV cameras. The metaphorical, yet real sacrifices displayed by players and fans (whether throwing one's body into a tackle or cheering in freezing weather with a shirtless body painted in team colors) raises the game's script to a metaphysical level, especially through the power of the TV broadcast to bring idolized figures into millions of homes. Even without an overtly religious context like the Aztecs had, today's sports stars perform as gods in the eyes of their fans, entering a sacrificial script so that the fans can feel godlike if their team wins. And yet, this metaphorical theatre of sacrifice also involves the hidden spectatorship of owners and politicians. They call the plays in other theatres whose sacrificial violence—for the sake of financial points, commercial territory, and corporate victory—is mimed, yet masked by the TV sports screen (or by the demand for public money to build a new stadium to keep the home team in town).

Props and gestures in the Aztec gladiator fight show further dimensions of sacrificial im-mortality, as well as politically scripted metaphysics, that relate to the Roman paradigm and illuminate the theatre of televised football today. Trumpets and conch shells were played to announce the start of the combat. The captive warrior was given a sacred wine to drink, a wooden shield to defend himself, and his offensive weapons: four pine cudgels to throw and a war club that had feathers on it, but not the usual obsidian blades. He was also tied by a rope to the center of the sacrificial stone on which he stood. Such props show that the focus of the Aztec script was not on a fair fight, but on the ritual meaning of the battle. A quail was sacrificed for the captive warrior, its throat cut open like the captive's chest would be at the end of the fight for the heart sacrifice. In fact, the object of the gladiatorial game for the home team— for the eagle and jaguar warriors who faced the captive one by one and swung bladed clubs—was to cut the visitor's body, to score by scarring the skin.[27] The Aztecs called this ritual sport Tlahuahuanaliztli, which could be translated as "Scoring with the Sword," a term that Durán compares to the European fencing goal of *touché* (or *toque* in Spanish).[28]

FIGURE 2.2. The Aztec gladiatorial combat from the Codex Magliabecchi. On the left is the captured warrior, tied by a rope to the sacrificial stone. (Notice the cone-shaped hat, emblematic of the god Xipe Totec.) On the right is a home-team warrior, wearing a jaguar skin. Reprinted from *Dances of Anáhuac*, by Gertrude Kurath and Samuel Martí (Viking Fund Publications in Anthropology #38, 1964), by permission of the Wenner-Gren Foundation for Anthropological Research, Inc., New York, New York.

When the captive could no longer stand, the game was over. As god-actors held the arms and legs of the scored body on the sacrificial stone, the priest playing the god Xipe Totec cut out the heart and placed it in the "eagle vessel" as an offering to the sun (Sahagún 52). A hollow "eagle cane" was set into the open chest so that the blood inside the body could also be offered to the sun "to drink." A bowl of the blood was carried by the original captor of the sacrificed warrior to various stone images of the gods in different temples. The blood was offered to these gods by placing the eagle cane to the statues' lips. The scarred body of the dead Aztec gladiator[29] was then flayed and transported to the original captor's home, where its flesh was eaten. After a series of gladiator battles and sacrifices, the decapitated heads of the fallen warriors were used as props in a final dance of the god-actors around the sacrificial stone.

These details of Aztec ritual differ greatly from the Roman gladiator fight as well as from American football. The reverent use of body parts to feed the gods and as props for further ritual and dance performances by god-actors and warriors was unlike the Romans' quick disposal of their dead gladiators. (However, the blood of dead Roman gladiators was reportedly poured onto a statue of Jupiter Latiaris, "perhaps into its throat" [Plass 29].) The Aztec sport of one-on-one combat to draw blood sounds more like the action of today's boxing ring than the gridiron game. And yet, through such distinctions in script and performance elements, certain uncanny similarities appear.

God-actors did perform as attendants in the Roman gladiatorial sacrifices. Mercury (as Hermes Psychopomp, conductor of the dead into Hades) tested the skin of fallen bodies with a red-hot iron, to prove they were not just playing dead. Another attendant, dressed as Charon (in a beaked mask), hit the dead body with a symbolic mallet, to take possession of it for Hades, before it was carried offstage, through the Gate of Death, toward the underworld.[30] And *larvae*, the dissatisfied spirits of the dead, gave a ritual beating to new gladiators in the arena before they fought (Barton, *Sorrows* 19). Were these costumed workers just lingering mythological references in an otherwise secular theatre of violent, mass-audience entertainment? Or do such minor characters, when compared with the major roles of god-actors in Aztec ritual theatre, show a common fascination with the stage edge of mortal/immortal identity—expressed through sacrificial scripts and mythological costumes? The differences are even greater with regard to the secular, nonfatal violence of American football. Yet, this familiar sport can become strangely revealing of current sacrificial and martial desires, when viewed through the theatrical terms of other cultures' violent rites and entertainments.

During a football game today, godlike stars and their colleagues fight to break through the collective skin of the other team: with a running back slicing through the defensive line, with a "Hail Mary" pass (or "bomb") cutting deep into enemy territory,[31] and ultimately with a run or pass play puncturing the imaginary plane above the goal line. The team that draws the most blood from such piercings—in the form of points—scores the fatal blow. Roman and Aztec societies were warrior cultures, in contrast to America's more commercial imperialism (at least until recently). Yet, in all three societies, a violent sport creates an ideal battlefield that abstracts certain types of individual and corporate performance from the theatre of war.[32] Costumed bodies carve out territory through strategic cuts in the Other's collective skin. This offers the mass audience a safely distant, yet intimate contact with brutality, through the flow of blood or points, and the dance of bodies with others' parts—or with the fetishized pigskin and its suturelike laces.

The little football as primary performance prop (Lacanian *objet petit a*), like the Aztec heart, head, and skin taken from the captive player's body, becomes a metaphysical object of pleasure and power around which the violence of the game circulates. Officials, in their black and white costumes, with whistles and yellow flags (plus slow-motion TV monitors) as props of the law, regulate the violent struggle for possession and movement of that primal object of desire. Yet their performance, as judicial spectators, frames the drama on the field where the warriors' violence exceeds the order of the game. Proper and improper violence frequently occurs in the "trenches," for example, as offensive linemen form a collective skin around the precious ball and its bearer (the quarterback or running back), which the defensive players attempt to cut through.[33] The ball also focuses the violent contact when it is thrown in the air or fumbled on the ground. Ecstatic jubilation or extreme frustration arises in a sudden turnover of the ball, even though each team politely returns the ball to the enemy team after success in scoring or failure to cross the first down line. In contrast to the chaotic bloodshed of war and its destructive fight for territory, football offers a focused flow of bodies and blood across the groomed grass—with alternate turns for each team, with uniforms and helmets as corporate skins and totemic skulls, and with the football as the heart of the violent dance.[34]

The Aztecs more directly expressed the metaphysical value of athletic warriors' bodies and body parts as sacrificial actors and props. But even an apparently incidental detail can illuminate a common contact point—in the personal experience of mortality—for Mesoamerican and modern American players and spectators. The priest who tied the captive warriors to the sacred stone was called "Old Wolf" (*Cuetlachtli*).[35] He was considered to be the "uncle" of each captive. After the series of fights and sacrifices, and the "Dance with the Severed Heads" by home warriors and god-actors, the Old Wolf as uncle would mourn the loss of the captive players, raising in the four cardinal directions the so-called sustenance rope that had bound them in the game.[36] "He went weeping and howling, like one bereaved; he wept for those who had suffered and died" (Sahagún 53). Why would an Aztec priest weep for enemy warriors sacrificed by his own city? All Aztec warriors who died on the battlefield or at the sacrificial stone were called "eagle men" and were thought to dwell in the presence of the sun after death, rather than in the underworld. (After four years with the sun, they became birds and butterflies, sucking honey from flowers.)[37] Why then were they mourned?

The prop of the sustenance rope, tying the captive warrior to the sacrificial stone during the gladiatorial game and raised by his "uncle" in ritual mourning afterward, shows a connection between the display of immortal energy in the sport, that energy's sacrificial expenditure, and its primal source. The untying of the rope for the postgame sacrifice, so that the eagle man could be sent upward, following his heart and blood, to dwell with the sun, parallels the primal scene in which an infant's umbilical cord is cut so that it may dwell outside the mother's womb. My interpretation here can be supported by other associations in Aztec ritual and myth. The umbilical cords of male infants were buried in the battlefield; the midwife greeted the newborn infant with war cries, calling it a "captive"; and mothers were considered to be warriors while giving birth.[38] Women who died in childbirth became warriors in the sky; they fought with the dead male warriors (dwelling with the rising sun) to bring the sun down to its setting. Thus, the bloody spectacle of the Aztec "Scoring with the Sword" not only represented the dominance of one city's warriors over the captives from another;[39] it showed the transformation of an enemy warrior into a sympathetic hero, especially if he performed well—reborn (like the sun each day) through gladiatorial labor and sacrificial death. This dramatic transformation through sport and dismemberment, repeated with each captive (whom the captor called his "son"),[40] then culminated in the paradoxical joy and sorrow of the chorus: the god-actors dancing with severed heads and the Old Wolf uncle weeping with the umbilical rope, celebrating and mourning the cycles of birth, death, and rebirth,[41] around the omphalos-like stone.[42]

None of this symbolism seems to occur in today's football game. Yet, each player and spectator shares a primal experience with their Aztec counterparts: the life and death struggle to be born, to pass outside the womb and its bloody show, beyond the reach of the umbilical rope.[43] Although the Aztecs (and Romans) imagined and symbolized that trip quite differently from us, Tlahuahuanaliztli points to the Real pain and triumph of that first moment of life in each person's unconscious memory reverberating in the jouissance of players and sympathetic spectators when winning points are scored, especially against a powerful defense, as the football crosses over the goal line or through the goal posts. This sport is not only a seasonal rite of passage for many Americans, through family traditions of playing or watching; it also becomes a theatre of rebirth in its dance of death.

STAR POWERS

As with the Roman and Aztec gladiatorial games, the current bodies at war in football are staged not only in relation to mythic history or dead ancestors, but also as figures of a past and future violence, at birth and at death, within each spectator's mortal body. Athletic bodies that perform well on the field become media celebrities—in the dances of death and rebirth while carrying, catching, or stopping the ball across the first down and goal lines. The limited life energy and playing ability of each spectator in the mass audience becomes hypostatized through the transcendent performance of the star's body. Yet, the star's immortal beauty and success, caught and replayed through the sacred aura of slow motion on the TV screen,[44] depends not only on athletic talent, training, effort, and teamwork, but also on the investment of desire by hundreds of thousands of mortals watching. Various views of star power and audience investment, involving the sacrificial athletes of different cultures, provide distinctive insights as to the potential for tragic catharsis in sports spectatorship. A Lacanian view of televised football might describe its sacrifice of identity as the painful and pleasurable, erotic and death drive *jouissance* within each spectator's body finding collective focus and expression in the athlete's performance.[45] A Roman view of gladiatorial performance would stress the sacred power of honor on display between the despised, yet idolized actor and the mass audience. But an Aztec view of the warrior's performance, tied to the sacrificial stone, would delineate the shared animistic powers within that godlike body and its spectators.

As mentioned in the previous chapter, Aztec *tonalli* was the force of heat, personal temperament, and destiny. It was drilled into the human embryo at conception, residing in the head, hair, and blood after fetal development and birth. It untwined (like a rope) during the course of one's life.[46] The greater the gladiatorial performer, as athlete and god-actor, the greater his *tonalli*—and the greater the force of divine heat offered to the spectators and the sun. The blood shed by the gladiator's body, as it was scored by the opponent's bladed club and then opened by the priest's knife, displayed the inner life force of *tonalli* in all those watching—greatly intensified, as divine nourishment.[47] The "feeding exchange" between the dead warrior's body and the hungry gods (including the sun) passed through the eyes of the audience as well.[48] An Aztec version of catharsis took place as the public watched *tonalli* appear in the blood of the performer's wounds during the fight, in the blood taken by the captor, with bowl and cane, to the lips of the gods' statues, and in the final dance of god-actors with decapitated heads (the *tonalli* receptacles of the sacrificed warriors). Mortal fears and immortal sympathies were thereby purged and purified. The feeding of the gods through these blood rites assured that the natural world would again feed the human community in return. If this ritual feeding did not take place, a much greater violence would occur: darkness (without the sun's rise), starvation (without food or water from the earth), and chaos (without the social order of sacrifice). Thus, the immortal *tonalli* in each watching mortal body was also purified, with each person's temperament and fate reoriented to the orders of society and cosmos.

Similarly, the inner force of *teyolia* was intensified, revealed, and purified through the cathartic performance of gladiatorial combat and sacrifice. *Teyolia* (divine energy and movement) gave shape to a person's thoughts and sensibilities, while residing in the human heart. It was thus expressed in the bravery and skill of a gladiator's athletic gestures, as well as in the subsequent extraction of his still beating heart. The warrior's personal *teyolia* rose to the sun through the heart sacrifice. But the audience's collective *teyolia* also became enriched through the gladiatorial spectacle, as this divine force was channeled into the heart of the community and its landscape through the body of the god-actor and warrior.[49]

While Aztec gladiatorial sacrifice valued the forces of heat (*tonalli*) and movement (*teyolia*), expressed through the athletic actor's body, the more secular Roman games fetishized the sacrificial performer in a different way. The Romans focused on the skill and bravery of the gladiator's fight to the death, not because he brought animistic forces into the heart of the community or fed the hungry gods, but because he exemplified a passion for honor and a freedom from mortal fears.[50] As I mentioned earlier in this chapter, Roman gladiatorial games began as funeral offerings—and blood was required to give the dead the strength to speak. But as the games developed into mass spectacles at public festivals, the shedding of a gladiator's blood related more directly to his own death and his strength in performing a fatal script. The best gladiators became idolized by the Roman audience, in their fearless passion and immortal (death-defying) freedom, like the Aztec warrior as a sacrificial god-actor. Some became even more like the NFL football player as mass media star—performing not just once at a fatal festival, but again and again, with skill and luck, year after year until retirement.

The first recorded *munus mortis* occurred at a private funeral in 264 BCE and involved three pairs of fighters. By the end of the Republic (27 BCE), the gladiator games had become vast public events, with hundreds of captured warriors, condemned criminals, slaves, and animals fighting to the death as an offering to the ruler and the mass audience watching in the amphitheatre.[51] Along with the monumental grandeur of so many warring bodies, certain settings, props, and costumes created a theatre of mythic proportions—magnifying the dramatic idealization of fighters (and hunters) as characters, whether individual or team players. Exotic habitats appeared, through lifts in the arena floor, for the wild animal hunts and executions *ad bestias*.[52] During a *naumachia* (staged sea battle) on the Fucine Lake under the emperor Claudius in 52 CE, 19,000 war captives and condemned criminals were forced to fight as "Sicilians" against "Rhodians"—after the starting signal was given by a silver image of the god Triton, who rose from the lake and blew a trumpet.[53] Individual criminals, executed between the acts of the beast hunts and gladiatorial games,[54] might also appear as mythological figures, with elaborate settings and costumes. Tertullian (a leader of the early Christian church) leaves a specific account of god-actors in both the executions and gladiator rites, while criticizing his fellow Romans not only for worshipping gods in the theatre, but also for being "still more religious in the amphitheatre . . . [where] often the guilty play the parts of gods" (15.4–5). He describes a criminal in the role of Atys being castrated and another in the guise of Hercules being burned alive,[55] as well as the actor (already mentioned above) playing Mercury to test the fallen gladiators with a burning iron, and Jove's brother, "hammer in hand," dragging the corpses away.[56]

Various types of characterization—with corresponding costumes and props—developed through the expansion of Roman gladiator games as a ritual theatre of death. Certain players became characterized by their particular equipment, whether fighting individually or in teams. The *essedarii* fought from chariots, with horses handled by other players, and with the accompaniment of flourishes from a hydraulic organ (like the organ music during a basketball game today, or the musical sound track that embellishes an action movie). The *equites* used lances to joust on horseback; unlike most gladiators, they wore a breastplate as well as thigh-pieces, and carried a round shield. The *dimachaeri* fought on foot without a shield, but with a sword in each hand. The *laquearii* used a lasso; *retiarii* a trident and net, without helmet or shield as protection. The *andabates,* on the other hand, wore helmets with full vizors and a coat of mail.[57] But along with these various possibilities for costumes and props, a gladiator's particular character and drama became scripted through his status when entering the arena.[58]

Unlike the Aztec gladiator, the Roman performer was not always a captive warrior. He or she might be a condemned criminal (with or without a sword),[59] an enslaved professional, or a free volunteer—even an aristocrat or emperor playing the game. If a captured warrior, he represented a specific conquered land in Rome's imperial expansion.[60] If a condemned criminal, he or she served to demonstrate the logic of the Roman judicial system— sometimes costumed as a mythic figure in relation to the specific violence of the sentence. If a professional gladiator, he or she[61] showed the Roman passion for a fearless confrontation with death, even in pre-scripted circumstances. (Professional gladiators might fight together one day and against each other the next, perhaps killing a former teammate or roommate.)[62] Gladiatorial sacrifices brought together the highest and lowest ranks of society, as well as foreigners and locals, as victims or players. The gladiator was, paradoxically, the most despised character in Roman society, yet also the most honorable.

Romans used the term *gladiator* to curse someone as a disgusting sensual-ist. However, gladiators exemplified the most severe asceticism in their train-ing and performance. "No other figure in Roman society embodied, in quite such extremes, punishment and impunity, constraint and abandon, asceticism and profligacy" (Barton, *Sorrows* 48).[63] A great gladiator became a sacred actor, "highly charged" with good and evil energy (Barton, "Savage" 45). He dis-played the boundary of honor around each Roman citizen, when he gambled his life in mortal combat. Even a condemned criminal (including a Christian martyr) could show the sacred power of honor in the way he faced humilia-tion, extreme torture, and death. "The criminal, like the gladiator, redeemed himself, the editor [producer of the spectacle], and the audience with his own blood—but only if he had their sympathy—only if they acknowledged his 'gift'" (53). In an ideal performance, the Roman criminal as gladiator, like the Aztec captive as god-actor, invested with great social meaning, sacrificed his life and blood as a spectacular gift for audience catharsis and communion.[64]

Of course, today's football star as warrior (and sometimes as criminal) does not offer his life and blood in the same way. But the magnification of his athletic sacrifice on the field through the myth-making lenses of the game's drama and the televisual apparatus does create a communal catharsis of audi-ence *jouissance*. Unfortunately, this catharsis (often more melodramatic than tragic) does not guarantee that violence will be exorcised in the exercise.[65] Various studies have shown that football players and their fans often express violence beyond the game's boundaries.[66] But the sacrificial intensity of the game, especially in the mythic theatre of its televisual presentation, focuses an enormous submission of mass audience energy (of erotic and mortal dri-ves) into three hours of controlled, dramatic conflict. This produces the illu-sion of transcendent beauty and honor, although without the high degree of brutality and nobility shown in the Roman games. For that higher degree of ego illusion, through explicit death and dismemberment, American specta-tors turn to other channels and screens.

In his study of Roman games, classical scholar Keith Hopkins briefly compares ancient gladiators to today's "pop-stars and athletes" (21).[67] Even though the professional life of the gladiator was often short, he was a glam-our figure, says Hopkins, a cultural hero like the current media stars whose screen lives can also be quite brief. "The transience of the fame of each does not diminish their collective importance." Gladiators received crowns as symbols of their bravery, as well as money for winning fights—and eventually their freedom from slavery, along with a symbolic stick (the *rudis*, a wooden sword used for gladiatorial training), if they survived long enough (25).[68] However, a famous gladiator might return to the arena for the right price, even after winning his freedom (Auguet 61).

Freeborn men who became voluntary gladiators took a sacred oath, the *sacramentum gladiatorium*, swearing to sacrifice themselves to be burned, bound, beaten, or slain by the sword (Barton, *Sorrows* 14). Why would a man of high class give up his freedom and descend into slavery, binding his body to public torture and death? According to the Roman disgust for, yet idealization of the "sacred" gladiator, he became freer than any free man, transcending the fear and fate of mortality, through this sacramental oath and his performances at the edge of death. He also joined other gladiators, from various classes, in becoming an idolized, eroticized body. The term *gladiator* came from *gladius*, which meant sword, but was also slang for the penis. A new bride might have her hair ritually parted by a spear dipped in the blood of a dead, defeated gladiator—so that she would be subject to her husband's commands, yet through intercourse with him bring forth a brave child (Hopkins 22). A gladiator's image has also been found at Pompeii on an ancient Roman baby bottle made of clay (7). Certain works of Roman art show the gladiator fighting a large penis (while the audience yells both "free him" and "kill him") or fighting his own elongated penis as it transforms into a wolf. The Roman satirist Juvenal ridicules a senator's wife, Eppia, for running away to Egypt with an ugly gladiator named Sergius, who had a scarred face, a big wart on his nose, and puss running from one eye. "But he was a Gladiator. That word makes the whole breed seem handsome, and made her prefer him to her children and country, her sister, her husband. Steel is what they fall in love with."[69]

The phallic beauty of the gladiator inspired both men and women to imitate or adore such stars. The beautiful wounds (*pulchra vulnera*) of Roman gladiators,[70] like the scars and blood sacrifices of captive Aztec warriors, opened the body and its im-mortal energies as spectacle, for a moment of godlike ecstasy in both actor and spectator.[71] Through the violent spectacle, the audience could bind—across the arena wall—with the performer's vulnerable body and sacred oath. While the gladiator's body heroically grappled with the phallic wolf of his own erotic death drive, he also took his vicarious spectators back to a stage edge *jouissance* within their psyches: the infantile experience of mortal vulnerability at the phallic mother's breast (or baby bottle). The Roman attitudes and artifacts of gladiator idolization show not just a melodramatic sympathy and fear in the catharsis of the contest, but also a tragic joy and terror at the primal fulcrum of symbiotic union or separation— in the earliest experiences of life and death against the mother's body.

Such primal experiences of vulnerability are preverbal and, to some extent, precultural, providing a link between ancient Roman subjectivity and our own today[72]—especially regarding the uncanny expression of the Real through violent entertainment. Thus, a Lacanian view of the idolized gladiator and his audience might show both sides of that stage edge as mirrors to the star athlete and TV spectator today. While an NFL player does not take a sacred oath to be "burned, bound, beaten, or slain by the sword," he does submit to the script of the game, which involves pain,[73] frequent injuries, scars, and occasionally being beaten by the other team. Through such masochistic submission, certain players become stars because they lead their team in taking control of the game. They become authors of their own fate, scripting key plays and thus shaping the dramatic score within the rules, white lines, and ticking clock. But outside the boundary lines and through the TV cameras, fans for each team also authorize the stars by submitting like them to the script of the game, binding their erotic and death-drive emotions to the vulnerable bodies in performance on the field. Both players and spectators submit to the power of football's theatre of violence, to find moments of empowering *jouissance*. Some moments might evoke an ecstasy beyond the usual melodramatic release of emotion in a sympathetic win or feared loss. To the degree that a football game expresses the star athlete's beauty and mortal fate, touching upon primal joys and terrors within the spectator's body—as with the idolized Roman and animistic Aztec gladiators—some in the audience might experience a tragic (or tragicomic) catharsis. But that would depend on how they watch, as well as how the game is played.[74]

AUDIENCE PARTICIPATION AND ALIENATION

Classical scholar Carlin Barton has elucidated several aspects of gladiatorial shows that drew a mass audience and lured some freeborn Romans to participate by taking the sacrificial oath. There was the im-mortal power of the emperor's thumb or, if the emperor was not present, of the editor's—influenced, up or down, by the cheers or jeers of the crowd. According to the rules of the game and its theatre, the gladiator would not kill his opponent until he received the signal from the emperor or editor. The audience contributed to the editing of the fatal script at its climactic moment, experiencing a godlike authority as communal voice. Yet, the best gladiators did not just submit as victims to that voice, thumb, and script. They were also consummate actors, "appear[ing] to take active pleasure in the struggle right up to the moment of death" (Barton, *Sorrows* 19–20). The choreography of the execution itself was rehearsed in advance as part of the players' training (Auguet 51). The gladiator's transfiguration into a godlike character, "an ideal type of the soldier/philosopher," came through his performance of joy in the game of life and death (Barton, *Sorrows* 20).[75] As his blood was being shed for his masters (and executioners) in the audience, "they provided each other with . . . mutual empowerment."

While Barton does not emphasize the theatrical or psychoanalytic elements in this relationship (as I have done), he does draw a brief parallel to today's athletic events. "Just as the clamoring fans at a football or basketball game like to feel that their team is playing the better for their shouting and that the athlete's strenuous exertions are an expression of the value they place on this esteem, so the gladiator's willingness to die in order to put on a 'good show' honored the audience in the extreme" (34). The gladiator paid a "high honor" to his audience, if he fought and died with bravery and joy; he received "glory" in return. This lured the spectator into participating in the joyful pain, "descending into the arena metaphorically or physically," as fan or voluntary gladiator, joining the sacred scapegoat as outcast, at the center of cultural meaning and power. Barton does not relate this aspect of the glad-iator and spectator dynamic to sports today. But one might see in the surplus enjoyment of Roman audience participation, with its *chora* of violent subli-mation, drawing spectators into the sacrificial vortex of cultural enjoy-meant (*jouis-sens*): an ancient parable for the surplus value that today's athlete achieves in the media marketplace, masking the Real sacrifice of his fans.[76] Star athletes receive enormous salaries, as well as greater glory, not only for their performance in the game, but also for a few seconds of symbolic *jouis-sens* during commercial interludes. Yet spectators are ultimately the ones who pay in this sacrificial game; they materialize the surplus value of great players (and teams) by consuming their sacred props, buying the brand-name prod-ucts that have the aura of star contact onscreen.[77] This gives greater meaning to the ordinary labor and lives in the mass audience, and holds the class struc-ture in place, as spectators become voluntary gladiators, metaphorically and physically. Enslaved by the voluntary oath of their own sacrificial jobs, they can still touch the honor and glory of star athletes, by cheering them in the game and possessing their props at home.

Barton presents further glimpses of Roman audience participation that might serve (though he does not make the move) to elucidate today's theatre of violent sports entertainment. With the failure of Rome's aristocrat Repub-lic, gladiators of the Empire came to represent the dishonor of the earlier free and privileged classes (*Sorrows* 27)—whose members could then rediscover honor by identifying with the gladiator's enslavement, vulgarity, and desper-ate joy at death. Set off from the disappointing theatre of daily life, the games played upon a collective nostalgia for the individual warrior of the early Republic: for "the imagined personal purity and self-vindication" of severe discipline and triumph over adversity in Rome's Golden Age (32–33).[78] In similar ways, football's rise as the dominant spectator sport in recent decades, especially among college-educated males (Guttmann, *From Ritual* 119), may reveal an uncanny American shame, despite the success of our imperial cor-porations and high-tech wars. Football plays upon the nostalgia for pure, physical combat and individual heroism, through the vanishing family values of honor, discipline, and teamwork.[79] Young American men and women, as players and cheerleaders, are initiated into the patriarchal rituals of foot-ball—by fathers, coaches, and schools systems—to maintain such nostalgic values.[80] They thus acquire personal memories of culturally sanctioned vio-lence that become sentimental hooks in the later enjoy-meant of watching the professionals perform.

And yet, the Roman audiences, like American fans today, expressed a collective wildness that belied the nostalgic values of honor and individual freedom. "The major and bloody battle that broke out between the Pompeian and the Nucerian spectators and their sympathizers in the amphitheatre at Pompeii in the year 59 CE was only an extreme version of the riotous behavior that had come to be expected at public spectacles" (Barton, *Sorrows* 63).[81] The stage edge between audience and actors in the amphitheatre became permeable—not only through violent claques and riots, but also in relation to the emperor as primary spectator, editor, and actor. Caligula picked spectators to be thrown into the arena when he ran out of criminals to feed to the wild animals and out of gladiators for fighting.[82] Nero sometimes entered the arena himself, performing the role of Hercules by killing a lion with a club (Wistrand 25). Commodus also performed in the animal hunts as that character (Köhne 26), though he is not shown that way in the recent film *Gladiator*. Many emperors acted as gladiators in the arena—or became the focus of spectators' cheers and jeers, while still in the *cavea* with them, thus forming another kind of permeable stage edge, around the elite seats in the *podium* section.[83] Emperors were expected to attend the gladiator shows, allowing the Roman public, as mass audience, its only form of democratic voice. Often, though, the collective energy of the audience turned not to the emperor's body as political focus, but to the performing bodies in the sand. According to Seneca, the spectators often voiced a violent rage, especially at the criminals sword-fighting until death (while surrounded by guards with swords and torches): "Kill him! Flog him! Burn him! Why is he so afraid to throw himself on the sword? Why does he not kill more boldly? Why does he not die more willingly?"[84]

These scenes and voices are more extreme than the usual expressions of crowds in an NFL stadium—or of politicians watching the game from box seats. Yet, a similar vehemence by fans, fueled by class resentment, occurs in the theatre of football (and other professional sports). We do not have strictly segregated seating, by class and gender, including box seats for aristocrats, like the Romans developed.[85] But we do have ticket prices that distinguish class areas in the stadium audience, with luxury boxes for the elite. Despite the American myth of social mobility and the illusion of communal participation in sports spectatorship, fans bring to the game their personal frustrations with particular class situations. They defer that social rage by identifying with the struggle of a certain team and its players against others—rather than against the wealthier spectators (or team owners) watching from higher-priced seats. Female fans also bring their social rage to the game, even though professional football, unlike basketball, remains strictly a male sport. (The patriarchal Romans were more liberal in this regard, offering opportunities for female gladiators.) Collectively, the social rage of fans at all levels and of both genders is channeled into the "fair fight" on the field. But the enthusiasm of a home-team win, especially in

a championship game, manifests a violent energy that may spill across the stadium's stage edge (to the tearing down of a goal post, for example) and beyond
the rituals of the game (with riots in the streets).[86]

Performing their class membership, the elite in the Roman audience
wore distinctive costumes and colors, while most citizens wore simple, white
togas (Edmondson 85). In the American football stadium, certain spectators
also become performers—especially for the TV audience—through strange
costuming or color-coded body makeup that expresses fanatical identifications. Such extremes today tend to show a common man's passions, unlike
the reserved spectatorship of the upper crust in luxury boxes, where the team
owner is also shown on TV. In Roman amphitheatres there were blocks of
seats for fans from foreign cities and for spectators from certain occupational
associations (collegia), somewhat like today with the visiting team's fans or a
certain company's workers seated together (100–101). Roman spectators
intensified their identification with gladiatorial performers, as well as with
their colleagues in the cavea, by gambling—as did Aztec spectators at the
sacred ball game. This is also a powerful mechanism for fan communion in
sports contests today.[87]

Ovid describes the sadomasochistic union of spectator and player, across
the stage edge of the Roman arena, through the ecstatic jouissance of gambling: "the spectator who has watched men being wounded is wounded himself . . . after he places a bet he groans from the blow, feels the dart and himself becomes part of the game."[88] The spectator sadistically enjoyed the pain
of the other if his bet-upon gladiator won; but he also expressed masochistic
pleasure while losing—as the player's wounds showed the bleeding of the
spectator's own gambled money and identity. For the Aztecs, their sacred ball
game involved the gambling of players' lives and spectators' money, yet also
reflected the world's order. A losing player would be sacrificed by decapita-
tion.[89] His head then symbolized the life and death passage of the sun, moon,
and other celestial bodies—as did the moving ball, especially when it passed
through the stone ring at the side of the court for a rare, game-ending score
(Gillespie).[90] Because they hit the hard rubber ball mostly with their hips,
players wore yokes at their waists, carved in the form of the earth monster,
thus positioning them at the entrance to the Underworld (Wilkerson, "In
Search" 116). The court itself, related in shape to the headless body of the
sacrificed player, was the navel of the earth and thus an actual entrance to
the Underworld (Gillespie 338–339, 345). Rulers might wager as much as
their entire annual income or several towns' tribute on the game—whether
as spectators or as players themselves.[91] The outcome of the game was thought
to be controlled by the gods and its playing was thus a mode of communication with the divine (Wilkerson, "And Then" 45).

Today's televised sports may not bear such cosmic significance for most
fans, even if they gamble on the game. But football stadiums do acquire a

sacred aura as powerful theatres for the competition between owners as well as fans—like the ancient amphitheatres in which Roman aristocrats spent huge sums, competing to impress the public and gain political status (Hopkins 8–9). The home field for a football game, reflecting the manicured lawns of the American dream, thus becomes, like the Aztec ball court, a "territorial possession . . . at the threshold of nature and culture" (Gillespie 341). Helmets, hip pads, and pigskin might also be seen as having a cosmic significance, like Mesoamerican heads, yokes, and ball, in relation to the stars' im-mortal struggle on the omphallic field. Fans, betting and identifying with their hearts, if not their wallets, are wounded along with the sacrificial players. Weekend bets on football games mimic the workday gambling of the stock market, which fuels the world economy. Spectators thus commune with the materialist, yet metaphysically tinged ideologies of our current world order, through the violent contest of opponents on the field and fights among fans in the mass audience.

MELODRAMATIC OR TRAGIC CATHARSIS

During Roman gladiatorial games, small wooden balls (missilia) were thrown into the crowd. Each could be exchanged for a specific prize: food, clothing, silver, or slaves (Hopkins 9).[92] One can imagine the unruly Roman audience fighting for these balls like football players scrambling for a fumble today (or like baseball fans when the ball goes into the stands)—with the jouissance of the ball's possession showing the luck as well as skill of the player, team, or spectator. Today's mass-media theatre has developed many similar games to pick out certain lucky spectators as prizewinners, in commercial contests related to the sport. But this chance transcendence for a few barely masks the abject insignificance of the rest of the mass audience. Spectators may experience a communal ecstasy, akin to the team spirit of the athletes, in rooting together for one team. But in exchange they must sacrifice their individuality to the crowd's collective voice and gestures. The theatre of sports provides a social safety-valve to manage personal abjection and collective rage through melodramatic fan identification with and against certain players and teams, as home-town heroes or foreign scapegoats. Yet it also stirs the fans' passions, sometimes to the point of rioting, as the game moves through the liminoid stages of social drama (demonstrating Turner's Aristotelian formula): the breach of opponents meeting, the crisis of points scored or bodies wounded, the redress of vengeful counter-attacks, and the reconciliation of conclusive victory and handshakes or the further schism of continued violence beyond the rite (108–109).[93] Thus, the expression of violent jouissance in sports can temporarily purge individual abjection and communal rage, but it can also lead to further aggression within and between spectators as they leave its theatre or switch to other violent channels.[94]

In his recent study of the Roman games, Alison Futrell argues that gladiatorial sports were ritual sacrifices as well as dramatic entertainments.[95] He
discounts a cathartic approach to the gladiatorial show, yet focuses on a "theatrical analogy" to describe the sacrificial and agonistic potential for audience
participation (49). Futrell sees amphitheatrical violence as melodramatic: it
gave "a simplistic portrayal of the victims as deserving of their fate" rather
than as tragic "victims of unjust, unrelieved violence." This more melodramatic violence encouraged spectators to identify with the "perpetrators,"
while the victim was "demonized or alienated" from audience sympathy.[96]
According to Futrell, the games served as a catalyst for Roman "bloodlust,"
with the audience "gaining an intense feeling of satisfaction, even joy, in
their vicarious 'revenge' upon the victim." Audience ecstasy came through
the agonistic conflict of right against wrong and through a sacrificial climax—both of which involved melodramatic, judgmental participation.
"Seen in this way, the arena spectators were meant to participate in the 'punishment' of the performer; they were his judges, inflicting the fate he merited,
both by his marginal status and by his actions in the arena." Apparently,
Futrell applies his melodramatic model to all types of gladiators: not just
criminals, but also slaves, freed professionals, and freeborn volunteers. He
thus presents an oversimplified characterization of the arena players, their
drama, and the audience's response.

And yet, Futrell's comparative terms of tragedy and melodrama, from
theatre to amphitheatre,[97] help to show potential dramatic types and audience relations—in Aztec and postmodern, as well as Roman sacrificial sports.
Melodramatic violence in the Roman arena, in contrast to the tragic exem-
plars of Greek theatre, could be seen as a regression from the Kleinian depressive position of integrating good and evil, back to the paranoid-schizoid stage
of splitting such objects.[98] But Barton's interpretation of Roman desire, which
I quoted earlier, points to a more complex dynamic of both melodramatic and
tragic representation. I agree with Futrell that a sacrificial force persisted in
the Roman games, from their funeral origins through their expansion as agonistic entertainment. But the perception of honor and individual heroism, as
gladiators acted out a fatal script, indicates a tragic sympathy and facing of
fear, not just melodramatic joy in the victim's punishment.

Roman spectators did view some gladiatorial performers as melodramatically alien, especially those of lowest status fighting at the lunchtime executions. The audience reveled in vengeful rage at the demonized convict's suffering, if he showed cowardice with his sword. The Stoic philosopher and
playwright Seneca characterized the melodramatic rage of execution spectators as bestial. "In the morning men are thrown before lions and bears, at noon
they are thrown before the spectators."[99] However, the violence of the games
could also ennoble the mass audience—much more, according to Roman writers, than the contemporary theatre.[100] Seneca, for example, valued the tragic

violence of brave gladiators, who embraced their fate. Bravery, even from the vilest criminal, engaged audience sympathy in a virtuous way, clarifying the fear of death through suicidal valor.[101] Such catharsis of pity and fear shows that the Roman games could be tragic as well as melodramatic, depending upon the particular script for violence, the character of the gladiator in performance, and the audience's mode of participation.[102] The games could also be experienced as cruel comedy in their satyrlike excesses.[103] But these various modes of dramatic representation and audience perception in the Roman amphitheatre all indicate a measure of alienation within the sacrificial desire of agonistic combat.

Like the captive warrior as god-actor in Aztec gladiatorial sacrifice, the Roman gladiator, whether criminal, professional, or captured foreigner, was both alien and supernatural to his audience. He evoked the death-drive alienation within each spectator: as spiteful, melodramatic villain, or justice-enforcing victor, or mythologically-dressed buffoon, or sympathetic, fear-purifying tragedian. These types of audience identification are also available to the sports fan today, with varying degrees of tragic awareness of one's own alienation while cheering, jeering, or laughing.[104] The collective aggression summoned by a melodramatic battle of good and evil forces, in the home and visiting teams, may not be fully purged by the cathartic *jouissance* of the final score, especially for the fans who lose. But the promise of another game or another season displaces the aggressive drive (for further ecstasy or revenge) into a perpetual drama of partial catharses across many games. This allows for more survival of violent players than in the Roman or Aztec games. Yet, it likewise channels communal competition and personal death-drives toward the field of ritual play, through the broadcast and screening devices particular to each culture's technomythology.

Futrell presents the Roman amphitheatre as a "politicized temple," in which criminals were sacrificed to the state gods and the gladiatorial performance celebrated the cults of Nemesis (Fortune) and imperial expansion.[105] American football shares a sense of both Roman cults in its melodramatic plot devices: (1) a collective struggle with the forces of fate and vengeance, regarding the specific script of a game or season, and (2) a territorial battle over yardage, reflecting the cultural script of capitalist ownership and Euro-American Manifest Destiny. However, the politics of participation in the amphitheatre of football, through player and fan self-sacrifice toward the team's greater glory, also expresses a primal, personal scene of tragic loss. The aggression that football (or another sport) activates and channels into a dramatic *agon* arises from the fundamental sacrifice of symbiotic *jouissance* in the mirror-stage infant's separation from the mother and alienation from itself, as it joins the symbolic and imaginary orders of identity.[106] Desire and terror—in that choral space of blissful belonging, yet Real disintegration—are evoked and sublimated by the theatre of sports violence. These affects of a sacrificial cut in identity fuel today's cult of Nemesis in the gridiron game,[107] which also reflects the culture of American imperialism in numerous scrimmage lines between competing brands in stores and on TV screens around the world—as well as in recent theatres of war.

The extremity of bloodshed, cruelty, and killing in the Roman arena may seem very alien in comparison with today's sports theatres. The Aztecs' ritual play with human blood, hearts, skins, and heads—in a theatre of cosmological communion—also appears otherworldly. However, each of these performance texts bears a palimpsest of ancestral ghosts who speak to our own culture's violent, agonistic desires. The past century's mass-audience shift from tragedy and melodrama onstage to drama and sports onscreen shows the expanding significance of such rites. This shift of the mass audience to screen violence, and the potential for some degree of catharsis through its ritual, tragic edges, will be explored through select examples of certain types of cinema (and types of spectators) in the next several chapters: classic and postmodern horror, serial killer, ethnic gangster, boxing, Vietnam war, and religious movies. While these genres and examples are not comprehensive of all screen violence, they are illustrative of the dominant, melodramatic mode, its sacrificial identifications involving spectators as fetishistic, mimetic consumers, and the possibility of a partial remedy to the media rite and real-life bloodshed, through tragic insights.

The tragic complexity of evil and goodness in the Aztec warrior as captured enemy yet sacrificial god-actor, or in the Roman gladiator as despised yet honorable, sensualist yet ascetic performer, appeared early in cinema's history with the mad scientist Frankenstein and his destructive yet sympathetic Monster in the 1931 film by James Whale. But this work, which developed out of various nineteenth-century melodramatic stagings of Mary Shelley's novel, also demonstrates the easier path of simplistic violence in most horror movies today. It offers the clear-cut *katharsis* of an obvious *katharma*, a villainous scapegoat as purely evil object, to be punished and expelled, ostensibly exorcising the community. This exemplifies the Frankensteinian magic and Faustian danger of cinema, not only to raise monstrous specters onscreen, but also to provoke the violent superego of the audience, justifying vigilante vengeance or triggering perverse imitations of the fetishized villain. More of this danger, plus its tragic repercussions, becomes displayed in theatre actor and director Kenneth Branagh's 1994 version of *Frankenstein*, which returns to Shelley's novel, responds to Whale's classic film, and adds some postmodern twists of its own.

The vast power of today's mass media to celebrate certain outlaws, as terrifying monsters yet also transcendent actors, is shown even more broadly in Oliver Stone's 1994 satire of "natural born" serial killers. The danger of that power, despite the film's tragicomic insights, was also demonstrated by the copycat killers in its audience, whose extension of cinematic sacrifice into the Real will be considered at the start of the next chapter. The final two chapters of this book will look at the tragic edges of melodramatic films by three directors in the 1970s and 1980s, to reveal further ties to the Real in *ixiptla* and gladiator sacrifices: with the zoot-suit skins of Valdez's *pachucos*; the sacramental bloodshed (*tonalli* and *teyolia*) of Scorsese's gangsters, athletes, assassins, and Christ-figures; and the ritual battles of Coppola's Mafia and Vietnam warriors. Valdez also depicts an Aztec god; Scorsese shows a heart extraction, as does Branagh, albeit as special effect; and Coppola displays the actual death of an animal in ritual sacrifice. They thus exemplify specific ties from current screen violence to ancient sacrificial performance, involving the Real edges of life and death within the actor and the audience.

PART II

Screening Real Monsters

THREE

Choral Edges in *Frankenstein* and *Natural Born Killers*

IN MARCH 1995, 23-year-old Angela Crosby and her boyfriend, Ronnie Beasley, reportedly watched the newly released video of Oliver Stone's *Natural Born Killers* 19 times and started calling each other Mickey and Mallory, the names of the film's homicidal characters. With the help of two friends, they then lured a 68-year-old handyman to their mobile home in rural Georgia and killed him (Cook). By November 1994, 17-year-old Nathan Martinez had already shaved his head and was wearing tinted glasses in imitation of Mickey. Then Martinez murdered his 42-year-old stepmother and 10-year-old stepsister in their Salt Lake City home (Macintyre). Many other killings have been tied to fans of the film: in Texas (by a 14-year-old boy who decapitated a 13-year-old girl), in Massachusetts, several in Georgia, and in France (Cook, Moss, and Ramos). The Columbine High School killers in Colorado were also fans of the film (Courtwright 191). But the most notorious case involved Ben Darras and his 16-year-old girlfriend, Sarah Edmondson, the daughter of a district-court judge in Oklahoma, the niece of that state's attorney general, and the granddaughter of a U.S. congressman (Shnayerson 100). They had watched the film together over a dozen times and watched it again on video the night of March 5, 1995 while taking 17 tabs of LSD (142). The next day they left on a road trip together, during which they each shot a stranger they encountered, like the fictional Mickey and Mallory in Stone's film. That was on March 7 and 8, the day of and the day after the 50th birthday of Sarah Edmondson's father (141–142).

One of the victims (the deceased William Savage) happened to be an old acquaintance of the famous lawyer-novelist John Grisham, who then encouraged the other, surviving victim (Patsy Byers, paralyzed from the neck down) to sue Oliver Stone for the dangerous effects of his film "product" (quoted in

FIGURE 3.1. The romantic outlaws and serial killers Mallory and Mickey Knox (Juliette Lewis and Woody Harrelson), who inspired many acts of real violence by their fans. *Natural Born Killers*, Warner Brothers, 1994.

Shnayerson 100). Verbal sparring in the media ensued between Grisham and Stone. Grisham called the film a damaging product "not too dissimilar from breast implants" and declared that Stone, his production company, and the studio should be liable for the resulting injuries, "whether by design or defect." Stone countered that Grisham was on a witch-hunt, that artists merely hold up the mirror to nature, that parents and schools are more to blame than cinema, and that our daily doses of TV violence are "far more pervasive than those of one two-hour film" (quoted in Shnayerson 143). Grisham has himself become wealthy and famous for his violent novels and the films made from them, as Stone pointed out. Yet Grisham compared Stone's film to "a loaded gun," which he has the right to keep in his home and leave on the coffee table, but if "the kid next door shoots himself with it, then I'll be held liable for my negligence" (quoted in Shnayerson 144). This is an ironic parallel for the lawyer to use, not only because he identifies himself with Stone, but also because Sarah Edmondson took her father's revolver with her for the LSD- and film-induced violence of her romantic road trip (Shnayerson 101).

The most violent scenes in Stone's film were cut out of the initial version, released in August 1994 (and the video seen by Edmondson and Darras), in order to get an "R" rating instead of "NC-17"; yet they were restored in the 1996 "director's cut" on video (Courtwright 314n5). Stone states in an interview at the start of that video that the initial film release was "censored" by the ratings board and excised of its "black humor," making the film "grimmer" and allowing "certain people to not completely grasp the attitude of the movie." The suit against Stone revealed that he and his staff, while making the film, had even joked about its excessive violence as a challenge to the ratings board: "Maybe this will be an NC-32" (Welkos). In March 2001, the Stone suit was dismissed by a state judge in Louisiana. Similar lawsuits in other states have also been thrown out of court (Stanley). However, Grisham's projection of legal guilt upon Stone and his different stance as a maker of violent fiction, plus the many copycat crimes related in some way to Stone's film, exemplify the significance of melodramatic versus tragic (or tragicomic) violence in recent screen sacrifices.

In Grisham's novels and the films made from them, the violence is presented within a conventional moral order of criminals brought to justice. In contrast, Stone calls his own film "an in-your-face satire of a moral order turned upside down, . . . a wake-up call to a schizophrenic country and culture which decries violence but just can't get enough of it. Viewers are bombarded day in and day out by tabloid trash shows, entertainment and news programs which convert tragedy into soap opera, replete with weepy musical sound tracks . . ." (quoted in Shnayerson 144). If Grisham's novels and films match a conventional moral order, by showing the melodramatic violence of the hero's justice prevailing in the end over the clear-cut villain, are they less likely to trigger a copycat crime than Stone's film, in which the killers are presented sympathetically and seem to escape the law in the end? Or might Grisham's moral violence also inspire acts of vigilante vengeance against supposed villains (or an imitation of their pure evil as outlaws)? As Stone puts it, "according to Mr. Grisham's logic, the next time a 'righteous' revenge murder takes place . . . he will be happy to assume the liability if it can be shown that the offender had read or seen [Grisham's novel/film] *A Time to Kill*." Stone seems to argue (as a twice-wounded Vietnam veteran)[1] that the numerous screenings of violence in the mass media today, converting real-life tragedy into soap operas and melodramas, create a pervasive culture of mimetic violence, which requires the homeopathic antidote of a tragicomic farce like *Natural Born Killers*. One violent film alone does not produce real monsters, converting the inert bodies of spectators into murderous zombies, like Frankenstein's disastrous invention. Yet, today's film and TV dramas do extend the risky experiment of theatre, its sublimation of prior ritual sacrifices into fictional violence and virtual reality for a mass audience. If the performances of Greek animal sacrifice, Roman gladiators, and Aztec *ixiptlas* involved both melodramatic and tragic elements, confirming or questioning the mass's moral order, then how do today's screen rites comfort us with conventional gods and goods—or challenge us to rediscover an ethics of the Real?

This problem goes beyond the legal-liability-versus-censorship debate of Grisham and Stone. A certain filmmaker or novelist should not, in my view, be held directly responsible for each act of copycat violence. If he were, the publicity of punishing him would probably increase, not stop, the mimetic interests of perverse or psychotic spectators.[2] According to Sarah Edmondson, Stone's film was only "one of many elements" leading to her and her boyfriend's violent road trip (quoted in Shnayerson 142). Yet, there was an influence. En route to their first homicidal act, her boyfriend "started talking about finding an isolated farm house and doing a home invasion, that is, robbing a family and killing them, leaving no witnesses . . . as if he was fantasizing from the movie *Natural Born Killers*" (quoted in Shnayerson 103). Stone's film even predicts such violent mimetic effects, while satirizing the mass media, of which it is also a tragicomic example. During a scene of the media's idolization of the serial killing couple, a teen fan says: "If I was a mass murderer, I'd be Mickey and Mallory."[3] Later, Mickey's live TV interview in prison inspires other prisoners into a mass riot when he describes his rejection by society at an early age and his eventual discovery of his life's role, his "calling" as a "natural born killer." The Dionysian riot climaxes with the off-screen *sparagmos* of the prison warden (Tommy Lee Jones), whose head is then displayed on a stick, like Pentheus' head in Euripides' *The Bacchae*.[4]

Does this film, in its tragicomic violence, evoke a cathartic clarification of the false moral order and dangerous melodrama of pervasive mass-media

rites and their daily screen sacrifices? Could it both contribute to the disease
for some spectators, like Sarah Edmondson and her boyfriend, yet also purify
the awareness of violence in others to prevent violent acts? Apparently, that
is Stone's gamble.[5] His film exemplifies a terrible risk in the last century's
invention and expansion of mass-media violence, as sublimated sacrifice and
cathartic entertainment. Like the fictional Frankenstein's disastrous experiment, cinema and TV give life to dead matter mechanically, through the
illusion of transcending life's sacrificial demands. And yet, more death may
thus be produced mimetically, through the unnatural birth of copycat killers
in the audience.

A MONSTROUS GAZE

The first half of this book explored how tragedy can work from ancient ritual
to today's stage and screen in complex, cathartic ways to clarify violent, sacrificial drives—so that spectators might become more aware of the violence
within them, rather than acting out violently in their own lives. But the dangers of melodramatic mimesis also continue in the postmodern, perhaps even
more for a growing mass audience. This second half of the book focuses on
specific screen monsters, criminals, and saviors, who reveal the structures of
cinema as a sacrificial theatre. To clarify potential audience effects, the current chapter will consider what lies behind the screen historically: the precedents for perceiving a credible reality, a transcendent communion, or a challenge to both—by engaging and manipulating the spectator's gaze, from
theatre to film. Then we will look at the edges of the screen and at uncanny
creases in certain films, as lures to the gaze, which point to the *chora* of Real
violence offscreen and in the audience as well.[6]

Feminists have long criticized the cinematic apparatus of mainstream
Hollywood for constructing a "male gaze."[7] Recently, however, that critique
has developed into a more optimistic celebration of diverse "viewing positions."[8] The former avenue of gaze theory was heavily invested in psychoanalytic speculation, yet misinterpreted the Lacanian gaze.[9] Both approaches
have failed to consider the complex parallels and historical precedents in theatrical apparatuses and their various ways of structuring the viewer's gaze.[10] In
this chapter I hope to provide some new illumination upon the liminal borders of perception in the cinematic frame, in film cuts, and in particular
uncanny points within the scene—using Lacan's sense of the Real as absence,
loss, and abjection beyond (or within) imaginary and symbolic representations.[11] I will explore such a cinematic threshold through various elements it
shares with the stage edge: spatial, temporal, visual, acoustic, and dramatic.[12]
I want to look especially at a certain effect which gaze theory has neglected,
the sense of a sacrificial community shaped by the stage or screen edge and
its focal range of spectator identifications:[13] from the alienated mirroring of

individual, narcissistic viewers to the transcendent, illusory communion of a choral audience—or both in some spectators who mimic the violence later on. No one can comprehensively define the innumerable, complex experiences of various spectators, even of the same film or of a single stage performance. Yet, one can analyze the desires engaged by certain stage or screen structures—and the compositional choices at a particular moment in a theatrical or cinematic work—to theorize those desires and choices, along with the potential audience catharsis, as more melodramatic or tragic.

This chapter will offer a detailed analysis of James Whale's *Frankenstein* (1931), a classic horror film inspired by a nineteenth-century novel and its subsequent stage versions. In the second half of the chapter, more recent films will be considered: Oliver Stone's *Natural Born Killers*, Kenneth Branagh's remake of *Frankenstein*, and various horror movies with females as the leading monsters. *Frankenstein* is emblematic not only of science gone awry, but also of cinema as an invention extending theatre's revision of ritual sacrifice: giving the creator and spectator an apparently godlike power over life and death, while sometimes creating mimetic monsters. And yet, despite the monstrous murders reportedly inspired by *Natural Born Killers*, I will argue that there are tragic aspects to it, as in both versions of *Frankenstein*, which produce positive, cathartic effects for some spectators, even if more melodramatic parts trigger copycat violence in others at the screen's edges.

SLICES OF SPACE AND TIME

Both theatre and film cut out and re-present combinations of life and fantasy, no matter how realistic or abstract, objective or subjective, the *mise-en-scène*. Of course, the slice and splice of life in theatre is different from that of film. The live bodies of theatre actors appear at the same time and in the same space as their audience. And yet, as with the cinema screen, theatre performers and spectators are always separated by some sense of a stage border— a spatial and temporal gap between them—even with postmodern environmental staging or medieval dispersed decor, in which actor and audience spaces might seem intricately mixed.[14] Theatre theorists, from the ancient Greek Aristotle to the Renaissance neoclassicists to their counterparts today, have long debated the unities of time and place, as well as action, in the presentation of drama onstage. Like cinema, theatre has often been tempted to abbreviate time dramatically, and to leap through space—which involves certain liabilities.

In 1570, Lodovico Castelvetro argued that stage time should be tied to that of its audience, rather than (as many of his colleagues argued) to Aristotle's limit for tragic action, "a single revolution of the sun" (35). Castelvetro said this was too long for credible action onstage, with too many gaps between the slices of time and place. The drama should be limited to "what-

ever place and time the actors actually use in the performance" (144).[15]
Castelvetro's ideal realism was thus an attempt to synchronize (and syn-
topize) the bodies performing and watching, despite the temptation to fly
godlike through time and space.

> Because of the needs of the body, such as eating, drinking, dismissing super-
> fluous burdens of the stomach and bladder, sleeping, and other necessities,
> the public cannot tolerate any kind of delay in the theatre beyond the afore-
> said limitation. Nor is it possible to make the spectators believe that many
> days and nights have passed when they sensibly know that only a few hours
> have elapsed.

But as Christian Metz observed about the cinematic experience 400 years later
(using the Freudian theory of fetishism),[16] it is precisely because we do know,
as sensible spectators, that what is on the stage or screen is not real—in time
and place—that we are so tempted to believe, in the moment, otherwise.

Today's cinema, despite its photographic enhancement of theatre's age-
old yearning for mimetic realism, usually cuts and splices far beyond the
fetishistic limits of Castelvetro's ideal re-presentation of life. This shows
another desire from centuries earlier, which Castelvetro's argument could
not restrain. Film offers a sacrificial temptation to the audience: the godlike
power to travel through time and space. Such a trick fixes the spectator in
place, offering a divine view (and monstrous gaze) in exchange for the
viewer's belief in a diegetic world on and beyond the screen. This technique
can be traced back to a much earlier technology in theatre's *trompe l'oeil* of
wings and shutters, painted with perspective scenes that gave the illusion of
great distances onstage. In the century following Castelvetro's time, in
France and England as well as Italy, audience desire increased for "machine
plays," along with court masques and *intermezzi*, specializing in such spectacle. Elaborate mythological scenes, capturing the infinity of single or multiple vanishing points,[17] became even more powerful through the new technology of smoothly changing the perspective scenery before the spectators'
eyes (with Torelli's chariot and pole system). The appeal of such genres and
techniques reveals a collective Renaissance and Baroque desire, as with
today's cinema, to transcend ordinary space and time, against the neoclassical rules of moral credibility set for regular drama and its realism.[18] One
might also find correlatives to current mass-media desire further back in theatre history: in the Roman invention of the stage curtain, the *auleum*, as a
device for making scene changes more sudden, somewhat like cinematic
cuts—and in various ancient Greek technologies for creating greater spectacle onstage, *contra* Aristotle. All of these devices culminate in the power of
cinematic illusion, which offers today's spectator the lure of a nearly omni-
scient, yet potentially monstrous, scenic view. Like the Aztec god-actor
(who attains a divine identity by submitting to the knife), the mass-media

viewer becomes an *Übermensch*, while playing the sacrificial role of submit-ting to the screen, especially when the spectator identifies with a transcen-dent character or star actor. The return then to mundane, mortal reality, at the drama's end, fuels the demand for another fix of illusory immortality onscreen—or the mimetic playing out of screen violence against others in real life.

Fairly early in cinema's history (1936), Allardyce Nicoll confronted the threat of film to kill theatre, its elder art, by better achieving the machine play dream. "Is, then, theater, as some have opined, truly dying? Must it suc-cumb to the rivalry with cinema?" (184). Unlike Castelvetro or the seven-teenth-century machine play fans, Nicoll finds his answer in "convention," theatre's distinctive ability to transcend reality through poetry as well as scenery. Aeschylus and Shakespeare, for example, "did not try to copy life, . . . their works have the quality of being independent of time and place" (185). This desire for theatre to be reborn out of its cinematic ashes, through tran-scendent poetic performance, echoes Friedrich Nietzsche's call (a half cen-tury before, in 1872, near the time of cinema's birth) for theatre to return to its pre-natal heritage of a ritual womb, already lost in classical Greek drama. Ironically, though, Nietzsche's dream of theatre's primal scene, whatever its historical validity,[19] has become realized in some ways today with the tran-scendent pleasures and dangers in cinema's extension of theatrical power over ordinary space and time.[20]

According to Nietzsche, the ancient chorus, singing and dancing in the orchestra, became a communal lens, focusing the wild, creative and destruc-tive, Dionysian passions of the audience into a sublime vision of Apollonian beauty on the actor's mask (56–67). The loss of individuality through this psychomythic womb at the stage edge meant, in Nietzsche's nostalgic dream, a communion of spectators with the ritual, sacrificial chorus.[21] The audience thus became (at least the illusion of) one body, mind, and soul. Despite their different technologies, theatre and cinema share the desire and ability to transcend individual space and time through shared meaning. Yet the extremity of Nietzsche's vision—and the inspiration he gave to Nazism and its mass theatrics—shows the destructive potential that theatre and cinema share (with other mass media) today. Such political danger, as well as poten-tial communal pleasure and metaphysical meaning, increases the significance of cinema's psychotheatrical effects, whether toward a more alienated, indi-vidual experience of time and space or towards a mystical, choral communion at the screen edge.

In 1951, André Bazin went beyond Nicoll's work, with a more percep-tive, yet still oversimplified look at the ghost of theatre at the screen edge. Bazin, like Nicoll, identifies the temporal (and thus spatial) difference of the-atrical versus cinematic "presence": film delays and distances the actual co-creativity of the spectator with the performer (97). But Bazin exaggerates this difference with a Nietzschean nostalgia for a distinct sense of theatre. Bazin describes the actor onstage as "the focus of a two-fold concave mirror" (106). The auditorium and scenery focus all theatrical energy on the live human body of the actor, which "lights up in each member of his audience an accomplice flame." Thus, according to Bazin, the communal experience of "infinity" in theatre "cannot be spatial . . . [for] its area can be none other than the human soul" (105). Here Bazin romanticizes the difference between theatre and cinema. He overlooks how they both involve a complex spatial dynamic between performance and perception, meeting at various stage and screen edges, drawn by a particular production and changing throughout the show, through each viewer's personal associations—even if that meeting of actor and spectator is delayed by the cinematic apparatus (and further manipulated by camera work and editing).

Bazin goes further, denying that the screen edge is like the proscenium picture-frame of Renaissance and modern theatre.[22] "The screen is not a frame like that of a picture but a mask which allows only a part of the action to be seen" (105).[23] Here, however, Bazin unveils again, despite such sharp distinctions, a Nietzschean vision of cinema. The film screen becomes the divine Apollonian mask of a Dionysian choral theatre: "to make of a revolver or of a face the very center of the universe." Bazin also gives the telling, patriarchal example of "chorus girls" who excite the "onlooker" differently when they are onstage, as compared to the screen (99). Unlike Nietzsche's theory of ancient choral and audience ecstasy, Bazin sees "jealousy and envy" in the male gaze of the stage audience; hence there is "no identification with the hero." Cinema, though, seems to recapture Nietzschean communion: identification between the spectator and "the film's hero" is so strong that it "turn[s] the audience into a 'mass' and . . . render[s] emotion uniform." If cinema has this potential today, for both male and female spectators, then the choral element that Nietzsche saw as crucial to sacrificial communion in ancient Greek theatre should be discernible at the screen edges of modern and postmodern films. The apparent uniformity of emotion in the mass audience—as orchestrated by the film's drama, camera work, editing, and soundtrack—may mask various Dionysian effects, involving both creative, cathartic insights and destructive, pathological passions (as with Darras and Edmondson, or other NBK fans) in the chora of different spectators.

The choral edges of cinema (and other forms of mass media) engage communal desires and sacrificial drives in various ways, like theatre,[24] with the potential for both ecstatic joy and painful delusion. When we go to a play or a film, we share an experience with other spectators in the same auditorium (even those we do not know); our individual lifetimes and spaces are spliced together for a while. Yet we also know that we each perceive the show, onstage or onscreen, through distinctively personal (conscious and unconscious) associations. More so in reading a novel or drama, or in watching a play onstage with fellow spectators at different angles and distances from the performance, but also in watching a film together—we do not see and hear the same thing. However, part of the joy of watching a great play or movie in the theatre is the sense that it brings all spectators together, especially in moments of contagious laughter or tense silence. Some plays and films are great, in fact, because they bring out our individual alienation as human beings communally. We experience a greater sense of personal aloneness through a collective identification with characters onscreen or onstage. We laugh or cry even more with the others watching, experiencing ourselves as collective Other to the characters, with our desires and theirs focused jointly by the stage or screen, toward a potential catharsis at its choral edges.[25] But the illusory transcendence of screen figures, beyond personal alienation and mortal fears, may inspire further sacrifices by some spectators offscreen, involving others as victims in real life.

The collective reaction to screen drama involves particular choral passions—and the potential eruption of the *chora* within individual spectators—even when viewing a film on video, as the overdose and imitation of Stone's work by Edmondson and Darras shows. (Their particular way of viewing the video, while alone together and using drugs, shaped their experience of Stone's film and their identifications with its romantically violent couple. They may have also, effectively, re-edited Stone's film through multiple video viewings, repeating the melodramatic parts and skipping the tragic.) Melodrama tends to unify the audience's emotional participation, with simple characters and a thrill-ride plot of good-versus-evil violence. But this may stimulate a traumatic paranoia and punitive rage, in the *chora* of certain spectators, to overflow the enclosed space of fictional becoming and the film's ostensibly moral resolution—with further acts of violence outside the cinema (or home video theatre), as preemptive strikes or vigilante vengeance. The more tragic the film, however, the more its audience communion also evokes a complex awareness of alienation in each spectator, opening the spatial and temporal sutures[26] of the collective diegesis. Particular visual, acoustic, and dramatic edges or creases of the screen[27] deconstruct the mirror-stage illusion of ego (revealing a fragmented body) in film's apparent, godlike power to transcend human mortality and lacking being. Cinema is a consummation of earlier theatrical dreams: Renaissance perspective scenery and Baroque vanishing points, nineteenth-century melodramatic spectacle, and modern, box-set, fourth-wall realism—all of which may backfire with mimetic violence in the postmodern, or fuel the cathartic clarification of violence, through such sacrificial tricks. Like Frankenstein's experiments, cinema offers the hope of transcending death through new forms of insightful violence and meaningful sacrifice. Yet it also creates real monsters.

EDGES OF COMMUNION IN *FRANKENSTEIN*

The potentially cathartic moments in James Whale's *Frankenstein* (1931) may have been inspired by Mary Shelley's nineteenth-century novel, but they are plotted out more like the stage adaptations which began to appear soon after the first (anonymous) publication of her book in 1818.[28] In 1823, Richard Brinsley Peake's *Presumption; or, The Fate of Frankenstein* hit the London stage, with an already wordless Monster—like the grunting and moaning Boris Karloff version a century later—instead of Shelley's very artic-ulate creature, who tells his own story to Victor Frankenstein, and also speaks of his extreme alienation to the ship captain (and letter writer), Robert Wal-ton. Rather than using such verbal narration and frame tales (the Monster's story within Frankenstein's story-telling, within Walton's letter-writing),[29] Peake's play excerpts certain climactic moments from the novel, displaying and extending them through dramatic tableaux, pantomimed action, and chase scenes—though such tense revelations are still set up by long speeches, much longer than those in the later film.[30] Peake also adds the character "Fritz," Frankenstein's assistant, who appears again as a comic villain in the Whale film.[31] Before the Monster is revealed, in Peake's version, Fritz sees and describes him to the audience, reacting to the monstrous sight in a farcical pratfall ("having fallen flat in fright" on the stage floor): "hob-goblin, seven-and-twenty feet high! Oh, my nerves . . ." (143). In Whale's film, a more sin-ister yet still comical Fritz (Dwight Frye) gives the Monster an "abnormal" brain, having dropped a jar containing the good brain; later he brings out the Monster's evil by taunting him with fire. Thus, melodramatic villainy, fight scenes, spectacular chases, and comic relief are used by the 1823 play[32] and 1931 film as dramatic edges, distinct from the novel, to frame the horror of the Monster's presence—and to evoke a choral thrill in the audience.

Like the original novel, the Peake and Whale versions present a Mon-ster suffering from an acute lack of being: made from dead body parts, rejected by his creator, rejected by all other adult humans who see him, and missing any other creature of his own species.[33] Yet these monstrous ideas, from novel to stageplay to film, are conveyed increasingly through visual and acoustic effects instead of words. In Peake's stage directions, the visual edge of the creature's monstrosity seems to be his inhuman color rather than form: his "bare" limbs and face, along with his tight fitting body suit, are "a light blue" (135–136).[34] Sketches of T. P. Cooke in that role show the Monster with a normal human face and body, in a classical tunic and cape (Forry 19–20), even though Frankenstein describes him more grotesquely, with words taken straight from the novel: "his cadaverous skin scarcely cov-ers the work of muscles and arteries beneath" (143).[35] In the 1931 film, developed from a contemporary stage version by Peggy Webling, none of Shelley's nor Peake's descriptive terms are spoken as a choral connection between spectator and mask. There is only Frankenstein's "It's alive!" performed in histrionic ecstasy by Colin Clive. For the body and mask of the Monster, Whale and Karloff created a stiff zombielike walk, a prominent forehead with scars, indented cheeks (through the removal of the actor's false teeth), and electrodes protruding from the neck. This image of the Monster is now so famous in popular American mythology that it is often confused with the name of the scientist, "Frankenstein." It has become a prophetic symbol for the vast spectrum of creative powers and destructive horrors in modern science: nuclear energy, robotics, genetic engineering, and the VR realms of film, television, and computer screens—all of which give birth to new powers and monsters.

The confusion about the name "Frankenstein" exemplifies how a film image and symbol (as Apollonian mask) can reveal, yet also repress, the Real (of Dionysian passion). For the imaginary and symbolic orders onscreen relate to the Real at the screen edge.[36] But that Real order is actually in the audience and in various communal powers outside the theatre that are merely represented by the symbols and images onscreen (as with Kristeva's symbolic realm and semiotic *chora*).[37] Thus, the imaginary and symbolic orders onscreen might be focused and intensified by the cinematic apparatus toward a greater, cathartic awareness of the Real at the screen's edges. Frankenstein's Monster would then become a monstrance, showing the sublime creativity and terrifying danger of human technology, involving a partial triumph over death and disease, yet also abject loss, alienation, and rage—in a sacrificial body visually consumed by the congregation, although to varying degrees by each spectator.

In Whale's *Frankenstein* certain choral holes at the edges of the screen reveal the divine and preternatural qualities of the Monster,[38] evoking the Dionysian *chora* embedded in the cinematic proscenium and its audience. After an introductory warning from an actor in front of a stage curtain, about the potential "strain" upon spectators' nerves,[39] and then a whirl of eyes behind the credits, the film shows a family mourning at a gravesite. When the cemetery is deserted, Frankenstein and Fritz dig up the grave and push the coffin out of the hole at the screen's bottom edge. Like a trap in the stage floor representing a grave or the underworld, this use of the screen threshold evokes an imaginary projection and symbolic bleeding beyond its visual and dramatic boundary, toward the Real offscreen object (the choral "Thing")[40] of the family's abjection—which Dr. Frankenstein would cure with his supernatural, scientific knowledge: "He's just resting. Waiting for new life." Frankenstein also tries to use the body parts of a hanged man, as Fritz climbs the pole and crawls along its crossbeam toward the cinema spectator (toward the screen's surface, where it meets the choral gaze) to cut the fatal rope. The cemetery scene begins, too, with a close-up of hands pulling a rope out of a grave, through the bottom of the screen. Thus, the first dramatic scene of the film involves several images of ropes and death sites, pointing offscreen through the mortal holes at the screen's edges, into the lacking gaze of the audience, who play the role of ghostly, spectatorial Other, driving Frankenstein's desire to create life out of death.

In Mary Shelley's novel, this desire in Frankenstein is explicitly tied to the loss of his mother. She saved his adopted sister, Elizabeth, from a fatal illness, then died from the disease (like Shelley's own mother, Mary Wollstonecraft, who died after giving birth to her). In fact, right after the first horrified glimpse of his creation coming alive, the exhausted Frankenstein falls asleep and dreams of Elizabeth turning into his dead mother while he kisses her: "I saw the graveworms crawling in the folds of the flannel [shroud she wore]" (57). This nightmare wakes him, yet takes him to another primal scene—the gaze of his Monster, standing at the stage edge of his dream space. "He held up the curtain of the bed; and his eyes, if eyes they may be called, were fixed on me." Neither Peake's play nor Whale's film shows this double primal scene. Yet both construct a parallel relation between monster, master, and spectator—with the viewer's gaze sutured through the creator's to identify, to some degree, with the horrifying lack of human life in the creature. The film calls attention to this role of the spectator, at the screen's abject edge, not only in its introductory warning before a stage curtain, but also in Frankenstein's manic setting of the scene for the monster's (re)birth.

Frankenstein places his teacher (Prof. Waldman, played by the same actor, Edward Van Sloan, who gave the frame/curtain warning), his friend Victor,[41] and fiancée Elizabeth (Mae Clark) in chairs near his laboratory table, with an intense: "Sit down!" The cinema screen places the table at its bottom edge—a sheet covering the still lifeless assemblage of dead body parts—as Frankenstein then says: "Quite a good scene, isn't it? One man crazy; three very sane spectators." Choral affirmation for this crazy/sane "scene" comes immediately from the diegetic storm above, through a sudden flash of light and the sound of thunder. While the novel's dead mother is missing here, the film elaborates upon Shelley's brief description of the Monster's creation to visually reveal more elements of choral fetishization and resurrection. The obscene immortal Thing rises out of the womb of Mother Earth (from the earlier graveyard scene), through the lightning force now of Mother Nature—which Frankenstein calls, regarding his revolutionary scientific discovery: "the great ray that first brought life into the world." Here the storm functions (like the earlier grave hole) as visual, acoustic, and dramatic *chora*, sparking the monstrous mask to life and resounding explosively at the upper edge of the proscenium screen, beyond the phallic tower of Frankenstein's operating theatre.

As the others watch, Frankenstein raises the table to a hole in the laboratory ceiling (at the top of the cinematic frame) to be touched by the maternal *chora* of the sky's electric storm, then lowers it again to the audience's

90

FIGURE 3.2. Henry Frankenstein (Colin Clive) with his creation and audience: Fritz (Dwight Frye), Doctor Wald-man (Edward Van Sloan), Victor Moritz (John Boles), and Elizabeth (Mae Clarke). *Frankenstein*, Universal, 1931.

level—for a close-up of the monster's fingers and forearm rising slowly from the table edge at mid-screen. A few scenes later, when the Monster's face is first shown onscreen, jump cuts from medium shot to close-up to extreme close-up intensify the imaginary horror of his face—as set up by the framework of symbolic/Real horizons (scientist/monster, culture/nature, life/living death) in preceding shots and scenes. The Monster's hands then reach upward into the sunlight, as he makes infantlike moans—again suggesting his origins in the "good breast" and womb of Mother Nature.[42] But soon the comic yet melodramatic villain, Fritz, tortures the Monster with fire, arousing the evil force of his abnormal brain, dead body parts, and immoral Promethean creation—the destructive side of the choral womb at the screen's sacrificial edge. Both displays of the Monster's tragically good and evil nature serve to arouse sympathy in the cinema spectator, demonstrating that the creative and destructive *chora,* for better and worse, also lies in the audience as Real offscreen.[43]

VIOLENCE IN THE HOUSE

Other uncanny sounds and onscreen audiences play significant roles elsewhere in the film, pointing beyond such edges to the violent desire of spectatorial communion, which haunts the movie theatre house. When Fritz attempts to steal a brain for the Monster from a medical school operating theatre (after the initial graveyard scene), he first watches from outside a window as a student audience laughs at a hanging skeleton, bumped by the teacher's assistant. Fritz then sneaks into the theatre/classroom, after students, instructors, and their dead-body prop have left. Fritz also bumps the skeleton, then clings to it in fright. This sets up an unidentified offscreen clatter, which frightens Fritz so much that he drops the good brain, breaking its container, and takes the evil one instead.

At a parallel point later in the film, the Monster appears at a window like Fritz, bearing an evil brain and fiery violence (both induced by Fritz) inside his head and body. Just prior to this visual edge of monstrous appearance, the uncanny presence of the Monster has already been revealed acoustically to an onscreen audience. While preparing for his wedding to Elizabeth, Frankenstein hears his Monster's moans somewhere in the house. He locks Elizabeth in the bedroom, so that he and his male friends can search for the source of the monstrous sounds elsewhere in the Baron's (Frankenstein's father's) mansion. We then see the Monster at the uncanny vanishing point of the window behind Elizabeth, as yet unseen by her.[44] (He appears and enters her dressing room through the window, like Fritz stealing into the classroom earlier, but as a more distant, background figure.) Like the obscene hole empowering the illusion of depth in Renaissance perspective staging, the smaller frame of the window within the proscenium frame of the screen reflects the audience's lacking gaze—which bears a distant choral emptiness and Dionysian creative/destructive urge toward immortal transcendence. This is the ecstatic horror the Monster brings to Elizabeth, as he climbs through the window (with a phallic cypress in the darkness behind him) and approaches her, as we watch. The climax of this sacrificial *jouissance* comes, of course, with his groan and her face in close-up, screaming.[45]

The Monster's earlier infantile moan at the sunlight and his mature groans of violent desire in this scene exemplify the acoustic edges of the screen, and the choral ghosts lurking there. Likewise, the vanishing point of the window/cypress, through which the Monster approaches Elizabeth (and the spectator), shows a distant, then intimate, visual edge or crease within the screen. It also reveals a particular dramatic edge as the audience antici-pates, though never sees, what he does to her physically. (We learn later that she survived, when she is happily reunited with Frankenstein at the film's end, unlike the novel's Elizabeth.) Lacan's theory of the Real as a terrifying lack in the viewer, reflected by the imaginary/symbolic "stain" in a painting,[46] could be applied to these uncanny visual points and edges (or creases) onscreen—to exemplify the "gaze *qua* object" coming from the screen (stain),[47] through the "mirror stage" experience of cinema. Such a moment might evoke a visual communion among movie spectators—if it involves a collective regression toward unconscious memories of a pre-mirror-stage sym-biosis, a lack of Self in union with the primal (m)Other.[48] This would also show a splicing of time and space between performance and audience, as each spectator's illusions and partial memories of that lost Real are given a com-mon focus via the cinematic projection.

However, the acoustic dimension in the above examples from *Franken-stein* relates even more directly to Kristeva's theory of the *chora*, which she finds in her adult patients' infantile "echolalias,"[49] and to Nietzsche's vision of the singing and dancing chorus at the ancient Greek stage edge. Both Kris-teva and Nietzsche stress the violent, destructive force—as well as loving, creative power—of the semiotic, Dionysian womb at the "borderline"[50] of symbolic, Apollonian performance. The violent eruption of such choral pas-sion, creating the pleasure and pain of destruction onscreen,[51] and how that relates to real-life violence, is thus the key sacrificial issue.

Whale's Monster kills two or three times: his torturer Fritz, the little girl Maria, and perhaps Waldman, when the professor is going to "dissect" (destroy) him. Shelley's original Monster murdered three other characters: Frankenstein's little brother William, his best friend Clerval, and his wife Elizabeth. All of them were innocent, and he killed them much more pre-meditatively. Instead, the film Monster seems to kill, despite his "criminal" brain, through self-defense and stupidity, rather than vengeance. Fritz and Waldman are torturing and destroying him, so the Monster's violence could be seen as a defense of his new fragile self. Even with the innocent Maria, the

Monster kills through playful ignorance, throwing her into a lake after she entices him into a similar game with flowers. And yet, this tragic scene, censored in the film's original release,[52] shows not so much the creature's low I.Q. as an abject *méconnaissance* (mirror-stage misrecognition).[53] The film may try to reassure the viewer about the Monster's otherness, through the distancing effect of his "abnormal" brain and the unusual circumstances driving him toward violence. But it also reveals a potential cruelty in our "normal" minds and lives, through the violent peripety of his *chora*[54]—with the plot suddenly twisting from beautiful pastoral play to obscene irrational brutality. Here the film Monster embodies the many vengeful reasons of Shelley's highly verbal creature, in a single preverbal gesture. His unconscious act of vengeance is thus "structured like a language" (Lacan, *Four* 20)—or, in Kristeva's terms, is an eruption of the "semiotic *chora*"—which the film audience reads, through its own desires of the (m)Other.[55]

In the next scene, the celebration of Frankenstein's wedding by Bavarian townspeople is interrupted by Maria's father, who carries her corpse through the dancing crowd. This disruption of communal joy becomes a distinct visual, acoustic, and dramatic edge—through the reaction of the chorus. Their dance and music stops, as the crowd parts in stunned silence. It then turns, through subsequent scenes, into a vengeful torch-bearing mob of men (while women cringe against a wall) with yelping dogs pursuing the Monster, after his visit with Elizabeth, toward an apparent execution inside the phallic cross of a burning windmill tower. (He survives, of course, into Whale's 1935 sequel, *The Bride of Frankenstein*, and many further spinoffs.) The murderous Monster, as living-dead scapegoat, embodies and attracts the vengeful rage of the maternal *chora,* at the Real edges of the cinematic apparatus. Just a few decades after cinema's birth as an art form, Mary Shelley's destructive creature is reborn as an imaginary/symbolic figure for—and onscreen victim of—the violent desire for revenge against a lacking and lack-giving Other. Frankenstein's creation is thus emblematic of the living-dead matter of cinema's machinery and its melodramatic paradigms. The Monster's primal alienation illuminates the screen itself as a cruelly sublime, Apollonian mask: a totemic, sacrificial fetish, fueled by the choral, Dionysian womb of apparatus and audience at its edges, involving tragic agony and irony.

Much more gender analysis might be applied to this film, made from the novel of an early feminist's daughter, via a woman's stage adaptation, and various male screenwriters. For the purposes of this chapter, I am particularly interested in the maternal rage of an abject mournful *chora*—repressed by (and subsumed in) the patriarchal proscenium,[56] yet embodied in certain male and female characters onscreen. Frankenstein becomes a male with a womb: his laboratory gestates and gives birth to the Monster. But Frankenstein fails to be (or have) a "good breast." Instead, his experiment in "male mothering" makes him a castrative "phallic mother," via Fritz's torch in the film, intensifying the Monster's own abject *chora*—even though he had just begun to learn obedience from his creator/mother, by sitting in a chair, after reaching for the sunlight.[57]

The long process in Shelley's novel of the creature's entry into the imaginary and symbolic realms (as he sees himself in a pool of water, while learning language, culture, and literature from the cottagers) is condensed by Whale's film. Frankenstein's creation turns into the Monster while still inside the laboratory womb. Although this monstrous, murderous child lacks a female counterpart who might normalize him (in both Shelley's novel and Whale's films), he thereby bears his own womb of violence.[58] He strikes back at his non-nurturing creator, hanging Fritz and choking Waldman. Then he shatters the idyllic mirror scene of Mother Nature, throwing little Maria into the water, in monstrous "self"-defense, yet abject innocence.

Such choral violence does not have its source in women (despite what Shelley's Monster says [137]), but rather in the fragile illusion of ego in the mirror stage and in the infant's extreme vulnerability to the phallic mother phantasm. The Monster is the "fragmented body" experienced by the infant, while perceiving the false sense, though necessary illusion, of a complete Self, in the mirror and mother's eyes (Lacan, *Écrits* 4). He kills because, cut off from the illusion of a human *imago*, he is being torn apart as he lives. Yet this also expresses the choral vulnerability and potential violence of all those watching him, including the spectators at the edges of the cinema mirror, partially suturing the monstrous apparatus as it acts out their fears and desires.

Female characters embody the abject *chora* in Whale's film, though in less active ways than Frankenstein and his creature. Elizabeth does act initially like a good (enough) mother,[59] as she tries to rescue Frankenstein and ignores the amorous pleas of Victor Moritz. She eventually succeeds: we see her at the end of the film, in the distance through a bedroom doorway, at the infinite vanishing point, as antidote to the Monster's evil entrance, nursing Frankenstein back to health. Yet such actions of the good Elizabeth are pushed offscreen throughout most of the film by the male characters, by their *chora* of creative experimentation and destructive revenge, allowing her only an abject scream at the monstrous climax. As Frankenstein said to her earlier, when she wanted to watch his experiment: "You'll ruin everything." Perhaps his locking her in the bedroom, where the Monster then catches her, says even more. Even the comical Baron (Frankenstein's father) treats his female servants with contempt, giving them champagne during the prenuptial celebration instead of a wine that is "too good for them." The film concludes (after the door to Elizabeth's maternal actions is closed) with the Baron again drinking such a special wine, his grandmother's favorite, which the servant girls have brought to help cure his son. Though not drinking with him, the obedient female chorus joins him in the patriarchal toast for "a son to the House of Frankenstein"—showing the *chora* as restored to an orderly, repressed place, with their supportive voices and Elizabeth's maternal care, which may eventually produce a rightful, male heir, instead of a monster.

CRUEL AFFECT AND A-EFFECT AS CATHARTIC CURES

Such choral investment in transcendent male heroes, by secondary females characters, exemplifies the traditional class and gender hierarchy of cinema's Apollonian screen. Yet the repressed, Dionysian *chora* does return with a raging vengeance in *Frankenstein*, even if only through the male creator, creature, and mob—like ancient Greek males taking the place of female maenads, in performing the chorus of Euripides' *The Bacchae*. However, while there were no female actors onstage and in the orchestra of Euripides' Greece, nor in Shakespeare's England, these male playwrights did create powerful, violent female characters, from Agave and Medea to Lady Macbeth and Lear's daughters—drawing, through the *chora* of their theatre work, upon the lives of actual women in such times.

For both men and women today, the temptation of choral rage—fueling individual violence—is evoked, displayed, and hopefully clarified by cinema as well as theatre. But such an Aristotelian hope hinges, in my view, on two modern theories that seem diametrically opposed: Bertolt Brecht's alienation effect and Antonin Artaud's theatre of cruelty. Brecht abhorred the communal catharsis of Aristotelian tragedy, whereby the audience, in sympathetic fear of the hero's catastrophe, believes in his inevitable fate—rather than questioning societal norms. As a witness to the theatrics of Nazism, with its power to create and mislead a mass communal audience, Brecht desired an alienation effect (A-effect) in his epic theatre, which would distance actor from character and spectator from both—to create a more critical view of the action onstage. Yet, such critical distance does not mean being out of touch. Rather than simply purging fear and pity through submission to fate, Brecht's non-Aristotelian homeopathy would use the spectator's alienation to purify communal emotion, toward social change. Thus, through the alienation effect, a Brechtian spectator would feel a part of the social structure forming the character's fate, yet also be wary of the temptation to lose one's head in vengeful, violent communion. But Brecht was also aware of the opposite temptation, toward the illusion of a transcendent ego, too powerfully distanced (onstage or politically) from choral concerns.[60]

In analyzing the origins of the aggressive ego, Lacan focuses on "transitivism": one infant cries, then others catch and express the choral emotion. Lacan relates this contagious effect of infantile affect to many forms of "identification with the other" at any age, including "the actor with the spectator" (*Écrits* 19). Lacan views such mirroring as a crucial step toward identification with a self that is also self-alienating (more in the other), as in the mirror-stage separation between image and body: "the individual fixes upon himself an image that alienates him from himself." And this sense of a misplaced or stolen self arouses "the desire for the object of the other's desire: here the primordial coming together (*concours*) is precipitated into aggressive competitiveness (*concurrence*)" of individual egos, onstage and in life—through the "specular communion" of transitivism. Clearly, the violence in *Frankenstein* arises through such "erotic" competition between male egos (Frankenstein, the Baron, Victor Moritz, Fritz, and the Monster), as well as the death-drive horror of the creature. Yet the escalation of violence also shows a regression to communal *concours* in the raging, fiery mob.[61]

Artaud desired such communal inflammation, through self-immolation, in his theatre of cruelty, with the actor (and the sympathetic spectator) as a martyr burning at the stake. Unlike Brecht's desire for critical distance from the stage (but more like Nietzsche's nostalgia for an ancient choral womb), Artaud wanted an apocalyptic "plague" in theatre—a mystical and physical contagion, ritually transforming self-alienated spectators and purifying their social *ressentiment*.[62] Thus, Artaud's sacred theatre of cruelty would use the spectator's self-alienation, like Brecht's political A-effect, yet intensify audience sympathies centripetally, through the intimacy of stage edge violence, evoking a cathartic return to transitivistic *concours*, rather than Brecht's centrifugal *concurrence*. "I propose then a theater in which violent physical images crush and hypnotize the sensibility of the spectator seized by the theater as by a whirlwind of higher forces" (Artaud, *Theater* 82–83).

Cinema seems to have inherent A-effects, when compared with live theatre: the screen itself, as well as long shots and odd angles, tend to distance the spectator from the original performance, scene, props, and actor's body.[63] And yet, film bears a greater technical ability to focus the spectator's gaze and to unite disparate views seamlessly onscreen—toward the potential communion of Artaudian cruelty. (Artaud acted in Gance's *Napoleon* and Dreyer's *Joan of Arc* before turning fully to theatre.) Brechtian effects are already well known in cinema studies, especially through the films of Jean-Luc Godard. But such A-effective films are not usually considered in relation to Artaudian cruelty, on the other side of the Brechtian mirror, nor in relation to both theorists as spectral doubles at the screen's edge.[64] In a Lacanian view, Brecht's approach would emphasize the symbolic order of stage/screen semiosis,[65] as a way to better perceive the imaginary illusion of ego and the Real lack of being. But it would also be wary of such individual masks and black holes, reflecting more on social constructions of identity, in order to analyze and improve that imaginary/symbolic realm. Artaud's approach, on the other hand, would stress Real lack and the imaginary world of myths and dreams—to conjure cruelly abject, yet transcendent symbols, and thus reach a symbolic level beyond ordinary social realities. "A violent and concentrated action is a kind of lyricism: it summons up supernatural images, a bloodstream of images, a bleeding spurt of images in the poet's head and in the spectator's as well" (*Theater* 82).[66]

Artaud's vision of theatrical communion and cruel catharsis might simply be dismissed as a psychotic delusion.[67] But Brecht's A-effect, though apparently more rational, also bears a risk of greater ego illusion at an aloof distance. Thus, both Artaud and Brecht haunt today's screen edge with dialectical temptations and cures: the homeopathic medicine/poison of dissolving into violent community or transcending that toward an even crueler alienation. Perhaps the best approach is a mixture of Artaud and Brecht, in film creation, spectatorship, and analysis. But the precise recipe for this volatile mixture depends upon the subject and situation of screen presentation. If we agree with Lacan and Kristeva that we all suffer from phallic lack, then we all (male and female) bear a creative/destructive *chora*, which conjoins as we watch, co-creating the scene onscreen. Yet we also create a distinct film in our heads as we each watch the same one together.

CHORAL BORN KILLERS

Abject choral violence has become a conspicuous symptom of the postmodern: circulating between actual criminals (male and female), their unfortunate victims, and their idolized representations in the current rites of mass-media spectatorship. Oliver Stone's *Natural Born Killers* (1994) shows this postmodern circulation of violent desire in a symbolic/imaginary frenzy very unlike Whale's *Frankenstein*, yet haunted likewise by Real ghosts. When the film's perverse romantic heroes, Mickey and Mallory Knox (Woody Harrelson[68] and Juliette Lewis), begin their first violent scene, Stone shows *Father Knows Best* playing on a TV screen in the diner they have just entered. An offscreen waitress's hand turns the old television knob, changing its screen to the figure of Richard Nixon and then to an anonymous, monstrous man screaming. Throughout the film, many shots of male monsters appear (including Mickey's own bloody face, his and Mallory's fathers, and Boris Karloff's famous creature)[69] as do other fantasy figures—sometimes for only a split second, just subliminally visible. In this first scene, the waitress changes visibly, through Mickey's highly subjective point of view, into a smiling seductress. As the killing starts, another woman appears behind the counter, a fat maternal figure in a hair net and white apron, raising a meat cleaver. Her expression changes from menace to surprise as Mickey's slow-motion bullet approaches her face. Such alluring, nightmarish, yet comical figures recur throughout the film, along with satirical extremes of violence (and a parody of tabloid TV dramatizations of such violent crimes), evoking both Artaudian ritual cruelty and Brechtian consciousness of artifice, at the screen's various edges. The audience is given Artaudian glimpses, halfway through the film, of Mickey's repressed memories, through his encounter with the magic fire of an Indian (played by activist Russell Means) and with his own snake totem. Black and white dream images show a boy being grabbed by his father (as the adult Mickey says, "Don't hit me," in his sleep), his mother being slapped by the father, and his mother yelling ("I hate you, you little ass hole"). In a more Brechtian vein, the latter half of the film stresses the role of the mass media and judicial system in creating serial killers—through several representative caricatures: a sadistic detective, a vain prison warden, and the "American Maniacs" TV host. Yet, there are also Artaudian revelations in the latter half: a flashback while Mickey is interviewed in prison by the TV host shows a man, perhaps his father, shooting himself in a field while a boy watches at a distance. Even the obnoxious TV host, Wayne Gale (Robert Downey, Jr.), a foolish figure of the media's villainy throughout most of the film, is given a sympathetic moment as sacrificial victim at the end, as he begs for his life, then accepts his martyrdom, replaced by his videocamera as sole witness to the killers' romantic escape.

Mallory's familial ghosts appear early in the film, along with depictions of the media's symbolic and imaginary pressures on her and her lover to perform as great killers. As they drive away from the film's first murder scene, the obviously artificial backdrop around the car turns into a rapid montage (in red tint, normal colors, and black and white) of their prior exploits acclaimed by the press, and other hallucinatory symbols. Shortly after that, the film shifts into a parody of a TV sitcom, "I Love Mallory," showing her sexually abusive father (played by Rodney Dangerfield) and complicit mother, accompanied by a similarly abusive laugh track. After Mickey kills Mallory's parents to end the sitcom, Stone plays again with the screen edges between various fictional genres and visual media in their romantic self-made marriage on a bridge over a deep river canyon. Mickey cuts his palm and hers, then joins their hands in a blood bond, with the drops of blood falling into the abyss and becoming a cartoon of intertwining snakelike spurts. A few scenes later, as Mickey and Mallory make love in their motel room (with a girl tied and gagged in the corner), the film intercuts their passion with violent scenes on the room's TV set, and on the room's windows behind their bed. (A praying mantis eats its mate, for example, in a nature show on the TV.) The media's imaginary and symbolic mirrors surround and pressure these romantic heroes—molding them into sacrificial idols like the Aztec *ixiptla*—to act out their fate as "natural born killers," reflecting as well the violent, perverse desires in the real-life media audience watching them. Yet, as sacred puppets, Mickey and Mallory are not only sacrificed by the media. They also sacrifice others in their gladiatorial games as outlaws onscreen, inspiring some spectators to mimic them in the Real and thus become monstrous god-actors themselves.

Like, but more explicitly than, Whale's film, Stone's demonstrates how abject violence arises from the Real ghosts of a particular perverse father and lost mother in an individual's "abnormal" brain. Yet these films also show violent desires circulating through the social Other—represented by the audience at the screen's edges. Viewed with cruel sympathy and critical alienation (Artaudian and Brechtian theatrics), such films might be experienced as symptoms of current violence, not only in fictional characters and rare real-life criminals, but in all of us. The passage through these films' edges might become a rite of communal purification, leading to less violence than they show onscreen. Or they might backfire for some in the mass audience, intensifying the violent sympathy and fear that could lead to the mimetic return of abject rage in real life—especially with the criminal stars and spectacular violence of Stone's film.[70]

Perverse and psychotic spectators may be particularly inclined to imitate the violence they see onscreen, copying the sadism or striking back at the demons in their own lives. Yet even an apparently normal, upper-class teenager like Sarah Edmondson can be pushed by a film like *Natural Born Killers* and the psychotic, hallucinatory effects of LSD (as well as by her homicidal boyfriend) to act out violently. "A woman was working [behind the counter]. As I looked at her, I did not see her, but I saw the demon. I shot it. She fell" (quoted in Shnayerson 104). Most viewers did not react like Edmondson to the demons in Stone's film. But all of us relate to other people, especially to strangers, through prototypes in our experience, partly shaped by media characterizations. And the danger of repeated, mimetic sacrifices from the screen to real life, in extreme and subtler ways, is revealed by the director's own comments on the two endings that he filmed. He first made a typical Hollywood finale, a "killers-receive-their-just-deserts ending" (247).[71] But instead he decided to show the killers escaping punishment because Mickey and Mallory were "the new Adam and Eve." Stone adds: "now that the media were dead, they would be the new model parents for a new culture." Yet that logic seems to justify and encourage the copycat violence by young fans of the film, as real-life children of its fictional heroes, continuing its romantic, melodramatic revolution against the media and other demons.

Stone's choice of romantic escape or just punishment, in the two melodramatic endings he filmed, belies another alternative: a more tragic awareness of repeated suffering within the heroic villains, their victims, and their families—perpetuated by vengeful communion and apparently transcendent violence. The film starts to unmask its ego illusions of screen romance as Mickey and Mallory fight on their road trip, taking further victims through their anger at each other. There is a further unmasking of their transcendent power as they feel remorse at killing the Indian shaman and start to see the demons growing within themselves, not just appearing on others to be destroyed. More honing of such tragic edges[72]—and of the tragicomic critique, rather than melodramatic demonizing, of the media—might have helped more of the film's audience toward a healthy catharsis, rather than inspiring some (already troubled) spectators to commit copycat monstrosities as further mass-media sacrifices, in apparent communion with the lovers' revolution. But with the case of Sarah Edmondson and her boyfriend, it is possible that their mimetic violence, after watching the perverse romance of Stone's film over a dozen times, may have also been due to the psychotic effects of the LSD they took—especially with the "demon" that Sarah remembers seeing in her victim.

MALE AND FEMALE MONSTERS

Stone appeals to the melodramatic expectations of his cinema audience, building on road movie and romantic outlaw stereotypes.[73] But he also creates various tragic edges that may snag viewers' identifications toward a more Artaudian sense of fatal cruelty, clarifying the self-destructive passion for revenge, or a Brechtian awareness of social pressures, inspiring the desire for change. In the same year as Stone's movie, a remake of Frankenstein hit the screens, by director and actor Kenneth Branagh (with the script adaptation by Steph Lady and Frank Darabont). It restored much of the plot from the original novel, yet also borrowed from Whale's classic, refocusing the melodramatic horror and revenge toward a more tragic climax. With Mary Shelley's Frankenstein, Branagh the director paralleled Victor Frankenstein, the character he played in the film: creating more complex monsters than James Whale had as director or Colin Clive did as Henry Frankenstein.[74] Branagh's film refocused audience sympathies and fears for Victor, for Victor's father (Ian Holm), and for a speaking Monster (Robert De Niro).[75] It also featured female characters more tragically, revealing their choral abjection at the edges of the screen—through the death of Victor's mother, a mob's lynching of Justine (servant and friend to Victor and Elizabeth), and Victor's creation of a mate for the Monster out of Elizabeth's and Justine's body parts.[76]

In contrast to Whale's prototype, Branagh shifts his version (as the full title indicates) back to the original novel and to the origins of Shelley's work as a ghost story. Whale does show a scene of the novel's historical origin at the opening of The Bride of Frankenstein: the ghost story contest between Mary Shelley, her husband Percy, and Lord Byron. Whale casts the same actress, Elsa Lanchester, as Mary Shelley in the beginning of the film and the female monster at its end. But in both parts, the woman has a small role to play, even as the original work's author and the title character. The Monster also begins to speak in Whale's sequel, yet says very little. Branagh, on the other hand, develops Victor, his father, and his monstrous creation as complex characters—and provides a stronger role for Elizabeth (Helena Bonham Carter) as both tragic figure and monster, by making the bride of Frankenstein into the Monster's mate, unlike the novel (or Whale's sequel, despite its

name). Instead of Whale's focus on the mad scientist, with his father as buffoon, and the robotic hulk of a manufactured Monster, with a tin-canlike
head,[77] Branagh's film expresses the ghostly *chora* of the dead mother in
Frankenstein's work. He thus raises the spectre of the dead author, Mary Shelley—as repressed by Whale's classic, the Karloff image, and the sequel's depiction of her onscreen. Mary Shelley's abject emotions from the loss of her
mother when she was born, and of her own children before and during her
writing and revision of the novel,[78] may filter through the father-son story in
Branagh's film: in the mourning for and obsessive rage to revive the dead, to
materialize the ghosts at the edges of the page and screen.

   Branagh is not strictly faithful to the book. However, he presents significant elements omitted in previous film versions, while adding new details
that are not in the novel, yet feature and extend its tragic spirit. For example, he restores the frame tale of Captain Walton meeting first Frankenstein
and then the Monster, while his ship is frozen in ice on a polar expedition.
The audience sees the Monster's story directly, in the middle of the film,
without seeing the Monster tell his story to Walton. But the film does return
to the Walton frame at the end, to show the Monster choosing to die with
the already dead body of his creator (staying with the funeral pyre, as the ice
breaks and Walton's ship leaves).

   Branagh's film shows some details of the Monster's learning of language
through, yet also his alienation from the De Lacey cottagers. It thus reveals
his double mirror-stage abjection: from both his male creator and the loving
De Lacey family whom he spies through a hole in their wall, while eating the
slop they throw to their pigs. (He makes a connection to the blind father, as
in the novel, but is thrown out of the cottage when the son returns and sees
his monstrosity.) Most importantly, Branagh focuses early in the film on Victor's relationship with his mother, adding certain details not in the novel. She
is shown dancing with Victor as a child and telling him that he will be an
even greater doctor than his father. She tells her adult son to enjoy life, not
just his studies, stealing his book to tease him. Yet she is also too full of life:
she dances with the adult Victor while she is pregnant and then she miscar-
ries, dying while giving birth to his brother, William.[79] Victor finds her lifeless body in the birthing chair, in blood-soaked clothes, after his father has
come down a huge, banisterless staircase with bloody hands and bare chest,
crying out his failure as a doctor to save her. Shortly before this, a lightning
bolt hits a tree outside the house, as Victor and Elizabeth watch—the only
detail from the novel that relates to the use of lightning in Whale's film
(although the scene is not shown by Whale).[80] Later in his film, Branagh also
adds a scene not in the novel, which recalls the experiments with lightning
in Whale's classic. Branagh's Frankenstein sets up an experiment on a hilltop,
using a lightning rod to gather electricity into his own body and that of Elizabeth and Justine. But the choral power of Mother Nature is tied much more

directly to maternal blood in the Branagh film, and to amniotic fluid, which he uses for his laboratory resurrections, along with acupuncture and electric eels (unlike the novel).

Branagh does not show Frankenstein's nightmare in the novel of Elizabeth turning into his mother's decaying body. But he does add a scene of Victor vowing at her grave site that he will realize his scientific dream for her sake: "Oh, mother. You should never have died. No one need ever die. I will stop this" (Branagh 53). Branagh also refers to today's medical technology to connect the novel's science fiction with his audience's reality. Victor tells his friends Henry and Professor Waldman that they, in the late eighteenth century, are "steps away" from replacing a sick heart with a healthy one (65). Yet it is his Monster who later removes a heart, like an Aztec surgeon, in sacrificing Elizabeth on his creator's wedding night, because Frankenstein refused to make the Monster a mate. The Monster's own creation in Branagh's film, unlike Whale's film or the novel, develops from the death of Victor's mentor, Waldman, as well as his mother. After failing to save the professor on the operating table, Victor cuts out Waldman's brain and later puts it into the skull of the man who murdered him and was hung for that crime. (It is not clear why Victor cannot use Waldman's entire body for his experiment.) Victor cuts down the hanged man, like Fritz in Whale's version, and cuts off the leg of someone else who died from cholera, to replace the one missing from the murderer's body. He follows Waldman's notebook, repeating the dead man's experiments to give life to a dead frog. He is also shown suturing the creature's bald head and face as he prepares the grotesque body for resurrection. But it is in the repetition of a life-and-death dance—along with abject notebooks and stitches—that Branagh shows the most significant choral edges and rhythms of his *Frankenstein*.

After Elizabeth visits and fails to dissuade Victor from continuing his experiments (more like the classic film than the novel), he sends her away and places the reconstructed body into a womblike, metal sarcophagus.[81] Working bare-chested like his father when he failed to save his mother, Victor succeeds in reviving the body with amniotic fluid and electric eels. But he cannot get it to stand, nor can he stand very well himself with the slippery fluid from his experimental womb spilled onto the floor. Victor wrestles with the adult-size baby, its body naked and restitched. Together they rise and fall, again and again, in a grotesque, abject dance. This abject double of creator and monster recalls the child's uncoordinated body in the mirror stage, contradicting its ideal, whole ego—as creation of the (m)Other's desire.[82] Victor then accidentally catches the body on some counterweighted chains and watches it rise to the ceiling, its head knocked unconscious by the falling counterweight. (This may also recall, to Victor and the audience, the hanging of that murderous body in an earlier scene.) Victor writes in his notebook that this creation is "malfunctional and pitiful, and dead" (Branagh 81). He then falls asleep exhausted (as in the novel), but wakes to see the Monster steal his coat, which held the notebook, and flee. That notebook will later explain to the Monster, when he learns to read, about his creator's use of dead bodies as "raw materials" and of Victor's disgust at seeing him. Thus, the Monster's tragic, mirror-stage awareness of his own abject, fragmented, and uncoordinated body, his *corps morcelé*, is shared with the film viewer through various symbolic and imaginary edges of the Real *chora*: the notebook's words (as in the novel), the grotesque sutures on his face and body, and the clumsy dance of this adult child unable to stand, while grasping at the ideal beauty of the Other, which ought to be his own.

Victor also encounters his mirror stage in this scene. He had followed the steps in his professor's notebook and then filled his own with an ideal formula to create life out of death. Yet he finishes the book by describing a repulsive Thing as the result. He finds a tragic reflection of the monstrous within the beautiful, through his dances with life and death, here and elsewhere in the film. The notebook that he completes yet fails to destroy, after hanging his creature and before staring at himself in a mirror, comes from his father in an earlier scene, a gift of his dead mother with the pages left blank for Victor to fill with his greatness, "with the deeds of a noble life" (Branagh 50). The ideal ego that she thus gave her son (through a desire of the Other that he inter- preted as a necrophilic demand) is now seen by the film audience as shat- tered, like the double he has birthed, with sutures and dance. But here Branagh also reveals the monstrous, mirror-stage mechanism of the cinematic apparatus: the audience's suturing of the film's diegesis, filling the book (per- formance text) beyond the screen and forming the *chora* of ideal and abject identifications at its edges.

A more elegant, yet also grotesquely tragic dance occurs near the end of the film, with Victor's second monstrous creation. After the Monster has killed Elizabeth by tearing out her heart (using the superhuman strength of his bare hand), Frankenstein chops the head off her body and sutures it to Jus- tine's. Victor stitches up Elizabeth's face as well, since it was cut and burned by an oil lamp when the body rolled off the sacrificial bed, after the Monster lay on top of her and literally stole her heart. Stitches are also obvious around the female monster's neck and wrist, as Victor tries to get her to dance with him—as the live Elizabeth had done, with similar music on the soundtrack earlier in the film, and as his mother had also done while pregnant and before that when he was a child. In retrospect, Victor's various dances with his mother and with Elizabeth, both as herself and as a head restitched to another body, become primal scenes of erotic and death drive *jouissance*, related also to the bloody scene of the mother's miscarriage and death—as well as to Vic- tor's dance with his male-child Monster. These dances also evoke the chorus of primal scene voyeurs at the screen's edges: the cinema (or video) audience, dancing vicariously through various visual and acoustic, personal and cultural

FIGURE 3.3. The Monster (Robert De Niro) lying on top of Elizabeth (Helena Bonham Carter), just before he steals her heart on her wedding night, tearing it out of her chest. *Mary Shelley's Frankenstein*, TriStar, 1994.

associations—like the Aztecs enacted more literally in their "Dance with the Severed Heads" after the heart extraction rite.

Branagh extends the sacrifice of Elizabeth beyond Shelley's novel, from the Monster's vengeful murder of her (along with little William, Justine indirectly, and Victor's father) to Victor's use of her head and Justine's body as raw material to make a female monster. Victor and the male Monster then fight over the abject, recreated Elizabeth/Justine—whereas in the original novel Frankenstein never finishes the female creature and in Whale's sequel she makes only a brief appearance at the end to hiss at everyone. In Branagh's version Victor tries to reawaken Elizabeth's memory of her (or the head's) identity, as he revives the creature, dresses her, puts the wedding ring on her finger, and asks her to say his name, and then says hers. After this imaginary and symbolic invocation, Elizabeth raises her head (or her head rises on Justine's body) and she touches Victor's face with her fingertips. Such a mirror-stage identification for this hybrid of two women's bodies shows both the idealizing desire of the male (m)Other recasting his creation's *Gestalt* and—with a burned head and large stitches across her face and around her neck and wrist—the abject, fragmented body and Real loss of being behind the mirror. At various points throughout the film, the male creature had also shown such mirror-stage edges: in the sutures across his face and body, in the notebook of his creator that he finds in the coat he wears, which calls him monstrous, and in his discovery that parts of him remember how to play a flute. Victor's father also faces the tragic edge of life and death in his own hands and mind, expressing his despair as a great physician at his wife's miscarriage. He says, "I can't," when she tells him to "cut" her and "save the baby"—then shows his son his bloody hands when he has failed to save the mother as well. Even at a moment of great joy, at his son's graduation party, his face suddenly changes, showing abject loss, as he recalls out loud that Victor's mother is not there to share his pride. But Branagh's film redoubles the tragic, mirror-stage edges with Elizabeth/Justine's rebirth.

Elizabeth was first introduced in the film, as in the novel, as an orphan adopted by Victor's parents after her own had died of cholera. She became his sister (or "cousin") and took the place of his mother in his parents' home after her death. Victor thus finds in her revived, hybrid face and body, as his monstrous wife, an incestuous,[83] Oedipal (m)Other and mirror. Justine is also shown early in the film as loving Victor, though at a distance as servant and friend. Then she is framed for the murder of William by the Monster, who puts a locket from the dead boy on her dress as she sleeps.[84] Justine is hung by a furious mob that sees her as a murderess (recalling the mob that chases the Monster in Whale's classic). Her abject death thus plays a role in her monstrous re-creation. But with all four of these characters, the various instances throughout the film of mirror-stage *méconnaissance* return at the climax, in Victor's creation of the Elizabeth/Justine figure and his battle against the Monster for identification with her.

After Victor revives the dead Elizabeth/Justine through the mirror of his face and voice, he dances with her as in the earlier scene when she was alive and whole. But her head and upper torso hang to the side as he twirls with her; she seems to be a puppet, or an erotic object as toy, rather than a separate, individual person. Her lacking being is then extended when the male Monster appears and demands her as his possession. Both Victor and his male creature woo the female: she stands between them and turns to each one as he says her name. The Monster tells her she is "beautiful" and she moves toward him (132). She touches the suture scars on his face, then sees the stitches around her wrist and touches the sutures on her own face. (She has a large stitch across her right eye and also over her lips.) Elizabeth/Justine is thus caught between two desiring mirrors:[85] the two monstrous men who want to repossess her, yet are also her male (m)Others, calling forth her head's identity as a sutured, lacking being. Victor gets her to speak, to say his name once. Then the male Monster starts to dance with her, as Victor had done before. But Victor stops their choral romance. They each tug at her arms, saying, "She's mine." She frees herself, breaks an oil lamp over her head, and runs ablaze through the Frankenstein mansion, setting it all on fire. Here Branagh puts a Brechtian twist on this mostly Artaudian film. He offers a gestic, feminist critique[86] of the possessive, objectifying, male gaze of Victor and his Monster (and of the cinematic apparatus). That gaze is revealed as trapping the newly reborn Elizabeth—with abject self-destruction as her only escape—thus showing the patriarchal and capitalist monstrosity of Frankenstein's society (and our own) in his reproductive machinery and sacrificial love triangle.[87]

Not all of the cinema audience will sympathize with the film's spectacular, Artaudian (and Aztec-like) cruelty, or its violent, somewhat Brechtian climax. Here and throughout the film it is easy to question the filmmaker's choices. Why does Victor use Waldman's brain and not his whole body to produce the first monster? Why are there stitches across the male Monster's face when he was never cut there—or why did Victor cut his face if just replacing the brain?[88] Why does he attach Elizabeth's head and hand to Justine's body, rather than transplanting the servant's heart to his wife's own body? But such questions resist the power of horror at this film's choral edges, evoked by the various stitches across faces, absurd uses of body parts, and grotesque dances with hybrid creatures. In contrast to Whale's *Frankenstein*, Branagh's characters are more fragmented, postmodern, and tragically complex—perhaps giving some spectators the uncanny sense of dead or unborn spirits from their own minds, reflected in the screen's mirror stagings. As psychoanalyst Bruce Fink says, "the unconscious is full of other people's talk . . . goals, aspirations, fantasies" (*Lacanian* 9–10). Spectators may find a cathartic engagement of their own split subjectivity through the drama onscreen, exemplified in the Monster's questions to his creator when they

meet in an ice cave. He asks Frankenstein whether his re-membered knowledge of how to play the flute (and to speak and to read) resides in his hands,
mind, or heart. He also asks who the others are "of which I am comprised"
(Branagh 115). And he asks his creator if he has a soul—or if that was a part
of him that Victor "left out." Frankenstein does not have an answer for him.
Yet the film audience does, at the edges of another world that the characters
cannot perceive.

There are many visual edges and creases of the Real in Branagh's film:
blood, wounds, scars, sutures, lightning at the tree and in the rod, electricity
in the lab circuits and eels, amniotic fluid, the ape arm in Waldman's lab that
comes alive with brutal strength, and the dead frog in Frankenstein's lab that
breaks its glass container, foreshadowing the Monster's erotic and death drive
power. There are also various acoustic edges throughout the film: thunder and
lightning strikes, the mother's birthing/dying screams, the Monster's flute
music outside Victor's honeymoon hotel (drawing him and his men away
from protecting her), and the dance music for Victor to hold his mother, Elizabeth, and his female creature. But the tragic edges of this film, with its
schizoid characters and reflective plot twists, demonstrate a further Lacanian
(as well as Artaudian and Brechtian) potential for Aristotle's ancient formula
to have postmodern relevance. Aristotle found the human impulse for theatre in the mimetic joy of the child: to both play at being other and watch
others becoming characters in a plot. Branagh's film shows the joy and horror of the mirror stage, of a whole and fragmented identity, in the adult scientist and his creatures—as the source of their dramatic conflict. Their split
subjectivity is their *hamartia*, their tragic flaw or missed aim in judgment and
identity. They each create a theatre of sacrifice, with the men sacrificing
themselves and others, and the female creature (Elizabeth/Justine) destroying
herself and the mansion. Thus, they show the cathartic potential of cinema,
like theatre, to restage the primal sacrifice behind Aristotle's mimetic mirror:
the loss of being in the human acquisition of an imaginary and symbolic identity, through family and society, involving the Other's desire and discourse.
The child may have no other choice, except autism, in that primal sacrifice.[89]
But through the cathartic, choral restagings of film and theatre, the audience
might see more: a sacrifice of the sacrifice, beyond tragic passions and actions.

Elizabeth/Justine's abject rebellion as female monster relates to many
other, more fully developed devils and warriors in films of the last three
decades, such as *The Exorcist* (1973), *Carrie* (1976), and the *Alien* series
(1979, 1986, 1992, 1997). In *The Exorcist*, Regan's abject revolt as possessed
girl shows to some spectators not a male devil controlling her, but rather her
own menstrual power as a threat to patriarchy.[90] *Carrie* also has a menstrual,
psychic power, but she becomes monstrously violent in revenge (more like
Shelley's and Branagh's creatures). The film shows her as a sympathetic victim of brutal peer pressure and perverse mothering, as others react with teen

mockery and religious horror at Carrie's menstrual bleeding. Her eventual rebellion seems a justified revenge, yet excessively violent and self-destructive. Ripley is a fully mature female warrior, but like Carrie she becomes alienated from her peers as she battles the monstrous alien mother, plus various male and android villains in all four films. Like Branagh's Elizabeth/Justine, Ripley is reborn, with each *Alien* sequel, becoming progressively more monstrous herself.[91] In the most recent film, she is a hybrid, human and alien creature, cloned by Frankenstein-like scientists, upon whom she and her offspring take violent revenge.

Branagh's *Frankenstein* does not show these abject dimensions of the female monster as menstruating, supernaturally violent teen (beautiful yet grotesque in her growth) or as alienated warrior and mother (fighting the patriarchy but also her own reproductive body)—which express specific tensions for real women today. But Branagh's monsters do reveal a violent horror behind the mirrors of beauty, involving the abject, choral rage for rebellious vengeance in both men and women.[92] The Artaudian cruelty of his *Frankenstein*, along with its Brechtian twists, does not reach the media reflexivity of Stone's *Killers*. Yet Branagh does present complex, composite creatures who reveal the mirror-stage edges of self and theatre, creating a potential cathartic effect through his tragic film.[93] (This also shows Branagh's experience as an actor and director of Shakespeare's tragedies.) Branagh's *Frankenstein* creates a bridge from the romantic, sublime horror of Shelley's novel and the modernist fear of technology in Whale's classic film, to the postmodern angst behind our current celebration of diverse, multicultural, and transgendered identities—as evidenced by the adoration and imitation of star's body parts, with product endorsements, exercise machines, plastic surgery, and anorexic horrors. Thus, he reveals how our age continues to bear the elements of preceding times and is not just "post."

The tragic and melodramatic edges of the various monster films analyzed in this chapter show a continued yearning for communal connection, from the modern alienated ego to the postmodern schizoid subject. The outcast's abject agony can turn into a criminal's destructive rage, with further acts of violence in vengeful retribution. But the degree to which the murderous villain (whether it is Frankenstein's Monster, Mickey and Mallory Knox, Carrie, Regan, or the alien mother) is also depicted as a tragic, sympathetic figure— as a victim of trauma, suffering too in the repetitions of violence—makes a crucial difference in the film's representation of the sacrificial *chora* and its potential cathartic effects. Both the modern independent ego and the premodern tribal community have become illusory identities in the postmodern, as ghostly lures to today's split and schizoid subjects. The movie theatre, especially with its screen edge monsters, provides the tempting illusion of ego transcendence and communal wholeness, yet also the abject terror of that mask's fragmentation and the Other's overwhelming, symbiotic *jouissance*. Clear-cut heroes, victims, and villains offer simple ego identifications and safe glimpses of terror (or terrorism). But the presentation of a complex, tragic hero—as victim and villain in the character's own violent choices—offers a greater potential for cathartic awareness of the violence in each spectator's ego and in the superego of poetic justice as communal revenge.

The next chapter will examine another type of movie (or an intersection of various types): a gang war, race riot, jail and courtroom, musical and historical drama—in a low-budget, ethnic-oriented, bilingual feature film made from a stage play. Its presentation of violence onstage and onscreen, through Hispanic and non-Hispanic, ego and superego figures, will be examined for potential cathartic effects on different kinds of spectators, with melodramatic conflicts, yet tragicomic twists of Aztec sacrifice and Brechtian gests. Then the final chapter will look at the possible cathartic effects or violent mimetic backfires of certain gangster, boxing, Bible, and war films by two mainstream directors—with their sacrificial displays of monstrous idols and modern gladiators onscreen.

FOUR

Brechtian and Aztec Violence in *Zoot Suit*

LUIS VALDEZ CATEGORIZES the plays he has developed with El Teatro Campesino as *actos* (political agit-prop to organize migrant farmworkers), *mitos* (mythic works to focus indigenous identity), and *corridos* (musical ballads acted out). His bilingual musical[1] *Zoot Suit* combined all three forms, as it moved from page to stage (1978) to screen (1981). *Zoot Suit* was a tremendous hit on the Los Angeles stage, and became the first Chicano play on Broadway, although it played much less successfully in New York. When Valdez made the musical into a feature film for Universal, on a modest budget, he created a unique mixture of stage and cinema production, of melodramatic types and conflicts with tragic figures and edges. He used the theatre space in Los Angeles where the play had been so popular, but transformed it into the 1940s setting of the drama. In significant ways the film reaches even further back to the Amerindian roots of Chicano culture, connecting the zoot-suited *pachuco* to Aztec mythology, as well as showing the modern influence of European theatre through Brechtian techniques.[2] It raises a powerful image of ethnic identity, yet critically questions the sacrificial urge in Chicano machismo.[3]

The phenomenal success of *Zoot Suit* onstage raised critical questions about Valdez as a leading *teatro* artist—although his grass-roots credentials were impecable. He had been a *campesino* himself, working as a migrant farm laborer in his childhood. Eventually, he developed the leading Chicano theatre company of the 1970s in affiliation with the United Farm Workers union of César Chávez.[4] But he then led El Teatro Campesino toward a search for ethnic identity in Aztec and Mayan mythology. This paradoxical combination of political activism with ethnomythic nostalgia[5] became further complicated as Valdez departed from his collective work and developed *Zoot Suit*

112

FIGURE 4.1. The stage setting of *Zoot Suit* as it was used in the film, with the judge, cops, and military at right, the *pachucos* in their zoot suits and leaning poses on the dance hall floor, plus El Pachuco above them all. Universal, 1981.

as a feature film. In the decades since the film was made, critics have accused Valdez of: (1) selling out to the white, mainstream, mass audience, (2) presenting reactionary stereotypes in his female characters, and (3) idealizing violence in the gangster paradigm of his male, zoot-suited pachucos. Yet, through these flaws, *Zoot Suit* expresses a current struggle within Chicano identity, becoming more valuable in a Brechtian sense by producing various political views—even as the film shows the opposite, Artaudian desire for a primal, unifying connection to lost, spiritual forces.[6]

Valdez's film developed as a very personal work, out of the collective practices of El Teatro Campesino. The film focuses more than the play on the relationship between the main character, Henry Reyna, and his mythic alter ego, El Pachuco, who also addresses the audience as narrator. But the film continues to be concerned with the social relations and historical events of the Sleepy Lagoon murder trial and zoot-suit riots.[7] *Zoot Suit* reveals a great deal about the drive toward violence, creative and destructive, in ghetto generations of the 1940s and in generations since then.[8] In its use of theatrical and ritual techniques, as well as historical and mythical images, *Zoot Suit* exemplifies how an ethnic film (in English and Spanish) can display violent stereotypes in complex ways, provoking critical thought, while also evoking ancestral passions—especially through the troublesome figure of El Pachuco.

PATRIARCHAL SACRIFICES

Valdez has been praised by prominent male scholars (Huerta, Brokaw, and Elam) as the main leader, or father, of the Chicano *teatro* movement. But he has been castigated by feminist scholars (Broyles-González; Fregoso, "*Zoot Suit*"; and Yarbro-Bejarano) for misrepresenting Chicanas and for usurping the collective work of *teatristas* through his patriarchal control of the company and by his publishing of their collaborative *actos* as his own. These positive and negative aspects of Valdez's patriarchal leadership culminate in the production history of *Zoot Suit*, with his hiring as an individual playwright and director by the Mark Taper Forum and by Universal Studios, although the play and film draw greatly on prior techniques and images of the Teatro Campesino collective. In its focus on Henry Reyna's choice between various father figures—his garbage collector father (Enrique), his white lawyer (George Shearer), a friendly cop (Lt. Edwards), and the Pachuco superego— *Zoot Suit* itself reflects a paradigm shift in the patriarchal inheritance of Chicano identity, which pivots on the perverse power of criminal violence.

Zoot Suit looks back to a time when young urban gangs were forming as an alternative ethnic ideal, prior to today's drug deals, automatic weapons, and drive-by shootings. This nostalgic ideal is exemplified onscreen with the highly stylized *pachuco* walk, the zoot-suit costume, and choreographed switchblade fights. As the Pachuco explains in his introduction to the audience (in a line added to the film): "Our *pachuco* realities will only make sense if you grasp their stylization." In the stage version of his introductory speech, the Pachuco describes in more detail how his stylized figure reveals contradictory ideals in Chicano identity: "A mythical, quizzical, frightening being / precursor of revolution / Or a piteous, hideous heroic joke / deserving of absolution?" (25–26). *Zoot Suit*, as play and film, hits at the heart of minority desires and mainstream fears in today's audience, using the Brechtian distancing effects of historification (displaying a current problem through a parallel situation in the past) and *Gestus* (showing a critical social attitude through an ironic stage gesture).[9]

El Pachuco appears as a purposefully problematic character in *Zoot Suit*, both onstage and onscreen.[10] As narrator he controls the sequencing and editing of scenes as they appear, by snapping his fingers, and thus becomes, like Shakespeare's Prospero, a figure of the playwright within the play. But he also becomes vulnerable to the actions of other characters during the drama. As Henry's alter ego, he pressures in various directions, stirring rebellious violence or coaching with *calma* or making Henry (and the audience) think at critical Brechtian moments. Except for another allegorical character named the Press, only Henry Reyna can see and talk to El Pachuco. But he incarnates the spirit of pride and defiance, violence and "cool," in all the zoot-suiters. He is directly affected when Henry and others embrace the *pachuco* style or turn against it. When the zoot-suit riots take place in the play, El Pachuco embodies Henry's many zoot-suited peers, who were attacked by uniformed sailors and marines in the streets of Los Angeles in 1943, while Henry (the historical Henry Leyva) was imprisoned in San Quentin for the Sleepy Lagoon murder.[11] In the climactic scene of the play and film, a group of sailors and marines, led by the character of the Press, overpower El Pachuco and his switchblade, then strip him of his zoot suit. But he arises in Aztec guise, turning a gestic moment into a mythic one with tragic resonance: the loss of prior gods, yet repetition of human sacrifice (with his zoot suit taking the place of a god-actor's flayed skin).

Zoot Suit prepares the audience for this complex climax through earlier gestic twists and ritual moments. In the first scene after the Pachuco's introduction in the film (the third scene in the published stage play), he reminds Henry and the watching audience of the historical circumstances of the drama. Although Henry has just been arrested for the Sleepy Lagoon murder of 1942, he had already volunteered to join the American war effort: "I'm supposed to report for the Navy tomorrow." El Pachuco mocks this potential change of costume, from the zoot-suit uniform to "tight *puto* pants" (film version), and gives Henry more ethnic-oriented orders (in both versions): "Rommel is kicking ass in Egypt but the Mayor of L.A. has declared all-out war on Chicanos. On you! . . . Forget the war overseas, carnal. Your war is on the homefront" (30). A little later in the film, after Henry is beat up during

Figure 4.2. El Pachuco (Edward James Olmos) as alter ego to Henry Reyna (Daniel Valdez) while he is in prison. Universal, 1981.

a police interrogation, El Pachuco takes him, with a snap of his fingers, to a flashback of home, "a lifetime ago, last Saturday night," prior to the Sleepy Lagoon murder of which he is now falsely accused. There, as Henry proudly dons his zoot-suit uniform, ostensibly for the last time, Pachuco hands him a switchblade to take to the dance. This is a glaring misrepresentation, according to one of Valdez's strongest critics, because the actual 38th Street Gang, led by Henry Leyva, did not carry switchblades, nor did most *pachucos* at that time (Broyles-González 183). Yet this anachronistic prop of the phallic switchblade figures prominently in the play and film, like the Pachuco's snapping fingers, as a fictional instrument symbolizing the perverse, ritual power of the zoot-suit image—and the exposed cuts (or switches) in the drama—rewriting memory and history to express the current, violent desire for a distinctive, costumed identity.

The flashback of home also shows Henry being lured away from his father, Enrique, and his mother, Dolores, from their ambiguous desires and lower-class status, through the diamondlike sharpness (as the Pachuco says later [80]) of the zoot-suit image and costume. Henry's father, a garbage man, is proud that his son will soon join the Navy and assimilate as an American hero. Just before Henry leaves home for a last night out as a *pachuco*, Enrique tells his son (in the film version) to take the switchblade from his pocket and "rip apart that goddamn silly zoot suit." This paternal desire takes an uncanny turn, later in the drama, when the zoot suit of El Pachuco is ripped from his body as he loses the switchblade fight with the uniformed American servicemen. In the earlier scene at home, Henry's mother also expresses her ambiguous desire, which will soon follow an uncanny path: "Bendito sea Dios. I still can't believe you're going off to war. I almost wish you were going back to jail" (34).

The film version retains this prophetic line, showing that the perverse *pachuco* route Henry takes, one too many times, arises from his mother's desire and father's rule, even as it defies and redefines them. But the film cuts out one of Henry's potential father figures, Lt. Edwards. In the stage play he reminds Henry of how he saved him from delinquency in the past. He then gives Henry: "One more chance, son," to escape from the Sleepy Lagoon arrest and still join the Navy (31–32). Henry instead obeys his alternative superego, El Pachuco, and says to Lt. Edwards: "I ain't your son, cop" (32). However, when the "People's Lawyer," George Shearer, offers his help as another white father figure (also calling Henry "son" [42]) and professes his belief in the American judicial system, Henry contradicts El Pachuco's defiance. In the film Henry argues more with El Pachuco than in the stage play, and a revealing line is added, giving a further gestic twist to the zoot-suit ideal. When Henry angrily asks, "Whose *pinche* side are you on?", El Pachuco responds, "The side of the heroes and the fools, Hank. Which one are you?" Henry is on his way to becoming both hero and fool in the theatre of the law, as he accepts George as lawyer for himself and his gang, while exchanging angry looks with the imaginary Pachuco. Thus, both Henry and El Pachuco become tragicomic figures—each a hero, villain, and fool.

BRECHTIAN *IXIPTLA* ONSCREEN

The contest of wills between Henry and his ethnic gangster superego intensifies in subsequent scenes, building to El Pachuco's zoot-suit *sparagmos* and Aztec reincarnation. Yet, as Henry's awareness of his own split-subjectivity grows, he is more and more able to use his raging *ressentiment*, as oppressed, lower-class minority, to fight judiciously, rather than self-destructively. Using El Pachuco's wisdom, as well as passion, Henry becomes heroic, although still playing the foolish scapegoat of American racism and injustice. This leads to potential insight for various types of spectators—through the ritual passion, yet Brechtian distancing effect of the Pachuco's influence and Henry's shifting awareness.

For example, in the gang fight scene during the Saturday night dance (prior to the Sleepy Lagoon murder), Valdez reminds the watching Latino and American audience of their participation in the theatrics of ethnic violence. The dramatic interest grows as tensions in the barrio dance hall increase, between male and female, between Henry's gang, a rival Chicano gang, and uniformed servicemen. Then the choreography of the mambo switches into that of a knife fight, as Henry takes the place of his younger brother, Rudy, to tangle with the other gang's leader. But at the climax of their sacrificial contest, with Henry's switchblade at the rival leader's throat, the Pachuco snaps his fingers and freezes the action. Here Valdez willingly *un*suspends disbelief, in a Brechtian gesture—a coitus interruptus of the tragic sacrifice—that makes both Henry and the audience think twice. With the other characters frozen, El Pachuco says to Henry: "Que mamada, Hank. That's exactly what the play needs right now. Two more Mexicans killing each other. Watcha . . . Everybody's looking at you" (46). El Pachuco then refers beyond the chorus of characters watching the fight onstage, to the sacrificial desires of the theatre audience: "That's exactly what they paid to see. Think about it."

In the film version El Pachuco refers instead to Henry's own sacrificial desire. Yet this also reflects the multicultural audience—and the Pachuco's own role.

> HENRY: Don't give me that bullshit, *ese*. I got this stilleto from you.
> PACHUCO: Did I tell you to kill the *bato*? Control yourself, Hank. Don't hate your *Raza* [people] more than you love the *gringo*.[12]

In both versions Henry chooses to let Rafas, the rival gang leader, go. This disappoints the *pachucos* and *pachucas* in his own gang, and eventually plays

FIGURE 4.3. Henry and his gang face off against Rafas and his in the dance hall. A sailor stands in the background between them. Universal, 1981.

into the prejudice of the gringo father's law. Henry's 38th Street Gang is later arrested for the murder at the Sleepy Lagoon, where it met to take vengeance on Rafas and the Downey Gang, after Henry was beaten up by those enemies, in revenge for their humiliation at the dance hall.

The actual killer at Sleepy Lagoon is not made clear in the play or the film. But El Pachuco is shown, onstage and onscreen, representing someone "hitting a man on the ground with a big stick," as Della, Henry's girlfriend, testifies during the courtroom scene (57). The clearly biased Judge and Prosecutor (played by the Press in the stageplay) pin the guilt on Henry and his gang, though they insist on their innocence. The Press/Prosecutor directly expresses the prejudicial rationale for the gang's arrest and conviction: the public's fear of *pachucos* as "forces of anarchy and destruction in our society" (62). The film makes this prejudice even more explicit through the testimony of a cop, who compares the Anglo gangsters' use of "fisticuffs" to the *pachuco's* weapon of choice: "all he knows and feels is a desire to use a knife to kill or to at least let blood. This inborn characteristic comes down from the blood-thirsty Aztecs. . . ." Similar testimony was given during the actual trial of the 38th Street Gang,[13] but Valdez does not just ridicule this racist view and its legal unfairness. Instead, he presents El Pachuco with his switchblade as indeed incarnating an Aztec spirit, both violent and wise.

El Pachuco, as onscreen editor of the film, then cuts, with a finger snap, from the cop's racist testimony to a romantic song about marijuana, with himself playing the piano and singing, while a chorus of *pachucas* surrounds him. In this Brechtian gest, Valdez juxtaposes the sacrificial prejudice and scapegoating of a white legal system with an ironic self-questioning of the Aztec heritage of sacrifice inside Chicano culture, which El Pachuco himself represents. Between the verses of his song, he says to Henry: "This is 1942, or is it 1492? Something inside you craves a punishment, a public humiliation, and a human sacrifice? There's no more pyramids, carnal, only the gas cham-ber." Henry responds, "But I didn't do it, *ese.* I didn't kill anybody!" And El Pachuco continues his song: "Mari . . . marijuana, that's my baby's name."

As Valdez has made clear in interviews, *Zoot Suit's* El Pachuco represents (and re-presents) the Aztec god Tezcatlipoca, with the red and black colors of his costume, his magical cutting and ordering of scenes, and his mirroring of Henry's sacrificial impulses.[14] The play and film suggest certain parallels between the sacrifice of *pachuco* characters and the Aztec ritual theatre of human sacrifice. They show the Chicano gang fights of the 1940s as a stylized spectator sport (and dance), feeding the judicial show trial. This is somewhat akin to the ritualized "flower wars" that the Aztecs conducted in order to cap-ture enemy warriors from neighboring city-states as future sacrificial actors. El Pachuco embodies the mythic role of the most ideal captured warrior, who was given the costume, character, and respect due to the god he played as he was sacrificed. The Pachuco's specific relation to the god Tezcatlipoca (Smoking

Mirror), and to the captured Aztec warrior who performed him, is shown through his colors, his magic, his giving of visions to Henry, his joint as "smoking tube" during his song about marijuana (with *pachucas* accompanying him like the *ixiptla's* four wives), his sacrificial knife, and his proud procession toward the rite of sacrifice, in spite of his apparent godlike ability to turn the play another way.[15] Although Pachuco critiques the sacrificial imperative within Henry ("There's no more pyramids, carnal"), he also walks proudly up the pyramid steps to be sacrificed.

Valdez attributed the terrific success of *Zoot Suit* to the mythic power and ancestry of the Pachuco figure, both as a character and as "master of ceremonies" for the stageplay. "That's why a half-million people came to see it in L.A. Because I had given a disenfranchised people their religion back" (quoted in Savran, *In Their Own Words* 265). But in the film version, Valdez plays up the Brechtian critique and metatheatrical reflection along with the religious déjà vu. When El Pachuco visits Henry in solitary confinement, he gives him a vision of the family and past reality that he has lost, telling him— à la Calderón—that he is "just a dream."[16] He shows Henry's family (and his lawyer) seated in an otherwise empty theatre auditorium. Then he snaps his fingers and they disappear. Henry suddenly sees who the Pachuco really is, as smoking mirror: "You're the one that got me here. . . . You're me. My worst enemy. And my best friend. Myself. So get lost." *Zoot Suit* may give Chicanos a glimpse of their lost religious and ethnic heritage, but it also unveils the Pachuco's machismo as a tragic illusion, with the potential for fatal self-destruction as well as rebellious, creative power.

El Pachuco responds to Henry's rejection, in the play and film, with a Brechtian gest: "Don't take the pinche play so seriously" (78). But the next scene brings El Pachuco's mythical role in the drama to a serious sacrificial climax, as the historical zoot-suit riots arrive onstage. Here again in the movie version Valdez shows the action taking place in a theatre to stress how the performance of violence implicates the desires of others who watch, onscreen and off. During a debate with the allegorical figure of the Press about its misrepresentation of the zoot-suit identity,[17] El Pachuco chases the Press through the theatre seats and watching audience. After he and Henry suddenly appear in the seats with the audience, on the other side of the Press, El Pachuco is chased by the rioting servicemen—to the merry beat of Glen Miller's "American Patrol." The soldiers chase him up the aisle and catch him in the lobby, standing on top of the refreshment bar. He waves his switchblade at them but then, with a look at Henry, lets it drop. The soldiers pull him down, carry him back to the stage floor, and strip him. His then reappears on the stage floor. When Henry reaches down to touch El Pachuco's naked, shivering body, it becomes that of his younger brother, Rudy, who says that he was wearing Henry's zoot suit when "they stripped me." Valdez thus intersects the historical riots of servicemen attacking anyone dressed in a zoot suit, sparked by a racist press and wartime xenophobia, with the specific drama of Henry's imprisonment, the judicial stereotyping, yet stripping, of his zoot-suit identity, and the separation from his family, as Rudy also asks: "Why didn't you take me with you?" However, this loss of family and *pachuco* identity catalyzes a resurrection of indigenous ancestry: the stripped body becomes El Pachuco again and he stands, wearing only a loincloth, as "an Aztec conch blows" (81). He then "exits backward with powerful calm into the shadows" (in the play's stage directions and in the film).

AUDIENCE EFFECTS OF THE PERVERSE SUPEREGO

El Pachuco reappears in a subsequent scene (wearing a white zoot suit in the film) to question the historical, happy ending of Henry's successful legal appeal and his release from prison. "But life ain't that way, Hank. / The barrio's still out there, waiting and wanting" (88). This eccentric Brechtian gesture, connecting the historical drama and its mythical power to the complications of the present social reality, continues at the postmodern conclusion of *Zoot Suit*.[18] After the Press announces the tragic end of the historical Henry (who "went back to prison . . . [and] died of the trauma of his life"), El Pachuco and other characters offer the audience various alternative identities and different endings for the fictional Henry and his life story (94). This disclosure, with a doubly tragicomic, historical, yet fictional, finish to the drama, may serve to inspire further critical thoughts in the audience—in the antiritual way that Brecht desired. That is, how can tragic fate be changed, in real life, through future political action? But it also involves the spectators, whether they identify themselves as the white majority, as Chicano/Chicana, or another minority,[19] in the ritual worship of a transcendent *pachuco* hero, who transforms his role and costume as "classic social victim" (51) through the traces of Aztec god-actor sacrifice. Each spectator thus experiences a varying degree of ritual involvement or Brechtian distance, which reflects his or her viewpoint as well as cultural identity—and provides a different sense of catharsis.

Can Valdez and his implied audiences really have it both ways? Can El Pachuco effect both a Brechtian critical conscience in the audience (questioning the performance of violence) and an inverse Artaudian morality of participatory cruelty? Valdez has insisted that El Pachuco is not simply a perverse alter ego, but also Henry's alternative superego, "both the devil and the angel" at his shoulders (Orona-Cordova 100). Yet, if Valdez presents a native Aztec superego to counter the flawed father figures and racist judicial system in Henry's drama, then Pachuco as Tezcatlipoca bears some heavy sacrificial baggage along with his legal briefs. Unlike Valdez's invocation of the more "positive" and "kinder" Aztec god, Quetzelcoatl, through the character of

Ritchie Valens in the subsequent film *La Bamba* (1987),[20] El Pachuco as a reincarnation of Tezcatlipoca reveals the fetish of the switchblade (linked to more recent gang weapons of choice) at the heart of Chicano machismo.[21] With either of these Aztec gods as alter-native superego, returning after the 500-year repression of the Conquest, there is a deceptive nostalgia—a mournful idealization of lost ethnic figures and rites, which masks the sacrificial impulse of today's multicultural superego.

Although there are "no more pyramids" today, inner-city *pachucos* continue to sacrifice one another through their machismo and gang rituals, as if to prove that Tezcatlipoca along with "El Pachuco . . . The man . . . the myth . . . still lives" (94). This final line of *Zoot Suit* refocuses the various potential endings for Henry's drama to show the lure of a lost myth reborn. Yet that ideal also runs the risk of fitting Chicanos, as *pachucos*, into a sacrificial rite in service of the gringo Father's Law—obeying the Other's desire through defiant violence. Rather than recovering a lost father-figure or superego, Valdez's multiethnic mix of stage and screen viewpoints demonstrates the dialectic between dominant and lost fathers as a perpetually shifting sacrificial demand. *Zoot Suit* provides Brechtian mirrors and Aztec ghosts, at various historical distances, to show the prismatic sublimation of identity today by Chicanos and many other Americans, as actors and spectators in ordinary life—refashioning their identities and roles through skin color, class heritage, generation gaps, and the double-bind of desire for both assimilation and difference.

Using Žižek's terms, El Pachuco might be viewed as the "non-sublated" part of Henry's Mexican-American sense of a father, arising from the lack in both Enrique and George (*For They* 134). Yet, in his zoot-suit sacrifice, El Pachuco also seems lacking, as he perversely induces, then submits to the Press and pressing rioters. In that sense he is "the obscene, cruel and oddly impotent agency of the superego." But when resurrected in his Aztec loincloth, the Pachuco as Tezcatlipoca becomes "the symbolic father [who] is a symptom," more powerful dead than alive, like the victim of primordial patricide in Freud's *Totem and Taboo* (Žižek, *For They* 134–135). However, the return of this repressed Aztec father/god, "the obscene and traumatic Father-Enjoyment," is a retrospective projection: "its original status is that of a leftover produced by the failure of the operation of sublation [*Aufhebung*] which establishes the rule of the Name-of-the-Father; its allegedly original status (primordial father) results from an illusion of perspective by means of which we perceive the remainder as the point of origins" (135). To his credit, Valdez shows the stripped Pachuco wearing a Christian cross at his neck—as he had throughout the film—along with the Aztec (or Christ-like) loincloth, thus recognizing a sticky mixture of superegos. The Aztec "Father-Enjoyment," with his alter-native sacrificial rule, emerges through a "structural insufficiency" in the Christian, Euro-American, legal order and symbolic network. He does not overturn it, nor return as purely prior to it.

How might such a perverse superego, as lost sacrificial god, affect various spectators? El Pachuco could be viewed as a symbolic father (in his Brechtian narration and editing of the play/film), as an imaginary father (in his zoot-suit style of authority), and as the Real father (in his obscene role as sacrificial victim). He also becomes the symbolic father as symptom (*sinthome*) in his Aztec resurrection.[22] Those in the audience who identify with El Pachuco as Hispanics, especially as Chicanos, might extend the questioning of tragic, ethnic sacrifices in judicial prejudices, race riots, and gang war melodramas, from Los Angeles in the 1940s to elsewhere today—through the Brechtian freezes and comments. Or they might idolize the zoot-suiter's criminal machismo. Or they might commune with his martyrdom and resurrection— as chased, beaten, and defrocked, native yet alien American, thus crossing a fundamental fantasy of nostalgic power to reconstruct that symptom with various new possibilities as stated for Henry at the end of the tragicomedy. "Henry Reyna went back to prison in 1947 for robbery and assault with a deadly weapon. While incarcerated, he killed another inmate and he wasn't released until 1955, when he got into hard drugs" (94). Or he "went to Korea in 1950 . . . [and] was killed at Inchon in 1952, being posthumously awarded the Congressional Medal of Honor." Or he "married Della in 1948 and they have five kids, three of them now going to the University, speaking calo and calling themselves Chicanos."

White spectators, or those of other ethnicities, could also identify with any of these *pachuco* positions and possible endings through other, personal associations. Or they could identify with the sympathetic white characters, George and Alice (and Lt. Edwards in the play)—or even with the villainous Press, Prosecutor, Judge, and servicemen. One member of Henry's gang is also white. These various potential identifications with major and minor characters may complicate the overall cathartic effect, especially with a mixed-race (and -gender) audience. There is still a danger of overly Artaudian pathos or overly Brechtian criticism, of an abject return to self-sacrifice or a demonizing critique of the dominant society and its authorities—with too much fatalism either way. But *Zoot Suit*'s many plot twists and discoveries encourage multiple associations, moving between melodramatic violence and tragicomic clarifications, for different types of spectators.

The perversely moral Pachuco, as resurrected Aztec god, desiring yet transcending sacrificial violence, has received mixed reviews from academics. Various scholars—white, Chicano, and Chicana—while applauding *Zoot Suit*'s postmodern ending, have criticized Valdez as modernist, patriarchal, and essentialist in his macho idealization of El Pachuco.[23] Although the film version enhances the roles of Della (Henry's Chicana girlfriend) and Alice (Henry's white savior and love interest), the roles of his mother, his sister, and the *pachucas* remain slight.[24] *Zoot Suit* onscreen continues to be a male-centered, father-son-brother story. However, through that limited focus, Valdez brings together diverse historical, mythical, and cultural elements, challenging audiences in multiple directions. In contrast to his earlier, agit-prop plays for farmworkers, Valdez may well have been seeking a larger, mainstream audience with this stage play and film. But he also raises ethical, political, and aesthetic questions about the desire for violence—in *la Raza* and in other audiences—with his unique mixing of theatre, cinema, and ritual sacrifice in *Zoot Suit*.

Mainstream, white directors have also drawn from ethnic wells in presenting violence onscreen. The next chapter will look at various violent films by Martin Scorsese and Francis Ford Coppola, who used their Italian-American and Roman Catholic heritage to create postmodern rites of sacrifice for the mass audience. Scorsese and Coppola made their characters, their actors, and themselves into stars and martyrs through the sacrifices demanded in making their films. Their work illustrates both the lure of melodrama in identifying and punishing certain scapegoats, as simply evil villains, and the potential of blockbuster movies, not just art films, to offer tragic, Artaudian and Brechtian edges for a complex catharsis of the latent paranoia and bloodlust in cinema spectators and their particular, ethnic communities.

FIVE

Martyrs and Scapegoats in the Films of Scorsese and Coppola

AFTER THE TERRORIST ACTS of 9/11/01 and the subsequent escalation of suicide bombings in the Middle East, including those by Iraqi assassins at American military checkpoints, our mass media are paying more attention to terrorists who sacrifice their own lives and the lives of others to send a political message. (The Arab news media have celebrated the bloodshed of terrorists, soldiers, and civilians even more explicitly.) Such martyrs are heroes to their subaltern communities, yet villains to the dominant governments and their threatened citizens. People on both sides view themselves as scapegoats to the evil of the Other. But only the most radical (or those radicalized by an invasion) take on the role of martyrs in a "holy war," as suicidal terrorists and insurgents.

The first two chapters of this book explored how animals and humans, in ancient Greece, Rome, and Aztec Mesoamerica, were persuaded to accept the divine role of martyrdom. But the spectacle of offering one's life and taking others' lives is greatly magnified in the postmodern. The Greeks offered animals to purify their Dionysian theatres. The Romans offered numerous animal hunts, human executions, and gladiator combats in their arenas. The Aztecs displayed multiple human sacrifices of god-actors. Yet only with our current mass media is human sacrifice—in the World Trade Center plane crashes, for example—displayed again and again as news onscreen. The sacrifices of terrorism and war are often performed for the sake of the TV audience: especially with the second plane crash, while news cameras were already focused on the Twin Towers, or with the "surgical strikes" of "smart bombs" that minimized "collateral damage" in Baghdad. Such acts shape the subsequent melodramatic figures and plots of film and TV fiction, and repeat the dramas already prefigured by Hollywood—as in the uncanny attacks on

125

New York and Washington in the film *Independence Day*, five years prior to 9/11/01. Life imitates art, which imitates the news and fantasy fears of real-life sacrifices. This mimetic perpetuation of violence is fueled by melodramatic scapegoats, until a more tragic offering suspends the reciprocal vengeance (as Girard theorized), raising the cathartic awareness of guilt on both sides, rather than continuing the blame game.

Apocalypse Now* and *Taxi Driver*, two of the most violent films in the 1970s, prefigured the current, millennial theatre of terrorism, with its loss of American innocence and perpetuation of superpower vengeance—through their ironic display of national and personal (im)morality during and after the Vietnam War. Inheriting the manifest destiny of Westerns, but troubled by postimperial alienation, the soldier assassin in *Apocalypse Now* and the Vietnam vet as domestic terrorist in *Taxi Driver* armed themselves onscreen and took aim at their scapegoat targets. In what ways did these films, and other violent works by the same auteurs,[1] not only express the guilt, rage, and fear of the nation's cultural unconscious in the 1970s, but also melodramatically encourage—or tragically clarify—the violent drive toward self-sacrifice and scapegoating in real life, then and now?

BODY AND BLOOD OFFERINGS

Between the gangster films *Mean Streets* (1973) and *GoodFellas* (1990), which depicted some of his own Sicilian-American upbringing in New York, Martin Scorsese made several other violent films based on characters cast a bit farther from home. None of the anti-heroes of *Taxi Driver* (1976), *Raging Bull* (1980), and *The Last Temptation of Christ* (1988) are Mafia wise guys. Yet, the protagonists in these films, while offering their bodies in heroic protest against social corruption, also succumb to violent temptations—reflecting the lure of blood for film audiences, like the role of that liquid prop in Greek, Roman, and Aztec sacrifices. Travis Bickle in *Taxi Driver*, disgusted at the disorganized crime of New York City streets, becomes a vigilante hit man under his own command. Jake La Motta in *Raging Bull* resists the mob influence in his sport, trying to "do it on his own." But eventually he throws a fight as ordered by the mob kingpin in order to gain a later shot at the title. Jesus in *Last Temptation* rebels against God's love and Roman oppression, then becomes tempted to accept the ordinary violence of human life, before returning to the cross as his divine destiny. In these films, there is no Pachuco as alter ego egging on defiance against a racist society, while providing an alternative gangster ideal tied to Aztec sacrifice, as in Valdez's *Zoot Suit*. Yet, Scorsese's anti-heroes display a will to sacrifice in distinctive ways that reflect both ancient and modern, ritual and screen, melodramatic and tragic martyrdom, for a mainstream American audience—through the director's specific ethnic and religious background.

In *Mean Streets*, based on characters and incidents from Scorsese's youth in Little Italy, Charlie (Harvey Keitel) tries to live a saintlike life, despite the temptations of organized crime and the reckless disruptions of his close friend, Johnny Boy (Robert De Niro). Charlie's relationship with his girl-friend, Teresa, also becomes "a formula for self-sacrifice" because she, as epileptic, is a neighborhood outcast, like Johnny Boy, her wild cousin (L. S. Friedman 34). The film ends with the three of them driving away from the neighborhood, trying to escape from Johnny's dangerous defiance and direct insults against his loan shark, which Charlie had tried earlier to prevent. While attempting to save Johnny, with Teresa joining their escape, Charlie finds the punishment for his own guilty conscience "in the streets," as his voice-over had prophesied at the film's beginning. In the final car chase, the loan shark nears the fleeing trio. His hit man (played by Scorsese) shoots at their car, hitting Johnny in the neck and Charlie in the hand, then wound-ing Teresa in the head when their car crashes into a fire hydrant.

Throughout the film a melodramatic revenge code in the Mafia neigh-borhood perpetuates the violence of reciprocal ego battles among the young male characters. But Johnny's foolish debts and barroom fights, combined with Teresa's epileptic yearning to escape her Italian-American ghetto and Charlie's vain hope for religious transcendence while praying in church (and mortifying his flesh with a finger over a match flame), mark their final, unex-pected sacrifice as a tragic, triple martyrdom, even if each survives. The sources of their suffering are displayed not just as fate or circumstances of birth, but also as errors of judgment. Rather than just being melodramatic scapegoats, chased by purely evil villains, and triumphing in the end through violence, they become tragic anti-heroes. They bring upon themselves the revenge plot against them, without a hint of victory, only a glimpse of redemption through cathartic pain and learning.

Before he turned to filmmaking at NYU, Scorsese attended the seminary as a teenager, studying to become a priest: "wanting that vocation, selfishly, so that I'd be saved. . . . I wound up finding a vocation in making movies with the same kind of passion" ("In the Streets" 92).[2] Scorsese made a bloody B-movie for Roger Corman (*Boxcar Bertha*, 1972) prior to *Mean Streets*.[3] But it was not until *Taxi Driver* that the director's penchant for sacrificial bodies and sacramental blood became fully displayed in mainstream film. Scorsese, as cinematic priest, offers the spectacular violence of a romantic outcast, Travis Bickle, finding his vocation as suicidal assassin. The shocking bloodiness of the film's climax became even more famous when John Hinckley was found "not guilty" in his assassination attempt upon President Reagan because of mental illness, involving his identification with Travis Bickle, after seeing the film 15 times (Taubin 20). The screenplay by Paul Schrader was likewise influenced by the published diary of Arthur Bremer, who shot George Wal-lace and claimed he was inspired by Stanley Kubrick's *A Clockwork Orange*

(Clarke 88–92). Thus, to some degree, Hinckley's real-life violence imitated an artwork (*Taxi Driver*) imitating a real-life assassin (Bremer) imitating the reel's display of violence onscreen. Kubrick made his film unavailable for showing in Britain after other copycat acts of violence there. But Scorsese claimed, like Oliver Stone with *Natural Born Killers*, that his vocation as filmmaker—showing the bloody results of the psychopath's vocation—produced a warning for society, not a cause of individual violence. "It's not cautionary for psychopaths because you can't caution a psychopath, but cautionary for the society that produces them and casts them out and ignores them until it's too late" (Scorsese, quoted in Taubin 40).[4] Thus, Scorsese wanted "to create a violent catharsis" with *Taxi Driver*. But he was disappointed and "shocked by the way audiences took the violence," when they cheered the film's bloody massacre, indicating a melodramatic view of heroic triumph, rather than a tragic response of cautionary disgust (*Scorsese* 63).

Both *Mean Streets* and *Taxi Driver* show protagonists trying to save others (Charlie with Teresa and Johnny, Travis with the child prostitute Iris). In the former film, the vocation to save potential victims draws the melodramatic hero toward his own tragic martyrdom. A real sense of pain, loss, and mortality might thus be evoked within spectators, beyond the mimetic temptation of cheering for and against the battling gangster egos—at the edges of broken metal and stage blood in the film's final car chase, shooting, and crash scenes. However, in *Taxi Driver*, Scorsese draws the audience inside the mind of Travis Bickle as he seeks the right scapegoat to sacrifice, along with himself, in his vengeful rage for martyrdom.[5] Paul Schrader has admitted that he wrote the script at a point in his life when he was very much like Travis Bickle or Arthur Bremer, and could have committed their violence. The writing of the script was cathartic for Schrader: "if I didn't write it, I was going to end up doing something like my protagonist was imagining, and it had to come out. You know, art does work" (16).[6] Scorsese did not find a full catharsis for himself in making this film,[7] but he offered it as a potential clarification for society about ignoring its outcasts. John Hinckley made the film work another way, taking the image of the outcast so much to heart that he imitated Travis's violence—repeating the film's sacrifices in the Real offscreen.

Hinckley did not follow the script precisely. He shot a president and others in his entourage,[8] while Travis planned to shoot a presidential candidate, but instead used his guns on the men abusing a child prostitute, Iris (Jodie Foster). Hinckley thus condensed and revised the script through his own romantic fantasies and violent actions. He idolized the actress Jodie Foster as the film shows Travis idealizing the campaign worker Betsy (Cybill Shepherd). When Betsy rejects Travis, he turns his violent rage against her ideal candidate, Palantine, whom he had already met in his cab. But Travis fails to get a good shot at Palantine, despite wearing various guns. So he changes his martyr's mission toward saving Iris instead. Hinckley directly worshipped the actress playing Iris and, when rejected by her, simply fired one gun at the president. Rather than saving a child prostitute, Hinckley got revenge upon Foster (and his own father) for ignoring him—sacrificing himself, along with the president and his aides, to become significant in history. "By sacrificing my freedom and possibly my life," Hinckley wrote in a letter to Foster one hour before his mission, "I hope to change your mind about me . . . with this historical deed, to gain your respect and love" (quoted in Clarke 59). Like an Aztec *ixiptla* offering his heart and skin while emulating a mythic character, Hinckley became a monstrous idol for the mass media, through his imitation and adoration of prior screen gods. James Brady was forced to pay a greater price, however, for his moment on the pyramid with the president, taking a bullet in his skull—because of Hinckley's sacrifice to transcend insignificance and alienation.

Scorsese shows Travis Bickle in a similar state of sacrificial alienation, even before he begins to worship Betsy. At first, Travis fills his empty life and sleepless nights with his taxicab work, expressing in his voice-over and his written journal an extreme disgust for the city sights around him. The film encourages empathy for this existential nausea, especially since Travis is a Vietnam veteran, perhaps with posttraumatic stress syndrome.[9] The young movie star Robert De Niro charms his audience with the role, just as Travis initially charms Betsy with his passionate interest in her, until he makes the naïve error of taking her to a porn movie on their first date. And yet, while involving the audience in the subjective despair of this sacrificial star (or *ixiptla*), the film objectifies and demonizes its other scapegoats, especially the pimp and his colleagues, whom Travis eventually kills. As Amy Taubin puts it: "The problem with *Taxi Driver* . . . is not that it gives Travis his humanity, but that it deprives others of theirs" (49).[10] His first meeting with Iris, when she enters his cab to escape from her pimp, evokes sympathy for both of them through the taxi driver's missed opportunity to help her. If he had driven away when she first asked, before the villainous pimp pulled her out of the cab, he might have saved her from further abuse. The crumpled twenty that Sport (Harvey Keitel) throws into the cab in exchange for the girl makes Travis complicit in her captivity. This fuels audience compassion for him as he later uses the same twenty, while posing as a john, to talk with Iris and advocate a return to her parents, instead of taking advantage of her body.

Eventually, the film draws its audience into the main character's violent madness. "Travis's paranoia infects the narrative, imbuing seemingly insignificant objects, words and gestures with multiple meanings" (Taubin 60). The ritualistic scenes of Travis preparing for battle also evoke sympathy for this gladiatorial hero, ready to die in his showdown with Palantine or Sport—like the melodramatic gunslinger going against the greater powers of evil and savagery in a Western.[11] Travis is shown doing push-ups and pull-ups, steeling his fist over an open flame, buying a suitcase of guns in various

FIGURE 5.1. Travis (Robert De Niro) tries to save the young prostitute Iris (Jodie Foster) by meeting with her at a diner and giving her money to return home to her parents. Eventually, however, he must find a more violent way to save her—inspiring Hinckley's idolization of Foster and self-sacrifice to prove his love for her as presidential assassin. *Taxi Driver*, Columbia Pictures, 1976.

sizes, then arranging them on his body with holsters and a mechanical device that slings a pistol into his hand, out of his sleeve. He also takes target practice with his gun, heats boot polish with a flame, and burns the dead flowers that Betsy rejected.[12]

But De Niro's improv in the mirror became the most emblematic of all these gestures, especially regarding the male gaze of the audience. "You talkin' to me?" exemplified the resurgence of a phallic (white) ego in America in the 1970s—after the castrating losses of the Vietnam War, of the feminist revolution, and of the civil rights movement (Taubin 21). Travis's playful ego-building with guns in a mirror eventually turns into a suicidal bloodbath to save Iris—after which he tries and fails to shoot himself in the head, then jokingly gestures at doing so with a bloody finger as the police arrive. And yet, the film may encourage identification with this suicidal martyrdom, especially for already paranoid spectators—despite the tragicomic survival of Travis and the ironic pan of his wall, which shows news clippings about the assassin's heroism and an appreciation letter from Iris's parents. The voice-over of her father reading the letter only begins to suggest, with its controlled tone, why she may have run away from home to escape others to whom Travis has now returned her. In the end, however, the gunslinger did save the girl. The gladiator was ready to die, yet lived to fight another day. The bloodletting scene was magnificent (through special effects) as in the Aztec warrior's skin striping and the god-actor's heart sacrifice. Thus, the film bears a double-edged potential: not only a tragicomic warning to society, but also a melodramatic call to arms, involving self and other sacrifices, as in the case of John W. Hinckley, Jr.[13]

Travis is celebrated for his violence against a street pimp and other criminals, as the newspaper clippings on his wall show. But the audience knows what his original target was. If he had hit the politician, that would have made him a negative celebrity, a Frankenstein monster—like Hinckley became in imitating him. (The film and Hinckley's abnormal brain were the cause of his monstrous violence, according to the court.) But instead Travis becomes a hero to the parents of Iris, to his fellow cabbies, and even to Betsy, whom he picks up in his taxi in the film's final scene. He has completely recovered from his wounds, telling Betsy there is only "a stiffness" now. She respects him, as Hinckley wanted Foster to do, although Travis does not propose another meeting with her (or take money for her fare) when he reaches her destination. The pain of Travis's victims is not shown, nor of their friends and relatives, nor of himself after his sacrifice. Scorsese makes the ironic point that society values the gunslinger's vigilante justice, while showing what a bloody mess it really was, and how easily it could have been the slaying of a politician instead. And yet, such ironies were lost on those, like Hinckley, who identified with Travis as a melodramatic hero purging society. The imaginary inflation of his ego with guns in the mirror and with the bloody showdown, plus his symbolic victory over purely evil villains, served to mask, more than reveal, the Real losses and continued abjection at the edges of the screen.

Both Scorsese and Schrader were raised, in the Catholic and Calvinist traditions, to believe in purification by Christ's blood.[14] Scorsese views the overhead tracking shots in *Taxi Driver* as suggesting the objects on a Catholic altar (Taubin 36, 72). Like the priest at mass, Scorsese offers the actors' bodies and the stage blood, especially in the final massacre, as incarnating a divine sacrifice onscreen.[15] He multiplies this transcendent food for millions of eyes through his medium, like Jesus' miracle of multiplying the loaves and fishes. The priest at the Catholic mass who consecrates the bread and wine says, in the role of Christ: "This is my body. This is my blood." However, he also prays, as leader of the congregation: "Let it not bring us condemnation, but health in mind and body." The carnage of bodies and fountains of blood in the climax of *Taxi Driver* could bring a tragic clarification of the horrible results of Travis's abjection, paranoia, disgust, and rage—bringing some degree of cathartic health to the spectator's mind and body (as the writing of the script helped Schrader). But depending on how the film is watched, it could offer the temptation to share in Travis's solution: to partake in the sacrificial edification of his body and blood onscreen by incarnating his violence in real life, purging the evil from oneself by projecting it on others, then punishing them as villains, while saving or avenging innocent victims.[16]

The sacramental violence of Scorsese's *Taxi Driver* sublimates the persistent drive of sacrifice—like the Dionysian animal or human actor as scapegoat, like the Roman gladiator in fatal competition, and like the Aztec *ixiptla*—but with fictional bodies and blood onscreen. However, such sublimation, especially as it spreads the spectacle of martyrdom to millions and can be viewed many times over (as in Hinckley's case), has an even greater potential today to perpetuate mimetic violence through melodramatic scapegoating, rather than raising tragic awareness of the real results of vigilante justice and vengeful violence. There is some sympathy evoked for Sport in Scorsese's film—in a scene added to Schrader's script "to show that Iris was not being held against her will" (Taubin 66). The pimp dances with Iris against his chest, showing tenderness with her, which later makes Travis's bloody battle to save her even more ironic. And yet, the scene is not enough to alleviate all suspicion that Iris might have lied when she told Travis that Sport never beat her. The pimp's dance with the child prostitute illustrates his subtle control of her, as well as his affection for her as valuable property, as "my woman." Later, Sport teases and kicks Travis, then is shot in the stomach at point blank range. But the pimp, as violent victim of violence, is not a sympathetic subject in the end. Despite the tender dance with Iris, he becomes an evil object, ripe for Travis's righteous rage.[17]

Likewise, Travis's point of view, given throughout the movie from within his cab, points to many black faces as melodramatic scapegoats. This racism culminates in the first shooting of the film, when Travis kills a black robber in a convenience store and the store's owner beats the body of the prone thief with a metal bar after Travis leaves the store. In Schrader's original script, Sport was also black. But the screenwriter and director decided they might produce a race riot and "fights in the theatres" if they cast the pimp that way (Schrader, quoted in Taubin 18).[18] The director himself played the role of a racist, misogynist passenger in Travis's cab, who tells the driver to watch a building near them, as the shadows behind a curtained window show his wife making love to a black man. The passenger then contributes to the driver's vengeful, virulent rage: "Did you ever see what a forty-four magnum can do to a woman's pussy?" Later, Travis buys that type of gun, along with others, for his eventual killing spree. The influence of the back-seat driver in Travis's cab[19]—along with the "voluptuous" massacre he later commits onscreen (Taubin 11)—may also direct some spectators, already on the edge of real violence, to focus their rage against persons of a certain gender or race, as well as politicians. The domestic terrorism in *Taxi Driver* might counteract its warning to society, especially in its encouragement to identify with a martyr's melodramatic, objectifying vengeance.[20] As much as the film helps us to understand the sources of Travis's violence, it also evokes a scapegoating of others as objects deserving a bloody sacrifice in the Real, through the desire and paranoia of the Other onscreen.

BETWEEN ANIMAL AND DIVINE

There is no denying the power of bloody bodies splattered across the screen. The climax of *Taxi Driver* not only shows Travis being shot in the neck and shoulder, while killing Sport, Iris's john, and her timekeeper. Sport is shot in the stomach and the john in the face and chest. The timekeeper's fingers are shot off, his other hand stabbed through with a knife, and then Travis puts a bullet through his head at point blank range, splattering blood and brains on the wall behind him, as Iris screams: "Don't kill him." Scorsese was forced to "desaturate" the color of the massacre, reducing the blood's redness in the final print to gain an "R" rating instead of an "X" (Grist 130). After the film's violence inspired Hinckley's in 1981, Scorsese considered giving up filmmaking, but then made *The King of Comedy* in 1982 (Taubin 74). Prior to that, Scorsese had made another extremely violent film, *Raging Bull* (1980). However, he shot that film in black and white, with brief displays of Jake La Motta's brutality in various fights in the ring and at home throughout the movie, rather than a final eruption of bloody vengeance as in Travis's showdown. The continuum of Jake's violence against others and himself—as victorious, competitive entertainment and as tragic, destructive passion—makes

FIGURE 5.2. Jake La Motta (Robert De Niro) with his wounded, bloody face and sacrificial body in the ring. *Raging Bull*, United Artists, 1980.

him a less enviable martyr than Travis. But he is thus even more illuminating as a scapegoat, exposing the guilty heroics and bloodlust of both boxing and cinema, in their monstrous idols and fans.

Raging Bull is not a typical boxing movie. While using documentary titles and dates, Scorsese devotes only a few minutes of screen time to the main La Motta fights, focusing on the brutal sacrifice of bodies in the ring, through jarring angles and brief close-ups. The director gives a considerable display of dark blood in the black and white fight scenes, spurting in slow motion from Jake's face or his opponents', and pouring from the sponge onto his body, as he is tended in his corner. But Scorsese offers a "stylized vision of this punishment" of Jake, especially in his final losing bout to Sugar Ray Robinson, which the director calls a "religious ritual" (Martin 96–97). "I had to use a lot of blood because we were shooting in black-and-white, but that's just secondary. The real violence is inside. . . . This vision became a mental projection." The film's stylized blood rites of the Bronx Bull in the ring, juxtaposed with his violence at home and in jail, point to the tragic edges of the Real within the character and throughout his life, not just to the melodramatic heroism of a middleweight champion.[21] The mental projections of the film viewers, like the director's, are focused upon a martyr's body and blood for the sake of cathartic awareness, not merely punch-drunk identification with the star. This is the film's tragicomic focus for its spectators, even when the washed-up Jake, as former champ and celebrity, tries to get his nightclub audience to sing joyfully with him: "That's entertainment."

Scorsese's own struggle with his filmmaking vocation helped him identify with the tragic side of this protagonist. Raging Bull begins and ends with a 50-pound overweight De Niro as an older La Motta, a has-been from the ring, practicing his stand-up comedy routine in a dressing room mirror and then struggling in vain to entertain his nightclub audiences. Scorsese himself had fallen from award-winning success with Mean Streets and Taxi Driver to failure with New York, New York. He was hospitalized in 1978, "hovering between life and death" (Scorsese, Martin 88).[22] After surviving this "suicide period," he decided to make Raging Bull, because the desire "to kill yourself over work, to dream of a tragic death," helped him to understand something of the real-life Jake La Motta, who had "known" that before him—with their common Catholic background, guilt feelings, and "hope for redemption" (88–89).[23] The Bronx Bull is the least articulate of all of Scorsese's protagonists, even less verbal than the same actor as Branagh's Monster. But the offering of De Niro's body, with bloody wounds and weight gain, provides a sacrifice of the human animal onscreen, in the modern context of the boxing ring and boxer's life, that speaks volumes about the drive toward martyrdom today, in the secular rites of god-actors in sports and the mass media.[24]

Raging Bull shows a modern gladiator fighting not to the death, but to the point of knocking his opponents unconscious onstage. Yet, it also shows the unconscious cycles of spousal abuse and self-destruction repeating in La Motta's life. The movie's violence points to an inherent tragic guilt, a profound alienation and lack of being, beyond any specific actions or social demands. As Scorsese explained in 1981: "If you had inherited this guilt from birth, what chance would you have had to escape? If in the deepest part of yourself, you're convinced that you're not worthy—as I have been, and as I might be again sometime—what can you do? You're condemned, no?" (*Martin* 89). This sense of original sin within oneself, as the lack of being "worthy," marks a crucial distinction between the melodramatic sacrifice of Travis Bickle, offering his life to purge the evils of society, and Jake's offering of himself to be punished, even while beating others in the ring. Scorsese presents his Bronx Bull, not as a melodramatic hero triumphing against all odds, but as a tragic animal, winning his fights, or narrowly losing, through his willingness to take extreme punishment with his "concrete head." Jake even takes pride in his title loss, letting Sugar Ray beat repeatedly on his face in the final round, but not falling down, as Robinson had fallen in their earlier match. After his face is brutalized onscreen and his blood showers the ring's spectators, Jake proudly proclaims: "You never got me down, Ray." The hubris of this masochism also expresses to the film audience the foolish nobility of La Motta's blood sacrifices, which are admirable, yet not enviable.[25]

Unlike Travis Bickle, Jake La Motta has already found his vocation at the start of the film, his mission of self (and other) sacrifice. The title credits show him shadowboxing in the ring, an apt image for the character's endless punishing of others, and of himself, for the entertainment of his boxing and cinema audiences. Jake's masochism in the ring also involves a sadism against his opponents, plus the fetishizing of his body and its bloody exhibitionism, for the boxing and film voyeurs. But all of these perverse traits point to a hollowness in the body image—an unworthy alienation or lack of being—shared by the movie spectators. Jake makes himself an object of admiration and punishment (like the actor playing him) to gain a celebrity identity in the eyes of others. Yet he appears as merely a shadow of himself onscreen, not only when he dances alone in the ring or performs his pathetic nightclub act, but also while exchanging punches with another fighter.

Jake's shadow play is emphasized by the structure of the film (with the screenplay by Paul Schrader and Mardik Martin, adapted from La Motta's memoir). From the opening title sequence of shadowboxing, to the frame-tale of his nightclub act, the film presents the struggling and triumphant La Motta as merely a memory, an illusion of transient success, with each bout dated by a supertitle and other fights outside the ring destroying his personal relationships. Jake fights with his first wife, overturning the dinner table, then finds a younger one (the 15-year-old Vickie) to idealize, marry, and fight with instead. He also fights with Joey (Joe Pesci), his manager and little brother, demanding to be hit by him, bare-fisted in the face, to demonstrate how he should be a heavyweight contender. He then argues with Joey (and punches him furiously in a practice session in the ring) about whether to submit to the mob boss, Tommy Como, or fight to the top on his own. Later, Jake punches his wife in the face and attacks his brother in a jealous rage, alienating both of them because he thinks they had an affair together.

All of these battles, within the ring and outside it, show Jake's struggle for significance, despite his success as a boxer. After he loses the title to Robinson, La Motta opens his own club, devoting his nights to entertaining his remaining fans. But his wife divorces him and he runs afoul of the law by giving drinks to underage girls. Jake pawns the jewels from his championship belt to get bribery money and ends up in a jail cell, pounding the stone wall and screaming in the darkness: "I'm not an animal." Yet, he is an animal in this sacrifice onscreen:[26] showing the human animal's loss of an instinctual place in nature, with the corresponding dependence on culture and the Other's view to give each individual an illusory identity.

The hollowness of Jake's identity as boxing gladiator, and his ephemeral triumph as champ, reveals the perverse violence of the ring and of his life as being akin to cinema itself, with its perverse pleasures for the spectator. The body and blood of this god-actor fetish (in the masochistic exhibitionism of both La Motta and De Niro) temporarily fills the hollowness of egos watching. They identify with him onscreen, while he finds an identity in that shadow role for them. But Jake's tragic flaws—unworthiness, guilt, jealousy, and rage against loved ones—also show the destructive dangers in sports and other media lures of greatness: for players, friends, and fans. In this way, Raging Bull may become cathartic for some spectators, crossing their own fundamental fantasies, while watching its fattened boxing star and frame-tale plot. The film displays a tragic sacrifice against the usual melodrama of sports and movie heroes. It thus offers an ethics of the Real, regarding our common submission to mass media rites.[27]

La Motta's willingness to be punished in the ring may be due to his guilt for abusing his wives, and his disgrace in obviously throwing the Billy Fox fight as the Mafia demanded (L. S. Friedman 116). The film also reveals the guilt-ridden, homoerotic component in Jake's intimacy with, and jealousy of, his opponents: not just in the hugs and hits of each bout, but especially in Jake's joking with his brother's gangster friends about his upcoming fight with the young Tony Janiro, saying he does not know whether to "fight 'im or fuck 'im." Here, as in Mean Streets, Scorsese shows a male bonding rite of violence. Yet, Jake's beating of Janiro's face also involves his jealousy about Vickie's comment, prior to the fight, that Janiro is "good looking." Like Travis more than Charlie, Jake seeks redemption in beautiful women, rather than in male camaraderie. After a fight he asks Vickie to kiss the wounds on his face. She does so and then continues down his torso and below the belt. But Jake cuts off the erotic foreplay and pours ice water into his shorts, to save his phallic energy for the ring. At the end of his boxing career, Jake allows under-aged girls to drink liquor when they give him a passionate kiss and thus he loses his nightclub. While he seeks redemption through physical contact with female beauty, and in the ring's homoerotic heroics, Jake fails to find it, except through further pain and punishment. He beats on others to rise above them and beyond his own guilty unworthiness. Yet he needs the kiss of a beautiful woman, or the punch of a man and the roar of the crowd, to become their martyr.

Like the Greek animal nodding assent, or the Roman gladiator taking an oath to fight till death in the arena, or the Aztec warrior walking up the pyramid steps to his heart sacrifice, the Bronx Bull finds his vocation in offering his body to the Other. But Scorsese's film also offers his audience the challenge of seeing Jake's tragic sacrifice as fated or chosen, as Artaudian cruelty of nature or Brechtian alienation by society. The symptomatic violence of Jake's erotic death drive repeats, inside and outside the ring, until he finds language to recite in his nightclub act, replacing the punches, and then finds his long-estranged brother, Joey, and gives him a kiss. After losing his nightclub and punching the wall in jail, Jake continues his verbal act to smaller audiences in seedy strip-joints, reciting Brando's lines in *On the Waterfront*. The fattened De Niro plays La Motta as a bad actor, mimicking Brando as a failed boxer. Yet he does entertain some spectators in his remaining audience, getting them to sing with him. Jake continues to be an Artaudian god-actor, exemplifying nature's cruelty by signaling through the flames, when he offers his wounds to Vickie's kisses, his blood to ringside spectators, and his fumbling recitations to a drunken audience. But Jake's tragic sacrifice is also presented in a Brechtian light, especially through the film's frame-tale memoir, showing the social pressures on him, as well as his inner drive: with his violent rise to the championship, his disgraceful compromise with the mob, his jealous beating of Vickie and Joey, his offering of his bloody body, yet concrete head, as a phallic totem to be beaten in the ring—and his gestic performance as a shadow of his former self in repeating a movie star's lines. It is only in the eyes of the Other that Jake becomes the Bronx Bull again. It is only with the ocular cannibalism of the film audience that his body and blood redeem onscreen, through Artaudian communion or Brechtian critique, depending upon the focus of each spectator's cathartic identification and awareness, as to one's own fate and choices.

LUCIFER WITHIN

Later in the 1980s, Scorsese made another sacrificial film that became famous, not for its violence, but for its perverse depiction of the ultimate martyr in Christianity (from the novel by Nikos Kazantzakis and screenplay by Paul Schrader and Jay Cocks). To the eyes and ears of many Christians, who

saw or merely heard about it, *The Last Temptation of Christ* (1988) was a sac-
rilege that they picketed at movie theatres across the United States. For others, it was an enlightening exploration of the human side of Jesus, sharing
fully in the lack of the Other. For both crowds it was a communal experience:
either by scapegoating the film and its director or by watching the screen
martyrdom of a god-actor.

Charlie and Travis discover their vocations; Jake already has his as a
fighter. But Scorsese's Jesus (Willem Dafoe) fights against the call itself,
unsure whether it is actually from God, the devil, or just his own existential
madness, both prophetic and alienating. Jake La Motta experiences his lack
of being as guilt and unworthiness. "I done a lot of bad things," he tells Joey
after an early loss to Robinson. "Maybe it's comin' back to me. Who knows?
I'm a jinx maybe." But Jesus' lack of being attacks him like a "claw" behind
his eyes. He writhes on the ground with the pain of his contact with the
Almighty. And yet, both characters, through their guilt, make the blind
see—as Scorsese indicates with his epigraph to *Raging Bull* (John 9:24–26),
connecting Jake La Motta as a "sinner" to Jesus Christ and the film's cathartic power to the miracle of a blind man's cure, at least for the director, if not
his audience.[28]

In Scorsese's *Last Temptation*, Jesus' cure of the blind man is one of several miracles shown, along with his changing of water into wine, expelling
demons, and raising Lazarus from the dead. However, before Jesus discovers
how to use his powers, he is plagued by his potential divinity and the schizoid
voices in his head. Scorsese depicts him (like Kazantzakis's novel) as a
betrayer of his own people, building crosses for the Romans and carrying the
crossbeam to the crucifixion site of someone referred to as "Lazarus" at the
start of the film. Judas (Harvey Keitel) criticizes Jesus for his carpentry and
slaps him in his workshop; other Jews throw stones at him as he carries the
crossbeam. Mary Magdalene (Barbara Hershey) spits at him. During the crucifixion, blood from Lazarus' feet squirts in Jesus' face as he helps the Roman
soldiers hold the other Jew's body for the nail to pierce it. But Jesus insists on
performing his abject role as crucifier—prefiguring, as the film audience
knows, his own ultimate sacrifice. This is not the Jesus of the gospels, as
Scorsese warns his film audience with an initial quote from Kazantzakis's
novel and an explicit statement onscreen that the character is based on a
work of fiction. And yet, Scorsese is working between fiction and conviction,
creating a very human Jesus, driven mad by the god within him.

In his overview of human sacrifice across many cultures, Nigel Davies
finds that "the victim, as a bridge between God and fallen man, must possess
the qualities of both, must be both pure and impure, . . . deliverer and wrong-
doer, . . . loved, but also in a sense hated" (275–276). Scorsese presents Jesus
as initially hated by all around him—especially Judas, the rebel fighter
against the Romans, who demands that Jesus stop building crosses and join

the resistance with him. Jesus becomes a scapegoat for Jewish hatred of the Roman oppressors when he carries the crossbeam for Lazarus' execution. Only his mother, Mary, tries to stop the other Jews from throwing stones at Jesus. That night, with Jesus' body writhing on the ground in torment from the voices inside his head, his voice-over calmly explains: "God loves me. I know He loves me. I want Him to stop. I can't take the pain. The voices and the pain. I want Him to hate me. I fight Him. I make crosses so He'll hate me. I want Him to find somebody else. I want to crucify every one of His messiahs." Jesus tells his mother he must leave her to discover whether the voices in his head are from God or the devil. Later, he says to a young monk that his god is fear and that Lucifer is inside him. Who is this confused Jesus, whom Michael Morris, a Dominican priest, has called "theologically wacko"[29]—yet Scorsese makes into his ultimate human sacrifice onscreen?

While *Raging Bull* displays its heroic martyr as a brutal masochist at the tragic edge of bestiality, *Last Temptation* presents Jesus as both animal and divine, as guilty of all human desires and unworthy of his role, yet still transcendent as god-actor. He is both pure and impure, telling the young monk in the desert that he wants to sin but cannot because he is a "coward." He is loved and hated by Mary Magdalene, whom he rejects twice in the film. The first time, after watching all day while she gave her body to other men, Jesus asks her forgiveness, but then refuses to touch her or stay the night with her, while she bitterly insists he has the same lusts as other men.[30] Later, after he saves her from being stoned to death (as a whore who works on the Sabbath), she wants to follow him along with his other disciples. Jesus will not allow her to be with him, yet he kneels and gently wipes her feet. His heroic act of saving Magdalene threatens to tip the film toward melodrama. But the conventional paradigm of saving the damsel (or femme fatale) in distress is undercut when Jesus later admits to Judas that he had wanted to "kill" Mary's attackers. And yet, when he opened his mouth, the word "love" came out instead.

Inspired in that moment, Jesus creates a tragicomic twist to the vengeful drive in Mary's persecutors and in his own desire to rescue her. Rather than seeing her as an evil object to be purged by stoning—or punishing the others instead, as melodramatic villains, by throwing stones back at them—Jesus evokes tragic sympathy and shared guilt, telling her attackers to throw stones only if they are without sin. That statement may be expected by film viewers who know their Bible. Yet, Jesus' later confession to Judas reveals the melodramatic temptation of this scene: to reverse and thus repeat the violence of the persecutors in punishing an evil object, by becoming the righteous hero who saves the threatened woman and destroys the villains (as in Travis Bickle's vigilante justice). This sheds a new light on the Biblical throwing of stones, although it is still the threat of God's punishment that Jesus uses to make the others drop theirs.

Jesus' initial temptation of masochistic despair as a cross maker turns toward desire for Magdalene's body, with a corresponding shift in the focus of his own guilt. But then his messianic vision changes the self-absorbed guilt into "pity for everything," even seeing the "face of God" in the shiny eye of an ant, as he tells Judas. Jesus preaches the answer of "love," sowing that seed (instead of the Word of God) in his sermon on the mount, right after saving Madgalene. But many of his listeners misunderstand and go off to fight for justice, as Judas wants. The few that remain as apostles are "weak" men, according to Judas, who debates with Jesus about whether to change the body and society first, or the soul. More Artaudian here than Brechtian, Jesus insists that the soul is the foundation, not the body or society. "If you don't change the spirit first, change what's inside, then you're only going to replace the Romans with somebody else and nothing ever changes. Even if you're victorious, you'll still be filled with the poison. You've got to break the chain of evil . . . with love." Here again Jesus challenges the melodramatic desires of the rebel Judas and of the movie viewer who wants to see the heroic underdog battle against the villainous oppressors. Jesus' tragic pity for all men, because he sees God in them, despite their evil or weakness, reveals a more complex sacrifice in his vocation. Thus, Scorsese's film shows a further cathartic hope with this scapegoat (pharmakos): to break the chain of reciprocal violence that most films promote, changing the poison into a remedy (pharmakon), from melodramatic revenge to another kind of passion onscreen—and inside the spectators.

Certain parts of Last Temptation seem somewhat silly. If the film is taken as a Biblical epic with historical realism, then Judas jumping up and down on the crossbeam in Jesus' carpentry shop, like a child in a tantrum, or Magdalene's voice in Jesus' hallucination of a cobra, telling him to look at her (its?) breasts, or the various New York and British accents of Jews and Romans, might make this movie not just offensive to some, but also farcical.[31] However, for many centuries in the Middle Ages, European towns presented passion plays showing the stages of Christ's journey to Golgotha, and longer epic cycles of his life and afterlife, along with many other Biblical events—all bearing anachronistic details that mixed the mythic past with the present time and apocalyptic future. Scorsese's film purposely mixes Biblical and fictional events, realistic settings and surreal visions, historical details in costumes and props, plus exotic scenery and extras (filmed in Morocco), with modern, Method actors and accents revealing more of character than period.[32] The film challenges its audience to see Jesus Christ as more fully human and thus divine, as existentially despairing and confused, questioning metaphysical providence and destiny, but finding his sacrificial fate through various temptations that reflect our own era, moving, with its mass-media passions, into a new millennium.[33]

Jesus' temptation toward violent melodrama—after the lures of despair, lust, and pity—is refocused in his meeting with John the Baptist (André

Gregory).³⁴ Despite Jesus' argument about love as the answer instead of violence, he now moves, after being baptized by John, back toward the political rage of his friend and nemesis, Judas. The Baptist likewise tells Jesus:
"Love is not enough. God demands anger." John encourages Jesus to test his
connection to God in the desert, yet warns him that he may also meet the
devil there. These plot twists and turns in Jesus' mission demonstrate his
tragic double-bind in the film. But they also reflect the philosophical dilem-
mas in various decades of our postmodern era. From his existential loss of
faith and focus, to his flower-child love as the universal answer, to his liber-
ation theology of violent revolution, Jesus' split subjectivity shows the conflicting responses of the twentieth century to the horrors created by post-
Enlightenment civilization.

   Jesus goes to the desert as the Baptist told him. He draws a circle in the
dirt and sits in it, telling God that he will not leave until he gets some
answers about his mission in life. His first vision is of a snake, along with the
voice of Mary Magdalene. Jesus had a similar hallucination when he went
into the desert the first time and talked with monks there. Now he is alone
and Magdalene's voice says she feels sorry for him. She (or the snake) claims
to be his "spirit" and invites him to care for women and have a family. She
calls his desire to save the world "arrogance" and tells him to save himself
instead—by loving a woman. But Jesus refuses to go with her and the snake
disappears. Then a lion visits him with the voice of Judas, saying he is his
"heart" and knows Jesus wants to conquer the world and have power. But
Jesus challenges the lion to enter the circle so he can rip out its tongue. The
lion disappears. Jesus then has a third vision: a column of fire appears and
speaks to him, reminding him of his cry to God as a little boy: "Make me a
god." The male voice of the flame invites Jesus to join him: "You are God.
The Baptist knew it; now it's time you admit it. You are His Son, the only Son
of God. Join me. Together we'll rule the living and the dead. You'll give life
and you'll take life. You'll sit in judgment. And I'll sit next to you. Imagine
how strong we'll be together." Jesus rejects this figure as "Satan." But a tree
appears at the edge of his circle. He takes the fruit from it and bites into it;
blood emerges from his mouth. The flame tells Jesus that they will meet again
and vanishes. Then Jesus finds an ax in the dirt and John the Baptist appears,
telling him to take "this message" to everyone. Jesus chops violently at the
trunk of the tree.³⁵

   These visions offer Jesus various solutions to his life's destiny and to his
mysterious attacks from God earlier in the film, which demanded he become
the Messiah, without showing him the way. Now Jesus must choose between
the temptations to love everyone and have a family, or to fight a revolution
and gain earthly power, or to rule with Satan. He seems to have chosen the
middle path when he returns to his apostles, after being restored to health by
Martha and Mary. He tells the men following him: "I'm inviting you to a

FIGURE 5.3. Jesus (Willem Dafoe), prior to his meeting with John the Baptist, holds an apple that he has just taken out of the robe over his chest, bit into, and opened with his hands. He then tosses a seed from it into the desert sand and a tree appears, already in bloom. This scene prefigures two others later in the film: (1) where Jesus takes an apple from a similar, suddenly appearing tree, during his desert temptations, and bites into it, with blood emerging from his mouth, and (2) where he takes his heart out of his chest and offers it to his apostles. *The Last Temptation of Christ*, Universal, 1988.

war." He reaches into his chest with his hand and takes out his own heart—a surreal moment which, according to Scorsese, "*could* be mass hallucination, mass hypnosis" (*Martin* 115). Then Jesus says, holding an ax in his hand instead of his heart: "God is inside us. The devil is outside us, in the world all around us. We'll pick up an ax and cut the devil's throat."

Combining the god-actor and the priest in the Aztec sacrifice, this Jesus removes his own heart onscreen—though offering it to his apostles, rather than the sun. Likewise, Scorsese, as cinematic priest, offers this scene to his bloodthirsty audience as the Other.[36] Indeed, there are many shocking images of blood in the film: squirting onto Jesus' face when he helps the Romans crucify Lazarus, pouring out of the fruit he bites from the hallucinated tree, dripping from his own heart, appearing when a goat is disemboweled at the wedding feast where Jesus performs his wine miracle, draining from the temple when he attacks the money changers there, dripping from his hands as his stigmata stops the revolution after he enters Jerusalem on a donkey, emerging from a lamb whose neck is slit at Passover, and pressed between Peter's lips and fingers after he tastes the wine that Jesus offers as his blood at the Last Supper—all prefiguring the blood lines on Jesus' face and body at his crucifixion. But the ocular cannibalism of the film audience at these various points involves shifting perspectives of cinematic communion. Jesus' offering of his heart relates not only to the Aztec *ixiptla,* but also to the Roman gladiators of his own historical period, with their vocation to die in the arena for the entertainment of others. Jesus leads his followers into battle against the Romans in Jerusalem, taking up the ax as Judas and John the Baptist wanted, and thus entertaining the melodramatic desires of action movie spectators. However, when he gets to the point of starting the fight, he stops and opens his hands, revealing the stigmata. Then he asks Judas to betray him in the garden, certain at last of God's plan that he be crucified and rise again in three days. Here, in effect, he returns to the heart offering, instead of the ax. And that night, at the Last Supper, he shares with his followers (including Mary Magdalene, Martha and Mary, and his mother) the bread as his body and the wine turned into blood. Through his final temptation on the cross, Scorsese's Jesus becomes a tragic scapegoat as Lamb of God: not a melodramatic gladiator fighting Romans to the death, but a god-actor walking up the steps of his pyramid to be sacrificed—to let immortal hopes arise again in believers' eyes.

The competing vocations of this Jesus may seem sacrilegious to many Christians. Yet his visions reveal a need for God, as both lost and revived, throughout history and in human evolution. Various cultures and religions, from ancient to modern, have substituted social orders and divine destinies for the loss of animal instincts in human beings, leading to the current, hollow illusions of self and Other in postmodern subjectivity and metaphysics. Scorsese's Jesus presents a postmodern lack of being in both self and Other, through his guilt-ridden confusion about, masochistic submission to, and psychotic hallucinations of God the Father. In his movement from madness to love, to war, to self-sacrifice, this Jesus might also display the yearning for cathartic consciousness within nature itself. Through chance and necessity, nature evolved a big-brained primate that has godlike powers of language and technology, with vast creativity and destructiveness, by virtue of its emptiness within and beyond nature. If the visions of gods in prior human cultures are manifestations of this common lack of being, then Jesus' hallucinations in Scorsese's film, and the bloody scenes shared with the audience, may show a drive toward self-awareness within all of nature as well as culture, from the eye of the ant or snake or lion to postmodern man's existential despair and diverse hopes for immortal transcendence.

Theatre, film, and other mass media today—along with prior artistic, religious, and scientific technologies—are extensions of the godlike drive within nature to become aware of one's earthly habitat as mortal limit, and yet to transcend it. Human beings have evolved as the species that bears the greatest burden of this divine drive, remaking their habitat and dreaming of worlds beyond nature and death. But humans have also become suicidal and tremendously destructive to their own species and the world around them, due to the freedoms of culture, language, art, and science—with the consequent lack of a definite destiny or meaning to life. Scorsese's depiction onscreen of Kazantzakis's fully human Christ shows this tragic flaw in the evolution of our own species and its divine aspirations. Yet the film also indulges in the temptation of theatre and ritual (as noted in earlier chapters here) to create a melodramatic, Manichean cosmos of good and evil forces in apocalyptic warfare, demanding perpetual sacrifices. Jesus' last temptation in the film is not just to get off the cross and live a full life by having a family, first with Mary Magdalene, and then with Mary and Martha. It is also the temptation of fighting a further melodramatic battle with Satan as the ultimate villain, rather than realizing that evil derives from the lack in his own being, as both god and man.

Jesus meets Satan in the column of fire during his desert visions. But his prior visitors, the snake and the lion, say they are parts of him: his spirit and his heart. Satan, as a speaking flame, does not remind Jesus that he is also within him. Yet Satan does recall Jesus' greed for divine power as a boy, his prayer to become a god. Satan offers a joining of their greedy powers to rule the entire cosmos now, both the living and the dead. In a postmodern sense, this Satan represents the lack within Jesus, as human and Other, twisting from hollow unworthiness and guilt into a maelstrom of potential violence and domination. The twisting tongue of fire depicts this better in the film than the monstrous Archangel with green wings who appears in the novel (262). And yet, there is a temptation here for the film audience, along with Jesus, to see Satan as the evil Other, the melodramatic villain who must be destroyed by violence, fighting fire with fire—or with the ax that Jesus shows his disciples, replacing his heart, as he invites them to war.

In nature there is violence. In life there is cruelty (as Artaud emphasized). So Jesus discovers blood in biting the fruit of the tree of knowledge and attacks that symbol of good and evil with an ax. But at the edge of a bloody battle with the Romans in Jerusalem, he realizes that the greater sacrifice is not in righteous warfare against the evil oppressor, breeding reciprocal violence that will also destroy the good. Instead, it is in his gift of divine mortality, as both good and evil, on the cross. Of course, the film audience expects this choice, along with Jesus' interrogation by Pilate and subsequent scourging, crowning with thorns, and carrying of the cross to Golgotha. There Scorsese shows a nail piercing Jesus' hand, his naked body raised on the cross, and (somewhat like the Aztec gladiator) blood striping his face and chest, while his onscreen audience gestures and jeers at him. The ultimate temptation of the cinema audience to see this ritual victim as a melodramatic hero, conquering Satan and death with his power on the cross, is then undercut—and yet reinvoked—in Jesus' final, tragic temptation.

Jesus speaks of God as his father throughout the film and rejects his earthly mother twice: when he first leaves her to discover his mission and later when she tries to follow him along with his disciples. (She is not shown at the wedding feast of Cana, yet is at the Last Supper.) But the last temptation—and the final half hour of the film—involves the ordinary, familial desires of the (m)Other, wanting Jesus to have a wife and children. After Jesus screams, "Father, why have you forsaken me?", a little girl appears (with a British accent), claiming to be his "guardian angel." She tells Jesus that his father is the God of mercy, not punishment, and that she was sent to save him, as when Abraham sacrificed Isaac, to "let him die in a dream, but let him live his life." She takes out the nails and invites Jesus to come down from the cross, telling him he does not need to be sacrificed, because he is not the Messiah. She gives him a different life: he marries Mary Magdalene and, when she dies, he also has a family with Mary and Martha, getting sons from the former but also sex with the latter—in what Scorsese has called "polygamy" rather than adultery (*Martin* 122).[37] The little girl, as guardian angel, stays with Jesus in his marriages and subsequent family. When Magdalene dies, Jesus takes up the ax again, hitting the ground with it, after the angel tells him: "God killed her." But the girl also consoles him with the idea that Magdalene is immortal and that there is "only one woman in the world, one woman with many faces." She encourages him to continue with Mary (who already bears his son) and with Martha, saying: "this is the way the savior comes, gradually, from embrace to embrace, from son to son." Scorsese's film, like Kazantzakis's novel, which shows even more of Jesus' love for nature as "mother" (455), provides a mother goddess alternative to patriarchal sacrifice—with the savior's gradual resurrection through females and families, in the *chora* away from the cross.

When Jesus meets Paul (Harry Dean Stanton), preaching about the cru-
cified Christ, the girl as guardian angel tries to keep Jesus from talking to him.
But Jesus insists on arguing with Paul about the truth of his life, contrary to
Paul's stories of his death and resurrection. Jesus says that he never died and
rose again, that he is just a man enjoying his life, and that he will denounce
Paul publicly as a liar. But Paul rejects this earthly, ordinary Jesus. He replies
that people are suffering and need a "resurrected Jesus," not the truth.
According to Paul, people need God to be happy. "He can make them happy
to die . . . all for the sake of Christ." Paul says he is glad he met the human
Jesus, because he can now forget him. "My Jesus is much more important and
much more powerful." This scene further distinguishes the split subjectivity
of Jesus' last temptation: the mother goddess option of an ordinary family life
or transcendence as patriarchal martyr. But it also points to the ordinary sacrifices in any human life. Jesus has not found a paradise away from the cross.
He enjoys a longer life in his last temptation, but he also encounters further
suffering: in his reunion with yet loss of Magdalene, in his loss of a true message with the hypocrisy of Paul, and in the destruction of Jerusalem, which
Jesus later witnesses as an old man nearing a natural death.

Paul's comments remind Jesus, and perhaps his film audience, that being
human is almost unbearable. Human minds mask the traumatic horrors of
memory and the terrifying potential of loss in each moment of life, to allow
some joy through the illusion of a stable ego and world. But all of life involves
perpetual change, from dying cells within the organism, to invasive diseases,
to the inevitable decay of oneself and loved ones, as well as transformations
of society and habitat. Paul offers the idea of a resurrected Jesus, even if
untrue, as an illusion of ego transcendence, to make ordinary people happy,
even as they are inevitably sacrificed by life. The challenge posed in Jesus' last
temptation is not just whether to finish his mission as Messiah or let Paul
preach a lie. He is also challenged to live and die as fully human, realizing the
true horror of mortality, with a god's tragic awareness, and thus to offer a
catharsis of nature itself on the cross. Jesus' final message in returning to the
cross might be to combine his dual lives: the joy of ordinary family love and
the transcendent pain of sacrifice, treasuring each moment of life as it is being
lost, with gratitude in one's heart, rather than a vengeful ax in one's hand.

Unfortunately, the last scene of Scorsese's film evokes the viewer's temptation of revenge, finding a melodramatic villain to blame for evil, suffering,
and loss—then punishing him in the hero's final victory. The guardian angel
turns out to be Satan, appearing as the same column of fire, and tells the
aging Jesus to just "die like a man." But our hero crawls from his deathbed, up
the steps of his home, and then outside. He returns to Calvary, asking God to
let him die on the cross after all. He is encouraged in this fight against Satan,
against the final temptation of a normal life and death, by his lost allies. Several apostles, including Peter and Judas, visit Jesus as an old man in his home,

while he is still lying on his deathbed, and summon his courage to win the spiritual battle. At the last moment of succumbing to ordinary life, Jesus regains his friends and his mission, dying instead on the cross, just when all that seemed to be lost. But this typical, melodramatic ending of a final victory of the hero and his allies, against the purely evil villain, is undercut by the specifics of the scene and its characters. Judas, an old man with blood on his hands from the battle in Jerusalem, condemns Jesus as a coward for not dying on the cross. Peter then tells Judas to let Jesus die in peace, because his crucifixion wounds are reappearing as stigmata, under the pressure of Judas' accusations. But Jesus combines the fighting spirit of Judas with the heartfelt pity of Peter to remake his ending.

Throughout the film Judas is Jesus' best friend and confidant. Even when arguing with Jesus about his cross making, even when sent by the Zealots (and Saul) to kill Jesus, Judas sees the potential Messiah in him and becomes instrumental in shaping his mission. Jesus finally tells Judas to betray him, according to God's plan, but admits that Judas has been given the more difficult job. These details from the novel, making Jesus and Judas into buddies for the film, challenge hundreds of years of passion plays that have made Judas the archvillain and exemplary excuse for anti-Semitic violence in real life. Instead, Scorsese's Judas is as much a hero as Jesus. Even if that tips the film's ending toward melodrama, with Satan as their immortal enemy, it also provides a tragic reminder of Jesus' shocking statement early in the film: "Lucifer is inside me." The film's last temptation shows the truth of this angel-*cum*-devil (the little girl and column of fire) as both good and evil, potentially. Lucifer is not an external, melodramatic villain, but the sacrificial lure in each of us, desiring immortality, yet lacking it with the Other—like Judas and Jesus, as enemies and friends.

Ironically, there were anti-Semitic attacks against the chairman and president of MCA (the parent company of Universal), Lew Wasserman and Sid Sheinberg, for producing *Last Temptation*. The protesters even staged passion plays outside Wasserman's home (Keyser 185). Scorsese responded: "the whole point of the movie is that nobody is to blame, not even the Romans. It's all part of the plan. Otherwise, it's insane. I mean, the Jewish people give us God, and we persecute them for 2000 years for it!" (*Martin* 119). A few years later, he remade the classic melodrama *Cape Fear* (1991), partly to repay Universal for its support of *Last Temptation*. *Cape Fear* turned out to be the biggest moneymaker of Scorsese's career. Yet the prior film, with its very human Christ, bears tragic edges that work against the moneymaking drive of Hollywood and the melodramatic prejudices of many in the mass audience, offering a powerful, spiritual and political challenge. The director and lead actor experienced what they each called a "mortification of the flesh" and "martyrdom" with this film (Scorsese, *Martin* 115; Dafoe, quoted in Keyser 179). Scorsese struggled for a decade, first with Paramount, and then with

Universal to make the film on a small budget. Dafoe nearly asphyxiated in filming the crucifixion scene. But both felt these trials purified the final product. Spectators might likewise find a catharsis in watching it, clarifying the temptation to violence in melodramatic entertainment and political extremism. When one picks up the ax in a just war against a clearly evil oppressor, as Judas and John the Baptist wanted (or as Christians believed in picketing the film), one is likely to become evil also—if villainy can be seen only in the Other, not in oneself. However, it is the way one handles the fact that "Lucifer is inside me" that makes the difference between paralyzing despair, reciprocal violence, and ethical sacrifice, as Scorsese's Jesus discovers in his various temptations of martyrdom.

In the 1990s, Scorsese made two more gangster films, *GoodFellas* (1990) and *Casino* (1995), both of which feature criminals at the edges of the Mafia who are not fully Italian. Scorsese admitted his admiration for the famous *Godfather* films of the 1970s, but insisted that his *Mean Streets* and *GoodFellas* were more "real" than Coppola's mythic Mafia epics (Scorsese, *Martin* 148). Scorsese called his own wise-guy films: "anthropology . . . how people live, what they ate, how they dressed." Yet, he also claimed there was a tragic side to *GoodFellas*, in Henry Hill's (Ray Liotta's) betrayal of his closest friends, testifying against them in court because they were ready to kill him. "Maybe that's the tragedy—what he had to do to survive, to enable his family to survive" (149). Throughout the film Henry's voice-over tells how much he enjoyed the life of crime and his camaraderie with the mob, yet the film shows the whimsical violence, brutal vengeance, greedy paranoia, and drug-selling/drug-taking madness of his chosen fate. At the climax of this, Henry is shown suffering through the intense, tragicomic craziness of a single, fateful day: shadowed by a helicopter while picking up relatives and cocaine, making dinner with his family, mixing drugs with his mistress, reselling guns, and being stopped with a gun to his head by narcotics cops.

Once again with this protagonist, Scorsese presents his audience with an ethical dilemma in the sacrifice onscreen. Like Charlie, Travis, Jake, and Jesus, Henry Hill becomes a sympathetic yet fearful, attractive but repulsive anti-hero caught between contradicting orders: the larger society and its laws, his rebellious friends and enemies with their own rules, and his lonely mission of sacrificing himself to save (and entertain) others. Henry chooses to give up the life he loves and offer up his friends to the court and the press. He saves his family through the witness protection program, but becomes an insignificant, anonymous, suburban homeowner in the end, picking up the newspaper in his bathrobe. He thus functions as a villainous scapegoat to his buddies and the law, yet a tragicomic martyr for the film audience. This path of Henry Hill, like that of other Scorsese anti-heroes, represents a difficult choice between conflicting rites of sacrifice (for some in the audience as well): to mediate one's lacking being with communal belonging, by submitting to others' demands, or to convert the inner emptiness into another, antagonistic calling.

SACRIFICES THAT CANNOT BE REFUSED

Scorsese never made a war movie, nor an epic, "Godfather" film (except for his Hamletic *Gangs of New York* in 2002). Even *The Last Temptation of Christ* features Jesus on a small scale, with personal visions and temptations. The cinematic violence of Francis Ford Coppola operates on another level, appealing to operatic tastes for romantic grandeur in family sagas and battlefield explosions, unlike the intimate bloodiness and anthropological insights of Scorsese's Grand Guignol. However, Coppola's large-scale gangster and war films, *The Godfather* (1972), *The Godfather, Part II* (1974), *Apocalypse Now* (1979), and *The Godfather, Part III* (1990), while using melodramatic formulas for mass-audience success, also create tragic edges that question the drive to perpetuate vengeance in personal vendettas and colonial wars. Coppola demonstrates, with *Apocalypse Now*, that cinema itself can be a mechanism for repetitive violence, behind and beyond the camera. With the recent realignment of American military might and capitalist, antiterrorist priorities, Coppola's Vietnam (as a "heart of darkness") and his Godfather films (where violence is "just business") become even more significant—from the theatres of war and "free trade" to mass entertainments today.

Coppola's large-scale cinematic violence shows a postmodern demand for human sacrifice, fictional and real, akin to the blood-rite logic of Aztec culture: screen offerings that keep the mass-media sun rising again each day, lighting the lacking being of current subjects with transcendent hopes. Coppola captures onscreen the mythic figures of today's underworld, with movie stars as god-actors pushed to their mortal limits, and the director himself (like Scorsese) mortifying his flesh, finances, and psyche in a filmmaking martyrdom for the Other in the audience.[38] With his Godfather films, Coppola recreates the vengeful warfare of Mafia families, sacrificing their own and others' children to maintain power in organized crime. Thus, the Italian-American Coppola (although Neapolitan, not Sicilian) found another kind of godfather power for himself, like Roman and Aztec rulers, in staging fictional flower-wars with actors as gladiators onscreen.

The first *Godfather*, taken from Mario Puzo's novel (but reset to the 1940s), has a melodramatic revenge plot. Yet, it also shows the unending horror of reciprocal violence.[39] Sympathy is created for the Corleone family from the beginning, as the patriarch (Marlon Brando) sits in his study during his daughter's wedding reception, hearing requests from others for help and promising to right their wrongs with violence or to make their enemies an offer they "can't refuse." The first petitioner tells how his daughter was brutally raped and disfigured, asking for the don's death sentence against her attackers, after the American judicial system let them go free. But the don's eye-for-an-eye justice does not allow such revenge. "Your daughter is still alive," he tells the petitioner. ("We are not murderers," the don also says.) Yet, he does promise to take care of the injustice when the other man calls him "Godfather" and kisses his hand, agreeing to do a "service" in return. The second petitioner, Johnny Fontane (modeled on Frank Sinatra), sings at the wedding reception of Don Corleone's daughter, then privately asks for help in getting cast in a movie. The vengeance of Hollywood is also shown in this case, as the don's lawyer and adopted son, Tom Hagen (Robert Duvall), meets with the movie producer, Jack Woltz. He refuses to give Fontane the role, even though it is "perfect for him," because the singer lured a young starlet away, making the producer, who was also her lover, "look ridiculous." But the don's more powerful and persuasive vengeance becomes apparent when Woltz wakes up in bed with the bloody, decapitated head of his $600,000 racehorse.

This scene offers a graphic example of animal sacrifice onscreen, although Coppola complained about being forced to film it as a famous detail in the original novel and claimed that the horse was already destined for the glue factory (unlike the animal sacrificed in *Apocalypse Now*). The shock of a real animal's bloody head, sacrificed for this film, sets the stage for the main revenge drama of the Corleone family, involving further tragic edges of Real violence. By showing the Mafia kingpin's nobility and vulnerability, the film encourages both sympathy and fear for Vito Corleone and his sons—as heroes, victims, and villains combined.[40] A rival gangster, Sollozzo, wants to make a deal to get protection for his narcotics trade. But the Godfather refuses to involve his family, and the judges and politicians in his pocket, with that kind of crime, because it is "a little dangerous." In return, Don Corleone is shot five times while buying fruit from a street vendor, but survives. While in the hospital, he is almost assassinated again, but his son Michael (Al Pacino) discovers that the police have left him alone there to be killed by the rival gangsters. Michael—who had been introduced through the wedding reception scene as a war hero in uniform with a WASP girlfriend, distancing himself from the family's "business"—vows to his father that he will stay with him and then saves his life. Thus, the audience's sympathies and fears are drawn toward the don as noble kingpin, who mediates vengeance, yet becomes a victim to it, and toward Michael as nearly too noble to be in the mob, but coming to the rescue of his father when needed. (The term *mafioso* means "beauty and honor.") These gangsters are presented as the good guys to root for—or at least not as bad as the villains on the other team—in this melodrama of "business" conflicts, family loyalties, and repeated sacrifices, both heroic and vengeful. But the mimetic, reciprocal

152

FIGURE 5.4. The Godfather (Marlon Brando) and his sons at his daughter's wedding reception in the first *Godfather* film. On the far left is Santino (James Caan). On the far right is Fredo (John Cazale). And in the middle is Michael (Al Pacino) in his very different uniform. Paramount, 1972.

violence is thus given a tragic dimension, through the ironic flaw of the gang-ster-gladiators: their noble bravery, yet monstrous destructiveness.

When his older brother Santino (James Caan) plots revenge against Sol-lozzo, Michael volunteers to kill both that rival and the corrupt police cap-tain who collaborated with him. Michael is accused by his teammates of vol-unteering for "personal" reasons, since the police captain also punched him in the face. (Pacino bears a swollen face and his speech is affected for several scenes afterward, unlike the typical victim of a bare-fisted punch in tradi-tional Westerns or gangster films.) Yet, the war-hero-turned-mobster insists he will kill the villains just for the sake of "business." At another level, he chooses the revenge plot for the sake of his cinema audience and the business of Hollywood. Coppola's *Godfather*, in fact, became the biggest blockbuster of its day, reviving a flagging film industry in the 1970s, which had not seen such a hit since television entered American homes decades earlier.

However, Coppola offers many tragic ironies within the melodramatic, blockbuster formula.[41] Despite what he says, Michael kills for personal as well as business reasons when avenging the assassination attempts. His success then produces the revenge killing of Santino by the other side, in a bloody overkill at the tollbooth, reminiscent of the famous death scene in Arthur Penn's *Bonnie and Clyde* (1967). Don Corleone, after weeping beside his son's corpse, then offers a truce to the other Mafia families, as a "reasonable man." He foregoes vengeance for Santino's death, showing tragic wisdom and heroic restraint in not perpetuating the sacrificial revenge—while trying also to spare his son Michael from violence when he returns from exile in Sicily. And yet, Michael is nearly killed there, on the island home of the Mafia, and loses his new bride, who is blown up in a car in his place. When Michael returns to New York and becomes head of the Corleone family, Vito deeply regrets involving his youngest son in the family business, having hoped, he says, that Michael would have become a senator or governor instead. The old don warns the new don that he will be invited to a peace meeting by a trai-tor within the family's organization and assassinated there. After Vito dies, apparently of natural causes while playing in the garden with his grandson, pretending to be a monster, Michael takes on the role of ruthless monster as "Godfather." This hero's tragic hypocrisy is intensified, during the film's melodramatic climax, by intercutting a baptismal rite—where Michael, speaking for his baby godson, renounces Satan and "all his works"—with the preemptive killings he has ordered of several rivals in various brutal ways. Michael then lies to his traitorous brother-in-law that he will not make his sister a widow, getting information from him that way before his garroting. Michael also lies to his WASP wife (Diane Keaton) when she asks him about his sister's accusation that he killed her husband.

Coppola shows the violence repeating, not only between feudal Mafia families, but also between generations, despite an earnest desire to end such sacrifices. Even when good men are in the role of "Godfather," the business of the Mafia family—reflecting both the Hollywood film industry and the geopolitics of American capitalism (with its military option)—demands the threat of revenge, and certain actions beyond bluffing, for those in power to stay in power.[42] And yet, the tragic sacrifices that patriarchs make, offering their sons' lives to save the family and business, also inevitably fail. As one gangster (Clemenza) tells Michael, while rehearsing his first mob killing with him, there will be even more violence against them in revenge for his act. "Probably all the other families will line up against us. But that's all right. These things gotta happen every five years or so. Ten years. Helps to get rid of the bad blood." Likewise, the predictable rhythm of a blockbuster action film demands a violent climax for melodramatic catharsis, with fans in the audience enjoying the temporary victory of their heroes over the other side as villains. Even while following this formula for screen success, Coppola tried to show the tragic irony of Michael's choices. But he found to his surprise (like Scorsese) that audiences cheered Michael in the end as a Manichean hero, a good-guy criminal beating the more evil Other (Lourdeaux 186–187).

Referring to ancient Greek drama and classic Westerns onscreen, philosopher Peter French has recently argued for the "virtue" of rational vengeance. Given the right authority, a deserving villain, and a fitting response, revenge maintains the system of honor in a particular community, according to French. "Simply, the light of honor illuminates the rationality of revenge for the avenger" (93). In Coppola's gangster revenge films, unlike Valdez's *Zoot Suit*, there is no surreal Pachuco, snapping his fingers to control the action, yet offering his body for sacrifice, as the honorable, ethnic alternative to America's unfair judicial system and racist society. But Coppola does create an ideal Mafioso figure in Don Vito Corleone, who rubs his cheek lightly with the back of his fingers as he controls others' lives with honorable, apparently virtuous revenge. He is a model of strength and honor for Michael, both as the "Godfather" and as counselor when Michael becomes don. Vito teaches his son to play the game of revenge in a rational and businesslike manner, rather than with hot-headed rage, as Santino mistakenly did.

However, Coppola presents a tragic irony in this father-son bond, showing Michael's fate seizing hold of him through his ethnic tradition and family, despite his initial attempts at American assimilation through a WASP wife and war-hero identity. (Likewise, Valdez's Henry Reyna tries to assimilate by joining the Navy in the 1940s, then finds himself fated to the *pachuco* ideal.) Michael had distanced himself from Vito as perverse father and superego, joining the Marines to fight in World War II, instead of becoming one of his father's commanders. But he is lured into the Mafia war after all, becoming a Godfather (and monstrous god-actor) very much like his father,

acting with ruthless precision in breaking the truce and eliminating all enemies and traitors after his alter ego's death. Such irony, along with Michael's
hypocrisy in lying to God (about renouncing Satan), his sister, and his wife
at the end of the film, may have been lost on the spectators who cheered him
in the final battle. Yet, in making the sequel, Coppola challenged his audiences even further, deconstructing the Godfather ideal with a double narrative and Brechtian anti-hero, who falls prey to the violent game of his own
business and loses his family while trying to save it (like a combination of
Brecht's Mack the Knife and Mother Courage).

THE SYMPATHETIC INHERITANCE OF EVIL

Whereas Scorsese's Jesus must choose between family, war, and martyrdom,
Coppola's Michael chooses all three in The Godfather, Part II.[43] But rather
than simply making a continuation of his first blockbuster hit, Coppola created Part II as both a prequel and a sequel, interweaving the backstory of Vito
Corleone in Sicily and New York, before he became an established Mafia
kingpin, with the continued struggle of Michael to maintain his family's
power after Vito's death. Coppola had already experienced a great deal of
conflict with Italian-Americans and Hollywood producers in making the first
Godfather film. Therefore, it was even more heroic (or arrogant) of him, after
the huge popularity of that film, to challenge the conventions of a sequel and
the expectations of his audience. Coppola's sacrificial desire to combine the
origins and extremes of the Corleone family, with its endless gang war and its
new patriarch's martyrdom—making a more artful film, more critical of its
heroes, instead of following the same successful formula—may be due to his
own mortifications with the first film and a sense of hypocrisy about himself
as its Godfather.

   Before Coppola was picked, many other directors refused to make the
first Godfather film, not wanting to involve themselves in a project that "glo-
rified or gave any kind of sympathetic treatment to the Mafia" (Schumacher
94). In fact, the young filmmaker was then chosen more for his Italian heritage than his track record. The producers' theory was that recent gangster
films had failed at the box office because they lacked authenticity, being
made by Jewish directors and actors. Throughout the preproduction meet-
ings, casting process, and filming, Coppola insisted on making his own
choices as co-writer and director, yet constantly feared he would be fired by
the producers—uncannily reflecting the conflict in both the novel and film,
between Corleone and Woltz, about Fontane's role.[44] The Italian-American
Civil Rights League, represented by the son of a reputed Brooklyn mobster,
complained that the film would "continue a hurtful trend of linking Italians
with organized crime" (Schumacher 104). Attempts were made by someone
to stop the production with bomb threats and by shooting up a car that

belonged to one of the producers (105). Coppola also had to fight for his casting choices, especially Brando and Pacino. The latter was then an obscure stage actor, whom Coppola eventually called his "Frankenstein" monster (109). Pacino and others in the cast, including Brando, Caan, and Duvall, met with real-life Mafiosos to gather authentic details for their roles (110–111). But the director took Puzo's advice, warning him against becoming friendly with Mafia members, because they "loved the glamour of show business and . . . if you let them, they'd get involved" (Coppola, Interview 62). Coppola not only kept the Mafia at a distance in making the original *Godfather*, he also undermined his glorification of their violence as melodramatic heroes, and sacrificed another potential hit, by making a more tragic sequel.[45]

The first *Godfather* begins with Don Vito Corleone granting an audience to his petitioners in his study in New York during his daughter's wedding reception. The second film starts much farther back in time, with the funeral of his father in Sicily in 1901, when Vito is nine years old. His father has been killed by the local don; his brother is also shot to death at the funeral. His mother then sacrifices her life to give Vito a chance to escape and he emigrates alone to America. Next, another plot thread begins with the first communion of Michael's son (Vito's grandson) in 1958, about five years after the original film ended. The double plot continues to interweave the backstory of Vito's rise to power and prestige—from an alienated child, having lost his family and home in Sicily, to criminal success as a young man (Robert De Niro), assassinating the prior mob patriarch and becoming Don Corleone in New York's Little Italy—with Michael's fight a generation later to maintain his father's legacy of family honor and organized crime.

Marlon Brando demanded more than Paramount was willing to pay, so his Vito does not appear in *Part II*. However, Brando's aging and soft-spoken, yet dominant and ruthless don haunts both plots in the second film. He is not an explicit ghost like Hamlet's father, nor a supernatural alter ego like El Pachuco. Yet, he is the ideal Mafia kingpin that the young Vito becomes in his plot, enjoying the success of a first-generation American immigrant. And he is the fading memory whose shoes the young Michael, as second-generation Godfather, struggles to fill. But in taking on his father's role, Michael discovers a tragic double-bind in its hypocrisies of nobility and criminality, family and business, sacrificial honor and Mafia revenge—while Coppola also shows his personal questioning of Italian/American ideals.[46]

As a third-generation Italian-American, Coppola was raised, he said, to strive for fame and wealth, to make his family proud, as an "immigrant thing" ("Coppola" 223). But with the phenomenal success of the first *Godfather* film, he found that he did not "wear well being famous or successful." Coppola's discomfort with filmmaking fame and his decision to sacrifice the previous blockbuster formula in making the second film show his kinship with the main characters in his script's double plot. He had risen to meteoric success like Don Vito and yet struggled with the hypocrisies of his business and Italian/American identity like Don Michael. Vito had told Michael toward the end of the first film that he did not apologize for his life, that everything he had done was for the sake of his family and because he refused to be the one "dancing on the strings" held by someone else, but wanted himself, and then his son, to pull the strings. However, with *Part II* Coppola stresses even more the sinister side to such a noble ideal of American immigrant success, having experienced the bitter battles to maintain control of the strings himself as a Hollywood director. In 1972, before making the second film, Coppola explained his view of the Mafia as a metaphor for America, both having their roots in Europe and both pretending to be "benevolent organizations" ("Coppola" 223). The Italian/American filmmaker then described the real, sacrificial identity of both communities. "Both the Mafia and America have their hands stained with blood from what it is necessary to do to protect their power and interests. Both are totally capitalistic phenomena and basically have a profit motive." The same might be said of Hollywood.[47] Coppola creates that parallel, too, with *The Godfather, Part II*.

After Coppola made *Godfather II*, he explained that its tragic hero, Michael, not just the Mafia in general, was a metaphor for America (and perhaps also for himself, with his prior hopes and hypocrisies as a filmmaker). "Like America, Michael began as a clean, brilliant young man endowed with incredible resources and believing in a humanistic idealism. Like America, Michael was the child of an older system, a child of Europe. Like America, Michael was an innocent who had tried to correct the ills and injustices of his progenitors" (Interview 60). But then Michael "got blood on his hands. He lied to himself and to others about what he was doing and why." And thus Michael is shown, in *Godfather II*, as "the mirror image of what he'd come from but worse." The director sees Michael, unlike America, as "doomed." He presents Michael as a tragic figure for the audience's catharsis and perhaps his own: "I thought it was healthy to make this horror-story statement—as a warning, if you like. . . ."[48]

In the sequel that Coppola scripted, beyond the plot in the Puzo novel, Michael's main battle turns out to be with Jewish mobsters in Las Vegas, Miami, and Havana. As Coppola recounted a half decade later: "because there was no story, I came to realize little by little that the subject treated in the script referred exactly to what was happening in my life at the time" (quoted and translated in Lourdeaux 189).[49] The second film reflects, along with his personal family struggles, Coppola's battle for power as the new don of gangster films, against Jewish directors and current executives,[50] while also fighting to resurrect his own studio, American Zoetrope, or to create another means for artistic filmmaking against commercial Hollywood. Coppola had opened Zoetrope in San Francisco in 1969, with money from Warner Brothers, producing his own film *The Rain People* and George Lucas's *THX-1138*. But a year later Warner Brothers pulled out because those films failed to make money. Zoetrope was already bankrupt when Paramount hired Coppola to direct *The Godfather* (Bergan 36–38). However, with the financial success of that film, Paramount made the young director an offer he could not refuse. Paramount executive Frank Yablans formed a "Director's Company," giving Coppola (with two other directors, William Friedkin and Peter Bogdanovich) creative autonomy, guaranteed funding, and 50% profit participation—in exchange for an exclusive contract to work only with Paramount for six years (Lewis, *Whom* 16). Sounding like a Godfather himself, Yablans touted the deal as a "family relationship" (quoted in Lewis, *Whom* 16). Coppola also described his desire "to take some control and own a piece of that film business, for lots of vindictive, Mafia-like reasons" ("Coppola" 223). He then disappointed Yablans with the experimental structure of *The Godfather, Part II* and its hour of subtitles—although it was not a Director's Company project and did become a big moneymaker (17). In the same year as that film's release (1974), Coppola released an art film, *The Conversation*, as his first Director's Company movie. Yablans hated it and a year later Paramount dissolved the Director's Company (18). Then, for the rest of the 1970s, Coppola worked on *Apocalypse Now*, risking his own fortune from the *Godfather* films and mortgaging all his personal assets for a $10 million loan to finish his masterpiece. In the 1980s he resurrected Zoetrope for a few years, but lost tens of millions in the films he directed there and elsewhere that decade.

Reflecting his own battle for success in the early 1970s as a filmmaking Mafioso and perhaps anticipating his fall from grace, Coppola positions Michael in *Godfather II* as being caught between political, Italian, and Jewish powers.[51] He has moved his family to Nevada to build a new casino empire, after his successful vengeance in New York at the end of the first film. (Coppola also moved his family to San Francisco to create his new studio, American Zoetrope.) But Michael is now fighting on several fronts: with a Nevada senator who wants to "squeeze" him financially, with the uncertain vestiges of his Mafia *familia* in New York, and in a new precarious alliance with the Jewish mobster Hyman Roth, who had worked with his father in the old days. (Roth, modeled on the Mafia kingpin Meyer Lansky, is played by the elder statesman of Method acting, Lee Strasberg.) Michael Corleone must also fight against the traitors within his own family: his wife, Kay, who aborts his son without his knowledge, and his older but weaker brother, Fredo, who betrays him to the Jewish mobsters and nearly gets him killed. Michael wants to be strong as his father was, as he tells his mother midway through the film, but fears he is losing his family at the same time. He pulls the strings to make others dance, as his father desired, yet finds himself tangled up, trapped, and sacrificed in those very strings (like a god-puppet).

With Michael's sense of honor comes debt and guilt. He tries to act the way his father would have done, legitimizing his criminal organization through gambling casinos in Las Vegas, instead of prostitution and narcotics in New York. He tries to pacify Frankie Pentangeli and others of the Corleone family in New York, while working with Roth to expand his operations into Cuba. But he is questioned by the U.S. Congress, barely escaping indictment, when evidence is given against him by his former New York colleagues. He discovers that Roth, who had befriended him like a father figure, is actually his enemy, and ordered his assassination, using information from his brother Fredo. Michael has been "careful," as his father told him in the previous film, to demand perfect loyalty—separating his wife from her children, when she wanted a divorce, and ordering the execution of Fredo, because he also betrayed him. Michael then survives and saves his father's business, but loses his family, and ends up alone. His tragic flaw of rational revenge, through virtuous, honorable violence, shows the greatness of character that he inherited from his father, allowing him to play the role of Mafia Godfather that he himself initially rejected. And yet, while playing it so well, he also fails miserably with his *familia*. He thus serves as Artaudian martyr for the film audience, with the cruelty of his violence returning to burn him, even as he wins the vengeance game. But Coppola also presents him through a Brechtian braiding of scenes, ironically juxtaposed in the double plot to provoke audience questions about the hero and the aspects of American ethnicity, family, and business that he represents.

The audience is brought inside Michael's tangled web of honor and debt, loyalty and betrayal, power and violence. Spectators are also drawn to sympathize with the sacrifices in Vito's early life. But they are distanced by the two narratives into comparing the regrowth of Vito's family (after he emigrates to America as a parentless child) with Michael's struggle to expand and legitimize the father's empire (which also alienates him). The sacrifice that Michael's grandmother made of her own life, so that his father could escape Sicily, and the sacrifices Vito then makes of others' lives to build his American legacy for Michael, weigh upon him, as unworthy successor, like the guilt trips of Scorsese's martyrs. Thus, the spectator sees the violent mission of Vito as immigrant businessman, overcoming his lack of identity (like De Niro in the subsequent roles of Travis and Jake, who gain fame through self and other sacrifice). But the audience also views a network of violence in the game of sacrifice that Michael plays. He is now an American monster created by his Old-World (God)father, Vito, whose Frankenstein-like drive made a life, for himself and his family, out of the dead.

The problem with rational, honorable vengeance (*contra* French) is that the right authority for violence, the desert of the recipient, and the fit of the response is all a matter of perspective. The view of the recipient of vengeance may be very different from that of the avenger. Perpetual revenge often results with both sides viewing each other as villains deserving further punishment (as in many cases of terrorism or warfare today). Ritual, theatrical, and cinematic violence may provide a catharsis, to some degree, of vengeful, communal passions—with a scapegoat offered on the sacrificial altar, stage, or screen. And yet, the drive to idealize and imitate heroic characters and actions, with further violence against those identified as villains, may perpetuate the vengeance beyond sacred rites or entertainment. Instead of containing and destroying evil in a villainous straw man as clear-cut *pharmakos*, a complex, homeopathic *pharmakon* is needed for tragic catharsis. The good and evil of heroic sacrifice in tragedy exposes the vengeful passions, rational choices, honorable insecurities, and fatal consequences of the hero's errors in judgment—through the villain's view as well. It thus displays the hero not just as a victim and righteous avenger, but also as a villain making mistakes with violence.

Each of Michael's five enemies in *Godfather II* is presented sympathetically. But Vito's are not. In his first act, the 9-year-old Vito is merely a victim of Don Ciccio in Sicily, though he escapes death through his mother's sacrifice and the help of others there, then emigrates to America. In his second act, 16 years later, Vito, already with a wife and baby (Santino) meets his New York nemesis, Don Fanucci, who forces his boss at the grocery store to fire him. Vito also spies Fanucci putting a knife to the throat of a young actress, threatening her father with extortion. (She had just appeared onstage in *Senza Mama*, a popular musical drama from the early 1900s, written by Coppola's maternal grandfather, about a man from Naples living in New York, who gets a letter saying his mother has died.) In his third act, Vito kills Fanucci during a religious festival rather than give him money from the crimes he and his friends commit. He then holds baby Michael in his arms and says he loves him very much. In his fourth act, Vito helps a widow whose landlord is evicting her. With charitable encouragement and the subtle threat of violence, he persuades the landlord to let her keep her apartment and to reduce her rent. In his final act, Vito, with his wife and three children, visits relatives and friends in Sicily. He then goes with a friend to see a weak, nearly deaf Don Ciccio, tells him his real name, and eviscerates the old man, avenging the deaths of his father, brother, and mother two decades before. Such a rational, patient revenge seems honorable, though still risky, as Vito's friend is shot while they leave the killing. The young Vito is thus presented as a melodramatic hero: a victim himself in the Old World, who overcomes his adversity through the American dream and defeats two villains, avenging other victims as well. This simple cathartic arc becomes much more complex, however, when braided through the tragic edges of Michael's story.

Michael's first enemy appears during the party on his Lake Tahoe property, after his son's first-communion rite in church. This also happens in the film just after the funeral rite of Vito's father, his mother's death, and his

escape to America. Instead of granting rational revenge to grateful petitioners, like Vito in the original *Godfather*, Michael is challenged in his study by
a Nevada senator, who does not like the family's "masquerade," with their oily
hair and silk suits, invading "this clean country." Some of the film's spectators may identify with Senator Geary's xenophobia, especially given the violence of the Mafia, even if Michael is trying to legalize his business by taking
over certain Reno and Las Vegas casinos. But after the senator threatens to
"squeeze" him financially (for the gaming license he needs), Michael
responds that they are both "part of the same hypocrisy" and demands that
his family be left out of it. The senator patronizingly calls this rhetoric a "little game." Later, however, Michael shows his own extortionist powers (like
his father taking over Fanucci's) by arranging for the senator to wake up from
his drunken pleasures in a bordello bedroom with the bloody corpse of a dead
prostitute. Geary says he knows he played a sex "game" with her and unlocks
her handcuffs. But he is uncertain whether he killed her. Then Tom Hagen
gives him an offer he cannot refuse: an alibi of having stayed at the Corleone
house that night instead of the bordello (which the family also operates). He
promises to make the problem of the dead girl go away, "as though she never
existed"—making the senator greatly indebted to the don. "All that's left is
our friendship," the Corleone lawyer says, smiling.

In his fear of the Mafia's invasion, his strong-arm threats of financial
extortion, and his later terror at the blood on his own hands, Senator Geary
represents the conjunction of criminal and political violence. But he also
becomes sympathetic for the audience, as both villain and victim, although
an enemy of the film's main hero. Other enemies are given even more of a
complete role. Early in the film, during the Lake Tahoe party, Michael is also
confronted in his study by Frankie Pentangeli, one of his leftover lieutenants
from the New York *familia*. Rather than respecting this young Godfather,
Pentangeli yells at Michael for giving his loyalty to Hyman Roth, a Jew,
"before your own blood." Michael responds that his father worked with Roth.
But the older *capo* reminds Michael that while his father did "business" with
Roth and respected him, he never trusted him. Thus, Pentangeli appears as a
potential counselor to Michael, as his father had been during the first film,
with wisdom from the older generation. However, Pentangeli's position under
Michael, in being left behind in New York and refusing to work with other
Mafiosi there who insulted him, makes him antagonistic. He may be the villain who then attempts to assassinate Michael in his own home, with
machine-gun fire through the windows of his bedroom. Or that could be Senator Geary. The film audience is left temporarily with a mystery, provoking a
reconsideration of each antagonist, as to how evil he really is.

Just after Vito's *Senza Mama* encounter with Don Fanucci's evil, Vito's
loss of a job, and his stealing of a rug with his friend Clemenza—Michael
meets with Roth in Miami to plan a new business venture together in Cuba.

Michael is offered a deal he apparently cannot refuse: the lure to "make history," according to Roth, surpassing his father with a plan even Vito could never have dreamed of. Michael tells Roth he is a "great man" and that there is much he can learn from him, as the elderly Jewish kingpin munches a sandwich in his modest living room. Michael then confides in this father figure, saying he will get revenge against Pentangeli for the attempted assassination. But Michael also meets with Pentangeli, saying he knows that Roth tried to kill him, but needs to discover who betrayed him in his own family, before taking revenge. The film audience is shown that it was Fredo, who then gets another call from the Jewish mobster Johnny Ola, an associate of Roth. Fredo refuses to give him more information. The mystery continues, however, of how much Michael knows and how he will play this game of business and family, friendship and betrayal, life and death.

When first seen at the party, Pentangeli is a likable old fool, alienated from Michael's other guests in Nevada and trying to teach the band to play Italian music, but getting only "Three Blind Mice" from them. Then he becomes an antagonist, instead of counselor, to Michael, and possibly the treacherous villain behind the assassination attempt. Eventually, however, Pentangeli evokes sympathy from the audience, as a pawn in Michael's high-stakes chess match with Hyman Roth. The Jewish mobster also uses that pawn against the Godfather, by having Pentangeli nearly strangled, with the killer giving the message: "Michael Corleone says, 'Hello.'" Later, Pentangeli agrees to testify against Michael in a Senate hearing on organized crime (after Vito is shown saving the widow in his new Godfather role). However, Pentangeli sees his Sicilian brother sitting next to Michael in the hearing room and changes his testimony to exonerate the Godfather. Tom Hagen later visits Pentangeli in prison. (They are filmed outdoors, between two sets of fences.) Tom recalls with him how the Mafia families were originally organized like "the old Roman legions." The elder gangster responds that the Corleone family used to be "like the Roman Empire." Tom indirectly suggests that Pentangeli could sacrifice himself now, as in ancient times "when a plot against the Roman Emperor failed." Pentangeli adds that the traitors' "families were taken care of"—if they died nobly, opening their veins in a hot bath. Tom agrees they had a "nice deal" and shakes hands with him, covering Pentangeli's wrist with his other hand. Later, Pentangeli is shown dead in a tub, his blood poured out from slit wrists, as villain, victim, and hero: both a scapegoat in the Mafia war and a noble martyr for his family.

Even Hyman Roth becomes sympathetic as the master villain and main opponent to Michael. He is a frail old man with a dream of business success he knows he will not live to fully realize. But he promises to give that legacy to Michael (in exchange for two million dollars) while befriending him like a son, as well as a business partner. Thus, Roth may charm the film audience as much as his rival, Michael, does. When Michael confronts him, however, with the question of who ordered the hit on Pentangeli, Roth responds with a story about Mo Green, who worked his way to the top with him. Roth is weak with a bad heart and has barely enough breath to speak, but he becomes passionate in recounting his loss. "I loved him and trusted him," Roth says. He was "a great man," who "invented" Las Vegas, but was killed there without any recognition of his achievements in that city. Roth says he did not take revenge when his friend was killed (as ordered by Michael in the first film). "I said to myself, this is the business we've chosen. I did not ask who gave the order, because it's business." Roth admits the hypocrisy in his own heroic villainy, of self and other sacrifice, but ties it to Michael's as well.

In the end Michael beats Roth at the game of rational revenge, by escaping alive from Cuba, where Roth had brought him to conclude the deal he almost could not refuse—and where he was going to be assassinated (as he told Fredo) before Castro's revolution intervened. Roth also escapes Michael's counterplan to assassinate him first in Cuba. However, Michael then avoids the Senate indictment, by changing Pentangeli's testimony, and Roth flees the country. When Roth fails to get asylum in Argentina and returns to Miami, Michael wants him killed. Tom Hagen tells Michael that he has already won, that Roth will die of natural causes soon and does not need to be killed in revenge. Yet here the Godfather, as tragic hero, insists on the assassination, becoming villainous as well in his ruthless violence against his enemies: "these things I have to do."

Michael also triumphs over his wife, Kay, shutting the door on her when she tries to stay longer in visiting her children, after being forced to leave without them in the divorce. Earlier, however, she struck a deeper blow by telling Michael her miscarriage had actually been an abortion of his next son. "I had it killed because this must all end . . . this Sicilian thing that's been going on for 2000 years." The film audience had seen her trapped in the marriage, not even allowed to leave her home at one point, because of her husband's "business." Michael had promised her (in the first film) that he would make it completely legal in five years, but failed to do so (as she reminds him in the second film). She is thus a very sympathetic figure, although married to the mob, because she believed Michael would eventually free them from it. But she also becomes a villain to him, killing his child—as he is a villain to her, in killing many others and lying to the world about his business and family, especially in the Senate hearing. Both characters become tragic figures, through the different perspectives that the film offers from each side of their revenge game.

Fredo wounded Michael the most deeply, early in the film, when the information he gave to Ola and Roth nearly resulted in the death of Michael and Kay in their bedroom. Michael eventually learns this truth in Cuba and confronts Fredo later at home. But once again the audience gets Fredo's side in the villainy: not as simply evil, but as the temptation of lifelong resentment

FIGURE 5.5. While having drinks with Michael in Havana, Fredo says that their father never considered him to be a true son and joked that he was left on the doorstep by Gypsies. Michael then tells Fredo about an assassination plan against him. Soon after this scene, however, Michael realizes that his brother, Fredo, is the one who has betrayed him. *The Godfather, Part II*, Paramount, 1974.

at his "kid brother" excelling beyond him and becoming his patriarchal boss in the family. Roth and Ola had charmed and nearly fooled Michael with the promise of a "real partnership with a government" in Batista's Cuba (along with various multinational corporations). So it is understandable that Fredo could have believed their promise to him of a partnership, with the "respect" his brother never gave him, if he helped them in the negotiations. Michael, however, sees these excuses as merely a confession of betrayal, not reasons to forgive or to forgo vengeance. "You're nothing to me now," he tells Fredo, and vows to never see him again. Later, Connie, their sister, tries to mediate between them. She succeeds in getting Michael to hug Fredo at their mother's wake.

The story might have ended there, with a partial reconciliation (like Jake's hugging of Joey in *Raging Bull*). But Coppola presents a further tragedy with Michael's complete vengeance. Like Euripides' Medea, Michael martyrs himself in order to get victory over his enemy. He cannot stop his revenge against his scapegoat—even if he learns that all Fredo wanted from him was the respect and honesty that Michael demanded from him as Godfather. So he lies in hugging Fredo (just after we see Vito's vengeance, eviscerating Don Ciccio). Later, Michael watches from the house as Fredo goes fishing on Lake Tahoe and prays the "Hail, Mary" to catch a big one, as he had promised Michael's son. Before Fredo can finish the final words to Mary ("pray for us now and at the hour of our death"), he is shot to death in the boat, presenting another ritualized sacrifice, like at the end of the first film. This time the Godfather is even more tragic as alienated monster, pulling the strings, but ending up alone in the monstrance of the large glass window of his home.

The final scene of the film provides a bridge between its two plots and a further link to the original *Godfather*. It offers a point in the saga prior to Michael's story in the first film, yet after Vito's prequel in the second. At a surprise birthday party for Don Vito Corleone, all of his sons gather at a table, talking about the bombing of Pearl Harbor that day and the 30,000 men who have enlisted for the war. Michael surprises his brothers by saying he has also enlisted. Santino calls this "stupid." He adds: "Your country ain't your blood." But Michael insists: "I have my own plans for the future." His brothers leave to surprise their father with his birthday cake, yet Michael stays alone at the table. Coppola thus focuses the end of the second film (like Valdez with his gangster film, *Zoot Suit*) on a basic cultural conflict of many Americans, between ethnic and assimilated identities. He also focuses on the dilemma of finding significance in life by following parental desires or forging a new path. Michael tries, between the end of the second film and the beginning of the first, to write a different script for himself: joining the Marines and becoming a war hero, instead of a Mafia warlord. Like Oedipus, though, he finds his tragic fate catching up with him.[52] Yet he still chooses how to play the violent game he inherits from his father—sacrificing the blood of family and friends, even after he wins.

Coppola has described how his own childhood, and the life of his siblings and mother, revolved around his father's career as a musician. "Our lives centered on what we all felt was the tragedy of his career" (Interview 185). Carmine Coppola was a very successful musician, playing first flute for the NBC Symphony under Toscanini. Yet, as a composer, "he felt that his own music never really emerged."[53] Francis eventually surpassed his father, the musician, and his maternal grandfather, the immigrant playwright, as a more famous Italian-American artist. But he also helped his father achieve his dream by using his music in both *Godfather* films—thus enabling Carmine Coppola to get an Oscar (with Nina Rota) for *Part II*.

Francis Ford Coppola did find it possible, unlike Michael Corleone, to expand his father's business and live out the immigrant dream in his own way. When he returned to the Corleone saga in 1990, he made a melodrama with purely evil villains for *Part III*. And yet, there are also tragic edges in this film: Michael's remorse without belief in redemption, when confessing to Cardinal Lamberto (who later becomes Pope John Paul I and is killed by Vatican crooks); Michael's partial reconciliation with Kay, weighing the losses of the past; and the death of his daughter, shot by accident in the Mafia attack upon him in Sicily, while all his enemies are also being killed.[54] Again, Coppola involved his personal experience of tragedy in making this film. He cast his own daughter Sophia in the role of Michael's daughter, Mary (as a last-minute replacement for an ill Winona Ryder). Mary's accidental death in the film's ending, with the father's silent scream, reflects the director's loss of his own son Gio in a boating accident just four years before. Part of the plot for *Part III* also derived from Paramount's involvement with a Sicilian financier and the Vatican-held company Immobiliare, in 1972, when the first *Godfather* film was being made (Lewis, "If History" 51). Coppola's own film company went bankrupt just as he began to shoot *Part III*, and he declared himself personally bankrupt with debts of six million dollars. "Michael Corleone . . . was like himself in being forced to contemplate a tragic fate" (Papke 15–16). But Coppola rebounded financially, and perhaps psychologically, with that film as his catharsis. He then created a huge hit with *Bram Stoker's Dracula* in 1992 and became a producer to other art-film directors through his Zoetrope dream, including Kenneth Branagh with *Mary Shelley's Frankenstein* in 1994.

In the 1970s, when Coppola was still in his thirties, at the height of his artistic power and his Godfather megalomania, he made his most spectacular film of tragic violence. Once again he showed the sacrifices of a loyal, yet guilt-ridden warrior, assassinating others to maintain the honor of his patriarchal order, as in the *Godfather* films. However, in *Apocalypse Now* Coppola reveals the full scope of national hubris, as the American dream of immigrant success becomes the imperialist nightmare of Vietnam. Here the son acts even more for and against the father. A dutiful, cynical soldier assassinates the savage, colonial Godfather, exposing the heart of darkness in both of them—under orders from other Godfathers. Kurtz is also a metaphor for American idealism, turned inside out, and Willard for the film viewer's sacrificial encounter with that legacy. Together they display the Western cults of rational individualism and Manifest Destiny as the reverberating vengeance of savage rites within and against civilized technologies (continuing today in the war on terrorism). But the film also reflects the director's own violent drive to capture the war onscreen and his concurrent, tragicomic fate as an anti-establishment martyr.

POSTMODERN FLOWER WAR

In making *Apocalypse Now*, following the artistic and financial success of his first two *Godfather* films, Coppola created even bigger scenes of violence en route to the climax of assassination. He staged mock battles in the Philippines, using helicopters from that country's Air Force, tons of explosive materials, 450 actors, and numerous technicians, during 238 days of shooting—to simulate the Vietnam War.[55] (The script's writer, John Milius, and co-producer, George Lucas, originally planned with Coppola to shoot the film in Vietnam during the war itself, but they could not get the funding in time.) Early in the shooting schedule, Coppola replaced his lead actor, Harvey Keitel, with the 36-year-old Martin Sheen, in the role of Capt. Willard. For the opening scene of the film, displaying the soldier-assassin's alienation and despair, Coppola pushed Sheen to explore the heart of darkness within himself—capturing the actor's psychological and physical agony onscreen, as he smashed the hotel room mirror, cut his finger, spread blood over his face, and sat naked beside his bed, crying. He then cried, sang, and prayed for hours after the cameras stopped rolling (Eleanor Coppola 85–87). As with Dafoe's crucifixion scene in Scorsese's film, this agony in the hotel room and in the rest of the shooting endangered the actor's life. Nearly a year after it began and two months before the Philippine shoot was finished, Sheen suffered a heart attack alone at night in his cabin and had to crawl a quarter mile before finding help. He spent three weeks in the hospital recovering, while Coppola tried to keep the news of his lead actor's mortal illness from leaking to the press and killing his movie project.[56]

Coppola also suffered a physical collapse and nervous breakdown after Sheen's. According to his wife, Eleanor, he said he "could see himself going down a dark tunnel and didn't know if he was dying or leaving this reality or what was happening to him. But he'd gone to the threshold, maybe, of his sanity or something. It was scary, but also . . . thrilling that he would take such risks with himself." Coppola said he contemplated suicide "as a graceful way out," because he feared he was bankrupting himself with a bad film that he "could not pull . . . out of." He had put his own personal wealth at risk, mortgaging all his assets to finish the film, with its budget nearly tripling in the three and half years of its completion. During the location shooting, the Philippine government repeatedly took away the helicopters it had rented him, in order to fight real rebels, and gave him different pilots from day to day, so that scenes had to be rehearsed all over again. One of the helicopters went out of control and hit the company's paint and prop shop. Hurricane Olga also hit the Philippines while the movie was being made, postponing the schedule and destroying many of the film's sets. But the director pushed forward to complete his recreated war, sacrificing himself and his personnel to find a personal catharsis through the tragedy of Vietnam.

In making this film, Coppola did not capture enemy warriors for heart sacrifices, or force slaves to fight to the death in the arena. But he did capture the destruction of war and the agony of soldiers and civilians onscreen, by demanding real sacrifices from his actors, extras, technicians, and himself. The movie climaxes with the actual sacrifice of a carabao (water buffalo), in a ritual hacking of its body by Filipino tribesmen, intercut with Willard's assassination of Col. Kurtz (Marlon Brando). Coppola created a postmodern flower war, blood offering, and gladiator show, with varying degrees of human and animal sacrifice, in making *Apocalypse Now*. As he later said of the film (rather ostentatiously, yet still to the point): "it's not about Vietnam; it *is* Vietnam. It's what it was really like; it was crazy. We were in the jungle, there were too many of us, we had access to too much money, too much equipment; and little by little, we went insane."

Despite being a film about the worst military loss in U.S. history, there are no purely evil villains in *Apocalypse Now*. The Viet Cong, as the enemy, rarely appears onscreen—except for one woman who throws an explosive device into an American helicopter while it is trying to airlift some wounded soldiers. But this is also shown as her reaction to the brutal American attack upon her peaceful village. Coppola's film is loosely based upon Joseph Conrad's novel *Heart of Darkness* (1902), which exposes the bestial violence within civilized Europeans, not just in the "savage" Africans they colonized. Like the novel, the film shows the brutality of American involvement in colonial oppression, through the microcosm of Willard's mission to assassinate Kurtz, a civilized man and military leader who has turned into a tribal warlord and terrorist. But during the voyage upriver into Cambodia, toward the darkness of Kurtz's heart, particular scenes represent the absurd heroics, naïve brutality, and wasteful erotics of America's neocolonialist spirit, as displayed in the Vietnam conflict (and more recent military exercises).

Willard is both hero and villain in his mission of self and other sacrifice. Kurtz is both heroic in his passion to explore the truth of human darkness and villainous in his betrayal of his culture and comrades. En route to Kurtz, Willard also meets Col. Kilgore (Robert Duvall), who heads the American air cavalry unit of helicopters that attacks a peasant village in enemy territory,

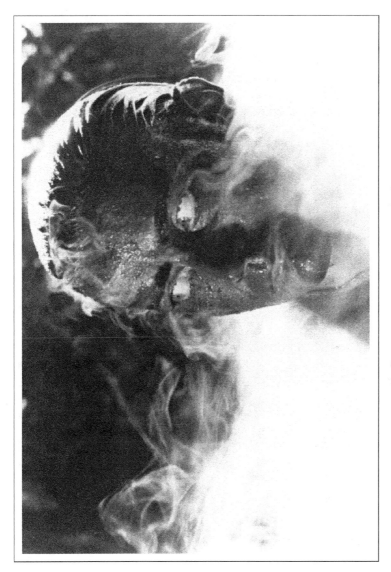

FIGURE 5.6. Willard (Martin Sheen) rises from the river to assassinate Kurtz, the Special Forces officer turned terrorist in *Apocalypse Now.* United Artists/Zoetrope, 1979.

not just to drop off Willard's boat and crew there, but also to surf the waves on that beach. Yet even the ruthless Kilgore—who enjoys the smell of napalm because it means "Victory"—is described by Willard's voice-over as caring and nurturing toward his men. "He loved his boys and they felt safe with him." He also offers water from his own canteen to a dying enemy, until distracted by the news that a famous surfer has arrived with Willard's crew. The most shockingly violent scene, later in the film, involves another member of Willard's crew, a teenage gunner who massacres all the Vietnamese on a small fishing boat they are inspecting, when a woman rushes forward to save a puppy. Only the woman survives the initial shooting, bleeding heavily. But Willard executes her, shooting her at close range, to prevent any further delay in his mission. The awful destruction here, as with Kilgore's air attack, arises through American foolishness, fearful bravado, and ruthless pragmatism, on the side of the film's protagonist, not in the pure evil of a melodramatic villain. Thus, the tragedy of American sacrifices in Vietnam, through the ostensible morality of saving people with democracy (as in Iraq today), is exposed in Coppola's film as the horror within sympathetic and partly good characters.[57]

Prior to the My Lai massacre on the fishing boat, Willard and his men stop at a supply depot and join the military audience for a Playboy Bunny USO show, with calendar girls in abbreviated cowboy and Indian costumes dancing for the troops. The soldiers' Dionysian passion erupts during the show, crossing the moat at the edge of the stage and forcing a premature ending, with the MC airlifting the girls away from the men, although two continue to dangle from the Playboy helicopter as it rises. This scene, however comical, reflects the erotic beauty of the setting and its burgeoning violence at other points in the film: a tiger charging in the jungle, explosions in trees, beaches, and bridges, tracers streaming over the river, or arrows and spears as the boat enters more primitive territory.[58] The Playboy girls as caricatures of cowboys and Indians, exciting the onscreen audience, parody the lure of voluptuous violence and tribal mystery for voyeurs and fetishists in the cinema audience as well. Coppola reminds his viewers that Hollywood appeals to the male gaze, from Westerns and film noirs to his own gangster and war movies, not only to entertain the mass audience, but also to excite passions that relate to real-life destruction. In demonstrating how cinema itself can become a femme fatale, evoking violence in the audience like the USO show, Coppola does not give more agency to women onscreen,[59] nor to Vietnamese characters and tribal figures. But he does show the dangerous connection between film melodrama and the theatre of war: in the erotic death drive to idealize, seize, and possess women or territory—while demonizing certain antagonists as primal villains and getting revenge for prior sacrifices by making more victims.

Apocalypse Now does more than critique the male gaze, however. It points to the animal instincts of the human species going radically awry,

especially with the godlike technologies of theatre and war in Western civilization. Rather than erotic displays and masculine bouts for the mating
purposes of natural selection, building the fittest genes in a particular environment, Coppola's flower war shows the divine whimsy of sex and violence
in human beings, destroying natural environments and other cultures, to
inflate hollow egos and ideologies. Bells ring in a peaceful, stone schoolyard
and children in uniforms are ushered into buildings, as Kilgore's choppers fly
over the waves that he fetishizes, blaring "The Ride of the Valkyries," then
sending bullets and bombs from the sky. Kilgore commends the helicopter
gunners who pick off the fleeing Vietnamese below them, including the
"bitch" who just planted a bomb in another chopper on the ground, exhort-
ing them to put bullets "up her ass." Jets are also called in to explode the tree
line by the beach and make it temporarily safe for surfing. Kilgore leaves
playing cards, with the insignia of his air cavalry unit, on the corpses to let
the enemy know, when they reclaim the territory later, who brought the fate
of destruction upon this particular village and its surrounding jungle. Then
he and his men turn the beach into their temporary playground, while drop-
ping Willard's boat on the water for its further journey upriver, according to
their civilizing "mission."

On a prior beach where Willard first meets Kilgore, Coppola himself
appears onscreen, as a TV news director. He tells Willard and other soldiers
walking into the battle scene on the beach: "Don't look at the camera. Just
go by like you're fighting." This double irony of Coppola not only simulat-
ing the war as film director offscreen, but also playing the role of a director
within it, capturing the soldiers on camera, while directing them to act nat-
urally for the TV audience, so as not to seem simulated, reminds the movie
viewer that parts of the real Vietnam war were actually staged—and that the
rest could never be completely covered by the news or recreated by this film.
Coppola's flower war of filmmaking stages mock battles to convince spectators they are experiencing something of the real war: capturing himself
onscreen, along with Sheen, Brando, Duvall, and others, as god-actors and
priests of the cinematic rite, sacrificing their bodies and causing actual
destruction, though in the Philippines, not Vietnam.[60] (This becomes even
more apparent with the subsequent documentary, Hearts of Darkness, about
the making of this movie, showing Coppola's personal sacrifices, along with
those of his actors in the location shooting.) And where does that leave the
audience of the tragic violence: as intimate worshippers in the rite or as distanced critics of what it represents?

At the beginning of Apocalypse Now, the audience is drawn into the
complicit, yet paranoid view of Capt. Willard, whose voice-over tells us that
he has already experienced one tour of duty in Vietnam and the return home
to America, only to long now for another mission in "the jungle." The film
begins with chopper sounds, palm trees exploding in napalm fire, and

Willard's face superimposed upside down, his eyes blinking and shifting their gaze, accompanied by the lyrics of Jim Morrison: "This is the end, beautiful friend." A close-up pan of Willard's personal items shows a letter and his wife's face in a black and white photo. As the chopper sounds continue, the ceiling fan in Willard's hotel room becomes superimposed over his face, its center at his left eye, revealing the beating blades within his brain. As Willard looks through the window blinds at the street below, his voice-over expresses disappointment at still being in Saigon and explains that he always thinks he will wake up in the jungle. "When I was back home after my first tour, it was worse. I'd wake up and there'd be nothing. I hardly said a word to my wife until I said, 'yes,' to a divorce." Home in America has become nothing to Capt. Willard. Nor is Saigon the place where his dreams lead him. Through Willard's subjectivity, in this very dreamlike opening of the film, the viewer already begins a journey into the darkness of the jungle, toward a *chora* of perverse animal instincts within the human heart and mind. Willard's place of rebirth from the dreamlike lie (and Nietzschean *maya*) of civilized life may be the particular jungle fire of his wartime experiences in Vietnam. But he also points to the lack of natural orders in the human brain, as the choral space of dreams and cinema. That *chora* of creativity and destruction bears the tremendous power to reinvent animal drives as social order and chaos, as love and violence, changing the environment into a theatre of cultural conflict.

Like Michael's tragedy in the *Godfather* films, Willard's loss of home and return to the trauma of the jungle becomes a metaphor for his homeland, America: the leading edge of Western civilization, losing its dream as a purely heroic melting pot, with democratic liberties, free-market success stories, and triumphant technologies.[61] Coppola returns his audience (in 1979 or today) to the loss of these ideals on the shores of Vietnam, deconstructing the melodramatic formula of traditional war movies, just as Vietnam challenged the righteous heroism of divinely blessed America and its victory over oriental villains in the Pacific theatre a generation before. Recent war movies (such as Steven Spielberg's *Saving Private Ryan*) often return to that melodramatic formula, displaying the horrors of war, yet also bolstering audience confidence about America's continued military ventures. However, through the release of *Apocalypse Now Redux* in 2001 with extra footage,[62] and through the tragic insights of the original version, Coppola may offer a homeopathic antidote to the American enthusiasm for vengeance in the current "war against terror."

Willard displays more of his loss of home, and yet its rediscovery as primal *chora*, in the jungle's terror and violence, while still in his Saigon hotel. "Every minute I sit in this room, I get weaker. And every minute Charlie squats in the bush, he gets stronger. Each time I looked around, the walls got tighter." Willard's paranoia, present and past tense, in this space of displacement, draws the audience inside his hollow martyrdom, especially through the lure of his voice-over. Then he assaults the audience, facing the camera with his fist extended in a martial arts pose. That gesture is revealed, in the next cut, as Willard facing himself in the hotel room mirror, which he suddenly punches. The body and blood of the Catholic actor, Marty Sheen, in his personal martyrdom of Method acting—with actual drunkenness, psychological pain, and physical injury—are thus offered on screen to the audience. But this communion is presented as both Sheen's attack upon himself, as character in the mirror, and his fight with the audience (through fighting with the director about being too bland in the role). Willard's paranoia in America as well as Saigon, with the walls closing in on him now, produces a sacrificial offering in the mirror: a shattering glimpse behind the mirror-stage illusion of ego wholeness, to the paranoid-schizoid background of the human mind and postmodern American culture.

The choral edges of Willard's broken mirror, with the real blood from Sheen's body, create a framework for the spectator's journey with him toward the parallel sacrifice of Kurtz (and Brando's improv) upriver. Despite his initial psychotic symptoms, Willard provides a rational voice-over for the rest of the trip, even when he leads the audience into further violence in his patriarchal mission, with reminders of the loss of home and temptations of paranoia in the maternal *chora* of the jungle. The surreal beginning of the film changes when Willard's mission papers are brought to him "like room service" and he is given a cold shower by the messengers. But his weird, ego-shattering introduction continues to haunt the journey, like the overlay of violent, yet beautiful images in that initial scene, until the tension between rational and Real, civil and primal, evokes further surrealism nearer to Kurtz and climaxes in the montage of his sacrifice with the carabao, its eyes staring at the spectator as it actually dies.[63]

This ultimate Coppolation (one might say) of filmic and Real, of patriarchal, military mission and maternal, jungle *chora*, is set up early on, when Willard receives his briefing in an orderly dining room, just after the passion play and cold shower in his hotel. As he approaches that briefing room, with its shades of home, inside a trailer on a military base, Willard says that he is "the caretaker of Col. Walter E. Kurtz's memory" and that Kurtz's "confession" also requires his own. The film audience, without knowing it yet, is put into the position of Kurtz's son—whom the jungle warlord wants the maieutic Willard to find (as Kurtz tells him in the end), as audience for his story. Through Willard, as executioner and narrator, the audience is given both an intimate, Artaudian experience of passionate martyrdom and a distanced, Brechtian mode of critical representation. Yet, Willard's critique throughout the film is not of Kurtz, but of his own commanders and of the war's hypocrisies.

This is signaled, even without the narrative voice-over, as Willard meets with a general and his aide, plus a man in a nonmilitary shirt and tie, who is probably with the CIA. Willard is asked about his own prior work with the

CIA, but he says he is not "disposed to discuss" it. Then the general breaks the ice by inviting Willard to sit down to lunch, with soft Muzak playing in the background. He politely asks "Gerry" (the CIA man) to pass the food both ways "to save time" and tells Willard that the shrimp will prove his "courage." The general thus offers an odd mixture of maternal nurturing and patriarchal challenge. The general's aide drops Kurtz's dossier on the floor as he hands it to Willard, spilling its contents and indicating a nervous clumsiness or chaos behind the almost comical attempt at back-home civility in the military base's mobile-home dining room. (Extreme close-ups of the shrimp and men's faces increase the uneasiness.) But then a tape of Kurtz is played, talking about orders to incinerate villages—as coming from "assassins" who call him "assassin." The Brechtian irony here is that Willard is being ordered now, because of such transmissions by Kurtz and his renegade violence, to assassinate him, thus proving his statement about the officers above him. Willard takes on this mission against Kurtz, like Scorsese's Judas in betraying Jesus, not because they are enemies, but because they are both martyrs for the truth of their missions. Kurtz is a villain to the military and CIA; he must be "terminated with extreme prejudice." But the film shows him, along with Willard, as both villainous and heroic in the tragedy of Vietnam and its military melodrama, which needs Kurtz as a scapegoat.

Even the general expresses sympathy for Kurtz as an "outstanding" soldier and "humanitarian," who succumbed to the "temptation to be God," and is reportedly worshipped now by his "natives." The general explains: "in this war things get confused" and there is "a conflict in every human heart . . . between good and evil." Sounding as though he knows him personally, he adds "every man has got a breaking point," including himself and Willard, but "Walt Kurtz has reached his and . . . gone insane." Unfortunately, the words of Kurtz himself when Willard reaches him, in the final part of the film, do not say much about why he became evil to his culture or a god-actor to the natives. Kurtz reads from T. S. Eliot's poem "The Hollow Men" and recounts a horror story of the Viet Cong hacking off children's arms after they had been inoculated by U.S. Special Forces. This gave him an insight, he says, like "a diamond bullet." They were "not monsters"; they were men with a "moral" strength to "use their primordial instincts to kill without passion, without judgment." He wants to have an army of men like that to win the war, "because it's judgment that defeats us." He tells Willard: "You have a right to kill me, but no right to judge me." The display of hanging bodies and decapitated heads around the Kurtz compound, along with his tribal worshippers and their sacrificial rites, says even more about this grotesque, Nietzschean superhero, posing as a God beyond judgments of good and evil.

Brando's 3.5 million-dollar performance, with lines more improvised than scripted, does not provide much insight on Kurtz's insanity. But his few coherent words, along with his hulking body and bald head, shot in the half darkness of a templelike structure deep in the jungle, still challenge the film spectators about their own moral judgments. En route to meeting Kurtz in the flesh, Willard also offers challenging comments about the American loss of home and morality through the Vietnam War—in a voice-over scripted by journalist Michael Herr, who had been there. After encountering Kilgore and his men, who brought as much of home with them as possible, while waiting to go back, Willard says: "Trouble is, I'd been back there, and I knew that it just didn't exist anymore." After the USO Bunny show, Willard comments: "No wonder Kurtz put a weed up someone's ass; the war was being run by some four-star clowns." After the boat massacre and Willard's ruthless execution of the sole survivor, he deconstructs the hypocrisy of the usual moral approach in getting medical help for someone like that. "It was a way we had over here of living with ourselves. We'd cut them in half with a machine gun and give 'em a band-aid. It was a lie." Thus, Willard becomes more and more like Kurtz as he moves upriver to kill him—putting a further Brechtian twist on the Artaudian tragedy of one warrior sacrificing himself to sacrifice another on his own side.

There are many mad ironies during Willard's mission, especially when the lives of his fellow crewmen are sacrificed to capture and terminate Kurtz, as warrior and god-actor, who exemplifies American individualism and imperialist genius in this war effort, "winning it his way." Chef, the cook from New Orleans, who goes into the jungle to get mangos for a sauce and almost gets eaten by a tiger, eventually ends up with his decapitated head dropped in Willard's lap, as a dish served by Kurtz. Lance, the surfer from San Diego, rides the waves as if he were still at home, saves the puppy after the massacre, drops acid and plays with colored smoke, then makes a gag arrow for his head out of the real ones shot from the jungle. He survives in the end, leaving with Willard, but only after going native like Kurtz. The seventeen-year-old Clean is not so lucky; he gets shot to death while listening to a tape of his mother telling him to "stay out of the way of the bullets" and come home "all in one piece." The Chief of the boat is also hit from the shore, but by a spear that goes through his chest. Then, with his dying grasp, he tries to pull Willard into its death point with him. Although many scholars have criticized the film for its lack of morality, especially with Willard as different from Conrad's Marlow,[64] these moments, like Willard's voice-over, involve spectators sympathetically, yet distance them ironically—in an ethical *Verfremdungseffekt* of the familiar made strange to provoke social critique.

Rather than providing answers to the moral ambiguities of the war and its generals, or about the heroic villains, Kurtz and Willard, *Apocalypse Now* challenges the audience to an ethical sacrifice beyond melodramatic morality and vengeful judgment. In my view, Brando as Kurtz says it best in the *Hearts of Darkness* documentary (with lines not used in the feature film): "It takes bravery. The deepest bullets are not to be feared. Phosphorus, napalm are nothing to be feared, but to look inward, to see that twisted mind that lies beneath the surface of all humans and to say, 'Yes, I accept you. I even love you because you're a part of me. You're an extension of me.'" This is the tragic sacrifice that *Apocalypse Now* poses for its audience: to cross fundamental fantasies of American righteousness that still tempt us today, as sole superpower and heroic police force of globalization and antiterrorism, of democracy and free trade. Sacrificing our neoimperialist illusions and clarifying the sacrificial demands of our current heroic identities means accepting the twisted hollowness of all human minds—not as a savage, alien evil to be cowed into submission with preemptive violence, but as the tragic flaw and potential brutality within us, as well as in the others we fear.

Many Vietnam films have been made since 1979, showing the horrors of war and the tragedies in returning home. But Coppola's film was the first to present postmodern warfare as a ritual game of martyrdom like the Aztec flower war and Roman gladiator fight, examined earlier in this book. The American Empire continues today to perform its wars for political gods, warrior ghosts, and terrorist victims back home (while also avenging an assassination attempt on the president's father). Wars are staged with increasing concern for the mass-media's display of sacrifice onscreen: from overexposed actors and body bags in Vietnam, to the videogame viewpoint of missiles approaching their targets in the first Gulf War, to "embedded" journalists reporting from inside the tank battles and "shock and awe" bombings of Gulf War II. Yet, these screenings of reality TV often serve to mask the Real heart of darkness perpetuating warfare: the ritual lures of vengeance and sacrifice, as *Apocalypse Now* shows.

Given the resurgence of U.S. hubris in destroying Islamic terrorists and their supporters overseas, like communists in Vietnam several decades ago, with threats of superior force through the latest military technology, with massive bombing campaigns to "soften" the enemy, and with American soldiers on the ground who are sometimes unsure which civilians to fight or save, Coppola's film gains a new relevance about the lessons forgotten in that earlier war theatre. Americans are still acting out the traumas and performing for the ghosts of prior wars, while believing in a God-given right and Manifest Destiny to recivilize the world. As in the old Westerns and many recent war movies, there is a renewed melodramatic demand today for American heroes to save helpless victims from purely evil villains—rather than a tragic awareness of the evil in the good, which Coppola's film presents—while Americans attempt, with both Gulf wars and the occupation of Iraq, to overcome their Vietnam Syndrome, yet find themselves repeating some of its sacrifices.

The films of Coppola and Scorsese, with their sacrificial gangsters and warriors, raise questions about immigrant entrepreneurs in the American dream, about sports stars in the arena, and even about Christ on the cross. Particular moments in these films caution the audience on the mimetic lure of violence by presenting ironic idols and their rites of vengeance. Jake uses his fists on his wife and brother between performances in the ring. Travis poses in the mirror, playing with his guns, and then, after using them against the bad guys, acquires newspaper fame as Iris's savior. Michael slays his enemies while enjoying the alibi of a baptism and opera at the climax of the first and third *Godfather* films.[65] Kilgore's wave-riding, Wagnerian beach assault is captured for the folks back home by a TV news director (played by Coppola himself), thus implicating the film viewer, too, in the sacrificial entertainment.[66] Then Kurtz, with his vicious genius, is fetishized by an American photojournalist and transformed into a totemic offering by Willard's military assassination of him. All of these ironic idols become tragicomic god-actors, like Scorsese's Jesus, through the temptation to sacrifice others as scapegoats, along with themselves as martyrs. They involve the film audience in various sadomasochistic desires, while exhibiting specific conflicts between communal and independent identities, through family bonds, business vocations, and warrior missions. These conflicts reveal the various sacrificial demands of patriarchy and capitalism in the postmodern—where all the world is even more a stage, with the Real of violence always being screened, and yet also taking place within the spectator.

Exodos

Long ago, theatre as an art form and the theatre of sports as violent enter-tainment gradually replaced the actual bloodshed of humans and animals in prior ritual performances with the fictional sacrifice of characters and the scoring of players. But that has also led to the current rites of our mass the-atrical media, masking Real sacrifices as mere play. Today, we do not use a pig's blood to purify our movie or TV theatres, as the ancient Greeks did with their rite of *katharsia*, sacrificing a piglet in the performance space before showing their tragedies (Ashby 123). Nor do we place an altar and temple just behind our live stages for the sacrifice of larger animals that are costumed and led in procession as performative offerings during a theatre festival. But we do raise Thespian stars as ideal egos with mythic media masks, empower-ing them with godlike immortality onscreen and onstage, while tearing apart their reputations as scapegoats in the tabloids. We are not spectators at yearly festivals honoring the god Dionysus, with competitions for the best tragic, comic, and satyr dramas that might provide a catharsis of terror and pity in the community. But we do create ordinary rites of watching new TV dramas (or favored reruns) in certain serial categories and of viewing the latest movies at the multiplex, or recent releases from the video store—every day or each week.

As we are lured empathetically toward violence at the screen's edges, we should recall the dancing hearts of the ancient Greek chorus, drawing spec-tator's emotions into the catastrophic f(r)iction of the hero's struggle against self, community, gods, and fate onstage. Although some of us today may lament the gratuitous excesses of sensational violence onscreen, the Greek celebration of tragic sacrifice as social catharsis shows that it is not how much violence but how it is presented and watched that matters. (Calls for censor-ship of film and TV violence today also forget how taboos may increase desire.) More violence on the screen or at its edges, if it shows the painful consequences and self-destructiveness of vengeance, will produce a more cathartic effect (with the right kind of audience), as too much violence to be simply pleasurable or temptingly repeatable in real life.

Just censoring or restricting certain degrees of violent display, with NC-17 ratings for movies or family viewing times on TV, does not turn the dangers of mimetic influence toward a more positive, cathartic clarification. As the power of the screen and its virtual reality grows, with its orgies of phallic knives and guns, as our personal identity and social awareness are shaped more and more by the characters and sacrifices of mass media rites, the difference between simple melodramatic thrills and complex tragic insights becomes even more crucial. For there are two dangers with melodramatic violence in the mass media: not only overt imitations of violent acts by already unbalanced minds, but also ideological framings that shape spectators' perceptions and projections in normative, stereotypical ways. The antidote to both lies in the more tragic presentation of motives and consequences for violence, along with a better education of viewers to watch the dominant melodrama more critically.

Nowadays, we do not watch gladiators battle to the death, nor do we tear out the hearts of god-actors to feed a hungry sun, as in Roman and Aztec times. But our capitalist culture does reinforce prejudices, or stimulate new allegiances, for and against certain character types through melodramatic screen fictions and sports battles. Such polar identification drives the commercial cannibalism of stars' brand endorsements. All sorts of consumer goods, along with film videos and televised games, become fetishized b(u)y-products of the performers' bodies, for the fans' communion. Yet, the best violence on the stage and screen today has the power to move us toward a radical questioning of sacrificial ideologies, especially of the movie, TV, or live theatre's own ritual apparatus. Melodrama's normative rite fuels transcendent illusions of ego and Other at the cost of real choices: when, where, and how to direct one's offering of life's inevitable mortality. Tragic pain, as cathartic learning, can benefit individuals and society more than melodramatic entertainment with its simple heroes and victims, its alien villains to blame, and its victorious, ostensibly moral violence—even if that clear-cut formula sells its screen deaths more easily.

Melodramatic violence onscreen may help children today to see their fears expressed in certain villains and monsters, like folktales of the past.[1] Ritual plot patterns and repeated mythic characters are needed in any culture to give individuals a sense of common meanings and shared identities. Each human brain builds its repertoire of thoughts and actions through a multitude of perceptions that form repeated patterns, as the otherwise random firing of neurons form likely pathways in chorus. Today, however, from cartoons to professional wrestling to computer and video games,[2] melodrama's justifying of violence against certain character types is rarely questioned. The development of a strong, heroic character in melodramatic plots corresponds to the goal of American ego psychology and drug therapy, which reduces the symptoms of lacking, depressed, or torn egos. This ideal of an essential Self can also be seen in the commonly used phrases of popular culture (and self-help psychology): "finding my self" and "being true to myself." But postmodern theory and Lacanian psychoanalysis challenge this ideal as an ego illusion that masks a fragmented psyche and lacking being. Melodramatic violence in cinema today, as in previous centuries of theatre and ritual sacrifice, supports the illusion of ego transcendence through clear-cut identifications with and against heroes and villains. This contributes to the casting of certain scapegoats, corresponding to villainous media types, as sacrificial victims in real life. Yet drama can also show more complex, tragic characters as both heroic and villainous, as victims of others and of themselves. Then the spectator—in watching tragic violence or seeing the screen through a more critical, tragicomic view—might move beyond simple, ritual identifications of good and evil, in the screen's numerous rehearsals of death. A crossing of such fantasies may eventually occur, changing repeated patterns of symptomatic perception and behavior.

If the Greeks could develop tragic drama out of melodramatic myths and rites (where humans were the pawns of warring gods and animals were surrogate victims),[3] if the Romans and Aztecs could create tragic dimensions in the melodrama of human sacrifice and fatal games, then our film and TV rituals can also produce tragic or tragicomic effects, against the grain of their commercial media. However, there are significant historical and psychological reasons why melodrama came to dominate the nineteenth-century stage and twentieth-century screen. The clear-cut characters, suspenseful plots, and spectacular violence of melodrama spoke across many language barriers in the theatres of immigrant America and continue to do so as Hollywood exports its products worldwide. If Lacan's theory of psychotic fragmentation, behind the mirrored mask of ego, is true for all of us, then we bear a melodramatic foundation to our psyches and a continued tendency to project good and evil characteristics on others.[4] Melodrama provides a container for, yet also feeds these schizoid projections, with violent fantasies and vengeful resolutions.[5] Multiple identifications by the audience and potentially fluid associations by each spectator are focused upon distinct stereotypes and simple justifications for violence. But rather than indulging such paranoid fears and clear-cut sympathies, tragedy moves viewers toward a more complex awareness of good and evil in all characters, as well as in the plot's violent twists and resolutions. Far from being dead today (as Steiner theorized in 1961),[6] tragedy returns through diverse, sacrificial edges in theatre and film characters—perverting the normative, melodramatic rites of violence with tragicomic reflexivity in open-ended, postmodern plots.[7]

Although the term *melodrama* developed much later in theatre's history, tragedy builds upon melodrama psychologically, transforming the good and evil, split projections of primal sacrifice toward the cathartic clarification of split-subjectivity within each human character. In the Artaudian mode, tragedy intensifies and complicates melodramatic passions for sympathetic, vulnerable, and lacking characters—to traverse fundamental fantasies through cathartic abjection.[8] In a Brechtian vein, tragicomedy exposes the foolishness of anti-heroes, despite their sympathetic struggle, revealing specific ego illusions as symptomatic problems in society. But both modes extend the primal pity and terror of melodrama's roles and rites, from simple characters and triumphant violence to complex, catastrophic sacrifices—enabling the potential catharsis in the audience of particular Oedipal complexes. Even Sophocles' *Oedipus the King,* the prototypical tragedy for Aristotle and Freud, begins as a detective melodrama, with the hero promising to save the plague-ridden people of Thebes by catching and punishing the killer of Laius, as Oedipus had saved them before by beating the Sphinx. Tragicomic anti-heroes nowadays are certainly different from ancient heroes. Yet Sophocles' *Oedipus* also begins to question its oracles, gods, and sacred dances.[9] Today, the subversive possibilities of tragedy against the dominance of melodrama in our mass media—and against the schizoid traits of postmodern life—can be clarified through a revision of Aristotelian catharsis, with the modern theories of Brecht and Artaud, in their opposing aims, and with the psychoanalytic insights of Lacan and Kristeva.[10]

Despite the recent cognitivist critique of Brechtian and Lacanian film studies from the 1970s,[11] I would argue that Brecht's theatre theories and Lacan's ideas of a psychoanalytic cure have not been fully considered by film scholars—especially in combination with a range of other cathartic theories, from Aristotle to Artaud and Kristeva, along with examples of sacrifice, from ancient rites to the modern stage and screen. This combination of psychotheatrical theories and intercultural examples bears further implications for the study of stage and screen violence, beyond what can be considered in this one volume. Not only could connections be drawn to various masculine melodramas, with or without tragic edges of complexity, but also to the domestic and maternal melodramas recently addressed by feminist film and TV theorists.[12] But I will leave it to others at this point to make further comparisons between today's sacrificial media and ancient rites—with the bloodshed of the animal as submissive actor, or the leaping heart of the choral dancer, or the gladiator's fight to the death in a spectator sport, or the Aztec offering of human blood, hearts, and bodies for the gods and mortal audience to consume.

Such sacrificial communion, from these primal rites to the consumer cultures of stage and screen, can be viewed through the lenses of specific art works. *Frankenstein's* various monsters, from page to stage to screen, reveal the sacrificial edges of the Real—and its cathartic potential—in the symbolic frames and imaginary mirrors of theatre and film. But Stone's *Natural Born*

Killers and the real-life violence it has inspired recall the danger of cathartic backfire, even with a complex, tragicomic film. The Frankenstein-like experiments of theatre, film, and television—transforming ritual and technological sacrifice into fictional immortality—may raise our awareness of the death-drive violence within us and in our society, thus working toward an ethics of the Real. But for some spectators and believers, these rites encourage a repetition of the virtual violence in real life, through a simpler view of villainous demons that inspires vengeance against certain scapegoats.

Valdez's *Zoot Suit* shows a direct attempt at tragicomic, Brechtian twists within melodrama onscreen, in a low-budget, ethnic film made by the playwright from his bilingual musical. As a film, *Zoot Suit* failed to attain the kind of popularity with a mainstream audience that it had onstage in Los Angeles with Chicanos. But it still reveals a potential combination of Artaudian and Brechtian devices in cinema—displaying an Aztec spirit of human sacrifice in gang warfare and *pachuco* identity, as a mythic heritage and theatre of cruelty to be valued, yet questioned, through gestic interruptions of melodramatic conflicts and stereotypes. The question of tragic fate is where the theories of Artaud and Brecht disagree most: whether theatre should draw the audience into deeper sympathy and fear with the martyred hero onstage, offering a transcendent clarification of life's fatal cruelty, or distance the spectator toward a critical view of the anti-hero's mistakes and of the changeable social problems that produce fatal suffering. *Zoot Suit,* onstage and onscreen, gives spectators of various ethnicities and different languages both of these angles for potential catharsis. Likewise, in the media theatre of terrorism today, two decades after Valdez's film, we need more questioning of self-sacrifice and ethnic warfare, when martyrdom and vengeance become tempting responses to geopolitical inequities and the fate of innocent victims.

For mainstream films today, the Los Angeles parents of the MPAA ratings board determine how the bloodshed onscreen has to be trimmed to get an "R" instead of an "NC-17." Ostensibly, this protects American children from the unhealthy effects of screen violence that is too real and disturbing for their immature minds. But it is actually Hollywood's system of self-censorship to preempt political attacks from offended customers, providing a safe thrill-ride for the majority of viewers, without upsetting the vocal minority too much. This commonplace dose of film violence reinforces the addictive pleasure of moral warfare onscreen, repeating a battle of good and evil forces through the anxiety, pain, vengeance, and victory of victims and heroes over villains. Melodramatic violence makes money through the adrenalin rush of danger, plus the reassurance of clear-cut characters, with good triumphing over evil in the end, especially when the sacrifices onscreen are well trimmed by the editor and ratings board. The simple characters, predictable plot, and voluptuous, yet trim violence reinforce not only the head rush of vicarious danger, but also the stereotypes of vigilante vengeance upon certain scapegoats of race, gender, and other antagonisms. This melodramatic formula has continued well beyond the demise of the Hays Code in the 1960s. However, the more real and disturbing violence of tragedy, tragicomic satire, and the tragic edges in melodrama sometimes challenges the postmodern audience beyond money-making, thrill-ride pleasures and the demands of the ratings board.[13]

Certain points in the films of Scorsese and Coppola, through dramatic context as well as explicit violence, expose the Real of social antagonism and spiritual agony, beyond the imaginary and symbolic conventions of stereotyped identities and virtuous vengeance. Their tragic martyrs also show great villainy, along with heroic struggle and fatal guilt. Sometimes the enemy's reasons for violence are presented, or the hero's remorse at the horrible consequences of his righteous acts. Despite the prophylactic process of the ratings board and the money-making agenda of Hollywood, these Italian-American directors, in their best works of the 1970s and 1980s, display a troubling reality of violence: within ethnic identities, vigilante justice, sports competition, religious messiahs, immigrant success stories, business loyalties, family values, and military duty—as well as the mass media's sacrificial apparatus and the filmmaker's ego.

I welcome a further dialogue on these examples, theories, and issues of human sacrifice and screen violence. I consider the analysis of dramas presented here, whether works available in print and video, or rites reconstructed with partial evidence, to be incomplete—without an audience as collaborators. So I hope to hear from the Other in this offering, especially with differing views of the sacrifices we share onstage, onscreen, and in life. Presently, as this book is being published, I can be reached at "mpizzato@email.uncc.edu"—with such an e-mail identity suggesting another stage of screen sacrifice, which we may share more and more in the future. We each are fated to repeat certain personal and social sacrifices, lured by rites of submission to the Other and illusions of ego transcendence. But we can change that fate to some degree, through exemplary works of art and the tragic edges of popular culture. These works and edges raise the awareness of cruelty within us—altering how we conform ourselves or alienate others in society, especially as we watch, desire, objectify, and identify with or against specific figures of stage and screen sacrifice.

Notes

PROLOGOS

1. Individual life is sacrificed by life itself (*bios* by *zoe*), through the erotic and death drives, as Freud pointed out: life uses and discards individuals to reproduce the species.

2. Cf. Derrida on "the sacrifice of others to avoid being sacrificed oneself" (86). Yet he also relates sacrifice to the Heideggerian idea of being-towards-death, as "the apprehension of the gift of death" (94).

3. My use of the term *death drive* involves the Freudian ideas of biological fate and of destructive repetitions beyond the pleasure principle, but also Jacques Lacan's symbolic and imaginary orders of language and culture, as they replace, or "kill," the Real of objects and nature. Yet, I also mean to invoke the Real of the death drive: (1) the terminal experience in the future, approaching each of us in some particular way, inaccessible to symbolic or imaginary representation, and (2) the passion of that and other losses, with the potential for revenge, already in each of us in the present, fueling symbolic and imaginary expressions of violence.

4. Cf. Mason 213: "Fear is . . . the emotion from which melodrama springs, inspiring first a conception of evil to rationalize the fear, and then a villain to mythologize that evil, giving it a form and a voice." See also Fietz 90–91 on the shift in European theatre from eighteenth-century tragedy and sentimental drama, involving heroic pity, yet potential weakness in the "man of feeling," to nineteenth-century melodrama with its "vultures," sacrificial lambs, and simpler, evil-fighting heroes. And see Metayer 242 on the sadistic violence, especially against female victims, in nineteenth-century stage melodrama, as related to "today's cinema."

5. Lacanian theory defines three orders of the mind and human reality (akin to Freud's superego, ego, and id): the symbolic order of language and law, plus the imaginary order of perception and fantasy, along with the Real order of lack and loss—repressed or replaced by, yet disrupting the other two.

6. Throughout this book my primary psychoanalytic approach is Lacanian, but I will occasionally use the object relations terms of Klein or Winnicott, along with

185

extensions of Lacan by Kristeva and Žižek, to show other possible perspectives—even if some followers within these Freudian camps see them as fundamentally opposed. There are many points of contact between Klein's and Lacan's theories. However, Klein (like Kristeva) stressed the maternal womb, while Lacan emphasized the paternal function. Klein focused on ego, body, and objects; Lacan on symbolic, imaginary, and Real structures. See Burgoyne and Sullivan for more comparisons. See also Julien 36–39 on the paranoic structure of the ego according to Lacan and Klein.

7. Cf. Prince, "Graphic" 19–22. He discredits the application of Aristotelian catharsis to cinema and does not make a distinction between melodramatic and tragic screen violence. Yet, while not using the term *mimetic*, he argues (along with others he cites) that "scenarios of righteous, justifiable aggression"—which I would call characteristic of melodrama—tend to "elicit more imitative aggression from viewers" (21). See also Whitmer 35 on the increase of aggression, rather than catharsis, demonstrated by studies of television spectatorship.

8. See Mueller for a survey of Brecht's influences. See Stam, *Film Theory* 145–149, for a list of Brecht's ideas, as applied to film, and their "dangers." See Elsaesser, "From," especially 177–179, on Brechtian and Lacanian film theories. In the 1970s Brecht was especially influential on British *Screen* theorists, such as Stephen Heath, and on the French poststructuralist Roland Barthes (see "Diderot"). See also Brewster, who directly addresses Brecht's "reproaches" against cinema for being controlled by businessmen, for delocalizing sound, for giving the audience only a fixed viewpoint, for its mechanical presentation of things as inalterable, and for not giving the audience a chance to change the performance (45). Yet Brewster argues, as I would, that Brecht's theatre theories can still be applied to cinema.

Artaud's theories of cinema from the 1920s (and his surrealist film scenarios), prior to his essays on the theatre of cruelty, were briefly reconsidered in the 1980s by Deleuze, *Cinema 2* 165–168; Flitterman; and Naomi Greene, "Artaud." Deleuze valued Artaud's "recognition of powerlessness . . . [as] the real object-subject of cinema" (166). He found in Artaud a deconstruction of Eisenstein's montage, pointing to the real cruelty and powerlessness "at the heart of thought," behind the imaginary/symbolic mirror of the dreamlike screen and its holistic illusions that steal thought. See also Rockett, who devotes an entire book to the transcendent values of Artaud's "cinema of cruelty," but does not relate Artaud to the Lacanian Real of the screen. On the Artaudian aspects of Polanski's *Macbeth*, see Reynolds. For an application of both Artaud and Brecht, as well as Aristotle, to Peckinpah's films, see Prince, *Savage Cinema* 109–113, 166–169.

9. See Armes 1–10 on the dominance of narrative over dramatic approaches in film theory.

10. See Staiger 63–68 for a summary of Bordwell's theory. See also the collection of essays edited by Bordwell and Carroll—especially Prince, "Psychoanalytic" 79–80, for a cognitivist critique of psychoanalytic film theory as "unidimensional." But cf. Walsh, who insists that "the Lacanian potential in cinema studies is far from exhausted" (23). Cf. also Greenberg for a non-Lacanian psychoanalytic approach to film studies.

11. For important exceptions, see Esslin's brief book on television and Auslander's argument that "film and video can be shown to have the same ontological characteristics as live performance" (159).

12. See Tan, Eitzen, McKinney, Murray Smith, and Zillmann. Tan and Eitzen argue for the validity of film catharsis, defined as the creation of and release from emotional tension (Tan 35; Eitzen 92). McKinney says that "strong violence" in film can create the effect of catharsis (17). Murray Smith, on the other hand, disregards the notion of catharsis as "vent[ing] the damaging emotions" of dangerous desires, because it shows a "psychoanalytic reflex response" in film studies ("Gangsters" 237). Zillmann defines catharsis as "relief" and says it has not been "proven" (183–186). None of these theorists makes a direct comparison to theatre, nor gives any specific consideration of Aristotle. Cf. social psychologist McCauley, who suggests that catharsis theory "deserves more careful attention" (148). He uses the ancient Indian text *Natyasastra* to consider the "purification" of unreal, artful, savored emotions (160–162).

13. See Nussbaum 388–391 on translating Aristotelian *katharsis* as "'purification'—or better, 'clarification', since the word obviously has a cognitive force" (389).

14. See also Brooks, "Idea" 14, where he argues, more generally, that the reader of a text, "caught up in the transference . . . becomes analysand as well as analyst." Cf. Green, "Double" 278.

15. Cf. Copjec's description of the "hysterical/melodramatic heroine . . . [who] sacrifices everything—all her claims *within* society" (267); Žižek's discussion of Euripides' Medea and Sethe in Toni Morrison's *Beloved* (*Fragile* 151–152); and Zupančič's analysis of Synge in Paul Claudel's *The Hostage* (213–216, 243–244). Each of these female characters, with her particular tragic drive, crosses a fundamental fantasy by sacrificing the very cause of her desire.

16. See Lang: "Tragedy . . . is a mode that [film] melodrama rejects but does not leave completely behind." He states that while film characters may be melodramatic, lacking self-awareness, "often the film itself will have a tragic point of view" (20). See also Singer 6–7, 57–58, and Linda Williams, *Playing*; they view melodrama as both a genre in its own right and a mode spanning many genres. Cf. Fowkes 29, 37, 43, and Doane, *Desire*, on the tragedy (or pathos) within melodrama. While Williams calls melodrama's pathos feminine and its action masculine (both involving lost innocence and a struggle for virtue, from theatre to film and news events); Fowkes rejects these binary gender identifications and theorizes tragicomic melodrama as masochistic.

17. See also Bourget 54 and Mulvey, "Notes" 77, for similar, generic distinctions.

18. See Bentley 217–218, 285–289, and Heilman 46–62 on melodrama and tragedy as a dialectical spectrum in theatre. Bentley describes a "continuous" scale between them, with tragedy as more mature, involving awe and compassion in its cathartic effect, rather than melodramatic fear and pity—and with the highest pattern of tragic action being "sacrifice and expiation." Heilman opposes the inner, "polypathic" dividedness of tragedy to the outer, "monopathic" conflict of melodrama. Yet he describes certain plays as "mixed types," with most "tragic heroes try[ing] to live in a melodrama." This also relates, perhaps, to the tragic "too late" within the melodramatic mode of "just in time" (Williams, *Playing*, and Fowkes).

19. Cf. Žižek, "Thing" 243–247. To this sacrificial goal of exchange, he adds the more basic notion of "ascertain[ing] that there *is* some Other out there who is able to reply," i.e., in more Lacanian terms, "to fill in the lack *in the Other*," which is also "to

dupe the Other." Žižek states the ultimate goal of Lacanian therapy as the opposite: "to *resist* the terrible attraction of sacrifice." See also Žižek, *On Belief* 69–74.

20. Cf. Girard's cathartic theory of sacrificial violence, from ritual to theatre and judicial performances, as offering a "scapegoat" in order to purge reciprocal vengeance within a community, thus confirming collective identity. See also Burkert, "Problem," for his theory that ritual sacrifice "preserves the image, the founding of community by communal eating," which he traces to the *Männerbund*, the primal male hunting group (165). For Burkert's view of the origin of Greek tragedy (goat-song) in goat sacrifice and the *Männerbund*, see "Greek" 111–115. See also Hubert and Mauss 93–94 on the "alternating rhythm of expiation and communion" in Christian and Hindu sacrifice. Cf. Myerhoff 170 on the goals of efficaciousness and communality in "all rituals."

21. Cf. Heath 92, on Oudart's theory of the cinematic suture as theological, involving the spectator as the Absent One, as having a God-like role.

22. Cf. Bell 211–215 on ritual's "negotiated participation and resistance" (211).

23. Cf. Richard Schechner's "infinity loop" as a diagram for Victor Turner's theory of the dialectic between social drama and stage drama, in Schechner, *Performance* 190–191, and Turner 73–74. See also my explication of a Möbius strip between modernist belief and postmodern perversity, hinging on the loss of ritual community, in Pizzato, *Edges* 7–8, 44.

24. This also relates to the historical shift in ancient Greece from a primarily oral to a predominantly literate culture. See Bacon 6; J. R. Green 2–6; and Wise. See also Goldhill 335, where he relates the form of tragedy, with its *agon* between hero and chorus, to "a tension between individual and collective responsibilities and duties, that is, a conflict central to the developing system of democracy, the rule of the collective." Green ties this conflict more directly to the "shadowy figure of Thespis" (16). Attacking ritual theory, Wise locates the new technology of distinct character voices in the "written version of Thespis' narrative [epic] inheritance" (31), which also produced performance reinterpretation, through tragic "alienation" (36, 53–54), as well as privileging sight over sound (56), history over myth (57–58), and fictional invention over collective memory (60). All of these shifts are aspects of what I am calling the "Thespian ego"—in conflict with the ritual chorus (and *chora*)—although I disagree with Wise's rejection of theatre's emergence from ritual.

25. See Bacon 8: "In the more individualistic society of the fourth century, tragedy with its chorus and its mythological stories was largely displaced by a new kind of drama, without chorus, about contemporary middle-class Athenians. . . ."

26. Cf. Nagy 49. He defines the chorus as "a mediating principle between the heroes of the there-and-then and the audience of the here-and-now." See also Henrichs, "Why" 58–59, where he argues that the chorus's "self-referentiality" encourages audience participation.

27. See, for example, the third episode (after the prologue) of Sophocles' *Oedipus the King* and the first ode of *Oedipus at Colonus*.

28. "Tragedy . . . certainly began in improvisations—as did also Comedy; the one originating with the authors of the Dithyramb, the other with those of the phallic songs . . ." (Aristotle, *Basic Works* 1458 [*Poetics*, chapter 4]).

29. Cf. Goldhill 336: "Tragedy . . . represents, redeploys, and comments on ritual."

30. The term *ego* here does not mean that the Greeks had a modern sense of self, but that the lure of heroic individualism in modernity begins to appear, retrospectively, in ancient theatre.

31. Cf. Morse 25 on the "manichaean moral structures" of melodrama, and Hauptman 287 on the "words, music, spectacle, and gesture" of nineteenth-century American melodrama "whose sensuous ambitions were a match for Antonin Artaud's."

32. Cf. Esslin 43, relating "the gods and heroes of ancient myth [to] . . . the heroes of present-day TV, with the important difference that they are infinitely more visible and accessible . . . , because they are living presences in our own homes." Esslin also relates TV commercials and their idealized products to religious animism (51).

33. Cf. Stacey 160, who argues for the "active and productive elements of the star-audience relationships," as evidenced by fan letters. See also Gledhill, "Signs" 213; she finds an intensification of stardom through "the emblematic, moral schemae of melodrama," in its rising popularity from stage to screen in recent centuries. Like Stacey (and Richard Dyer), Gledhill views stars as embodying ideological contradiction, "values felt to be under threat or in flux," even in their "drive as melodramatic personae towards emblematic monopathy" (217).

34. On the modern "death of tragedy," see Krutch; Steiner; and Brooks, *Melodramatic* 206. Cf. Žižek, *Plague* 158–159, on Lacan's view that classical tragedy took place in a frame of cosmic Destiny, which no longer preordains our "modern, post-Christian" lives. But this absence of Destiny "imposes on us an even more radical tragic guilt," says Žižek, with the "tragic fate" of being "hostage[s] of the Word," that is, of the "ideological doctrine which has lost its substantial bearings." Thus, the subject is asked to "sacrifice himself, . . . not for the True Cause, but for a pure semblance." See also Žižek, *Fragile* 43–44, on the shift from "*tragique* to *mock-comique*" in ancient drama and modern times, and *On Belief* 91–92, on desire as tragic and the drive as comic.

35. Cf. Tan and Frijda, who find a common thread in various sentimental film themes: "a paradisiac state . . . [like that] designated by Freud as the *oceanic feeling*, presumably stemming from a stage that precedes the development of individuality in young infants" (63). See also Doane, "Voice" 339, on how cinematic sound "envelops" the spectator, in a womblike way, beyond the visual frame.

36. For a similar (but simpler) Lacanian view of theatre, see Baal 56. He also points out that the "legendary origin of theatre has common roots with the most archaic forms of psychotherapy"—the shaman in various cultures (36).

37. Lacan's theory of mimetic identity bears the influence of phenomenologists Hegel, Kojève, and Merleau-Ponty. See, for example, Lacan, *Four* 71–76, for his references to Merleau-Ponty. For a more direct application of Merleau-Ponty to performance space, see Garner.

38. Cf. Mellard, "Lacan" 405–406, on the ethics of "Lacanian tragedy." In a recent conversation (Feb. 2003), I learned directly from Slavoj Žižek that he and

Alenka Zupančič have become more critical about their theory of an "ethics of the Real." He sees a problem in Lacan's simplistic idealization of Antigone in *Seminar VII*, with her sublime, blinding beauty. Žižek cautioned me that an ethics of the Real, in his view, does not involve the heroic approach to the edge of an abyss, to get a glimpse of the Real, and then withdraw. Rather, it is a discovery of the Real within oneself, of a blind spot in the viewer, not some external place beyond symbolic and imaginary screens. This distinction parallels my theory of melodramatic versus tragic catharsis: the viewer's simplistic, "moral" identification with a purely good hero, who fights at the cliff's edge and beats the evil villain, or the more complex, ethical challenge of the hero also discovering the tragic flaw within himself, of evil in the good—evoking in the spectator not just a purgation of fear and pity, but also a purification of desire, clarifying the drive that encircles the void of the Real.

39. For more on the (mirror) stage edges within the mind and in theatre's history, see Pizzato, "Edges of Perception." See also Green, *Tragic* 1–5, on the reversals of the spectator's gaze at the stage edge.

40. Cf. Wells 474, on the experience of tragic drama and psychoanalysis, "in which emotional catharsis is only an accompaniment to the dramatic re-working of repressed material."

41. Cf. Dahl's focus on sacrificial violence, communion, and catharsis in classical and modern drama within the European canon, especially her use of Girard (9–10). See also Slocum 18–23, on the application of Artaud and Girard to cinematic sacrifice.

42. Cf. Kellner 231–238, on the differences between premodern, modern, and postmodern subjectivity in relation to television.

43. On the simulacra and "hyperreal" of the mass media, see Baudrillard. See also Ang on the historical shift from modern to postmodern TV audiences: from "a symbolic 'imagined community' of the nation" (6) to "the 'active audience' as a sign of heightened cultural contradiction in contemporary society" (9). He also suggests a sacrificial trap in the latter: "the 'active audience' represents a state of being *condemned* to freedom of choice" (13). Cf. Dienst on televisual "flow" (26–33) regarding Heideggerian "Enframing" (122–124).

44. Cf. Eckhardt on various theories of mimesis, negative and positive, including those of René Girard, Arnold Gehlen, and Helmuth Plessner. My own view is most influenced by Girard's theory that mimetic violence will repeat between persons and groups, until it is focused and sublimated, through a sacrificial scapegoat. (This also relates to Lacan's view of the source of aggression in ego friction against the mimetic desire of the Other.) Yet mimesis can also have a positive side, whether in the Aristotelian sense of playful, instructive imitation or in the ritual practice of shared gestures. See also Soule on the Dionysian actor as more ritual than mimetic.

45. See Kristeva, *Revolution* 25–28, 46–59, for her reinterpretation of the *chora* from Plato's cosmological "space of becoming" in *The Timaeus*—and from Lacan's notion of the Real, in relation to the child's experience of the womb. She calls the *chora* a "rhythmic space," yet also "the process by which signifiance is constituted. Plato himself leads us to such a process," she says, "when he calls this receptacle or

chora nourishing and maternal . . ." (26). Kristeva focuses on the "mother's body . . . [as] the ordering principle of the semiotic *chora*," describing both ecstasy and horror at its edges: "the place where the subject is both generated and negated" (28). She thus redefines Plato's philosophical term to address the perennial influence of primal memories of the maternal body (and heart beat) within the subject's mind, which she also relates to cathartic rites of purification in various cultures (*Powers*, 14–17). See also Kristeva, "Modern Theater," and *Powers* 26–29, for her discussion of theatre semiotics and catharsis without reference to the *chora*.

46. Lacan himself redefines Aristotelian catharsis, with regard to Sophocles' *Antigone*, as a "purification of desire . . . crossing not only all fear but all pity" (*Seminar VII* 323). Lacan also calls catharsis, in relation to Freudian treatment: "a purification, a decantation or isolation of levels," as he discusses the ethics of psychoanalysis "expressed in what we call the tragic sense of life" (311–312). Cf. Mellard, "Other" 17–19; he emphasizes Lacan's view of tragic catharsis as purging the imaginary order. See also Žižek, *Looking* 138–139; Zupancic 3–4; and Fink, *Clinical* 208–216; on Lacan's reformulation of the psychoanalytic cure as a purification of desire toward identification with the drive's *sinthome*.

47. Cf. Elin Diamond, "Shudder," for a Lacanian and Brechtian revision of catharsis theory, as applied to certain female performers (Duse, Weigel, and Finley) and their audiences.

48. The issue of gender will be addressed briefly in all chapters, although most of the material features male characters as sacrificial figures. And yet, within the patriarchal framework and implied "male gaze" of each case, there is a repressed maternal *chora* and excess feminine (nonphallic, Other) *jouissance*, which I hope at times to discern. On the latter see Lacan, *Seminar XX* 77, and Fink, *Lacanian* 107, 120–121. See also Kristeva's warning for fellow feminists, in her essay, "Women's Time," to let go of melodramatic victims and patriarchal blame—to move instead toward a tragic clarification of sacrifice. "This in such a way that the habitual and increasingly explicit attempt to fabricate a scapegoat victim as foundress of a society or a counter-society may be replaced by the analysis of the potentialities of *victim/executioner* which characterize each identity, each subject, each sex" (*Kristeva* 210). In a revised version of this essay, she also warns that patriarchal sacrifice cannot be rejected without dangerous consequences (*New* 217).

49. Cf. Žižek's parallel of Aztec sacrifice with "our immersion into VR": as the big Other guarantees the sun's rise or the movement of an object in virtual space ("Cyberspace" 113–114). See also Žižek, *Plague* 99, on Marx's view of fetishism in both primitive and developed societies.

CHAPTER ONE
BLOOD SACRIFICE IN ANCIENT GREECE
AND AZTEC AMERICA

1. For a survey of modern theories on the origins of theatre, see Vince. The theory of tragedy's birth from a ritual Dionysian chorus can be traced back to Aristotle's *Poetics*, but it received a particular emphasis through Nietzsche's *The Birth of Tragedy*.

See also Weiner on the Brechtian as well as Nietzschean effects of the ancient Greek communal chorus. Cf. Rozik, who challenges the conventional theory of theatre's ritual origin, yet uses Nietzsche to develop an alternative theory of "the spontaneous creation of immaterial images in the psyche [as] the genuine roots of theatre" (344)—shown in dreams, daydreams, imaginative play, and formal ritual, as well as theatre.

2. Cf. Kubiak 151–152. See also Burkert 23–24 on the "two basic characteristics of ritual behavior, namely, repetition and theatrical exaggeration," both of which he relates to "aggression . . . repeated and exaggerated as a demonstration whereby the individual proclaims his membership and place in the community." Yet Burkert also points out that the "theatrical character of ritual . . . imperils its necessary function . . . question[ing] the acceptance of tradition" (42).

3. Cf. Padel 336: "Dionysos' specialty is to connect interior violence . . . with performed, exterior violence. . . ." She then charts the development of theatrical space, out of the *agora* orchestra (dancing-floor in the marketplace), as it continued to involve a sacred altar and religious audience (337, 340). See also Ashby, who argues that the "primal" Greek orchestra was "rectangular/trapezoidal" (40) and that the stage altar *(thymele)* was at the periphery rather than the center of the orchestra (57).

4. The Greek theatre festival in honor of Dionysus continued to involve the ritual slaying of a sacrificial goat. According to Burkert, *Homo Necans* 68, the goat-song of tragedy involved an offering of both life and gender: "the goat sacrificed to Dionysos was castrated by an assistant at the very moment it received its death-blow."

5. Cf. Girard. See also Hamerton-Kelly for a debate between the literary anthropologist Girard, the classicist Burkert, and historian Jonathan Z. Smith on the scapegoat and other issues of ritual sacrifice.

6. See Otto 113–114 on Dionysus as "render of men" and "eater of raw flesh," as related to other Greek man-eating monsters. See also Burkert, *Homo Necans*, on the primal male hunting pack, the *Männerbund*, as persisting within agrarian, civilized societies through certain sacrificial rites—involving cannibalism or the substitution of an animal for the human victim. And see Sagan, *Honey* 243, on Aristotle's justification for slavery and war as related to the continuation of "cannibalistic urges." But cf. Hughes, who distinguishes between various types of ritual killing and human sacrifice (8). The latter was rarely performed in ancient Greece, according to Hughes, and "did not as a rule involve consumption [cannibalism]" (11). Hughes also argues: "there is no truly reliable evidence for the practice of sparagmos and omophagy of *animals* in Dionysiac ritual" (89). Yet, even Hughes admits, "it remains possible that human sacrifice was a practice of the prehistoric Greeks" (191). And, as he puts it, "human sacrifice flourished . . . upon the tragic stage" (189).

7. For a recent theory of ancient and modern tragedy as based in *sparagmos* (the tearing apart of a sacrificial victim), see Storm.

8. See Padel 354–365 on the "dialectics of inside and outside" that developed in Greek theatre through the technology of *skene* door and *ekkuklema*. See also Paris 49: "Dionysos is not the God behind the mask. He is the mask." As Easterling notes, "masks were dedicated to the god after the performance was over and hung from the

temple in his sanctuary," perhaps to show their powerful otherness, their potential danger and disruptiveness to society (51).

9. See Cole 27. At the start of the City Dionysia (as a ritual prelude to the the-atre performances), a wooden statue of Dionysus was carried in an evening, torch-lit procession, along with many sacrificial animals, "to the sanctuary of Dionysus Eleuthereus near the theater in the center of the city. The climax of this evening cer-emony was the sacrifice of a bull." The theatre itself was ritually purified by carrying a bleeding pig around its perimeter (*katharsia*) and there were other opening-day sac-rifices at the shrine of Dionysus behind the scene house (Ashby 123). See also Wiles, *Tragedy* 26, 75. He notes that "the smell of dead animals must have lingered during the days of tragic performance" (59).

10. Cf. Friedrich's description of the evolution of Greek tragedy, as "an art form which . . . emancipated itself from religious ritual" by replacing the myth and cult practices of Dionysus with the performance of myths about other gods and human heroes (185–186).

11. Cf. Paris 27, on the motive of Pisistratus, "tyrant of Athens," for instituting theatre at the City Dionysia: "these celebrations maintained the tyrant's popularity by giving the people the illusion of participation." Yet Paris also mentions the "revolu-tionary, law-breaking, destructive," Dionysian impulse, only partly tamed by theatre's institutionalization.

12. Cf. the four stages of "social drama" (breach, crisis, redress, and reintegration) by which theatre emerges out of ritual, according to Victor Turner.

13. Durán admires Aztec religious rigor and becomes so fascinated by parallels with Judeo-Christian practices that he eventually views the Aztecs as the lost tribe of Israel, though under the Devil's influence. See also Todorov, especially 210.

14. See Durán 42, where his translators explain that part of his manuscript was published by another author in 1591, a few years after Durán's death.

15. Some scholars today prefer Sahagún's more expansive and apparently objec-tive study, but I (like Todorov) value Durán's subjective insights as well. See also Har-ris, *Dialogical* 136–141.

16. Cf. Sagan, *Cannibalism*. He finds a "similarity of psychological emotion" in Aztec and Christian sacrifice, but with a further sublimation (affection increasing, aggression decreasing) in the symbolic act of the latter's communion (60–61). See also Noble on medicinal cannibalism in Europe.

17. See also Rundin.

18. Detienne, "Between" 223: "Both in Dionysiac cult and in Cynicism canni-balism is seen as an extension of 'eating raw' [which was also considered savage] and becomes a means of achieving that subversion of the order of the *polis* which is their shared aim, a subversion from within, the one at a religious level, the other at a socio-political one." Cf. Burkert, *Ancient* 110–112.

19. Cf. Sanday 195, for her conclusions about the Aztec regulation of cannibal-ism.

20. See Ravicz 1–25. See also Durán 135.

21. Cf. Versényi 8–12. "The spectacle inherent in Aztec ritual warfare and sacrifice contained within it many elements of an incipient theater the mendicant orders skillfully used to their advantage as they undertook the task of Christianizing the New World" (8). See also Harris, *Aztecs*, and Potter.

22. See Kurath and Martí 88: "there were human sacrifices in all months [of the 18-month Aztec calendar] except month 9."

23. Cf. Durán's description of a theatre for dances and farces, which was also set up in the temple courtyard, with "a small stage or platform," adorned with branches and with arches of flowers and "rich featherwork" (134–135).

24. See Clendinnen, *Aztecs* 148, on the meaning of Tezcatlipoca's name in relation to the fate of the Aztec warrior and the obsidian mirror used by shamans. See also Olivier, especially 114–115.

25. See Anawalt for further details on the costuming of Aztec god and goddess actors.

26. See Clendinnen, "Ways," especially 121–130. She compares the human *ixiptlas* to other god-representatives made of wood, clay, stone, and maize dough. See also Kurath and Martí 81–83, on how Aztec priests "masqueraded as gods." Cf. Rostas on today's performances by "Mexica" Concheros, which involve "an invocation to the deity of the dance to enter the dancer; an indication that what is about to happen is occurring by consensus and not according to the dictates of one person's will" (93).

27. See Robicsek and Hales 49–90, on probable techniques of Maya and Aztec heart extraction.

28. See Durán 92, 107, concerning specific ritual sacrifices in honor of the gods Huitzilopochtli (the Sun) and Tezcatlipoca (Smoking Mirror).

29. See Hassig and Hicks. See also Durán 93.

30. Durán also describes "slaves" performing in the Aztec marketplace in order to be sold as future god-actors, if they sang and danced well (280).

31. Cf. Durán 131, on the actor that "the merchants bought" to play the god Quetzalcoatl for 40 days before being sacrificed.

32. See the answer given by Clendinnen, "Ways" 122–123. Although noting that "drink or drugs" may have been used in making the victim compliant, she finds something else at the heart of Aztec sacrificial desire, in both actor and audience: a "deep cultural predeliction for seeking the sacred through the extinction of the self." See also Clendinnen, *Aztecs* 92–93.

33. The Aztec god-actor thus resembles the *Übermarionette*, desired by the nineteenth-century theatre designer E. Gordon Craig, replacing the human body with an ideal "superpuppet." Cf. Clendinnen, "Ways" 122, where she calls the Aztec god-actors "dancing puppets." She also says of them: "Increasingly invaded, then obliterated by the sacred power, 'possessed' in the fullest possible sense, they had ceased to exist as persons well before they met their physical deaths."

34. Cf. Carrasco 90: "the impersonator is given four wives, who are impersonating goddesses of agriculture, with whom he apparently has orgiastic sexual relations for twenty days prior to this sacrifice."

35. Sahagún reports this name, along with the ritual gesture of putting the extracted heart in the "eagle-vessel" and calling the dead victims "eagle men," in his chapter on the festival of Tlacaxipeualiztli (47). See also Sanday 173–181.

36. See Read, "Sacred" 54: "Each evening the earth monster swallows the sun as it sets in the west, digests it, and emits it as sacred excrement in the morning, but only after a group of male warriors who have died as sacrificial offerings battle to capture it."

37. For a description of the skull rack, see Durán 79.

38. One might question the historical validity of Aztec memory in Sahagún's (or Durán's) reports. But see Todorov 77–86, on the significance of oratorical memory in the Aztec educational system, since the Aztecs lacked a written language, yet had a cyclical sense of time, with the past always repeating in the future.

39. Along with an increase in Aztec mass sacrifice, under the leadership of Tlacaelel, foremost advisor to three Aztec emperors, new rules were instituted requiring military service of all males. See Clendinnen, "Cost" 50: "Any male who failed to go to war, even if he were the king's son, would be deprived of all signs of rank and would live as a despised commoner, while great warriors would eat from the king's dish." See also Clendinnen, Aztecs, especially chapter 4. For more on Tlacaelel's leadership in the military expansion of the Aztec empire, see Padden 49.

40. Rehearsals included using a tortilla as a prop for practicing the heart extraction rite. See Carrasco, "Give" 5.

41. See John J. Winkler on the translation of tragoidoi as "billy goat singers." See also Lawler on the characteristic movements of the dancing/marching Greek chorus.

42. Cf. Clendinnen, Aztecs 180, and Read, "Sacred" 47–48, on the Aztec belief in fate, from the placing of a child in its mother's womb by the god Tezcatlipoca, to the significance of the date of the naming ceremony. See also Todorov 63–69.

43. Lacan also describes the infant's ideal self-image in the mirror in relation to its polymorphously perverse body: "in contrast with the turbulent movements that the subject feels are animating him."

44. Cf. Boothby, "Altar-Egos" 55: "Sacrificial dismemberment and ritual offering virtualize the play of the three Lacanian registers, the imaginary, the symbolic, and the real."

45. See Furst 137: "The loser in battle was destined by his time of birth to be conquered; it was his fate, or tonalli."

46. The term extimate comes from Lacan's neologism extimité, meaning external intimacy. See Lacan, Seminar VII 139. See also Žižek, Sublime 132, 180.

47. See also Carrasco, History 6.

48. Durán explains that although the festival of Tlacaxipeualiztli was performed in honor of the god Xipe Totec (the Flayed One), it involved the impersonation of

many other gods by "slaves" (captured warriors) who were costumed in the gods' "insignia" before being sacrificed, and then by the "owners" of those actors who wore their skins (174–176).

49. See also Clendinnen, "Cost" 78–79, on the "agony of identification" between captor and captive, as the former wore the latter's skin. "In a society which passionately valued cleanliness and treasured sweet scents, he and his kin had to live in a stench of corruption for the full twenty days."

50. Cf. Durán 79–80. According to Sahagún, these practices occurred at Tlacaxipeualiztli in honor of the moon god Xipe Totec; but Durán's parallel account relates them to the festival in honor of the sun god, Huitzilopochtli.

51. Cf. Willard C. Booth, who delineates the "dramatic" elements of Aztec festivals: incarnation, agon, sacrifice, and epiphany.

52. Certain children were sacrificed, after being reared in the temple, in order to nourish the rain god Tlaloc, who would then nourish the earth and the Aztecs. In fact, blood was called by the Aztecs: "most precious water." See Sahagún 5, and Durán 157, 164–167. See also Durán 250, on the children sacrificed to the goddess Iztaccihuatl.

53. For summaries of these Aztec origin myths, see Taube 33–36, 41–44. On the parallel between the gods' mass sacrifice to make the sun move and the Aztec practice of human sacrifice, see Moctezuma 44–49, and Carrasco, "Myth" 143–146.

54. Cf. Sanday 181, who notes that in another version of the same myth it is the monster god, Xolotl, who executes the other gods.

55. See also Clendinnen, *Aztecs* 183, and Taube 37.

56. According to Melanie Klein, the suckling infant fantasizes that it is taking "the breast *in bits*" (180), dismembering the mother—as in the Aztec origin myth about the gods tearing apart the earth goddess. In the anal stage, says Klein, "The child desires to get possession of the mother's faeces, by penetrating her body, cutting it to pieces, devouring and destroying it" (73).

57. Cf. Ragland-Sullivan 294: "In Lacan's 'more correct formulation' there is no penian part-object inside the [phallic] mother's body, but there is a signifier or, albeit unconscious, an attitude toward the Phallus." See also Ragland, *Essays* 57–58, where she makes a distinction between the theories of Klein and Lacan regarding infantile aggression toward the mother.

58. Cf. Neumann 202–203. His Jungian view interprets the Aztec victim as "the generative feminine earth principle, the woman dying in childbirth." Thus, the sun's mythic rise from the earth, reflected in the heart extraction rite, shows "the relative independence of an ego endowed with such attributes as free will"—through the "'symbolic slaying' of the Great Mother." This, in my view, projects too much of an ideal, Euro-American ego upon Aztec myth and ritual. See also Sanday 184–186, who borrows from Neumann's interpretation, but does a better job of showing the other side of the sun's (or ego's) path.

59. Cf. López Austin 376–380, on the theological and political reasons for Aztec sacrifice.

60. See also Alford 139: "In fact, if Lacan and Klein are correct, the Greeks were simply less repressed . . . about what we all do unconsciously: we live much of our lives as though we were living in the minds of others."

61. In analyzing ancient Greek sacrifice, precedent to theatre, as "the paranoid-schizoid defense, aimed at restoring the breached boundary" caused by a "contamination of good by bad, of love by hate" (67), Alford misses an opportunity to relate the cannibalistic fears and desires, which Klein describes in that stage of human infancy, to the collective ritual or theatrical experience of cannibalistic communion, literal or figurative. He also does not consider a parallel between that paranoid-schizoid stage and the characteristics of melodrama, as a foundation for tragedy (in ritual sacrifice, theatre, film, and TV). Cf. Alford 163–164, where he does mention the mimetic blood rites of revenge in Greek tragedy, but without applying the modern formula of melodramatic revenge.

62. This Aztec psychology could be compared with the significance of certain body parts and semiotic forces in Kristeva's theory of the womblike *chora*, Klein's of the good/bad breast and womb, and Lacan's Real order—behind and beneath the mirror stage of individualistic, mimetic (symbolic and imaginary) identity. However, those current psychoanalytic views refer to the mother's (or Other's) body parts in primal, infantile experience as setting up unconscious relations of desire. The Aztecs viewed psychic energy as invested in the child's head, hair, heart, and blood at birth, then drained—or returned to nature—as the body aged or as it was sacrificed.

63. On the ancient Greek sense of a multiple, corporeal soul with various emotions (or "soul words") located in distinct body parts, see Alford 100: "Greeks characterized most emotions in terms of their physical location in the body, as we speak of heartache." See also Claus 97, on *psyche* as "soul" related to breath and blood.

64. See Aristotle, *Basic Works* 554 (the end of *On the Soul,* Book I): "the several parts of the soul are indisseverable from one another, although the whole soul is divisible." See also Furst 4–9, on Aristotle's three parts of the soul and the Spaniards' view, with reference to Aristotle, that the Aztecs they encountered were at a pagan stage prior to the single-soul belief of Christian humanism. Cf. Sor Juana's *loa*, scene 4, lines 68–75, where the allegorical character of Religion (a Spanish lady) tries to convince the Aztec character, America, that the Christian God is also there in the New World, because "Providence" breathes a "vegetative soul" into the farmer's arm, the sky's rain, and the sun's warmth.

65. As Carrasco points out, the animistic force of teyolia pervaded both natural and man-made worlds. "Teyolia resided in mountains, lakes, towns, and temples" (*Religions* 70). See also López Austin 230–232. He translates the literal meaning of the Nahautl root word *yolia* as "he who animates" (230). According to Aztec myth, the gods themselves sacrificed their lives to give the sun animation.

66. See Read, "Sacred" 48–49, regarding *teyolia* in the "feeding exchanges" of Aztec human sacrifice.

67. *Tonalli* also bore the ancestral force of fate in the child's name (López Austin 212–213), somewhat akin to Lacan's *Nom-du-Père* (Name/No of the Father).

68. See also Furst 136–137. *Tonalli*, the life force as "heat" and personal destiny, was drilled by the god, Ometeotl, into the human embryo at conception. After the

child's birth *tonalli* could be increased through ritual exposure to fire and sun (or to other human beings). For further details on *tonalli* and *teyolia*, as well as the third animistic power, the foul-smelling *ihiyotl*, centered in the liver, see López Austin 204–236.

69. According to Carrasco, *Religions* 69, *tonalli* "infiltrated animals, gods, plants, humans, and objects used in rituals," i.e., both human and nonhuman objects. See also Furst 137: "The gods implanted the tonalli in the body [before birth] in a process similar to the drilling of gemstones, objects also believed to carry or receive life force." Clouds in the sky also carried the *tonalli* of dead ancestors, which then revitalized Aztec crops and culture through rain that fell from the clouds (178).

70. See Read, "Sun" 384, on the aesthetic arrangement of dead body parts in temple burial sites to "manipulate and take advantage of" animistic powers.

71. See, for example, Durán 80–81, 86–89, 94–95, on the rites for (and images of) the god Huitzilopochtli. See also Sor Juana's comparison of such rites to Catholic communion in her *loa* to *The Divine Narcissus*.

72. Aztec god-acting sometimes crossed gender lines, showing another relation to the feminine, maternal *chora*. For example, after a woman victim danced as Ilama tecuhtli, an aspect of the earth goddess, a priest costumed as the same goddess sacrificed her and then danced with her severed head (the center of her human/divine *tonalli*), while wearing a mask with huge lips and large eyes, "looking in two directions" (Sahagún 144). See also Clendinnen, *Aztecs* 249–250. For another example, see Durán 244, on the male Aztec performer wearing the skin of a woman who had been costumed and sacrificed as the goddess Xochiquetzalli.

73. Cf. Lupton 48, for her Lacanian view of the Renaissance iconography of flayed skin of St. Bartholomew (as imaginary other).

74. Cf. Carrasco, "Give" 15, on the "condensation of battlefield to city" through the Aztec use of blood, taken from the temple sacrifice to paint the lips of icons throughout the city.

75. See Wiles, *Tragedy* 202, where he argues that Euripides may have used sheep skulls as part of the set for his *Iphigeneia in Tauris*: "Orestes could well have seen hanging objects on the *skene*, permanent reminders of the threat of human sacrifice."

76. Cf. Read, "Sacred" 49: "From within this tightly knit cosmic *community*, [Aztec] people have a *moral* duty, then, to feed the hands that feed them. Without this necessarily bloody exchange [of human sacrifice], a worse violence will happen. . . ."

77. See also Boothby, "Altar-Egos," for a critique of Girard's model.

78. Cf. Michael Davis 42. He interprets Aristotelian catharsis as a purification of purity, revealing a similar sense of loss: "In exposing the dangers of idealizing, it is a pure critique of purity. . . . Tragedy thus beautifully depicts for us the consequences of the disparity between the beautiful and the real."

79. Cf. Moore 163, on the "animistic power" of cinema. See also Read, *Time*, especially 31–42, 197–198.

80. Cf. Lacan, *Seminar VII* 224: "What relation can there be between man and the return of the sunrise, if it is not the case that as a speaking man he is sustained in a direct relation to the signifier?"

81. See Londré and Watermeier, for a recent theatre history textbook that moves from the preconquest Maya and Aztec to the North American postmodern.

CHAPTER TWO
ROMAN, AZTEC, AND NFL "GLADIATORS"

1. Cf. Beacham 151. He refers to the complaints of Terence and Horace, yet develops a more complex view of the Roman audience. See also Harley 89, on the tendency of historiography to marginalize Roman "blood spectacles."

2. Cf. Plass 27. He briefly compares the theatricality of Roman gladiatorial games to various modern sports, especially professional wrestling as a "choreo-graphed . . . melodrama of good against evil violence, whose manifest artificiality calls for a special kind of involvement through self-deception on the part of the spectators." See also Jenkins, on WWF wrestling as a "fascist" melodrama that yet "lends it voice to the voiceless and champions the powerless" (76).

3. Cf. Skocpol and Somers 175. They outline three types of comparative his-tory: macro-causal analysis, parallel demonstration of theory, and contrast of contexts (175). My comparison of Roman, Aztec, and NFL gladiators primarily uses the second approach, though I will also consider contrasting contexts and psychocultural causes.

4. Cf. Futrell. He uses the approach of "enthnographic analogy" (169) to ana-lyze the Roman gladiatorial game as human sacrifice, by finding common patterns in many ancient cultures, including the Aztecs (171–173)—although his comparisons are brief. See also Plass 23–24, for a brief comparison of Roman and Aztec gladiators. He finds a similar purpose in both rituals: to exorcise violence by "taming" death. And see Kyle 220 on the display of decapitated heads by the Romans as well as Aztecs.

5. The royal decree in 1577 by Philip II of Spain to confiscate the bilingual ethnography of Spanish missionary Bernardino de Sahagún shows the threat of his work to his home culture, even if his ostensible purpose was to document Aztec ritual sacrifice and other cultural practices in order to convert native Mesoamericans to Christianity. See Taube 21.

6. A version of the ancient Mesoamerican ballgame is still played in certain areas of Mexico today, with aspects of modern soccer and basketball. See Scarborough and Wilcox vii; Santley, et al. 3.

7. Cf. Plass 30–32 and Futrell 48–49. The former (using Victor Turner's sense of "liminoid ritual") favors a cathartic theory of gladiatorial violence; the latter discredits it.

8. See Auguet 22: "The soothsayer Tiresias, moreover, formulates the implaca-ble law which rules the other world; only the souls who drink the blood of the sacri-fices will find once more some spark of life and the strength to speak."

9. See Auguet 22–23: "In the end, human blood, spilt in honour of the dead, could assure a permanent revival, that is to say a real deification."

10. This is the title that Mike Holovak, a former NFL coach, has given to his biography. Holovak's story begins with his memories as a soldier in World War II, then shifts to his football career.

11. For a Jungian view of team names and uniforms, see Odell 237–238.

12. For more on theatrical "ghosting," see Blau, *Audience*, and chapter 5 of *Take*.

13. On the greater aesthetic value of televised football, see Kostelanetz's 1969 essay, "Artistry in Football" (252–257).

14. Cf. Barton, *Sorrows* 5: "I have no way of knowing, finally, whether the Romans experienced desire the way that I myself or my contemporaries experience desire, but the assumption of a provisional comparability of human experience has given me the key to the decipherment of many particular behaviors. I may posit and desire difference, but I require comparability in order to interpret."

15. See Wistrand 13–19. Pliny valued arena sports and executions more than the art of theatre; he praised the emperor Trajan for sponsoring such edifying shows rather than theatrical plays (and for banning pantomimes). Even the Stoic philosopher and dramatist Seneca, while critical of arena violence as sadistic amusement, praised the example set by gladiators and criminals who demonstrated the freedom of dying bravely.

16. Cf. Wiles, *Masks* 130, on the Roman cult of the *imago:* "When a man of noble family died, a death mask was made using a wax mould. A person who had the same physique as the dead man, and had been trained in life to imitate him, sometimes a professional actor, would participate in the funeral as the living incarnation of the dead man."

17. See Fink, *Lacanian* 60, on second order *jouissance,* an "excitation due to sex, seeing, and/or violence," which substitutes for the lost, primal *jouissance* of mother-child unity. See also Whannel 199, for a distinction, applying Roland Barthes's theory of reading, between live audience *jouissance* (ecstasy) and the TV spectator's *plaisir* (pleasure) in watching sports.

18. On the relationship between *jouissance* and the death drive, see Ragland, *Essays* 33, 62, 80, 94–95.

19. On drama as an element in the ritual of modern sports, see Cheska.

20. Cf. Bloom's discussion of televised sports as unscripted, yet scripted (150–151).

21. For a full description of the festival, see Broda de Casas. See also Carrasco, "Give."

22. On the development of artificial turf in the football amphitheatre, see Rooney and Davidson, though they offer a "landscape perspective"—not a theatrical view.

23. On the historical development of home-team identification by NFL fans, see Oriard.

24. Cf. Guttmann, *Games* 113, on the nineteenth-century origins of American football: "The new game was immensely attractive to boisterous young men in need of some way to demonstrate the masculinity that their fathers and older brothers had recently proved on the bloody battlefields of the Civil War." See also Volkan, for an international, psychoanalytic view of how community identification depends upon hostility toward other groups.

25. This character in Sahagún's narrative was not a gladiator, but he was a captured warrior facing a similar sacrifice by heart extraction.

26. Sahagún reports that the visiting rulers from various cities (emperor Moctezuma's guests) were "confounded . . . undone and disunited" as they watched the gladiator fight and sacrifice (53). But this is certainly just one dimension of the effect of the spectacle on its elite spectators. Presumably the rival leaders also took pride in (even if not openly cheering) the skills demonstrated by fighters from their own city-state. This secret rooting would then relate to plans for further flower wars to capture more gladiators, on either side, for subsequent sacrificial spectacles. While the populace was entertained by a sports contest, given greater meaning through mythological costuming and the sacrificial climax of a divine script, the realpolitik of future warfare was rescripted—through further ritual arrangements by leaders of the dominant Tenochtitlan (Moctezuma's city) and its neighboring city-states. Some of those dominated cities and rulers also gave their warriors to Cortés, when he arrived and changed the game plan—a crucial contribution to the overthrow of Tenochtitlan's ritual theatre.

27. Sahagún's account suggests multiple scarring of the captive warrior by each of the four hometown Aztecs before the final score and fall. "Carefully they studied where they would smite him in a dangerous place, and cut him—perchance the calf of the leg, or the thigh, or his head, or his middle" (51). According to Sahagún if a captive beat all four attackers, he then faced a left-handed warrior who "wounded his arm and threw him flat upon the surface." See also the parallel account of Durán 179, which mentions that some captive warriors killed their attackers, despite having only a feathered club. Cf. Clendinnen, "Cost." She argues that there "must have been a system of timing of rounds or of counting passes or exchanges" (70). See also Clendinnen, *Aztecs* 94–95, where she describes the captive as having certain advantages, even though facing bladed clubs with just a feathered club, shield, and wooden balls. Also, she says, the attackers' goal was not to overpower him, but rather "in an exquisitely prolonged performance to cut the victim delicately, . . . to lace the living skin with blood," until the victim fell. Broda, however, reconstructs a briefer fight (215).

28. See Durán 179, where Fernando Horcasitas translates Tlahuahuanaliztli as "Marking or Scratching with the Sword." I offer an alternative translation to better fit my argument: one of the current meanings of the noun *score* (from the Anglo-Saxon *sceran*, to cut) is a scratch or mark.

29. The warrior's body would have born many scars, not just from the gladiatorial fight and battlefield. Every year, young Aztec males (including infants) were "cut on stomach, chest, and arms by the priests, to sign their commitment to Huitzilopochtli, god of the Sun and of War." Clendinnen, *Aztecs* 112.

30. Auguet 55 and Plass 43. See also Hopkins 4–5 and Futrell 14.

31. Indicating a parallel between football and modern warfare, General Schwarzkopf used the term "Hail Mary play" to describe America's final tank battle against Iraqi forces in the first Gulf War. This parallel resurfaced in the mass media when NFL player Pat Tillman gave up a multimillion dollar contract with the Arizona Cardinals to join the American military team in Afghanistan and was killed there, in spring 2004, by "friendly fire."

32. Cf. Carrasco's argument that the structuring of the gladiator spectacle and other events in Tlacaxipeualitzli created an "ideal battlefield" for the Aztec public to see warfare in a "dramatically controlled environment" ("Give" 15). See also Barton, *Sorrows* 37, on the Roman arena as an "apt metaphor for civil war"; and Edmonson on the "martial exploits" of gladiator fights as a fundamental theme of Roman culture. And see Guttmann, *From Ritual*, chapter 5, on the relationship between American football and war.

33. For an offensive lineman's testimony about the warlike violence of the NFL and his particular position, see Dobler and Carucci 18. For the views of a defensive player also well known for his violence on the field, see Tatum and Kushner. Jack Tatum, known as "the Assassin," is famous for "accidentally" breaking the neck of Darryl Stingley during a tackle in 1978, causing permanent paralysis and nearly killing the wide receiver (137–138). In August 2001, a veteran Minnesota Viking lineman, Korey Stringer, actually died during training camp due to the rigors of the sport and "heat exhaustion." Several college football players also died that summer during voluntary practice sessions.

34. Cf. Vince, "Ritual." He interrelates the dance elements of ancient Greek theatre, sports, and warrior training.

35. See Sahagún 51. *Cuetlachtli* is translated as "Old Mountain Lion" in Durán 178 and as "Old Bear" by Carrasco, "Give" 7, who says this figure was dressed in a bear skin. See also Broda 213.

36. The term "sustenance rope" is mentioned by Carrasco, "Give" 7.

37. See Clendinnen, "Cost" 83–84.

38. See Clendinnen, *Aztecs* 112, 174–179.

39. Clendinnen, "Cost" 76, offers further interpretations. The slitting of the captive's skin (in the role of Xipe) "represented the early spring, when the husk of the seed must be pierced if the sprouting life within is to break through, and when the winter-hardened skin of the earth is pierced by the new growth." She also emphasizes "the effusion of warrior blood" as sacred water to nourish the gods and the human community.

40. See Sahagún 52–53: "For when he took [the captive], he had said: 'He is my beloved son.' And the captive had said: 'He is as my beloved father.'" This is the reason Sahagún gives why the captor would not eat the flesh of the captive, in the ritual meal prepared by the captor's family. "He said: 'Shall I, then, eat my own flesh?'" See also Clendinnen, *Aztecs* 94: "The captive was in a deep sense the reflex of his captor, who accordingly took a tense and proprietary interest in the final performance." However, she argues that the father-son identification and the mourning of the "uncle" do not show tenderness or grief for the victim, but rather a blurring of the boundaries of the self: "the tears shed are shed for the victim, and his putative fate" (95).

41. See León-Portilla 203 on the Nahua (Aztec) sense of "life as a kind of dream, and time, *cahuitl*, as 'what is abandoning' us."

42. The Greek term *omphalos* refers to both the human navel and the navel of the earth, a sacred stone in the temple of Apollo at Delphi. Cf. Bronfen who ties the

omphalos, as "knotted scar," to birth and death (and to the Lacanian Real): "to the mortality of the child that sets in with birth" (84).

43. Cf. Puleo, who borrows from the research of Lloyd deMause to argue that the physical distress of the fetus in the third trimester and at birth, leaves "powerful memory traces" that Puleo ties to the myths and rituals of Judeo-Christianity, ancient Greece, and the Aztecs. In my view, though, Puleo oversimplifies ritual sacrifice: "the constant flow of blood among the Aztecs was a substitute for mothers' breast milk" (455). For another psychoanalytic oversimplification of Aztec sacrifice, see Reichbart 86.

44. Cf. Benjamin on the loss of ritual "aura" (unique presence) through the mechanical reproduction of art. But he also finds (in 1936) that "film responds to the shriveling of the aura with an artificial build-up of the 'personality' outside the studio," resulting in the "cult of the movie star" (231).

45. Cf. the conclusion of Boothby's essay, "Altar-Egos," on the "space of jouissance" as the essence of sacrifice (60).

46. See Carrasco, *Religions* 68–69. See also Furst 136–137 and López Austin 209–218.

47. Cf. Duverger, who likens the Aztec release of *tonalli* through blood sacrifice to today's release of nuclear energy by atom splitting (369–370). He also points out that Aztec heart extraction would have produced 5–6 litres of blood, "the most dramatic hemorrhaging that could be obtained by any means of slaughter" (383). Cf. also Ingham, who asserts that "in human sacrifice the victim's fear released part of his or her *tonalli* and concentrated the remainder in the heart" (392); but he does not account for the significance of the victim's blood during the gladiatorial combat.

48. See Read, "Sacred Commoners" 49. Cf. the statement by Salvian, a fifth-century bishop, about the Roman games: "the victims seem devoured almost as much by the eyes of the audience as by the teeth of beasts" (160). Also qtd. in Guttmann, "Roman" 13.

49. See Carrasco, *Religions* 70: "All important landscapes and living entities had *teyolia* or 'heart.' Each community had an *altepeyollotl* or heart of the town, a living divine force sometimes represented in a sculpture or decorated image."

50. Cf. Vince, "Ritual" 74–75, on the brutality, yet "patient endurance" (*kartereia*) of Greek combat sports.

51. See Barton, *Sorrows* 13–14, 25–31. On the possibility of gladiatorial combats prior to 264 BCE (in Etruscan rites), see Futrell 14–19. He also notes that Roman funeral *munera* probably began in the public space of the Forum, which influenced the development of the public games (35).

52. See Coleman, who lists from various sources: a forest that rose into view along with rain falling from a sprinkling system above (and perfumed water for the audience); a wooden mountain with real plants, a stream flowing, and wild goats, which sank out of sight; and a cage in the shape of a ship that broke open to release hundreds of animals (52).

53. Coleman describes this battle and others staged by various Roman emperors between fictional Tyrians and Egyptians, Athenians and Persians, Corcyreans and Corinthians, Athenians and Syracusans (71).

54. See Edmondson 74 on the standard "classical" program: "morning beast-hunts, followed by lunchtime executions, completed by gladiatorial combats in the afternoon."

55. For other examples (from various sources) of mythic characters in public executions, see Coleman 60–70. See also Edmondson 73 and Barton, *Sorrows* 61. Barton calls such executions in mythological guise "snuff plays."

56. Glover, in a footnote, translates "Jove's brother" as Pluto. Cf. Auguet 55 and Futrell 232–233n20, who see the Etruscan Charon (or Charun) in this role.

57. See Auguet 59–60, Hopkins 25, and Junkelmann 45–64.

58. See Edmondson 96 on specific classes of gladiators.

59. See Auguet 65, who notes that "only criminals of free condition had the right to this noble weapon [the sword]. . . ."

60. See Edmondson 72: "Certain types of gladiators were identified as Rome's toughest adversaries: Samnites, Gauls, and Thracians. . . . The repeated appearance in the arena of these once potent military threats warned the Romans against relaxing their imperial grip. . . ."

61. "Women as well as men played at being gladiators and *venatores* (wild-beast hunters), both in and out of the arena" (Barton, *Sorrows* 66). See also Hopkins 23: "Women, even women of high status, fought in the arena." See Guttman, "Appeal" 12, and "Roman" 12, for examples from the Roman writers Petronius, Dio, and Juvenal, of women who fought from chariots, were pitted against dwarves, and faced wild boars.

62. See Barton, *Sorrows* 37. See also Junkelmann 33.

63. See also Auguet 196–197.

64. Cf. Bataille 55–57 on Aztec sacrifice as consumption or "communion," seeking a lost intimacy. See also Roach 131, 146–148.

65. Cf. Russell, "Violent," and Guttmann, *From Ritual* 134. Russell directly refutes the catharsis theory of sports violence. Guttmann presents a "modified version" of it as valid, specifically with regard to football spectatorship, in the "release of normally proscribed and inhibited behavior." See also Russell, "Psychological" 168–171, for a survey of catharsis research in sports media.

66. See Welch, and Simons and Taylor. Welch finds that "touchdown scorers" (NFL receivers and running backs) are more often involved in violent crimes against women than are players at other positions. Simons and Taylor offer a survey of sociological research on fan violence and delineate specific factors, such as "dehumanization of the opposition," "modeling," and "score configuration." See also Bryant, who summarizes various studies and concludes that "hatred [of the other team] . . . can propel viewers to enjoy extreme violence, even that resulting in mutilation and death, as long as the hated foe is the victim" (288).

67. See also Auguet's chapter 6, "The Reign of the Star," especially 162. And see Ewigleben 133, on the souvenirs of gladiator scenes that were sold to fans.

68. According to Auguet 60–61, two gladiators who fought long enough to satisfy the crowd, without either overcoming the other, might both receive "the palm of victory" and live to fight another day. But gladiator battles designated as *munera sine missione* could only end in death.

69. Juvenal, *Satires* 6.102. I have used the translation in Hopkins 23. See also Auguet 166–170.

70. See Wistrand 15 on Pliny's praise of the emperor Trajan for supplying arena spectators with such a spectacle. See also Barton, *Sorrows* 32, on the glory of wounds for Roman soldiers and gladiators.

71. Cf. Kerr, *Motivation* 127–128, on the practice in rugby of "raking" an opposing player's back (with cleats).

72. Cf. deMause, who goes farther than I in describing the primal joy and terror inside the mother's body—of the fetus attached to and fighting with the nurturant and poisonous placenta—prior to the separating oedipal father (Freud) or the castrative phallic mother (Klein). DeMause interprets both ancient sacrifice and current political events in relation to the collective memory of a poisonous placenta.

73. On high school and college football as a masculine initiation rite, involving the infliction of pain by coaches, see Sabo and Panepinto.

74. A great player might evoke tragic emotions if he chokes on the fatal play, or shows he has aged past his former glory days. A severe injury on the field, stopping the action of the game, may cause players and fans to contemplate their own mortality. A referee's bad call, especially as shown through slow-motion replay, might set up a team's tragic, yet heroic struggle against the unfairness of higher powers or their apparent fate that day. Certain NFL players, such as O. J. Simpson, have become even more famous for their tragic lives off the field in conflict with the law and mortality. Simpson had already retired from a record-breaking career when his stardom changed through his murder trial. Recently, though, the football careers of two Carolina Panthers, Fred Lane and Rae Carruth, ended prematurely as the former became a victim and the latter a convicted perpetrator in separate murder cases.

75. Cf. Auguet 196–197.

76. See Fink, *Lacanian* 96–97, 99–100, on Lacan's theory of surplus *jouissance* and Marx's of surplus value. See also Boothby, *Death* 173–174, on the symbolic death drive of *jouis-sens* (ecstatic meaning) as a sublimation of the imaginary and actual violence of *jouissance*.

77. A certain TV commerical, showing the basketball star Michael Jordan drinking Gatorade, directly expressed the goal of identification between star, fan, and product: "Be like Mike."

78. See Futrell 50, who notes that imperial Rome had a professional army of largely non-Roman soldiers. "The Roman urbanite was no longer required to serve on the front lines. He could perhaps now find the emotional equivalent of actual warfare at the arena."

79. Cf. Megen.

80. Cf. Sabo and Panepinto, Beisser, Bianchi, and Farrell.

81. See also Edmondson 100 and Auguet 52.

82. See Edmondson 83 and Barton, *Sorrows* 63–64.

83. Hopkins notes that at least nine emperors "practised as gladiators or fought in gladiatorial contests" (20). He describes the gladiatorial games as "political theatre" and the vocal relations between audience and emperor as a kind of "parliament" (16–17). Cf. Plass 76 and Auguet 170–173, 184–190.

84. From Seneca's letter to Lucilius, *Epistle* 7.3–5, quoted and translated in Wistrand 17. See also Hopkins 3 and Auguet 66–67, who quotes the same passage and then calls the crowd: "the leading actor in these bloody dramas." See Coleman 57–59 and Wistrand 35 for further evidence of audience participation.

85. See Edmondson 86 and Auguet 35–36. While seating was segregated, the Roman games were free, paid for by magistrates competing for public status, or by the emperor. See Coleman 50–51 and Hopkins 6–7.

86. In European football, fan violence has become a regular part of the sport's ritual, especially in Great Britain. See Kerr, *Understanding*, and also *Motivation* chapter 7, which analyze fans' and players' arousal and "addiction" to violence in soccer and rugby, using "reversal theory." For a Jungian view of player and fan addiction to sports violence, cf. Heyman 197.

87. Cf. the brief discussion of sports "communion" in Goethals 6–7.

88. Ovid, *The Art of Love* 1.165–170. Qtd. and trans. in Plass 31. Cf. Edmondson 98–99.

89. Cf. Wilkerson, "And Then" 63, about an Aztec sculpture of the sacred ballgame that shows the ball itself as a skull.

90. Cf. Thayer A. Greene, who relates the Mesoamerican ballgame to ball play in ancient Egypt as a "fertility rite"—and thus to modern sports as an "archetypal source for the activation of the libido" (38).

91. See Santley et al. 14–15. See also Wilkerson, "And Then" 45, on the prophetic significance of a ballgame played between two Aztec rulers shortly before the arrival of the Spanish conquistadors.

92. See also Edmondson 99.

93. See also Plass 64–65 for a specific application of Turner's formula to Roman gladiatorial games.

94. Cf. Russell, "Psychological"; Crabb and Goldstein; and Schweitzer et al.

95. Futrell concludes her book by relating gladiatorial combat to the mythical "foundation sacrifice" of Romulus killing his twin brother Remus and to the "purgative" blood spilt in the Roman civil war (210–212).

96. Cf. Coleman 47: "the public nature of Roman execution shows that one purpose of humiliating the miscreant was to alienate him from his entire social context,

so that the spectators, regardless of class, were united in a feeling of moral superiority as they ridiculed the miscreant."

97. See also Gould, where Futrell finds his "paradigm" of tragic and melodramatic identification (246n191). Gould actually describes a third type of audience identification not mentioned by Futrell (and not so applicable to the Roman games): sentimental, as opposed to tragic or melodramatic. Gould argues that the effect of violence on film and television, as well as in literature and theatre, is worse when tearfully sentimental rather than truthfully tragic, and worst of all when vengefully melodramatic.

98. Cf. Bryant and Zillman's concluding question on today's media theatre: "Are we, then, regressing toward more violence in sports—toward gladiator-like combat?" (209).

99. Seneca, *Epistles* 7.4. Qtd. in Wistrand 17. See also Hopkins 3 and Plass 68.

100. In his survey of various Roman writers, including the dramatist Seneca, Wistrand concludes that they valued the gladiatorial shows more than theatre because the former exemplified social control, while the latter exhibited softness and indecency (69). Cf. Auguet 190–199.

101. See Wistrand 16–20 on Seneca's stoic attitude toward the gladiatorial audience and players. Wistrand mentions three examples of Seneca praising suicidal gladiators, including a convict who killed himself by sticking his head into the spokes of a cart en route to his arena execution (19). See also Barton, *Sorrows* 21, on Seneca's praise for gladiators fighting without regard to their own wounds, and 31–32 on his philosophical emulation of gladiatorial fierceness, shown by the warrior's glory in his wounds.

102. The recent Oscar-winning film *Gladiator* begins as a potential tragedy, with a dying emperor, Marcus Aurelius, who has failed as a father, and the triumphant, yet exhausted general, Maximus, who wants to return home to his family. But it soon turns into a conventional melodrama about the general's revenge as heroic gladiator against the villainous emperor, Commodos, who kills his father, Marcus Aurelius, and orders the execution of Maximus's family.

103. Tertullian gives this account of watching criminals executed as god-actors: "We laughed at the mockery of the gods in the lunch-hour spectacle" (trans. in Coleman 55). See also Coleman 68. Tertullian similarly says of the gladiatorial attendant as god-actor: "We have laughed, amid the noon's blend of cruelty and absurdity, at Mercury using his burning iron to see who was dead" (*Apology* 15.5).

104. See Rose and Friedman on sports programs as "open-ended, cyclical, and melodramatic" (2), producing multiple identifications and a "distracted" male viewer, very much like the female viewer of melodramatic soap operas, who relates to the characters as intimates and extensions of her own world (7). They also suggest, using Kracauer, that the distraction of TV sports usually masks truth, yet it can also be "redemptive" by exposing "true disorder" (11); perhaps this relates to what I am calling tragic awareness. Cf. Russell's brief mention of tragic moods in "Psychological" 167–168.

105. See Futrell 78–79, 170, 189. He explains that the Romans transformed Nemesis into the "goddess of athletic competition"—not as "a vindictive judge and

jury [like the Greek goddess] but as the power of changing fortune" (113–114). In my view, this would support the argument that the Roman games were tragic as well as melodramatic theatre, although Futrell does not make that connection. See also his description of Roman alienation in the "faceless individual" for whom the games and goddess "offered a release" (117–118)—which I would parallel to the mass-media spectator of sports today.

106. See Bracher, "Editor's" 4: "every instance in which a subject accepts an identity (or aspect of identity) from an Other demands a sacrifice of part of the subject's own being and enjoyment, and this forced sacrifice produces aggressivity, because it is experienced (unconsciously if not consciously) as a wounding attack by the Other."

107. On the expansion of American "gridiron football" to Europe, to compete with other sports for TV fans, see Guttmann, *Games* 113–119. Guttmann's research shows that, as of 1990, there were over a hundred American football teams in each of the following countries: Italy, Germany, and Britain (and 60 in France). In the 1990s the NFL created its own professional league in Europe with an April-to-June season (climaxing in a "World Bowl") involving six teams: Rhein Fire, Frankfurt Galaxy, Berlin Thunder, Scottish Claymores, Amsterdam Admirals, and Barcelona Dragons. The Arena Football League (AFL) also emerged in the 1990s in the United States with a spring season played on an indoor field, half the length of the NFL's.

CHAPTER THREE
CHORAL EDGES IN *FRANKENSTEIN*
AND *NATURAL BORN KILLERS*

1. In an interview on the 1996 "director's cut" video, Stone says that many younger filmmakers think violence is "cool and hip" and make a career out of that. But to him this is "morally . . . repugnant" because he has been in Vietnam and seen "the effects of guns."

2. Cf. Perlmutter on the Judeo-Christian repression of pagan nature religions in this film (135–136) and in calls for censorship of media violence more generally. Perlmutter boldly states that "violence in the media does not reflect or inspire violence in real life. The depiction of violence in film is a theological form of idolatry that invokes a cathartic form of ritual participation in its viewers" (140). But she does not consider various aspects of catharsis, nor degrees of participation, nor types of spectators, nor modes of plot and character onscreen.

3. In Quentin Tarantino's original screenplay, there is a similar line (38). Yet much of his script between the opening and ending scenes was changed by Stone and other writers (David Veloz and Richard Rutowski), who added the tragicomic romance and furthered the social critique. See Kagan 227–229, 246–247, and Salewicz 95–97.

4. The image of the warden's disembodied head was edited out to get the "R" rating for the initial release, but restored in the 1996 "director's cut" on video. According to Stone, 150 trims and cuts were made, mostly in the riot and initial cafe scenes (Bouzereau 61).

5. Cf. Kagan 234–235, 246; Courtwright; and Stone 242–248. Stone's own view of the film sounds Brechtian, as well as "deconstructivist" (the term he uses). In the 1996 director's cut video, Stone says: "You're aware of watching a movie . . . so you're constantly aware of the shifting points of view." More recently, Stone wrote: "it's violent . . . it's also *looking at* violence in our contemporary society and *showing* at the same time, through its weird graphics and montage, just how nutty it's gotten" (242). Claiming it is "the best film" he has made, he adds: "I can't be blamed for the literal interpretation of it by certain morons and unstable people, any more than the Bible can be blamed for its culture of violence" (244). See also his comments in Silet 126–129 and in Bouzereau 64–67, where Stone mentions Nietzsche's theory of "beyond good and evil," while presenting a more Artaudian view of cinematic catharsis as a sickening, burning, and cleansing—in his own *Natural Born Killers* and in Kubrick's *A Clockwork Orange*.

6. Kristeva's sense of the semiotic *chora,* as "Enclosed Space of Becoming," ties the disruptive function of the Lacanian Real to the role of the mother's body, as primary lost object, in the development of the infant's ego through imaginary and symbolic orders. I extend that connection to the role of a Dionysian chorus, as birthplace (Nietzschean "womb") of theatre's imaginary ego and symbolic frame—as the lost Real of ritual sacrifice, repressed by the art form, yet returning and disrupting it at specific edges and creases of the stage or screen. This relates also to the abject experiences, creative fantasies, and destructive potentials of any current audience, as choral element, watching at the edges of the stage or screen and carrying its effects into real life.

7. See, for example, Kaplan, *Women* 23–35, and Mulvey.

8. See the collection edited by Linda Williams, *Viewing Positions.*

9. Cf. Ragland, "Relation" 195, for a direct Lacanian critique of the feminist theory of the male gaze. See also the summary of various psychoanalytic critiques of feminist gaze theory (by Jacqueline Rose, Constance Penley, and Joan Copjec) in Stam, et al. 172–174.

10. See, for example, Vanessa R. Schwartz 105–111, who investigates the popularity of panoramas, but not their use in presenting plays onstage. See also Gunning 117–129, who relies greatly upon Maxim Gorky's comments (after watching Lumière's *The Arrival of a Train*) to alter the "myth" of precinematic spectatorship—without considering that Russian playwright's theatrical experiences and tastes.

11. Cf. Metz 73–78, on the play of presence and absence in cinematic fetishism, through "the *boundary* that bars the look" (77). See also 87n6, where Metz considers "the edge of the screen."

12. Cf. Perez's criticism of Lacanian film theory for not taking "proper cognizance of the screen as a space of representation . . . an imitation or mimesis in the Aristotelian sense" (17–18).

13. I mean "focal range" metaphorically and phenomenologically. But for a physical, historical comparison of theatre's "scalar" ranges as influential upon the development of early cinema, see Brewster and Jacobs, chapters 8 and 9.

14. On environmental theatre, see McNamara, Rojo, and Schechner, especially Schechner's essay. With the more obvious stage outline of proscenium theatre, actors and spectators also cross the border at times, redefining the edge. See Mittman for early historical examples.

15. See also Carlson, *Theories* 49.

16. See Metz 69–78. Cf. Brewster and Jacobs 12–13, for a brief reference to Diderot's eighteenth-century ideal of the invisible, fourth-wall spectator, as related to Metz's modern, fetishistic, film voyeur.

17. Cf. Lacan, *Seminar VII* 136, on the vanishing point in Renaissance perspective painting and architecture, including Palladio's Teatro Olimpico, which are "organized around emptiness"—anamorphically showing "that what we seek in the illusion is something . . . [that] transcends itself, destroys itself." See also Lupton and Reinhard 219–220 and Freedman. On Freud's "vanishing point" (or navel) of the dream, in relation to the art image, the Lacanian Real, and the ancient Greek *omphalos*, see Bronfen.

18. See Banham 999 on Torelli's seventeenth-century technology: "a swift, magical transformation of one scene to the next, creating an illusion akin to a cinematic dissolve which had a profound effect not only on design but on the evolution of theatrical forms."

19. For a recent reappraisal of Nietzsche's theory, see Hinden. For critiques of Nietzsche's theory, see Henrichs, "Loss," and Else (10–11). See also Silk and Stern's defense of Nietzsche, especially their refutation of Else (147). For an overview of others in this debate, see Hardin.

20. On Nietzsche's significance to postmodern theory, see Koelb, especially Higgins's essay. On the continued validity of *The Birth of Tragedy*, throughout Nietzsche's work and for philosophy today, see Porter. See also Lacoue-Labarthe 180–182.

21. Nietzsche's theory also corresponds to current social psychology on the loss of self in communal engulfment (or enmeshment). See Scheff, *Emotions* 49, 79, 101–104. He defines catharsis as a balance of Apollonian and Dionysian, thought and feeling—regarding stage and screen spectatorship (153–154). Cf. David Wiles, *Tragedy* 43.

22. Cf. Brewster and Jacobs, who trace theatre's influence on film to the historical development of early cinema directly from proscenium melodrama: "filmmakers, like pictorialist theatrical producers, saw themselves as presenting to audiences pictures of spaces in a represented world through a more or less fixed frame" (147). They argue that the convention of a rectangular film screen mimics the proscenium stage opening, although it was not initially the best shape for the use of light from a point source, which would have been a circle or square (168). They also discern a certain bias in current film studies against this connection to theatre (5).

23. Cf. Heath 11, where he finds in this quote from Bazin a "confirmation of the force of the frame, its definition as a 'view' that has ceaselessly to counter absence by the assertion of the coherence of its presence, its 'being-in-frame'." See also Deleuze, "Cinema" 177, for his analysis of the "out-of-frame" in relation to Bazin's screen as "mask."

24. Cf. Dixon, *It Looks*. He applies Kristeva's theory of the *chora* in his revision of gaze theory, but locates it simply in the "chorascular space" of the camera obscura (82)—missing the various technical and compositional elements involved in the *chora* of the gaze and its theatrical past.

25. Cf. Scheff, *Catharsis* 136: "An individual who is crying in the presence of others who are also crying is more able to be both a participant in, and an observer of, his or her own distress. It is in respect to social facilitation that television is the least advantageous form of mass entertainment for the purposes of catharsis."

26. See Oudart for his Lacanian theory of the cinematic suture, plus Heath, *Questions* 13–15, 87–101, and Silverman 200–206.

27. For an exploration of creases in the scene onstage, as designating female space in various periods of Western drama, see Scolnicov.

28. The film credits several male screenwriters, but also Peggy Webling's 1927–1930 stage play and "the novel of Mrs. Percy B. Shelley." Cf. Dixon, "Films" 169.

29. On the frame narratives of the novel, see Newman.

30. Compare, for example, how little Frankenstein says about his creature in the Whale film with his long description of the Monster and further troubled thoughts in Peake's play (143), taken almost verbatim from Mary Shelley's *Frankenstein*, chapter 5.

31. See Lavalley 246–250. He relates the melodramatic *Presumption* and comical Fritz to subsequent burlesques of the play and Shelley's novel, onstage and onscreen, from *Frankenstitch* and *Frank-n-steam* to Mel Brook's *Young Frankenstein* and the transsexual Frank-n-furter of *The Rocky Horror Picture Show*.

32. Peake's play moves from the Monster's creation, rejection, fight with his creator, and flight; to the DeLacey encounter (changed to a game with and murder of a child in Whale's first film version); to the monster's kidnapping of Frankenstein's young brother, William (somewhat like the novel); to a mob chase (like the film, unlike the novel); to an avalanche overcoming both Frankenstein and the monster onstage (like Whale's flaming windmill).

33. This last aspect is brought out more in Whale's 1935 sequel, *The Bride of Frankenstein*.

34. A contemporary critic stated: "I would not take my wife . . . to see this blue-devil" (quoted in Forry 4).

35. Peake has Frankenstein give the same description as in Shelley (56), with identical details about hair, teeth, and limbs—yet substitutes "cadaverous" for "yellow" skin, perhaps to better match the blue stage makeup and body suit.

36. Cf. Walsh 23: "film scholars have elaborated enthusiastically on the dialectic between the Imaginary and the Symbolic, while neglecting the dialectic between the Symbolic and the Real."

37. Kristeva's two realms derive from, yet do not simply parallel Lacan's three orders. See Allen 39–42, for a summary of Kristeva's theory of the *chora*, "where the

[Lacanian] real meets the imaginary." Unfortunately, Allen disavows the lacking, Lacanian spectator, in the mirror stage *méconnaissance* of cinema, as an "unlikely hypothesis" (142).

38. Cf. chapter 15 of Shelley's novel, where the Monster compares himself to both Adam and Satan, after reading *Paradise Lost*.

39. Cf. L. D. Friedman 61. While stressing "the intricate pattern of light and dark" throughout Whale's film, Friedman quickly represses the stage ghost here, calling the introduction "theatrical and readily dismissible."

40. Cf. Žižek, *Sublime* 79, 119–120, 132, 135, for his discussion of the "maternal Thing" (Freud's *das Ding*) in Lacanian theory.

41. Whale's film switches the first names of Victor Frankenstein and Henry Clerval (renaming them Henry Frankenstein and Victor Moritz), and makes Clerval/Moritz (played by matinee idol John Boles) a handsome, normal contrast to the hysterical, abnormal Frankenstein. Victor's shocked face in this scene, as he watches Frankenstein's experimental theatrics, also reflects the cinema spectator's normal male gaze—as double to the monstrous creator and creature.

42. See Klein 69–94, on the infant's fantasies of the mother's good/bad breast and womb.

43. The depiction of the Monster's primal alienation may also reflect the director's own experience of ostracism as a homosexual. See Curtis's biography and Condon's recent film about James Whale.

44. Cf. Shelley 186–187 (chapter 23), where Frankenstein sees the Monster at the window just after discovering Elizabeth's murdered body. See also 159 (chapter 20), where Frankenstein sees "the daemon at the casement" while he is creating a female monster for it, and is thus inspired, by the Monster's voyeuristic gaze and grin, to destroy the second creature.

45. Cf. Mulvey 203, who describes the gendered power of fetishism in cinema, with a female star's legs or face in close-up as "part of a fragmented body [that] destroys Renaissance space, the illusion of depth demanded by narrative." With *Frankenstein*, however, I would argue that the face and scream of Elizabeth (Mae Clark) invert the illusion of depth into the horror of proximity; the power of the screen's vanishing point is not destroyed, but rather intensified at the moment of her scream, as she sees the Monster who is now offscreen. Such an image (and sound) not only stops the "flow of the narrative," but also propels the story toward further illusions of depth in the subsequent chase and execution of the Monster. Cf. Zakharieva 740–741, on the Monster's "composite body" as related to cinematic montage.

46. See Lacan, *Four*, chapters 6–9, on the "gaze" as coming from the object, not just the spectator, and on the "stain" in Holbein's painting *The Ambassadors* (with its uncanny skull) as a prime example. See also Quinet.

47. Cf. Žižek, *Enjoy*, especially chapter 4, with specific examples from the films of Alfred Hitchcock and David Lynch. See also Žižek, *Looking* 88–106, on the "Hitchcockian blot" (i.e., stain) and 116–122 on the "Hitchcockian cut," producing the "gaze *qua* object."

48. This pre-mirror symbiosis is also illusory. See Ragland, *Essays* 43: "there is no symbiosis between the mother and child *qua* persons. Symbiosis occurs, rather, between signifiers, between objects, and within the order of signifiers Lacan calls the Other."

49. See Kristeva, "Within" 37–38, and *Desire* 133. See also Kristeva, "Ellipsis" 237, where she relates "echolalia" to cinema.

50. Cf. Barzilai 300–302, on Kristeva's own treatment of borderline patients, in which the analyst "echoes the echolalia of the patient."

51. Cf. Kristeva, "Ellipsis" 237: "At the intersection between the vision of a real object and hallucination, the cinematographic object brings into the *identifiable* . . . that which remains beyond identification: the drive unsymbolized, unfixed in the object—the sign—language, or, in more brutal terms, it brings in aggressivity."

52. See Dixon, "Films" 170–171. See also Prince, *Classical* 52–64, on various cuts that censors demanded due to suggestions of violence offscreen.

53. Cf. Shelley 108 (chapter 12), where the Monster gets a mirror stage view of himself by observing the "perfect forms of my cottagers," then the shock of his real, fragmented monstrosity in the "mirror" of a pool of water. This leads to his vengeful, envious gaze at the child William and woman Justine (and at the portrait of Franken-stein's dead mother) in chapter 16.

54. Peripety (plot twist) and recognition (discovery scene) are two essential ele-ments of tragic drama, according to chapters 10 and 11 of Aristotle's *Poetics*.

55. See Kristeva, "Ellipsis" 237, on the edges of tracking/terror in film: "once *frayage/frayeur* erupts into the *seen*, that *seen* stops being simply reassuring, trompe-l'oeil, or invitation to speculation, and becomes *fascinating specular*. Cinema seizes us precisely in this place."

56. Cf. Kristeva, *Powers* 14: "The sign represses the *chora* and its eternal return." See also 3: "as in true theater, without makeup and masks, refuse and corpses *show me* what I permanently thrust aside in order to live."

57. Cf. Klein 74. Disagreeing with Freud, she posits an earlier castration com-plex, in the infant's experience of a phallic mother through weaning and toilet train-ing: "in terms of psychic reality, she *is* also already the *castrator*."

58. See Kristeva, *Powers* 15: "The abject is the violence of mourning for an 'object' that has always already been lost."

59. The term "good enough mother" comes from objection-relations theorist D. W. Winnicott, attempting to cure the good/bad breast that Klein discovered. See Winnicott's *Playing and Reality*.

60. See Brecht's Lacanian statement before Lacan: "The continuity of the ego is a myth. A man is an atom that perpetually breaks up and forms anew. We have to show things as they are" (15).

61. The Bavarian character of the *Frankenstein* mob (and its setting in "Gold-stadt") may also reflect the real Nietzschean danger of a German *chora* in 1931, sensed by Whale's film.

62. See Artaud, *Theater* 15–32, 82. Also, cf. Nietzsche, *Genealogy*, on the slave's power of *ressentiment* against the master.

63. Cf. Bazin 105: "In contrast to the stage, the space of the screen is centrifugal."

64. For an exception, see Stam, *Reflexivity* 181–184, which considers the Artaudian roots of Godard's films.

65. See Brecht's call for the "literarization" of theatrical performance (43–44), as well as his use of scene legends and ironic song lyrics.

66. See also Artaud, *Theater* 48–67, on his desire for alchemical symbols (49) and hieroglyphic gestures (61).

67. Artaud was actually diagnosed as psychotic, while under the care of Jacques Lacan at the Sainte Anne asylum in Paris (1938–1939). See Barber 9, 99–100.

68. This role allowed Harrelson to show another side to his personality, very different from his comical "Woody" on the TV show *Cheers*. His own real-life father, Charles Voyde Harrelson, was convicted twice for murder, in 1968 and 1978 (when Woody was a child and teenager).

69. Stone joked about the prison setting in the film as "Frankenstein's castle" (Silet 127).

70. For critiques of this film, see Simpson 123–129; Caputi, "Small" 150–155; and Kinder, "Violence" 81.

71. Although Stone has described the alternate ending this way in print, it is, as shown in the director's cut video, far from a typical melodramatic ending. Instead of the cops catching Mickey and Mallory, they are shot by Owen, a fellow prison inmate who helped them escape during the riot. Sitting behind them, while Mickey drives the van, Owen shoots both killers—after Mallory refuses to have sex with him, briefly threatens him with her handgun, and Mickey pulls over, telling him to leave. This finale, with surreal imagery on the van's windows and flashes of Mickey driving with a pregnant Mallory and children, is an ironic and somewhat tragicomic ending, after the killers' triumphant manipulation of the villainous media and romantic escape from prison with Owen as their ally.

72. Cf. Horsley 2: 306, on the dimension of "tragedy" in the film's "I Love Mallory" scene.

73. Stone's *Natural Born Killers* parodies earlier films about outlaw lovers on the road, such as Arthur Penn's *Bonnie and Clyde* (1967) and Terrence Malick's *Badlands* (1973).

74. Cf. Heffernan, who mentions, while analyzing the *Frankenstein* films by Whale and Branagh, that the cinematic medium itself is like the Monster: "filmmaking itself is a Frankensteinian exercise in artificial reproduction" (139).

75. Cf. Branagh 21–23 on the casting and makeup of De Niro in the role, to overcome popular preconceptions about the Frankenstein monster, from Karloff's classic image to the Munsters and Addams Family—with a current, recognizable star "of medium height" and makeup that allowed his "face and expressions to be very clearly read." See also 174.

76. Cf. Branagh 26: "we have Victor and Elizabeth truly growing up in the course of two hours, and I think that that can happen when tragedy enters into people's lives in a major way. It forces them to think about what is meaningful."

77. See Lavalley 262–263 on why makeup man Jack Pierce chose to shape the head of Karloff's monster "like a lid," using tin and putty, to show it as reconstructed by Frankenstein in "the simplest way to open and recap the brain."

78. Mary Wollstonecraft Godwin died from postpartum hemorrhage eleven days after Mary Godwin (later Shelley) was born in 1797. In 1815 Mary Shelley gave birth to a premature female child who died within two weeks. A couple of weeks later she wrote in her journal: "Dream that my little baby came to life again; that it had only been cold, and that we rubbed it before the fire, and it lived" (qtd. in Scott xviii). In 1816 she gave birth to another child, William. About 6 months later she began writing Frankenstein, after Byron proposed a story-telling competition. Later that year her half-sister, Fanny, died, and Mary read her mother's book, A Vindication of the Rights of Woman. In 1817 she gave birth to Clara, who died the next year, the same year the novel was first published anonymously. Mary Shelley continued to revise it, after the death of William in 1819, after a miscarriage when she almost died herself in 1822, and after her husband Percy's death a few weeks later. She published a second and third edition of the novel in 1823 and 1831. Cf. Branagh 20–21 on his awareness of such details.

79. In chapter 3 of the novel, the mother dies in a different way. Frankenstein tells how she caught the scarlet fever from Elizabeth, curing her daughter but not herself. On her deathbed she told her son and adopted daughter to marry each other—and that she wanted Elizabeth to take her place as mother to her younger children. Thus, the novel presents a double incest between Victor and his sister Elizabeth, who becomes his wife and mother-substitute, through his dying mother's desire. Branagh's film ties the mother's death directly to Victor's drive to give birth himself, using dead bodies, without these incestuous twists. Cf. Lehmann 178–179 on Branagh's "matricide" and "hysterical hardbody" in this film.

80. On the relation between lightning (and the light/darkness motif) in Whale's film and in Shelley's novel, see L. D. Friedman.

81. Cf. Frost 81, who describes Branagh's "Iron Maiden" womb, giving birth to the creature, as a "sinister mechanistic parody of female anatomy [that] harks back to the evil robot in Fritz Lang's silent sf classic Metropolis (1926)." See also Branagh 166, on the scrotumlike sack above the metal womb, containing electric eels that were released through a phallic shoot into the rebirthing sarcophagus.

82. Cf. Laplace-Sinatra 262–263, who views Victor's dance with his Monster as "an enticing parody of sexual intercourse which reflects the homosexual side of his character in the film as well as the novel." Cf. also Frost 81: "the two of them slip and flounder around like a couple of geriatric waltzers."

83. Cf. Branagh 27, where he briefly mentions the "incestuous side" of the relationship between Victor and Elizabeth in his film.

84. This planting of false evidence is similar to the novel, but the film shows Victor's picture in the locket rather than his mother's. Chapter 16 of Shelley's novel also

more clearly expresses the creature's mirror-stage motive for putting the blame on Justine: his admiration for and erotic attraction to, yet alienation from and vengeance against, her beauty. Cf. Heffernan 137–139, 150–152.

85. Cf. Heffernan 154, who emphasizes the male Monster's mirror stage in this scene, rather than Elizabeth/Justine's.

86. Cf. Elin Diamond, *Unmaking*, on her theory of gestic feminist criticism. The Brechtian idea of gest, or *Gestus*, involves specific gestures an actor makes onstage that express and critique social attitudes.

87. Cf. Zakharieva 750–751 for a more melodramatic, feminist view of Elizabeth's self-destruction. "Branagh's film . . . maintains this dichotomy of wronged and violated Nature/Woman/Good *versus* Science/Man/Evil." See also Badley, who mentions that Branagh's film brings "a feminist reading to the forefront" (91).

88. Cf. Parker et al. 6–8 on various details of make-up design and technology for the Monster's face (and body), from stitches in the early scenes to scarring in later scenes. But the question of why Frankenstein cut and restitched the face is not addressed—except in the idea that "this is not one man" (11).

89. See Fink, *Lacanian* 99–100.

90. See Creed, chapter 3, on Regan's semiotic *chora* and devilish rebellion, as a menstruating female—not possessed by a male demon.

91. In *Alien* Ripley becomes the sole survivor on a spaceship infected by the alien creature, as she fights against it and against an android crewman (Ash) to "purge" the ship of the monster. In *Aliens* Ripley leads other soldiers (and a male android) to fight the alien creatures who have taken over a human settlement on a distant planet, also battling the inept commander and the villainous company man. In *Alien3* Ripley battles a brotherhood of convicts on another planet where she has crash-landed (losing the child Newt, whom she saved in the previous film). She eventually turns the male criminals into an organized fighting force to eradicate the alien creatures from their prison. In *Alien: Resurrection* Ripley is reborn as a clone of the alien creature, with her body's womb used to create an alien-human hybrid, as biological weapon. She joins forces with a female android (who had been sent to kill her) and several male space-pirates to fight the alien monsters that are her own children and grandchildren. Thus, the first film presents the horror of the death drive in outer-space life; the second in the home settlement invaded by nature; the third in society's criminal element; the fourth in biological experimentation (more like *Frankenstein*).

92. Cf. Crane 30, who uses Kristeva's theory of the abject to specify a certain cathartic effect (without using that term) beyond the simple purging of emotion. See also Badley, chapter 3, for a look at various "progeny" of *Frankenstein*, "in the post-Lacanian mirror of the mass media," with the Monster as "body myth and cultural icon," from zombie to cyborg to serial killer (70).

93. Perhaps because of its challenging, tragic edges, Branagh's *Frankenstein* was not successful commercially. According to the Internet Movie Database, it cost $45 million to produce in 1994, yet grossed only $22 million in the United States and much less than that in Europe. Whale's more melodramatic original, on the other hand, cost $291,000 in 1931, yet grossed $12 million.

CHAPTER FOUR
BRECHTIAN AND AZTEC VIOLENCE IN ZOOT SUIT

1. See Martin for a linguistic analysis of the use of Spanish in Zoot Suit.

2. Zoot Suit also shows the influence of the American theatre's Living Newspaper technique of the 1930s and of the Mexican-American carpa (tent-show) tradition. See Ramírez 195–198, Worthen 106–113, and Huerta, "Chicano Agit-Prop." See also Huerta, Chicano Theater 188–189, on the Aztec tlaquetzque as "ancient predecessors of Chicano teatros in the United States."

3. Cf. the positive reviews of the film by Aufderheide and Berg.

4. See Bruce-Novoa on the "origin myth" (constructed by historian Jorge Huerta) of Valdez's leadership of El Teatro Campesino.

5. Cf. Brokaw 252: "Some charged that he [Valdez] had lost touch with the Chicanos' past; that in fact he was idealizing it by ignoring the rather unsavory parts and exaggerating or inventing the good." See also the more recent critique by Sanchez-Tranquilino and Tagg 562, 569.

6. Artaud (like Valdez) even went so far as to invoke Aztec ritual sacrifice in his outline for a play he never staged, called The Conquest of Mexico: "Montezuma cuts the living space, rips it open like the sex of a woman in order to cause the invisible to spring forth" (130).

7. See Broyles-González 210, who critiques the film version as more internalized than the stage version, "subordinat[ing] the historical reality to a self-absorbed individual psyche." Cf. Valdez's own view of this internal focus in Orona-Cordova 108. See also Valdez's comparison of the audience relationship to the stage play and film: "You couldn't get that close to El Pachuco on stage and now you'll be into his nostrils" (Barrios 160).

8. See Orona-Cordova 101–104, for Valdez's personal account of the pachucos that he met in the 1950s, who gave rural Chicanos an urban identity. Valdez offers as an example the farm worker union leader César Chávez, "who was a Pachuco" (104). See also the Herms interview from 1978, where Valdez states: "the Pachuco to this day among Chicano youth is still a symbol, because he represents all of those qualities that they need in order to go on in the streets" (268). The zoot-suited pachuco also appears in Valdez's earlier works with El Teatro Campesino; see Los Vendidos and Bernabé in Early Works. See also Huerta, Chicano Theater 197, about a certain scene in Bernabé "that recalls the Aztec [heart] sacrifices."

9. Cf. Valdez's statement in Savran, In Their Own Words 261: "Brecht looms huge in my orientation." See also Huerta, "Chicano Agit-Prop," 48, 53.

10. See Valdez's own statements on the Pachuco in his interview with Orona-Cordova (98). Valdez calls him "the rebel"—and says he is both good and bad as Henry's "internal authority."

11. For a psychoritual analysis of the historical zoot-suit riots and Sleepy Lagoon case, see Mazón. On Valdez's personal contact with members of the Leyva family (after the death of Henry), during his research for Zoot Suit, see the Burciaga interview.

12. Valdez comments on this added dialogue in Orona-Cordova 104: "Unfortunately we still see a lot of people that court the Gringo and go after the Gringo, and they can't do the same thing with their Raza out of some failure in themselves to be able to deal with who they are and accept that." Here Valdez also responds to critics who have charged him with courting the Gringo in making mainstream Hollywood films; he implies that he is courting la Raza, too, and helping his people to deal with who they are.

13. See Davis and Diamond 124.

14. See Valdez in Orona-Cordova 100. See also Broyles-González 199. Tezcatlipoca also appears in Valdez's poem "Pensamiento Serpentino," but there he is associated with the devil and with Hernán Cortés (*Early Works* 196–198). Cf. Jorge Huerta's introduction to *Zoot Suit*, where he relates El Pachuco, as Henry's alter ego, to the Aztec concept of *nahual* or "other self" (15).

15. The zoot suit ideal and the stripping of El Pachuco might also be related to the god Xipe Totec (the Flayed One) and the wearing of human skins in Aztec rites. See *La Conquista de Mexico* (1968), a puppet show by Valdez and El Teatro Campesino, for a brief, satirical scene of Aztec human sacrifice (*Early Works* 55).

16. I am referring, of course, to Calderón's *Life Is a Dream*. But Valdez himself has related this point in the film to Shakespeare's *The Tempest* (Orona-Cordova 105).

17. See Gutiérrez-Jones 72, for a Foucauldian view of El Pachuco's reversal of the Press's panoptic gaze.

18. For Valdez's own explanation of this aesthetic choice, in relation to past and present social realities, see the Herms interview 270.

19. See Tyler on the popularity of the zoot suit among blacks and the response of the black press in the 1940s.

20. See the Valdez interview in Savran, *In Their Own Words* 265. See also Huerta, *Chicano Theater* 201, and Herms 260, on the appearance of Quetzelcoatl in Valdez's *La Gran Carpa de los Rasquachis*.

21. Cf. Booth 425 on Tezcatlipoca, "whose fetish was the flint knife."

22. See Žižek, *For They* 139–140n25. See also Boothby, *Death* 171–172 on the "force of the real" in the superego as "representative of the id" and "engine of the death-drive."

23. See Babcock 223; Sanchez-Tranquilino and Tagg 562, 569; Mazón 119; and Broyles-González 203–204.

24. See Fregoso, "Homegirls," for other films that fully explore the *pachuca* character.

CHAPTER FIVE
MARTYRS AND SCAPEGOATS
IN THE FILMS OF SCORSESE AND COPPOLA

1. Of course, Scorsese and Coppola are not the sole creators of their films. But they did strive for full creative control, while working with or fighting against their

co-writers and producers. See Chown, especially 8–15 and 143–147, on auteur theory in relation to Coppola.

2. For a brief comparison of Martin Scorsese and James Joyce as would-be priests, see Kelly 124.

3. Ronald Librach argues that Big Bill Shelley in *Boxcar Bertha* is the only one of Scorsese's heroes "granted the privilege of consummated martyrdom," unlike Travis Bickle in *Taxi Driver*, whose suicidal shot fails (15). Apparently, Librach does not consider Jesus' death in Scorsese's *The Last Temptation of Christ* as a consummated martyrdom.

4. See also Prince, "Aesthetic" 198–199.

5. Scorsese compares Travis to both St. Paul and Charles Manson: "It's the power of the spirit on the wrong road"—also pointing out Travis's "paranoia" as a war veteran (*Scorsese* 62).

6. Schrader did not see the script as cathartic for Travis, despite the bloody purge of his enemies. "I think the syndrome is just going to start all over again" (qtd. in L. S. Friedman 73).

7. "You think that you're gonna, in a way—exorcise those feelings. . . . [But] it isn't enough just to put it on the screen. You've still got to work at changing . . . the feelings of anger . . ." (Scorsese, *Martin* 65).

8. Hinckley fired six bullets at Reagan as he entered his limousine. The first hit secretary Jim Brady in the head; the second hit police officer Tom Delahanty in the neck; the third almost hit presidential aide Michael Deaver; the fourth hit Secret Service agent Tim McCarthy in the stomach; the fifth hit the limousine window; the last bounced of the rear fender and entered Reagan's chest (Clarke 7–8).

9. Before his killing spree, Travis shaves the sides of his head in a way, according to Scorsese, that the Special Forces did "before they went out on patrol in North Vietnam" (*Martin* 61). See also Keyser 73.

10. See also Taubin 20, where she calls Travis's date with Betsy at the porn theatre: "psychological rape."

11. See Grist 145; L. S. Friedman 69, 149–150; and Taubin 62. Sport looks like an Indian with his long hair and calls Travis a "cowboy" in their second meeting. But Travis wears a Mohawk haircut when he faces Sport for the final showdown and Sport does not recognize the cowboy disguised as an Indian. Cf. Slotkin on the myth of regeneration through Western movie violence.

12. Cf. Grist 149, who finds "ritual purification," "intimations of martyrdom," and "a predetermined, self-sacrificial but implicitly redeeming fate" in this scene.

13. Cf. Sharrett 223, 228, and 231, about *Taxi Driver* showing "the failure of American sacrificial violence," with Travis assuming "the position of God but also of simple aggressor," and by acquiescing to "martyrdom . . . in the tradition of American melodrama." See also Keyser 81–84 on the film's struggle to transcend melodrama and on Scorsese's denial of responsibility for Hinckley's crime.

14. See Scorsese, *Martin* 68: "I like the idea of spurting blood . . . it's like a purification, you know, the fountains of blood." See also Schrader 20.

15. Scorsese himself calls the scene a "blood sacrifice" and relates it to Christ on the cross as a "human sacrifice" that replaces animal sacrifice: "you know, no more ritualistic sacrifice of lambs" (Martin 60–61). He also sees Travis as "a would-be saint, a Saint Paul," like Charlie in Mean Streets (qtd. in L. S. Friedman 67).

16. See Taubin 74 on another killer, in addition to Hinckley, who possibly copied Travis Bickle. Cf. Grist 152, who sees the overhead shot at the end of the massacre as distancing the audience "to contemplate the implications of our identification." He argues that the film "exposes Travis's moral crusade . . . as destructive fanaticism," but does not consider further fan identification leading to real-life destructiveness, as with Hinckley.

17. Cf. Horsley 1: 153, who sees this scene as fixing a weak spot in the film's classic Western precursor, The Searchers.

18. Schrader also says this in an interview at the end of a videocassette version of the film.

19. Cf. L. S. Friedman 79–80, who calls this "perhaps the moment that turns him into a killer."

20. Cf. Horsley 1: 159, who views Travis as a "martyr to modern alienation" and Taxi Driver as a "tragedy."

21. Cf. Kolker 215, on Raging Bull: "Memory is a killer of melodrama . . . [through] a textual and perceptual complexity . . . that withdraws us from simple identification with the character. . . ."

22. Scorsese was in and out of the hospital for asthma attacks, then hospitalized for four days in September 1978 with internal bleeding, due to a "self-destructive lifestyle" involving cocaine (L. S. Friedman 112). After shooting New York, New York, Scorsese also made a feature-length documentary, The Last Waltz, about the farewell concert of The Band in 1976, and directed Liza Minnelli in a stage show, The Act, which bombed on Broadway in 1977, the same year his second wife filed for divorce, citing his affair with Minnelli and use of cocaine (111).

23. As Tomasulo points out ("Raging" 188–190), there are many differences between the historical La Motta depicted in his autobiography and the character in the film, which is also about the director himself, his actor, and his audience.

24. Cf. Keyser 108 on how Scorsese and De Niro removed the "literary dialogue" of the Paul Schrader and Mardik Martin script, replacing it with "non sequitors, half-formed ideas, angry blasphemies, poetic insults, and sustained cursing."

25. Cf. Horsley 2: 11–12, for a critique of the "masochistic brilliance" in Raging Bull.

26. Cf. Scorsese's view of Jake as being "on a higher spiritual level" because he is on a primitive, animal level as a fighter. "Which means that maybe animals are closer to God than we are" (qtd. in Kelly 32).

27. Cf. Tomasulo, "Raging." He argues that screen violence today (in Taxi Driver, Apocalypse Now, and Natural Born Killers, as well as Raging Bull) has become so graphic and exaggerated "that it no longer provides the Aristotelian emotional

catharsis and narrative closure that characterized previous eras" of cinema (175). Tomasulo argues that La Motta does not display tragic flaws (179) and that "any rhetoric against violence [in the film] is lost in the stylization" (193). And yet, he concedes that the film is both progressive and reactionary (194).

28. Scorsese explains the biblical epigraph in reference to himself: "Jake La Motta, at least as he appears in the film, is someone who allowed me to see clearly" (*Martin* 99). See also 91, where Scorsese calls Jake's wall punching in the prison cell "a catharsis" for the character, and says: "it happened to me too." And see 253: "I found myself through him. . . . I died and came back to life." Scorsese also relates this to his work on *Last Temptation*.

29. Morris 45. He also says, in his otherwise favorable article about the film: "heretics have been burnt at the stake for less."

30. "You're the same as all the others only you won't admit it," Magdalene says. "You're pitiful. I hate you." She then puts Jesus' hand on her naked body, but he moves away. After that, she clothes herself, telling him not to watch, and then says she has loved him tenderly since they were children. He agrees but leaves.

31. Cf. Keyser 173 and Scorsese, *Martin* 117.

32. See Scorsese, *Martin* 116, for his explanation about wanting "to break away from the sound of the old biblical epics, to make the dialogue plainer, more contemporary"—in rewriting the script with Jay Cocks. But see also Keyser 170–171 on Scorsese's extensive historical research for the film.

33. Cf. *Scorsese* 124, on the director's sense of Christ as both fully human and divine, in a debate that "goes back to the Council of Chalcedon in 451," but also forces today's audience "to take Jesus seriously—at least re-evaluate His teachings."

34. Gregory, a well-known avant-garde theatre director, also appeared as an inspirational figure in the Louis Malle film *My Dinner with André* (1981). Scorsese's Jesus, Willem Dafoe, had previously been an avant-garde theatre actor as well, especially as a company member of the Wooster Group since 1977. See Savran, *Breaking*.

35. Cf. Kazantzakis 263–266, where Jesus does not pick up an ax and attack the pomegranate tree, nor is he visited by John the Baptist in his desert visions, as in the film.

36. The scene appeared in Schrader's screenplay, but not in Kazantzakis's novel. Cf. Scorsese, *Martin* 114–115, on his inspiration for the heart offering in his grandmother's portrait of the Sacred Heart of Jesus.

37. Cf. Kazantzakis 444–467, where the guardian angel begins as a winged creature, then becomes a Negro boy, and Jesus has many sons and daughters with both Mary and Martha. The novel also has Saul and his cohorts kill Magdalene by stoning her (454), instead of her natural death in the film.

38. See Lewis, *Whom* 53, on Coppola's view of himself as "a tragic hero" in making *Apocalypse Now* and as being like Willard: "moving up river in a faraway jungle, looking for answers and hoping for some kind of catharsis" (qtd. in Lewis, *Whom* 50).

39. Cf. Johnson 116–121 on the weak parts of Puzo's novel that were not included in the film, with its less brutal, more sympathetic Corleone family and yet variety of violent scenes.

40. Cf. Schumacher 88–89 about the Puzo novel also creating sympathy for Don Corleone, because he prefers negotiation to firepower and finds prostitution and narcotics "beneath him."

41. See Camon 65, on how the breakdown of the Hays Code in the 1960s allowed for a "multilayered hero" in *The Godfather*, rather than just a simple "battle of good and evil where evil always got punished in the end." Camon also analyzes how the film's popularity affected the Mafia itself—as both a "critique and reaffirmation of the Mafia myth" (75). Cf. Papke 6.

42. In a real-life example of this, a threat was made by a Mafia lawyer, on behalf of Paramount, to get Pacino released from a prior contract so that he could play *The Godfather* role (Lewis, "If History" 28). See Man for a defense of all three *Godfather* films as "progressive" in their critique of capitalism (128). Man directly contradicts Jameson, who faults the first film for presenting the problem as ethical, instead of economic, through the "pure Evil of the Mafiosi" (32).

43. At first, Coppola balked at the idea of making a sequel to *The Godfather* (Schumacher 153). Then he agreed to produce it, but proposed Martin Scorsese as director. At last, he decided to direct it himself, with the idea of the double plot about Vito's rise and Michael's fall.

44. See Coppola's *Playboy* interview: "I made another pitch for Brando. Jaffe replied, and these are his exact words, 'As president of Paramount Pictures, I assure you that Marlon Brando will never appear in this motion picture and . . . I will no longer allow you to discuss it'" (56). Woltz makes a similar statement, but with more colorful language, about Fontane. See also 58, where Coppola says he nearly got fired for insisting on Pacino for the role of Michael.

45. See Coppola, Interview 60: "if the statement I was trying to make was outbalanced by the charismatic aspects of the characters, I felt *Godfather II* was an opportunity to rectify that." See also Ferraro 195–199 and Papke for critiques of Coppola's attempted demythologizing of the Mafia in his second and third *Godfather* films.

46. See Lourdeaux 172–174 on Coppola's "Italian/American" double identity as "both an Italian familial individual and a WASP individualist," through his father's independence as a musician and his family's many moves, in contrast with Scorsese's more communal experience of Little Italy in his teen years.

47. See Coppola, Interview 65, where he describes "a lot of bright young writers and directors in Hollywood who are very successful. . . . They've become the very people they were criticizing three years ago. Like Michael, they've become their fathers."

48. See also William Simon 76, for his interpretation of Michael as metaphor: "emerging from World War II as an innocent hero, becoming progressively corrupted . . . as a representation of America's post-war history."

49. Cf. Eleanor Coppola 26.

50. During the filming of the first *Godfather,* producer Robert Evans "hired Elia Kazan to stand by in case he eventually had to replace Coppola" (Lewis, "If History" 31).

51. Cf. Papke 13.

52. Cf. Horsley 1: 174–177. He calls the first two *Godfather* films: "the Great American Tragedy." See also Krapp, for a comparison of Coppola's *Godfather* trilogy and Aeschylus' *Oresteia.*

53. See also Schumacher 4–9.

54. Coppola hoped to make the third *Godfather* film about the death of Vito's adopted son, Tom Hagen, like the first two showing the deaths of Sonny and Fredo. But Coppola could not get Robert Duvall to play the role. See Ondaatje 258.

55. See Eleanor Coppola 170 on one of the scenes created for the film: "the biggest explosion . . . ever staged in the world before, outside a real war."

56. Most of the details in this and the following two paragraphs, including the quotes, are given in *Hearts of Darkness,* a documentary about the making of Coppola's film. See also Schumacher 202–253 and Bergan 53–59.

57. Cf. Elsaesser and Wedel, who call Coppola a "tragic" figure as director and find an "incommensurability across the handy trope of villains and victims" in this film, especially through its use of sound, as in the Kilgore scenes (156, 167–169).

58. Cf. Hagen, "*Apocalypse*" 238–239, for a critique of Coppola's failure to make the jungle more of a "character," rather than just a setting, as the screenwriter John Milius wanted. See also Hagen, "*Heart,*" for a further critique of the film as an unfaithful adaptation of Conrad's novel.

59. In the expanded version of the film, *Apocalypse Now Redux* (2001), Coppola adds a scene of Willard's crew getting personal time after the show with two of the Playboy Bunnies in exchange for canisters of diesel fuel from the boat. When the soldiers meet and touch the girls they had idolized, they find characters who depart from their pin-up images: women crying about the loneliness of being Playmate of the Year or reminiscing about a better job as a bird trainer at Busch Gardens. The former Playmate of theYear also screams when she knocks over a casket and a dead body rolls out. Yet this double tryst scene, despite its tragicomic insights about feminine subjectivity and mortal lust, is a confusing detour from the main story, as it shows Willard veering off course from his mission with uncharacteristic generosity to his men. See Ondaatje's interviews with Walter Murch, who wedited *Redux.*

60. Cf. Kinder, "Power," on the film's "elaborate promotion . . . [that] encourages us to identify Coppola both with Willard and Kurtz," through the publication of Eleanor Coppola's *Notes,* her journal in the Philippines, "coordinated with the opening of the film."

61. Cf. Burke, especially paragraphs 15, 26, and 32–34.

62. See San Filippo for details of the extra footage, which does not significantly improve the film.

63. Cf. Hagen, "*Apocalypse*" 233–234, and Kinder, "Power" 14–15, for their disagreement about the dreamlike quality of the entire film.

64. See Hagen, *"Heart"* 46–51; Jacobs 215–217; Kinder, "Power" 13; and Tomasulo. Cf. Chatman 209–218.

65. For more relations between the *Godfather* trilogy and opera, see Greene, "Family."

66. Cf. Hagen, *"Apocalypse"* 234–235. "The film initiates the viewer into a Vietnam outside the television screen . . . [with] a personal, involved view that tends to sacrifice moral distance for perceptual overload."

EXODOS

1. See Bettelheim for a Freudian theory of the folktale's cathartic effect on its readers. For a critique of this theory, see Tatar 70–71. See also Jones on the value of cartoon violence and Jenkin's application of Bettelheim to video game violence (Scholder and Zimmerman 127).

2. On computers and video games as theatre, see Janet Murray and Laurel. See also Žižek, *Art* 36–38, on the potential experience of cyberspace as "tragic," with the impossible Real at its center.

3. Cf. Seaford on ancient Greek tragedy as emerging from ritual and elevating the virtue of self-restraint "above the transient pleasures of vengeance" (405).

4. Cf. Klein 176–191, on the "paranoid-schizoid" stage of infancy and the "depressive-integrative" phase beyond that. See also Weatherill 78–79, 101, for parallels with Lacan's theory of the mirror stage and its sacrifice of being.

5. Cf. Weatherill 55–57, 106.

6. Steiner theorized the "death of tragedy" by defining the modern Christian worldview in its departure from the ancient. But he found hope for tragedy's revival in Brecht's *Mother Courage*. Cf. Brooks, *Melodramatic* 206, on "the death of tragedy and the rise of melodrama." See also Grodal, whose cognitivist approach to film barely mentions "tragedy," and then only in a chart where he places it with "passive melodrama" (161), while not showing the term at all in a subsequent list of genres (180–181), although he also refers to "tragic 'object' destruction in schizoid fiction" and "tragic melodrama" (176).

7. On current, postmodern theory as related to modern drama, yet perverse to modernist beliefs and ritual ideals, see Pizzato, *Edges*. See also Seaford on ancient tragedy as a perversion of ritual, developing from the contradiction in ritual between order and ambiguity (365).

8. Cf. Grant, who considers various serial-killer novels and films, especially Bret Easton Elis's *American Psycho*, to be Artaudian theatre of cruelty because they "work in a profoundly moral way insofar as they shock us by *not* shocking us" and leave us "to find our own way back from the land of the dead" (38–39).

9. See, for example, the third choral ode (second after the parodos).

10. Cf. R. K. Simon, who calls the journalism in today's tabloids "a new form of tragedy" as postmodern collage (69), but with no reference to Aristotelian or Freudian catharsis.

11. See Grodal 9, 82–83, 90, 111–114, 215.

12. See Kaplan, *Motherhood,* and Linda Williams, "Film Bodies," and "Melo-drama." Cf. also Gledhill, "Speculations" 109, on her broad sense of melodrama, while focusing on women's films and TV soap operas: "the melodramatic as an imaginative mode that can inform any genre whether 'male' or 'female.'" And see Copjec, "More!" 265, for a distinction between the elements of "early melodrama" onscreen, e.g. "stereotypical polarizations of characters," and the "narratives of self-sacrifice" in later, "more realistic melodrama."

13. See Stone's explanation, in the *Natural Born Killers* "director's cut" video, that he was forced to remove certain shots of extreme violence for the film's initial release, in order to get the "R" rating, making it less satirically insightful.

Bibliography

Alford, C. Fred. *The Psychoanalytic Theory of Greek Tragedy*. New Haven: Yale University Press, 1992.

Alien. Dir. Ridley Scott. 20th Century Fox, 1979.

Alien: Resurrection. Dir. Jean-Pierre Jeunet. 20th Century Fox, 1997.

Aliens. Dir. James Cameron. 20th Century Fox, 1986.

Alien3. Dir. David Fincher. 20th Century Fox, 1992.

Allen, Richard. *Projecting Illusion: Film Spectatorship and the Impression of Reality*. Cambridge: Cambridge University Press, 1995.

Anawalt, Patricia Rieff. "Memory Clothing: Costumes Associated with Aztec Human Sacrifice." *Ritual Human Sacrifice in Mesoamerica*. Ed. Elizabeth H. Boone. Washington, D.C.: Dumbarton Oaks Research Library and Collection, 1984. 165–194.

Ang, Ien. *Living Room Wars: Rethinking Media Audiences for a Postmodern World*. London: Routledge, 1996.

Aristotle. *The Basic Works of Aristotle*. Ed. Richard McKeon. New York: Random, 1941.

———. *Poetics*. Trans. S. H. Butcher. *Dramatic Theory and Criticism: Greeks to Grotowski*. Ed. Bernard F. Dukore. New York: Holt, 1974. 31–55.

Armes, Roy. *Action and Image: Dramatic Structure in Cinema*. Manchester: Manchester University Press, 1994.

Artaud, Antonin. *Collected Works*. Vol. 3. Trans. Alastair Hamilton. London: Calder and Boyars, 1972.

———. *The Theater and Its Double*. Trans. Mary Caroline Richards. New York: Grove, 1958.

Ashby, Clifford. *Classical Greek Theatre: New Views of an Old Subject*. Iowa City: University of Iowa Press, 1999.

Aufderheide, Pat. Review of *Zoot Suit*. *Film Quarterly* 36.2 (1982): 44–47.

Auguet, Roland. *Cruelty and Civilization: The Roman Games*. London: Routledge, 1994.

Auslander, Philip. *Liveness: Performance in a Mediatized Culture*. London: Routledge, 1999.

Baal, Georges. "Toward a Freudian and Lacanian Psychoanalytical Theory for Theatre, Centered on the Actor's Role." *Assaph* 7 (1991): 35–59.

Babcock, Granger. "Looking for a Third Space: El Pachuco and Chicano Nationalism in Luis Valdez's Zoot Suit." *Staging Difference: Cultural Pluralism in American Theatre and Drama*. Ed. Marc Maufort. New York: Peter Lang, 1995. 215–25.

Badley, Linda. *Film, Horror, and the Body Fantastic*. Westport, Conn.: Greenwood, 1995.

Bacon, Helen H. "The Chorus in Greek Life and Drama." *Arion* 3.1 (1995): 6–24.

Banham, Martin, ed. *The Cambridge Guide to Theatre*. Cambridge: Cambridge University Press, 1992.

Barber, Stephen. *Antonin Artaud: Blows and Bombs*. London: Faber, 1993.

Barrios, Gregg. "*Zoot Suit*: The Man, the Myth, Still Lives (A Conversation With Luis Valdez)." *The Bilingual Review* 10.2–3 (1983): 159–164.

Barthes, Roland. "The Death of the Author." *Image, Music, Text*. Trans. Stephen Heath. New York: Hill, 1977. 142–148.

———. "Diderot, Brecht, Eisenstein." *Image, Music, Text*. Trans. Stephen Heath. New York: Hill, 1977. 69–78.

Barton, Carlin. "Savage Miracles: The Redemption of Lost Honor in Roman Society and the Sacrament of the Gladiator and the Martyr." *Representations* 45 (Winter 1994): 41–71.

———. *The Sorrows of the Ancient Romans*. Princeton: Princeton University Press, 1993.

Barzilai, Shuli. "Borders of Language: Kristeva's Critique of Lacan." *PMLA* 106.2 (Mar. 1991): 294–305.

Bataille, Georges. *The Accursed Share*. Vol. 1. Trans. Robert Hurley. New York: Zone, 1988.

Baudrillard, Jean. *Simulations*. Trans. Paul Foss, Paul Patton, and Philip Beitchman. New York: Semiotext(e), 1983.

Bazin, André. "Theater and Cinema." *What is Cinema?* Berkeley: University of California Press, 1967. 76–124.

Beacham, Richard C. *The Roman Theatre and Its Audience*. Cambridge: Harvard University Press, 1992.

Beisser, Arnold. "The American Seasonal Masculinity Rites." *Jock: Sports and Male Identity*. Ed. Donald F. Sabo, Jr. and Ross Runfola. Englewood Cliffs, N.J.: Prentice-Hall, 1980. 166–177.

Bell, Catherine. *Ritual Theory, Ritual Practice.* Oxford: Oxford University Press, 1992.

Benjamin, Walter. "The Work of Art in the Age of Mechanical Reproduction." *Illuminations.* Ed. Hannah Arendt. New York: Schocken, 1969. 217–251.

Bentley, Eric. *The Life of the Drama.* New York: Atheneum, 1964.

Berg, Charles Ramírez. Review of *Zoot Suit. The Bilingual Review* 10.2–3 (1983): 189–190.

Bergan, Ronald. *Francis Coppola.* New York: Thunder's Mouth, 1998.

Bettelheim, Bruno. *The Uses of Enchantment : The Meaning and Importance of Fairy Tales.* New York: Knopf, 1976.

Bianchi, Eugene. "The Super-Bowl Culture of Male Violence." *Jock: Sports and Male Identity.* Ed. Donald F. Sabo, Jr. and Ross Runfola. Englewood Cliffs, New Jersey: Prentice-Hall, 1980. 117–130.

Blau, Herbert. *The Audience.* Baltimore: Johns Hopkins University Press, 1990.

———. *Take Up the Bodies: Theater at the Vanishing Point.* Urbana: University of Illinois Press, 1982.

Bloom, John. "Muscular Culture: The Cultural Significance of Sports." *American Studies* 37.1 (Spring 1996): 149–158.

Booth, Willard C. "Dramatic Aspects of Aztec Rituals." *Educational Theatre Journal* 18.4 (Dec. 1966): 421–428.

Boothby, Richard. "Altar-Egos: Psychoanalysis and the Theory of Sacrifice." *Journal for the Psychoanalysis of Culture and Society* 1.2 (Fall 1996): 47–61.

———. *Death and Desire: Psychoanalytic Theory in Lacan's Return to Freud.* New York: Routledge, 1991.

Bordwell, David, and Noël Carroll, eds. *Post-Theory: Reconstructing Film Studies.* Madison: University of Wisconsin Press, 1996.

Bourget, Jean-Loup. "Social Implications in the Hollywood Genres." 1973. *Film Genre Reader II.* Ed. Barry Keith Grant. Austin: University of Texas Press, 1995. 50–58.

Bouzereau, Laurent. *Ultraviolent Movies.* Seacaucus, N.J.: Carol, 1996.

Bracher, Mark. "Editor's Column: Lacan's 'Civilization and Its Discontents.'" *Journal for the Psychoanalysis of Culture and Society* 1.2 (Fall 1996): 1–12.

———. *The Writing Cure: Psychoanalysis, Composition, and the Aims of Education.* Carbondale: Southern Illinois University Press, 1999.

Branagh, Kenneth, dir. *Mary Shelley's Frankenstein.* Columbia TriStar/American Zoetrope, 1994.

———. *Mary Shelley's Frankenstein: The Classic Tale of Terror Reborn on Film.* Ed. Diana Landau. New York: Newmarket, 1994.

Brecht, Bertolt. *Brecht on Theatre.* Trans. John Willett. New York: Hill, 1964.

Brewster, Ben. "The Fundamental Reproach (Brecht)." *Cine-Tracts* 1.2 (Summer 1977): 44–53.

Brewster, Ben, and Lea Jacobs. *Theatre to Cinema: Stage Pictorialism and the Early Feature Film*. Oxford: Oxford University Press, 1997.

Brockett, Oscar G. *History of the Theatre*. Boston: Allyn, 1995.

Broda de Casas, Johanna. "Tlacaxipeualiztli: A Reconstruction of an Aztec Calendar Festival From 16th Century Sources," *Revista Español de Antropologia Americana* 5 (1970): 197–273.

Brokaw, John W. "Mexican-American Drama." *Essays on Contemporary American Drama*. Ed. Hedwig Bock and Albert Wertheim. Munich: Max Hueber, 1981. 241–256.

Bronfen, Elisabeth. "Death: The Navel of the Image." *The Point of Theory: Practices of Cultural Analysis*. Ed. Mieke Bal and Inge E. Boer. New York: Continuum, 1994. 79–90.

Brooks, Peter. "The Idea of a Psychoanalytic Literary Criticism." *Discourse in Psychoanalysis and Literature*. Ed. Shlomith Rimmon-Kenan. London: Methuen, 1987. 1–18.

——— . *The Melodramatic Imagination: Balzac, Henry James, Melodrama and the Mode of Excess*. New Haven: Yale University Press, 1976.

Brousse, Marie-Hélène. "The Drive (II)." *Reading Seminar XI*. Ed. Richard Feldstein, Bruce Fink, and Maire Jaanus. Albany: State University of New York Press, 1995. 109–117.

Broyles-Gonzales, Yolanda. *El Teatro Campesino: Theater in the Chicano Movement*. Austin: University of Texas Press, 1994.

Bruce-Novoa, Juan. "Chicano Theater: Editing the Origin Myth." *Gestos* 14 (Nov. 1992): 105–116.

Bryant, Jennings. "Viewers' Enjoyment of Televised Sports Violence." *Media, Sports, and Society*. Ed. Lawrence A. Wenner. Newbury Park, Calif.: Sage Publications, 1989. 270–289.

Burciaga, José Antonio. "A Conversation with Luis Valdez." *Imagine* 2.2 (1985): 127–141.

Burgoyne, Bernard, and Mary Sullivan, eds. *The Klein-Lacan Dialogues*. New York: Other Press, 1999.

Burke, Anthony. "Violence and Reason on the Shoals of Vietnam." *Postmodern Culture* 9.3 (May 1999): 38 paragraphs. Online.

Burkert, Walter. *Ancient Mystery Cults*. Cambridge: Harvard University Press, 1987.

——— . "Greek Tragedy and Sacrificial Ritual." *Greek, Roman and Byzantine Studies* 7 (1966): 87–121.

——— . *Homo Necans: The Anthropology of Ancient Greek Sacrificial Ritual and Myth*. Berkeley: University of California Press, 1983.

——— . "The Problem of Ritual Killing." Hamerton-Kelly 149–176.

Butler, Judith. *Bodies That Matter: On the Discursive Limits of "Sex."* New York: Routledge, 1993.

Camon, Alessandro. "*The Godfather* and the Mythology of the Mafia." *Francis Ford Coppola's* Godfather *Trilogy*. Ed. Nick Browne. Cambridge: Cambridge University Press, 2000. 57–75.

Caputi, Jane. "Small Ceremonies: Ritual in *Forrest Gump, Natural Born Killers, Seven,* and *Follow Me Home*." *Mythologies of Violence in Postmodern Media*. Ed. Christopher Sharrett. Detroit: Wayne State University Press, 1999. 147–174.

Carlson, Marvin. *Theatre Semiotics: Signs of Life*. Bloomington: Indiana University Press, 1990.

———. *Theories of the Theatre*. Ithaca: Cornell University Press, 1993.

Carrasco, Davíd. "Give Me Some Skin: The Charisma of the Aztec Warrior." *History of Religions* 35.1 (Aug. 1995): 1–26.

———. "Myth, Cosmic Terror, and the Templo Mayor." *The Great Temple of Tenochtitlan*. Ed. Johanna Broda, Davíd Carrasco, and Eduardo Matos Moctezuma. Berkeley: University of California Press, 1987. 124–162.

———. *Religions of Mesoamerica*. New York: Harper, 1990.

Carrie. Dir. Brian De Palma. United Artists, 1976.

Castelvetro, Lodovico. *On Aristotle's Poetics*. Trans. Charles Gattnig. *Dramatic Theory and Criticism: Greeks to Grotowski*. Ed. Bernard F. Dukore. New York: Holt, 1974. 143–149.

Cavell, Stanley. "The Fact of Television." *Daedalus* 111.4 (1982): 75–96.

Chatman, Seymour. "2 ½ Film Versions of *Heart of Darkness*." *Conrad on Film*. Ed. Gene M. Moore. Cambridge: Cambridge University Press, 1997. 207–223.

Cheska, Alyce Taylor. "Sports Spectacular: The Social Ritual of Power." *Sport in the Sociocultural Process*. Ed. Marie Hart and Susan Birrell. Dubuque: Brown, 1972. 368–383.

Chown, Jeffrey. *Hollywood Auteur: Francis Coppola*. New York: Praeger, 1988.

Clarke, James W. *On Being Mad or Merely Angry: John W. Hinckley, Jr., and Other Dangerous People*. Princeton: Princeton University Press, 1990.

Claus, David. *Toward the Soul: An Inquire into the Meaning of Psyche before Plato*. New Haven: Yale University Press, 1981.

Clendinnen, Inga. *Aztecs: An Interpretation*. Cambridge: Cambridge University Press, 1991.

———. "The Cost of Courage in Aztec Society." *Past and Present* 94 (May 1985): 44–89.

———. "Ways to the Sacred: Reconstructing 'Religion' in Sixteenth Century Mexico." *History and Anthropology* 5 (1990): 105–141.

Clover, Carol J. *Men, Women, and Chainsaws: Gender in the Modern Horror Film*. Princeton: Princeton University Press, 1992.

Cole, Susan Guettel. "Procession and Celebration at the Dionysia," *Theater and Society in the Classical World*. Ed. Ruth Scodel. Ann Arbor: University of Michigan Press, 1993. 25–38.

Coleman, K. M. "Fatal Charades: Roman Executions Staged as Mythological Enactments." *Journal of Roman Studies* 80 (1990): 44–73.

Condon, Bill, dir. *Gods and Monsters*. Universal, 1999.

Cook, Rhonda. "Woman on Trial for Murder Said to be Fan of Violent Film." *The Atlanta Journal and Constitution* 10 Feb. 1997, constitution ed.: 4B.

Copjec, Joan. "More! From Melodrama to Magnitude." *Endless Night: Cinema and Psychoanalysis, Parallel Histories*. Ed. Janet Bergstrom. Berkeley: University of California Press, 1999. 249–272.

Coppola, Eleanor. *Notes*. New York: Pocket, 1980.

Coppola, Francis Ford, dir. *Apocalypse Now*. United Artists/Zoetrope, 1979.

———, dir. *Apocalypse Now Redux*. Miramax, 2001.

———. "Coppola and *The Godfather*." (Interview with Stephen Farber.) *Sight and Sound* 41 (1972): 217–223.

———, dir. *The Godfather*. Paramount, 1972.

———, dir. *The Godfather, Part II*. Paramount, 1974.

———, dir. *The Godfather, Part III*. Paramount/Zoetrope, 1990.

———. Interview. *Playboy* 22.7 (July 1975): 53–54, 56, 58, 60, 62, 64, 68, 184–185.

Courtwright, David T. "Way Cooler Than Manson: *Natural Born Killers*." *Oliver Stone's USA: Film, History, and Controversy*. Ed. Robert Brent Toplin. Lawrence: University Press of Kansas, 2000. 188–201.

Cowie, Elizabeth. "Fantasia." *m/f* 9 (1984): 71–105.

Crabb, Peter B., and Jeffrey H. Goldstein. "The Social Psychology of Watching Sports: From Ilium to Living Room." *Responding to the Screen: Reception and Reaction Processes*. Ed. Jennings Bryant and Dolf Zillmann. Hillsdale, N.J.: Lawrence Erlbaum Associates, 1991. 355–71.

Crane, Jonathan Lake. *Terror and Everyday Life: Singular Moments in the History of the Horror Film*. London: Sage, 1994.

Creed, Barbara. *The Monstrous-Feminine: Film, Feminism, Psychoanalysis*. London: Routledge, 1993.

Curtis, James. *James Whale: A New World of Gods and Monsters*. Boston: Faber, 1998.

Dahl, Mary Karen. *Political Violence in Drama: Classical Models, Contemporary Variations*. Ann Arbor: UMI Research Press, 1987.

Daly, Mary. *Gyn/Ecology: The Metaethics of Radical Feminism*. Boston: Beacon Press, 1978.

Damasio, Antonio R. *Descartes' Error*. New York: Putnam, 1994.

Davies, Nigel. *Human Sacrifice: In History and Today*. New York: William Morrow, 1981.

Davis, Michael. *Aristotle's Poetics: the Poetry of Philosophy*. Lanham, Maryland: Rowman and Littlefield, 1992.

Davis, R. G. and Betty Diamond. "*Zoot Suit*: From the Barrio to Broadway." *Ideologies and Literature* 3.15 (Jan.–Mar. 1981): 124–133.

Dean, William. *The American Spiritual Culture and the Invention of Jazz, Football, and the Movies*. New York: Continuum, 2002.

de Certeau, Michel. *The Writing of History*. New York: Columbia University Press, 1988.

Deleuze, Gilles. "Cinema and Space: The Frame." *The Deleuze Reader*. Ed. Constantin V. Boundas. New York: Columbia University Press, 1983. 173–179.

———. *Cinema 2: The Time-Image*. Minneapolis: University of Minnesota Press, 1985.

deMause, Lloyd. *Foundations of Psychohistory*. New York: Creative Roots, 1982.

Dennett, Daniel. *Consciousness Explained*. Boston: Little, 1991.

Derrida, Jacques. *The Gift of Death*. Trans. David Wills. Chicago: University of Chicago Press, 1995.

Detienne, Marcel. "Between Beasts and Gods." *Myth, Religion, and Society*. Ed. R. L. Gordon. Cambridge: Cambridge University Press, 1981. 215–228.

———. *Dionysos at Large*. Trans. Arthur Goldhammer. Cambridge: Harvard University Press, 1989.

Diamond, Elin. "The Shudder of Catharsis in Twentieth Century Performance." *Performance and Performativity*. Ed. Andrew Parker and Eve Kosofsky Sedgwick. New York: Routledge, 1995. 172–192.

———. *Unmaking Mimesis: Essays on Feminism and Theater*. London: Routledge, 1997.

Dienst, Richard. *Still Life in Real Time: Theory After Television*. Durham: Duke University Press, 1994.

Dixon, Wheeler Winston. "The Films of *Frankenstein*." *Approaches to Teaching Shelley's Frankenstein*. Ed. Stephen C. Behrendt. New York: Modern Language Association, 1990. 166–179.

———. *It Looks At You: The Returned Gaze of Cinema*. Albany: State University of New York Press, 1995.

Doane, Mary Ann. *The Desire to Desire: The Woman's Film of the 1940s*. Bloomington: Indiana University Press, 1987.

———. "The Voice in Cinema: The Articulation of Body and Space." *Narrative, Apparatus, Ideology: A Film Theory Reader*. Ed. Philip Rosen. New York: Columbia University Press, 1986. 335–348.

Dobler, Conrad, and Vic Carucci. *They Call Me Dirty*. New York: Jove, 1989.

Durán, Diego. *Book of the Gods and Rites*. Trans. Fernando Horcasitas and Doris Heyden. Norman: University of Oklahoma Press, 1971.

Duverger, Christian. "The Meaning of Sacrifice." *Zone* 5 (1989): 367–385.

Earl, James W. "Identification and Catharsis." *Pragmatism's Freud: The Moral Disposition of Psychoanalysis.* Baltimore: Johns Hopkins University Press, 1986. 79–92.

Easterling, P. E. "A Show for Dionysus." *The Cambride Companion to Greek Tragedy.* Ed. P. E. Easterling. Cambridge: Cambridge University Press, 1997. 36–53.

Eckhardt, Karl. "Concepts of Mimesis in French and German Philosophical and Anthropological Theory." *The Play of the Self.* Ed. Ronald Bogue and Mihai I. Spariosu. Albany: State University of New York Press, 1994. 67–86.

Edmondson, J. C. "Dynamic Arenas: Gladiatorial Presentations in the City of Rome and the Construction of Roman Society during the Early Empire." *Roman Theater and Society.* Ed. William J. Slater. Ann Arbor: University of Michigan Press, 1996. 69–112.

Eitzen, Dirk. "The Emotional Basis of Film Comedy." Plantinga and Smith 84–99.

Elam, Harry J., Jr. *Taking It to the Streets: The Social Protest Theater of Luis Valdez and Amiri Baraka.* Ann Arbor: University of Michigan Press, 1997.

Elsaesser, Thomas. "From Anti-Illusionism to Hyper-Realism: Bertolt Brecht and Contemporary Film." *Re-interpreting Brecht: His Influence on Contemporary Drama and Film.* Ed. Pia Kleber and Colin Visser. Cambridge: Cambridge University Press, 1990. 170–185.

———. "Tales of Sound and Fury: Observations on the Family Melodrama." 1973. *Film Genre Reader II.* Ed. Barry Keith Grant. Austin: University of Texas Press, 1995. 350–380.

Elsaesser, Thomas, and Michael Wedel. "The Hollow Heart of Hollywood: *Apocalypse Now* and the New Sound Space." *Conrad on Film.* Ed. Gene M. Moore. Cambridge: Cambridge University Press, 1997. 151–175.

Else, Gerald F. *The Origin and Early Form of Ancient Greek Tragedy.* Cambridge: Harvard University Press, 1967.

Esslin, Martin. *The Age of Television.* San Francisco: W. H. Freeman and Company, 1982.

Ewigleben, Cornelia. "'What these Women Love is the Sword': The Performers and their Audiences." *Gladiators and Caesars: The Power of Spectacle in Ancient Rome.* Ed. Eckart Köhne and Cornelia Ewigleben. Berkeley: University of California Press, 2000. 125–139.

The Exorcist. Dir. William Friedkin. Warner Brothers, 1973.

Farrell, Warren. "The Super-Bowl Phenomenon: Machismo as Ritual." *Jock: Sports and Male Identity.* Ed. Donald F. Sabo, Jr. and Ross Runfola. Englewood Cliffs, N.J.: Prentice-Hall, 1980. 19–30.

Ferraro, Thomas J. "Blood in the Marketplace: The Business of Family in the *Godfather* Narratives." *The Invention of Ethnicity.* Oxford: Oxford University Press, 1989. 176–207.

Fietz, Lothar. "On the Origins of the English Melodrama in the Tradition of Bourgeois Tragedy and Sentimental Drama: Lillo, Schröder, Kotzebue, Sheridan, Thompson, Jerrold." *Melodrama: The Cultural Emergence of a Genre*. Ed. Michael Hays and Anastasia Nikolopoulou. New York: St. Martin's, 1996. 83–101.

Fink, Bruce. *A Clinical Introduction to Lacanian Psychoanalysis*. Cambridge: Harvard University Press, 1997.

———. *The Lacanian Subject*. Princeton: Princeton University Press, 1995.

Fiske, John. *Television Culture*. London: Methuen, 1987.

Flitterman, Sandy. "Theorizing 'The Feminine': Woman as the Figure of Desire in *The Seashell and the Clergyman*." *Wide Angle* 6.3 (1984): 32–39.

Forry, Steven Earl. *Hideous Progeny*. Philadelphia: University of Pennsylvania Press, 1990.

Fortier, Mark. *Theory/Theatre: An Introduction*. London: Routledge, 1997.

Foucault, Michel. "What Is an Author?" 1969. *Language, Counter-Memory, Practice*. Ithaca: Cornell University Press, 1977. 113–138.

Fowkes, Katherine A. *Giving Up the Ghost: Spirits, Ghosts, and Angels in Mainstream Comedy Films*. Detroit: Wayne State University Press, 1998.

Freedman, Barbara. *Staging the Gaze: Postmodernism, Psychoanalysis and Shakespearean Comedy*. Ithaca: Cornell University Press, 1991.

Fregoso, Rosa Linda. "Homegirls, *Cholas*, and *Pachucas* in Cinema: Taking Over the Public Sphere." *California History* 74.3 (Fall 1995): 316–327.

———. "*Zoot Suit*: The 'Return to the Beginning.'" *Mediating Two Worlds: Cinematic Encounters in the Americas*. Ed. John King, Ana M. López, and Manuel Alvarado. London: British Film Institute, 1993. 269–278.

French, Peter A. *The Virtues of Vengeance*. Lawrence: University Press of Kansas, 2001.

Friedman, Lawrence S. *The Cinema of Martin Scorsese*. New York: Continuum, 1999.

Friedman, Lester D. "The Blasted Tree." *The English Novel and the Movies*. Ed. Michael Klein and Gillian Parker. New York: Ungar, 1981. 52–66.

Friedrich, Rainer. "Drama and Ritual." *Drama and Religion*. Ed. James Redmond. Cambridge: Cambridge University Press, 1983. 159–223.

Frost, R. J. "'It's Alive!' *Frankenstein*: the Film, the Feminist Novel and Science Fiction." *Foundation* 67 (Summer 1996): 75–94.

Furst, Jill Leslie McKeever. *The Natural History of the Soul in Ancient Mexico*. New Haven: Yale University Press, 1995.

Futrell, Alison. *Blood in the Arena: The Spectacle of Roman Power*. Austin: University of Texas Press, 1997.

Garner, Stanton B., Jr. *Bodied Spaces*. Ithaca: Cornell University Press, 1994.

Gillespie, Susan. "Ballgames and Boundaries." *The Mesoamerican Ballgame*. Ed. Vernon L. Scarborough and David R. Wilcox. Tucson: University of Arizona Press, 1991. 317–345.

Girard, René. *Violence and the Sacred*. Trans. Patrick Gregory. Baltimore: Johns Hopkins, 1977.

Gladiator. Dir. Ridley Scott. Writ. David H. Franzoni. Universal, 2000.

Gledhill, Christine. "Signs of Melodrama." *Stardom: Industry of Desire*. Ed. Christine Gledhill. London: Routledge, 1991. 207–231.

———. "Speculations on the Relationship between Soap Opera and Melodrama." *Quarterly Review of Film and Video* 14.1–2 (1992): 103–124.

Goethals, Gregor T. *The TV Ritual: Worship at the Video Altar*. Boston: Beacon, 1981.

Goldhill, Simon. "Modern Critical Approaches to Greek Tragedy." *The Cambridge Companion to Greek Tragedy*. Ed. P. E. Easterling. Cambridge: Cambridge University Press, 1997. 324–347.

Gould, Thomas. "The Uses of Violence in Drama." *Violence in Drama*. Ed. James Redmond. Cambridge: Cambridge University Press, 1991. 1–14.

Grant, Barry Keith. "American Psycho/sis: The Pure Products of America Go Crazy." *Mythologies of Violence in Postmodern Media*. Ed. Christopher Sharrett. Detroit: Wayne State University Press, 1999. 23–40.

Green, André. "The Double and the Absent." *Psychoanalysis, Creativity, and Literature*. Ed. Alan Roland. New York: Columbia University Press, 1978. 271–292.

———. *The Tragic Effect*. Cambridge: Cambridge University Press, 1979.

Green, J. R. *Theatre in Ancient Greek Society*. London: Routledge, 1994.

Greenberg, Harvey Roy. *Screen Memories: Hollywood Cinema on the Psychoanalytic Couch*. New York: Columbia University Press, 1993.

Greene, Naomi. "Artaud and Film: A Reconsideration." *Cinema Journal* 23.4 (Summer 1984): 28–40.

———. "Family Ceremonies: or, Opera in *The Godfather* Trilogy." *Francis Ford Coppola's The Godfather Trilogy*. Ed. Nick Browne. Cambridge: Cambridge University Press, 2000. 133–155.

Greene, Thayer A. "The Archetype of the Game: Sports as a Reflection of Psyche." *Psyche and Sports*. Ed. Murray Stein and John Hollwitz. Wilmette, Ill.: Chiron Publications, 1994. 34–48.

Grist, Leighton. *The Films of Martin Scorsese, 1963–77*. London: Macmillan, 2000.

Grodal, Torben. *Moving Pictures: A New Theory of Film Genres, Feelings, and Cognition*. Oxford: Clarendon, 1997.

Gunning, Tom. "An Aesthetics of Astonishment: Early Film and the (In)Credulous Spectator." Williams, *Viewing Positions* 114–133.

Guthrie, W. K. C. *The Greeks and Their Gods*. Boston: Beacon, 1955.

Gutiérrez-Jones, Carl. "Legal Rhetoric and Cultural Critique: Notes Toward Guerrilla Writing." *diacritics* 20.4 (Winter 1990): 57–73.

Guttmann, Allen. "The Appeal of Violent Sports." *Why We Watch: The Attractions of Violent Entertainment*. Ed. Jeffrey Goldstein. Oxford: Oxford University Press, 1998. 7–26.

———. *From Ritual to Record: The Nature of Modern Sports*. New York: Columbia University Press, 1978.

———. *Games and Empires: Modern Sports and Cultural Imperialism*. New York: Columbia University Press, 1994.

———. "Roman Sports Violence." *Sports Violence*. Ed. Jeffrey H. Goldstein. New York: Springer, 1983. 7–20.

Hagen, William M. "*Apocalypse Now* (1979): Joseph Conrad and the Television War." *Hollywood as Historian*. Ed. Peter C. Rollins. Lexington: University of Kentucky Press, 1983. 230–245.

———. "*Heart of Darkness* and the Process of *Apocalypse Now*." *Conradiana* 13.1 (1981): 45–53.

Hamerton-Kelly, Robert G., ed. *Violent Origins: Ritual Killing and Cultural Formation*. Stanford: Stanford University Press, 1987.

Hardin, Richard F. "'Ritual' in Recent Criticism: The Elusive Sense of Community." *PMLA* 98.5 (1983): 846–862.

———. *The Dialogical Theatre*. New York: St. Martin's Press, 1993.

Harley, James. "The Aesthetics of Death: The Theatrical Elaboration of Ancient Roman Blood Spectacles." *Theatre History Studies* 18 (June 1998): 89–97.

Harris, Max. *Aztecs, Moors, and Christians: Festivals of Reconquest in Mexico and Spain*. Austin: University of Texas Press, 2000.

Hassig, Ronald. *War and Society in Ancient Mesoamerica*. Berkeley: University of California Press, 1992.

Hauptman, Ira. "Defending Melodrama." *Melodrama*. Ed. James Redmond. Cambridge: Cambridge University Press, 1992. 281–290.

Hearts of Darkness. Dir. Fax Bahr, Eleanor Coppola, and George Hickenlooper. American Zoetrope, 1991.

Heath, Stephen. *Questions of Cinema*. Bloomington: Indiana University Press, 1981.

Heffernan, James A. W. "Looking at the Monster: *Frankenstein* and Film." *Critical Inquiry* 24 (Autumn 1997): 133–158.

Heilman, Robert Bechtold. *The Iceman, the Arsonist, and the Troubled Agent: Tragedy and Melodrama on the Modern Stage*. Seattle: University of Washington Press, 1973.

Henrichs, Albert. "Loss of Self, Suffering, Violence: The Modern View of Dionysus from Nietzsche to Girard." *Harvard Studies in Classical Philology* 88: 305–340.

———. "'Why Should I Dance?': Choral Self-Referentiality in Greek Tragedy." *Arion* 3.1 (1995): 56–111.

Herms, Dieter. "Luis Valdez, Chicano Dramatist: An Introduction and an Interview." *Essays on Contemporary American Drama*. Ed. Hedwig Bock and Albert Wertheim. Munich: Max Hueber, 1981. 257–278.

Heyman, Stephen R. "The Hero Archetype and High-Risk Sports Participants." *Psyche and Sports*. Ed. Murray Stein and John Hollwitz. Wilmette, Ill.: Chiron Publications, 1994. 188–201.

Hicks, Frederic. "'Flowery War' in Aztec History." *American Ethnologist* 6 (1979): 87–91.

Higgins, Kathleen. "Nietzsche and Postmodern Subjectivity." Koelb 189–215.

Hinden, Michael. "Drama and Ritual Once Again: Notes Toward a Revival of Tragic Theory." *Comparative Drama* 29.2 (Summer 1995): 183–202.

Holovak, Mike, and Bill McSweeny. *Violence Every Sunday: The Story of a Professional Football Coach*. New York: Coward-McCann, 1967.

Hopkins, Keith. *Death and Renewal*. Cambridge: Cambridge University Press, 1983.

Horsley, Jake. *The Blood Poets: A Cinema of Savagery 1958–1999*. 2 vols. London: Scarecrow Press, 1999.

Hubert, Henri, and Marcel Mauss. *Sacrifice: Its Nature and Function*. 1898. Trans. W. D. Halls. London: Cohen and West, 1964.

Huerta, Jorge A. "Concerning Teatro Chicano." *Latin American Theatre Review* 6.2 (Spring 1973): 13–20.

———. "Luis Valdez's *Zoot Suit*: A New Direction for Chicano Theatre?" *Latin American Theatre Review* 13.2 supplement (Summer 1980): 69–76.

Hughes, Dennis D. *Human Sacrifice in Ancient Greece*. London: Routledge, 1991.

Hunt, Albert. "Amateurs in Horror." *Critical Perspectives* 5 (1980): 113–115.

Ingham, John M. "Human Sacrifice in Tenochtitlan." *Comparative Studies in Society and History* 26 (1984): 379–400.

Jacobs, Diane. "Coppola Films Conrad in Vietnam." *The English Novel and the Movies*. Ed. Michael Klein and Gillian Parker. New York: Frederick Ungar, 1981. 211–217.

Jameson, Fredric. *Signatures of the Visible*. New York: Routledge, 1990.

Jenkins, Henry. "'Never Trust a Snake': WWF Wrestling as Masculine Melodrama." *Out of Bounds: Sports, Media, and the Politics of Identity*. Ed. Aaron Baker and Todd Boyd. Bloomington: Indiana University Press, 1997. 48–76.

Johnson, Robert K. *Francis Ford Coppola*. Boston: Twayne, 1977.

Jones, Gerard. *Killing Monsters: Why Children Need Fantasy, Super Heroes, and Make-Believe Violence*. New York: Basic, 2002.

Julien, Philippe. *Jacques Lacan's Return to Freud*. New York: New York University Press, 1994.

Junkelmann, Marcus. "*Familia Gladiatoria*: The Heroes of the Amphitheatre." *Gladiators and Caesars: The Power of Spectacle in Ancient Rome*. Ed. Eckart Köhne and Cornelia Ewigleben. Berkeley: University of California Press, 2000. 31–74.

Kagan, Norman. *The Cinema of Oliver Stone*. New York: Continuum, 2000.

Kaplan, E. Ann. *Motherhood and Representation: The Mother in Popular Culture and Melodrama*. London: Routledge, 1992.

———— . *Women and Film: Both Sides of the Camera*. New York: Methuen, 1983.

Kaster, Joseph. *Putnam's Concise Mythological Dictionary*. New York: Putnam, 1963.

Kazantzakis, Nikos. *The Last Temptation of Christ*. New York: Simon, 1960.

Kellner, Douglas. *Media Culture*. London: Routledge, 1995.

Kelly, Mary Pat. *Martin Scorsese: The First Decade*. Pleasantville, NY: Redgrave, 1980.

Kerr, John H. *Motivation and Emotion in Sport Reversal Theory*. Hove, East Sussex, U.K.: Psychology Press, 1997.

———— . *Understanding Soccer Hooliganism*. Buckingham, U.K.: Open University Press, 1994.

Keyser, Les. *Martin Scorsese*. New York: Twayne, 1992.

Kinder, Marsha. "The Power of Adaptation in *Apocalypse Now*." *Film Quarterly* 33 (1979–80): 12–20.

———— . "Violence American Style." *Violence and American Cinema*. Ed. J. David Slocum. New York: Routledge, 2001. 63–100.

Klein, Melanie. *The Selected Melanie Klein*. Ed. Juliet Mitchell. New York: Macmillan, 1986.

Knapp, Bettina L. "Mexico: The Myth of *Renovatio*." *Substance* 50 (1986): 61–68.

Koelb, Clayton, ed. *Nietzsche as Postmodernist: Essays Pro and Con*. Albany: State University of New York Press, 1990.

Köhne, Eckart. "Bread and Circuses: The Politics of Entertainment." *Gladiators and Caesars: The Power of Spectacle in Ancient Rome*. Ed. Eckart Köhne and Cornelia Ewigleben. Berkeley: University of California Press, 2000. 8–30.

Kolker, Robert. *A Cinema of Loneliness*. 3rd ed. Oxford: Oxford University Press, 2000.

Kostelanetz, Richard. *On Innovative Performance(s): Three Decades of Recollections on Alternative Theater*. Jefferson, North Carolina: McFarland, 1994.

Krapp, John. "Ideology, Rhetoric, and Blood-Ties: From *The Oresteia* to *The Godfather*." *Mosaic* 32.1 (1999): 1–16.

Kristeva, Julia. "Ellipsis on Dread and the Specular Seduction." *Narrative, Apparatus, Ideology: A Film Theory Reader*. Ed. Philip Rosen. New York: Columbia University Press, 1986. 236–243.

———— . *The Kristeva Reader*. Ed. Toril Moy. New York: Columbia University Press, 1986.

———— . "Modern Theater Does Not Take (A) Place." *Sub-Stance* 18/19 (1977): 131–134.

———— . *New Maladies of the Soul*. New York: Columbia University Press, 1995.

———— . *Powers of Horror: An Essay on Abjection*. New York: Columbia University Press, 1982.

————— . *Revolution in Poetic Language*. New York: Columbia University Press, 1984.

————— . "Within the Microcosm of the 'Talking Cure.'" *Interpreting Lacan*. Ed. Joseph H. Smith and William Kerrigan. New Haven: Yale University Press, 1983. 33–48.

Krutch, Joseph Wood. "The Tragic Fallacy." *The Modern Temper: A Study and A Confession*. New York: Harcourt, 1929. 115–143.

Kubiak, Anthony. *Agitated States: Performance in the American Theater of Cruelty*. Ann Arbor: University of Michigan Press, 2002.

————— . *Stages of Terror: Terror, Ideology, and Coercion as Theatre History*. Bloomington: Indiana University Press, 1991.

Kurath, Gertrude Prokosch, and Samuel Martí. *Dances of Anáhuac: The Choreography and Music of Precortesian Dances*. New York: Wenner-Gren Foundation for Anthropological Research, 1964.

Kyle, Donald G. *Spectacles of Death in Ancient Rome*. London: Routledge, 1998.

Lacan, Jacques. *Écrits: A Selection*. Trans. Alan Sheridan. New York: Norton, 1977.

————— . *Feminine Sexuality*. Trans. Jacqueline Rose. New York: Norton, 1982.

————— . *The Four Fundamental Concepts*. Trans. Alan Sheridan. New York: Norton, 1978.

————— . "Position of the Unconscious." *Reading Seminar XI*. Ed. Richard Feldstein, Bruce Fink, and Maire Jaanus. Albany: State University of New York Press, 1995. 259–282.

————— . *The Seminar of Jacques Lacan: Book VII, The Ethics of Psychoanalysis, 1959–1960*. Trans. Dennis Porter. New York: Norton, 1997.

————— . *The Seminar of Jacques Lacan: Book XX, On Feminine Sexuality, The Limits of Love and Knowledge (Encore), 1972–73*. Trans. Bruce Fink. New York: Norton, 1998.

Lacoue-Labarthe, Philippe. "Theatrum Analyticum." *Mimesis, Masochism, and Mime*. Ed. Timothy Murray. Ann Arbor: University of Michigan Press, 1997. 175–196.

Lang, Robert. *American Film Melodrama: Griffith, Vidor, Minnelli*. Princeton: Princeton University Press, 1989.

Laplace-Sinatra, Michael. "Science, Gender and Otherness in Shelley's *Frankenstein* and Kenneth Branagh's Film Adaptation." *European Romantic Review* 9.2 (Spring 1998): 253–270.

Laughlin, Charles. "Revealing the Hidden: The Epiphanic Dimension of Games and Sport." *Journal of Ritual Studies* 7.1 (Winter 1993): 85–104.

Laurel, Brenda. *Computers as Theatre*. Reading, Massachusetts: Addison-Wesley, 1991.

Lavalley, Albert J. "The Stage and Film Children of *Frankenstein*: A Survey." *The Endurance of* Frankenstein: *Essays on Mary Shelley's Novel*. Ed. George Levine and U. C. Knoepflmacher. Berkeley: University of California Press, 1979. 243–289.

Lawler, Lillian B. *The Dance of the Ancient Greek Theatre*. Iowa City: University of Iowa Press, 1964.

Lehmann, Courtney. *Shakespeare Remains: Theater to Film, Early Modern to Postmodern.* Ithaca: Cornell University Press, 2002.

León-Portilla, Miguel. *The Aztec Image of Self and Society.* Salt Lake City: University of Utah Press, 1992.

Lewis, Jon. "If History Has Taught Us Anything . . . Francis Coppola, Paramount Studios, and *The Godfather Parts I, II, and III.*" *Francis Ford Coppola's Godfather Trilogy.* Ed. Nick Browne. Cambridge: Cambridge University Press, 2000. 23–56.

———. *Whom God Wishes to Destroy . . . : Francis Coppola and the New Hollywood.* Durham: Duke University Press, 1995.

Librach, Ronald S. "The Last Temptation in *Mean Streets* and *Raging Bull.*" *Literature Film Quarterly* 20.1 (1992): 14–24.

Londré, Felicia Hardison, and Daniel J. Watermeier. *The History of North American Theater: From Pre-Columbian Times to the Present.* New York: Continuum, 1998.

Lonsdale, Steven H. *Dance and Ritual Play in Greek Religion.* Baltimore: Johns Hopkins University Press, 1993.

López Austin, Alfredo. *The Human Body and Ideology: Concepts of the Ancient Nahuas.* Vol. 1. Trans. Thelma Ortiz de Montellano and Bernard Ortiz de Montellano. Salt Lake City: University of Utah Press, 1988.

Lourdeaux, Lee. *Italian and Irish Filmmakers in America.* Philadelphia: Temple University Press, 1990.

Lupton, Julia Reinhard. *Afterlives of the Saints: Hagiography, Typology, and Renaissance Literature.* Stanford: Stanford University Press, 1996.

Lupton, Julia Reinhard, and Kenneth Reinhard. *After Oedipus: Shakespeare in Psychoanalysis.* Ithaca: Cornell University Press, 1993.

Macintyre, Ben. "Copycat Killer Held in Nebraska." *The Times* (London) 5 Nov. 1994.

Man, Glenn. "Ideology and Genre in the *Godfather* Films." *Francis Ford Coppola's Godfather Trilogy.* Ed. Nick Browne. Cambridge: Cambridge University Press, 2000. 109–132.

Martin, Laura. "Language Form and Language Function in *Zoot Suit* and *The Border:* A Contribution to the Analysis of the Role of Foreign Language in Film." *Studies in Latin American Popular Culture* 3 (1984): 57–69.

Mason, Jeffrey D. "The Face of Fear." *Melodrama.* Ed. James Redmond. Cambridge: Cambridge University Press, 1992. 213–222.

Mazón, Mauricio. *The Zoot-Suit Riots.* Austin: University of Texas Press, 1984.

McCauley, Clark. "When Screen Violence Is Not Attractive." *Why We Watch: The Attractions of Violent Entertainment.* Ed. Jeffrey Goldstein. Oxford: Oxford University Press, 1998. 144–162.

McConachie, Bruce. "Doing Things with Image Schemas: The Cognitive Turn in Theatre Studies and the Problem of Experience for Historians." *Theatre Journal* 53.4 (Dec. 2001): 569–594.

McKinney, Devin. "Violence: The Strong and the Weak." *Film Quarterly* 46.4 (1993): 16–22.

McNamara, Brooks, Jerry Rojo, and Richard Schechner. *Theatres, Spaces, Environments: Eighteen Projects*. New York: Drama Book Specialists, 1975.

Megen, Bernard. "Riesman Redux: Football as Work, Play, Ritual and Metaphor." *Play and Its Cultural Context*. Ed. Alyce Taylor Cheska. West Point, New York: Leisure Press, 1981. 106–117.

Mellard, James M. "Lacan and the New Lacanians: Josephine Hart's *Damage*, Lacanian Tragedy, and the Ethics of *Jouissance*." *PMLA* 113.3 (1998): 395–407.

———. "The Other Desire: God, Beauty, Death and the Thing in Lacan's *Antigone*." *Clinical Studies: International Journal of Psychoanalysis*. 3.1 (1997): 11–30.

Metayer, Léon. "What the Heroine Taught, 1830–1870." *Melodrama: The Cultural Emergence of a Genre*. Ed. Michael Hays and Anastasia Nikolopoulou. New York: St. Martin's, 1996. 235–244.

Metz, Christian. *The Imaginary Signifier*. Bloomington: Indiana University Press, 1982.

Miller, Jacques-Alain. "The Desire of Lacan and His Complex Relation to Freud." *Lacanian Ink* 14 (Spring 1999): 4–23.

———. "On the Semblance in the Relation Between the Sexes." *Sexuation*. Ed. Renata Salecl. Durham: Duke University Press, 2000. 13–27.

Mills, Judson. "The Appeal of Tragedy: An Attitude Interpretation." *Basic and Applied Social Psychology* 14.3 (1993): 255–271.

Mittman, Barbara G. *Spectators on the Paris Stage in the Seventeenth and Eighteenth Centuries*. Ann Arbor: UMI, 1983.

Moctezuma, Eduardo Matos. *Life and Death in the Templo Mayor*. Niwot: University Press of Colorado, 1995.

Moore, Rachel O. *Savage Theory: Cinema as Modern Magic*. Durham: Duke University Press, 2000.

Moore-Gilbert, Bart. *Postcolonial Theory: Contexts, Practices, Politics*. London: Verso, 1997.

Morgan, William, and Per Brask. "Towards a Conceptual Understanding of the Transformation from Ritual to Theatre." *Anthropologica* 30 (1988): 175–202.

Morris, Michael. "Of God and Man." *American Film* 14.1 (Oct. 1988): 44–50.

Morse, William R. "Desire and the Limits of Melodrama." *Melodrama*. Ed. James Redmond. Cambridge: Cambridge University Press, 1992. 17–30.

Moss, Stephen. "Movie Shots." *The Guardian* (London) 7 Oct. 1998: 4.

Mueller, Roswitha. *Bertolt Brecht and the Theory of Media*. Lincoln: University of Nebraska Press, 1989.

Mulvey, Laura. "Notes on Sirk and Melodrama." *Home is Where the Heart Is: Studies in Melodrama and the Woman's Film*. Ed. Christine Gledhill. London: British Film Institute, 1987. 75–79.

———. "Visual Pleasure and Narrative Cinema." *Narrative, Apparatus, Ideology: A Film Theory Reader*. Ed. Philip Rosen. New York: Columbia University Press, 1986. 198–209.

Murray, Janet Horowitz. *Hamlet on the Holodeck: The Future of Narrative in Cyberspace*. Cambridge: MIT Press, 1998.

Myerhoff, Barbara G. "A Death in Due Time: Construction of Self and Culture in Ritual Drama." *Rite, Drama, Festival, Spectacle: Rehearsals Toward a Theory of Cultural Performance*. Ed. John J. MacAloon. Philadelphia: Institue for the Study of Human Issues, 1984. 149–178.

Nagy, Gregory. "Transformations of Choral Lyric Traditions." *Arion* 3.1 (1995): 41–55.

Neumann, Erich. *The Great Mother*. Princeton: Princeton University Press, 1983.

Newman, Beth. "Narratives of Seduction and the Seduction of Narrative: The Frame Structure of *Frankenstein*." *English Literary History* 53.1 (1986): 141–163.

Nicoll, Allardyce. *Film and Theatre*. New York: Thomas Y. Cromwell, 1936.

Nietzsche, Friedrich. *The Birth of Tragedy and The Case of Wagner*. Trans. Walter Kaufmann. New York: Random, 1967.

———. *On the Genealogy of Morals*. Trans. Walter Kaufmann. New York: Random, 1967.

Noble, Louise. "'And make two pasties of your shameful heads': Medicinal Cannibalism and Healing the Body Politic in *Titus Andronicus*." *ELH* 70 (2003): 677–708.

Nussbaum, Martha C. *The Fragility of Goodness: Luck and Ethics in Greek Tragedy and Philosophy*. Cambridge: Cambridge University Press, 1986.

Odell, Carol F. "Sports and the Archetypal Hero." *Psyche and Sports*. Ed. Murray Stein and John Hollwitz. Wilmette, Illinois: Chiron Publications, 1994. 235–250.

Olivier, Guilhem. "The Hidden King and the Broken Flutes: Mythical and Royal Dimensions of the Feast of Tezcatlipoca in Toxcatl." *Representing Aztec Ritual*. Ed. Eloise Quiñones Keber. Boulder: University of Colorado Press, 2002. 107–142.

Ondaatje, Michael. *The Conversations: Walter Murch and the Art of Editing Film*. New York: Knopf, 2002.

Oriard, Michael. "Home Teams." *South Atlantic Quarterly* 95.2 (Spring 1996): 471–500.

Orona-Cordova, Roberta. "Zoot Suit and the Pachuco Phenomenon: An Interview with Luis Valdez." *Mexican American Theatre: Then and Now*. Ed. Nicolás Kanellos. Houston: Arte Público Press, 1983. 95–111.

Osborne, Carol. "Fashioning an Identity." *Popular Culture Review* 7.1 (1996): 97–109.

Otto, Walter F. *Dionysus: Myth and Cult*. Bloomington: Indiana University Press, 1965.

Oudart, Jean-Pierre. "Cinema and Suture." *Screen* 18.4 (1977–1978): 35–47.

Padden, R. C. *The Hummingbird and the Hawk*. New York: Harper, 1970.

Padel, Ruth. "Making Space Speak." *Nothing to Do with Dionysus?: Athenian Drama in Its Social Context.* Ed. John J. Winkler and Froma I. Zeitlin. Princeton: Princeton University Press, 1990. 337–365.

Papke, David Ray. "Myth and Meaning: Francis Ford Coppola and Popular Response to the *Godfather* Trilogy." *Legal Reelism.* Ed. John Denvir. Urbana: University of Chicago Press, 1996. 1–22.

Paris, Ginette. *Pagan Grace: Dionysos, Hermes, and Goddess Memory in Daily Life.* Dallas, Spring Publications, 1990.

Parker, Daniel, et al. "Making Frankenstein and the Monster." *Sight and Sound* 4.11 (Nov. 1994): 6–9.

Parker, Kim Ian. "Mirror, Mirror on the Wall, Must We Leave Eden, Once and For All? A Lacanian Pleasure Trip Through the Garden." *Journal for the Study of the Old Testament* 83 (1999): 19–29.

Peake, Richard Brinsley. *Presumption; or, The Fate of Frankenstein.* Forry 135–160.

Perez, Gilberto. *The Material Ghost: Films and Their Medium.* Baltimore: Johns Hopkins University Press, 1998.

Perlmutter, Dawn. "Postmodern Idolatry: The Media and Violent Acts of Participation." *Reclaiming the Spiritual in Art.* Ed. Dawn Perlmutter and Debra Koppman. Albany: State University of New York Press, 1999. 129–144.

Pinedo, Isabel Cristina. *Recreational Terror: Women and the Pleasures of Horror Film Viewing.* Albany: State University of New York Press, 1997.

Pizzato, Mark. *Edges of Loss: From Modern Drama to Postmodern Theory.* Ann Arbor: University of Michigan Press, 1998.

——— . "Edges of Perception in Performance and Audience." *Performing Arts International* 1.4 (1999): 47–58.

Plantinga, Carl, and Greg. M. Smith, eds. *Passionate Views: Film, Cognition, and Emotion.* Baltimore: Johns Hopkins University Press, 1999.

Plass, Paul. *The Game of Death in Ancient Rome: Arena Sport and Political Suicide.* Madison: University of Wisconsin Press, 1995.

Porter, James I. "The Invention of Dionysus and the Platonic Midwife." *Journal of the History of Philosophy* 33.3 (1995): 1967–1997.

Potter, Robert. "Abraham and Human Sacrifice: The Exfoliation of Medieval Drama in Aztec Mexico." *Fifteenth Century Studies* 13 (1988): 543–553.

Prince, Stephen. "The Aesthetic of Slow-Motion Violence in the Films of Sam Peckinpah." *Screening Violence.* Ed. Prince. New Brunswick: Rutgers University Press, 2000. 175–201.

——— . *Classical Film Violence.* New Brunswick: Rutgers University Press, 2003.

——— . "Graphic Violence in the Cinema: Origins, Aesthetic Design, and Social Effects." *Screening Violence.* Ed. Prince. New Brunswick: Rutgers University Press, 2000. 1–44.

————. "Psychoanalytic Film Theory and the Problem of the Missing Spectator." *Post-Theory: Reconstructing Film Studies*. Ed. David Bordwell and Noël Carroll. Madison: University of Wisconsin Press, 1996. 71–86.

————. *Savage Cinema: Sam Peckinpah and the Rise of Ultraviolent Movies*. Austin: University of Texas Press, 1998.

Puleo, Bruce. "Fear of Maternal Engulfment in Christianity and Other Religions." *Journal of Psychohistory* 22.4 (Spring 1995): 440–460.

Quinet, Antonio. "The Gaze as an Object." *Reading Seminar XI*. Ed. Richard Feldstein, Bruce Fink, and Maire Jaanus. Albany: State University of New York Press, 1995. 139–147.

Ragland, Ellie. *Essays on the Pleasures of Death*. New York: Routledge, 1995.

————. "The Relation Between the Voice and the Gaze." *Reading Seminar XI*. Ed. Richard Feldstein, Bruce Fink, and Maire Jaanus. Albany: State University of New York Press, 1995. 187–203.

Ragland-Sullivan, Ellie. *Jacques Lacan and the Philosophy of Psychoanalysis*. Urbana: University of Illinois Press, 1986.

Ramírez, Elizabeth. "Chicano Theatre Reaches the Professional Stage: Luis Valdez's *Zoot Suit*." *Teaching American Ethnic Literatures*. Ed. John R. Maitino and David R. Peck. Albuquerque: University of New Mexico Press, 1996. 193–207.

Ramos, Dante. "Screening Violence." *The Times-Picayune* 6 Aug. 1996: A1.

Ravicz, Marilyn Ekdahl. *Early Colonial Religious Drama in Mexico: From Tzompantli to Golgotha*. Washington, D.C.: Catholic University of America Press, 1970.

Read, Kay. "Sacred Commoners: The Motion of Cosmic Powers in Mexica Rulership." *History of Religions* 34.1 (Aug. 1994): 39–69.

————. "Sun and Earth Rulers: What the Eyes Cannot See in Mesoamerica." *History of Religions* 34.4 (May 1995): 351–384.

————. *Time and Sacrifice in the Aztec Cosmos*. Bloomington: Indiana University Press, 1998.

Regnault, François. "The Name-of-the-Father." *Reading Seminar XI*. Ed. Richard Feldstein, Bruce Fink, and Maire Jaanus. Albany: State University of New York Press, 1995. 65–74.

Reichbart, Richard. "Heart Symbolism: The Heart-Breast and Heart-Penis Equation." *Psychoanalytic Review* 68.1 (1981): 75–104.

Reynolds, Bryan. "Untimely Ripped." *Social Semiotics* 7.2 (1997): 201–218.

Rinehart, Robert E. *Players All: Performances in Contemporary Sport*. Bloomington: Indiana University Press, 1998.

Roach, Joseph. *Cities of the Dead: Circum-Atlantic Performance*. New York: Columbia University Press, 1996.

Robicsek, Francis, and Donald Hales. "Maya Heart Sacrifice: Cultural Perspective and Surgical Technique." *Ritual Human Sacrifice in Mesoamerica*. Ed. Elizabeth H.

Boone. Washington, D.C.: Dumbarton Oaks Research Library and Collection, 1984. 49–90.

Rockett, Will H. *Devouring Whirlwind: Terror and Transcendence in the Cinema of Cruelty.* New York: Greenwood Press, 1988.

Rooney, John F., Jr., and Audrey B. Davidson. "Football." *The Theater of Sport.* Ed. Karl B. Raitz. Baltimore: Johns Hopkins University Press, 1995. 208–230.

Rose, Ava, and James Friedman. "Television Sports as Mas(s)culine Cult of Distraction." *Out of Bounds: Sports, Media, and the Politics of Identity.* Ed. Aaron Baker and Todd Boyd. Bloomington: Indiana University Press, 1997. 1–15.

Rostas, Susanna. "From Ritualization to Performativity: the Concheros of Mexico." *Ritual, Performance, Media.* Ed. Felicia Hughes-Freeland. London: Routledge, 1998. 85–103.

Rozik, Eli. *The Roots of Theatre.* Iowa City: University of Iowa Press, 2002.

Rundin, John. "A Politics of Eating: Feasting in Early Greek Society." *American Journal of Philology* 117.2 (1996): 179–215.

Russell, Gordon W. "Psychological Issues in Sports Aggression." *Sports Violence.* Ed. Jeffrey H. Goldstein. New York: Springer, 1983. 157–181.

———. "Violent Sports Entertainment and the Promise of Catharsis." *Medienpsychologie* 5.2 (1993): 101–105.

Sabo, Donald F., and Joe Panepinto. "Football Ritual and the Social Reproduction of Masculinity." *Sport, Men, and the Gender Order: Critical Feminist Perspectives.* Ed. Michael A. Messner and Donald F. Sabo. Champaign, Ill.: Human Kinetics Books, 1990. 115–126.

Sagan, Eli. *Cannibalism: Human Aggression and Cultural Form.* New York: Harper, 1974.

———. *The Honey and the Hemlock: Democracy and Paranoia in Ancient Athens and Modern America.* New York: Harper, 1991.

Sahagún, Bernardino de. *Florentine Codex: General History of the Things of New Spain.* Book 2. *The Ceremonies.* Trans. Arthur J. O. Anderson and Charles E. Dibble. Sante Fe: School of American Research, 1951.

Salewicz, Chris. *Oliver Stone.* London: Orion, 1997.

Salkever, Stephen G. "Tragedy and the Education of the *Demos:* Aristotle's Response to Plato." *Greek Tragedy and Political Theory.* Ed. J. Peter Euben. Berkeley: University of California Press, 1986. 274–303.

Salvian. *On the Government of God.* Trans. Eva M. Sanford. New York: Octagon Books, 1966.

Sanchez-Tranquilino, Marcos, and John Tagg. "The Pachuco's Flayed Hide: Mobility, Identity, and *Buenas Garras.*" *Cultural Studies.* Ed. Lawrence Grossberger, Cary Nelson, and Paula A. Treichler. New York: Routledge, 1992. 556–570.

Sanday, Peggy Reeves. *Divine Hunger: Cannibalism as a Cultural System.* Cambridge: Cambridge University Press, 1986.

San Filippo, Maria. "Reflections on Coppola, Director's Cuts, and *Apocalypse Now Redux*." *Senses of Cinema* 16 (Sept.–Oct. 2001): n. pag. Online.

Santley, Robert S., Michael J. Berman, and Rani T. Alexander. "The Politicization of the Mesoamerican Ballgame and Its Implications for the Interpretation of the Distribution of Ballcourts in Central Mexico." Scarborough and Wilcox 3–24.

Savran, David. *Breaking the Rules: The Wooster Group*. New York: Theatre Communications Group, 1988.

———. *In Their Own Words: Contemporary American Playwrights*. New York: Theatre Communications Group, 1988.

Scarborough, Vernon L., and David R. Wilcox, eds. *The Mesoamerican Ballgame*. Tucson: University of Arizona Press, 1991.

Schechner, Richard. *Performance Theory*. New York: Routledge, 1988.

Scheff, Thomas J. *Catharsis in Healing, Ritual, and Drama*. Berkeley: University of California Press, 1979.

———. *Emotions, The Social Bond, and Human Reality: Part/Whole Analysis*. Cambridge: Cambridge University Press, 1997.

Scholder, Amy, and Eric Zimmerman, eds. *Re: Play*. New York: Peter Lang, 2003.

Schrader, Paul. Interview. *American Film* 14.9 (July/Aug. 1989): 16–21.

Schumacher, Michael. *Francis Ford Coppola: A Filmmaker's Life*. New York: Crown, 1999.

Schwartz, Vanessa R. "Cinematic Spectatorship before the Apparatus: The Public Taste for Reality in Fin-de-Siècle Paris." Williams, *Viewing Positions* 87–113.

Schweitzer, Karla, Dolf Zillmann, James B. Weaver, and Elizabeth S. Luttrell. "Perception of Threatening Events in the Emotional Aftermath of a Televised College Football Game." *Journal of Broadcasting and Electronic Media* 36 (Winter 1992): 75–82.

Scolnicov, Hana. *Woman's Theatrical Space*. Cambridge: Cambridge University Press, 1994.

Scorsese, Martin, dir. *GoodFellas*. Warner Brothers, 1990.

———. "In the Streets." *Once a Catholic*. Ed. Peter Occhiogrosso. Boston: Houghten, 1987. 88–101.

———, dir. *The Last Temptation of Christ*. Universal, 1988.

———. *Martin Scorsese: Interviews*. Ed. Peter Brunette. Jackson: University of Mississippi Press, 1999.

———, dir. *Mean Streets*. Warner Brothers, 1973.

———, dir. *Raging Bull*. United Artists, 1980.

———. *Scorsese on Scorsese*. Ed. David Thompson and Ian Christie. London: Faber, 1989.

———, dir. *Taxi Driver*. Columbia Pictures, 1976.

Scott, Peter Dale. "Mary Wollstonecraft Godwin Shelley and *Frankenstein:* A Chronology." *The Endurance of* Frankenstein: *Essays on Mary Shelley's Novel.* Ed. George Levine and U. C. Knoepflmacher. Berkeley: University of California Press, 1979. xvii–xx.

Seaford, Richard. *Reciprocity and Ritual: Homer and Tragedy in the Developing City-State.* Oxford: Clarendon, 1994.

Seneca, Lucius Annaeus. *Thyestes.* Trans. Caryl Churchill. London: Nick Hern, 1995.

Shaffer, Peter. *Amadeus.* New York: Harper, 1981.

Sharrett, Christopher. "The American Apocalypse: Scorsese's *Taxi Driver.*" *Crisis Cinema.* Ed. Sharrett. Washington: Maisonneuve Press, 1993. 221–236.

Shelley, Mary. *Frankenstein Or, The Modern Prometheus.* 1831. New York: NAL-Penguin, 1965.

Shnayerson, Michael. "Natural Born Opponents." *Vanity Fair* July 1996: 100+.

Silet, Charles L. P., ed. *Oliver Stone Interviews.* Jackson: University Press of Mississippi, 2001.

Silk, M. S. and J. P. Stern. *Nietzsche on Tragedy.* Cambridge: Cambridge University Press, 1988.

Silverman, Kaja. *The Subject of Semiotics.* New York: Oxford University Press, 1983.

Simon, Richard Keller. *Trash Culture: Popular Culture and the Great Tradition.* Berkeley: University of California Press, 1999.

Simon, William. "An Analysis of the Structure of *The Godfather, Part One.*" *Studies in the Literary Imagination* 16.1 (1983): 75–89.

Simons, Yaron, and Jim Taylor. "A Psychosocial Model of Fan Violence in Sports." *International Journal of Sport Psychology* 23 (1992): 207–226.

Simpson, Philip L. "The Politics of Apocalypse in the Cinema of Serial Murder." *Mythologies of Violence in Postmodern Media.* Ed. Christopher Sharrett. Detroit: Wayne State University Press, 1999. 119–44.

Singer, Ben. *Melodrama and Modernity: Early Sensational Cinema and Its Contexts.* New York: Columbia University Press, 2001.

Skocpol, Theda, and Margaret Somers. "The Uses of Comparative History in Macrosocial Inquiry." *Comparative Studies in Society and History* 22 (1980): 174–197.

Slocum, J. David. Introduction. *Violence and American Cinema.* Ed. Slocum. New York: Routledge, 2001. 1–34.

Slotkin, Richard. *Gunfighter Nation: The Myth of the Frontier in Twentieth-Century America.* New York: Atheneum, 1992.

Smith, Murray. "Gangsters, Cannibals, Aesthetes, or Apparently Perverse Allegiances." Plantinga and Smith 217–238.

———. "The Logic and Legacy of Brechtianism." *Post-Theory: Reconstructing Film Studies.* Ed. David Bordwell and Noël Carroll. Madison: University of Wisconsin Press, 1996. 130–148.

Sophocles. *The Oedipus Cycle*, trans. Dudley Fitts and Robert Fitzgerald (New York: Harcourt, 1969), 1–78.

Sor Juana Inés de la Cruz. *The Divine Narcissus/El Divino Narciso*. Trans. Patricia A. Peters and Renée Domeier. Albuquerque: University of New Mexico Press, 1998.

Soule, Lesley Wade. *Actor as Anti-Character: Dionysus, the Devil, and the Boy Rosalind*. Westport, Conn.: Greenwood Press, 2000.

Stacey, Jackie. "Feminine Fascinations: Forms of Identification in Star-Audience Relations." *Stardom: Industry of Desire*. Ed. Christine Gledhill. London: Routledge, 1991. 141–165.

Staiger, Janet. *Interpreting Films*. Princeton: Princeton University Press, 1992.

Stam, Robert. *Film Theory: An Introduction*. New York: Blackwell, 2000.

———. *Reflexivity in Film and Literature: From Don Quixote to Jean-Luc Godard*. New York: Columbia University Press, 1992.

Stam, Robert, Robert Burgoyne, and Sandy Flitterman-Lewis. *New Vocabularies in Film Semiotics*. New York: Routledge, 1992.

Stanley, Stephanie A. "Filmmaker Cleared in Shooting Trial." *The Times-Picayune* 13 Mar. 2001: 1.

Steiner, George. *The Death of Tragedy*. New York: Knopf, 1961.

Stone, Oliver, dir. *Any Given Sunday*. Warner Brothers, 1999.

———, dir. *Natural Born Killers*. Warner Brothers, 1994.

———. "On Seven Films." *Oliver Stone's USA: Film, History, and Controversy*. Ed. Robert Brent Toplin. Lawrence: University Press of Kansas, 2000. 219–248.

Storm, William. *After Dionysus: A Theory of the Tragic*. Ithaca: Cornell University Press, 1998.

Studlar, Gaylyn. *In the Realm of Pleasure: Von Sternberg, Dietrich, and the Masochistic Aesthetic*. Chicago: University of Illinois Press, 1988.

Tan, Ed S. H., and Nico H. Frijda. "Sentiment in Film Viewing." Plantinga and Smith 48–64.

Tarantino, Quentin. *Natural Born Killers*. London: Faber, 1995.

Tatar, Maria. "'Violent Delights' in Children's Literature." *Why We Watch: The Attractions of Violent Entertainment*. Ed. Jeffrey Goldstein. Oxford: Oxford University Press, 1998. 69–87.

Tatum, Jack, and Bill Kushner. *Final Confessions of NFL Assassin Jack Tatum*. Coal Valley, Ill.: Quality Sports Publications, 1996.

Taube, Karl. *Aztec and Maya Myths*. Austin: University of Texas Press, 1993.

Taubin, Amy. *Taxi Driver*. London: British Film Institute, 2000.

Tertullian. *Apology*. Trans. T. R. Glover. Cambridge: Harvard University Press, 1931.

Theweleit, Klaus. "100 Years of the Dream Book, 100 Years of Psychoanalysis." Interpretations of Dreams/Dreams of Interpretation. Humanities Institute, University of Minnesota, Twin Cities. Radisson Metrodome Hotel, Minneapolis. 8 Oct. 2000.

Todorov, Tzvetan. *The Conquest of America: The Question of the Other*. Trans. Richard Howard. New York: Harper, 1984.

Tomasulo, Frank P. "The Politics of Ambivalence: *Apocalypse Now* as Prowar and Antiwar Film." *From Hanoi to Hollywood*. Ed. Linda Dittmar and Gene Michaud. New Brunswick: Rutgers University Press, 1990. 145–158.

———. "Raging Bully: Postmodern Violence and Masculinity in *Raging Bull*." *Mythologies of Violence in Postmodern Media*. Ed. Christopher Sharrett. Detroit: Wayne State University Press, 1999. 175–197.

Turner, Victor. *From Ritual to Theatre: The Human Seriousness of Play*. New York: PAJ Publications, 1982.

Tyler, Bruce. "Zoot-Suit Culture and the Black Press." *Journal of American Culture* 17.2 (1994): 21–33.

Valdez, Luis. *Luis Valdez—Early Works*. Houston: Arte Público Press, 1990.

———. *Zoot Suit and Other Plays*. Houston: Arte Público Press, 1992.

———, dir. *Zoot Suit*. Universal, 1981.

Versényi, Adam. *Theatre in Latin America: Religion, Politics, and Culture from Cortés to the 1980s*. Cambridge: Cambridge University Press, 1993.

Vince, Ronald W. *Ancient and Medieval Theatre: A Historiographical Handbook*. Westport, Conn.: Greenwood Press, 1984.

———. "The Ritual and Performative Basis of Greek Combat Sport and Hoplite Warfare." *Theatre Annual* 50 (1997): 72–82.

Volkan, Vamik D. *The Need to Have Enemies and Allies*. North Vale, N.J.: Jacob Aronson, 1988.

"Voluntary or Not, Is it Censorship?" *National Journal* 29.29 (19 July 1997): 1490.

Walsh, Michael. "Returns of the Real: Lacan and the Future of Psychoanalysis in Film Studies." *Post Script* 14.1–2 (1994–1995): 22–32.

Weatherill, Rob. *Sovereignty of Death*. London: Rebus, 1998.

Weiner, Albert. "The Function of the Tragic Greek Chorus." *Theatre Journal* 32.2 (May 1980): 205–212.

Welch, Michael. "Violence Against Women by Professional Football Players: A Gender Analysis of Hypermasculinity, Positional Status, Narcissism, and Entitlement." *Journal of Sport & Social Issues* 21.4 (Nov. 1997): 392–411.

Welcos, Robert W. "Judge Throws Out Lawsuit Against Oliver Stone." *Los Angeles Times* 13 Mar. 2001: C7.

Wells, David. "Tragedy, Catharsis and Creativity: From Aristotle to Freud to Winnicott." *Free Associations* 9.3 (2002): 463–478.

Whale, James, dir. *The Bride of Frankenstein*. Universal, 1935.

———. *Frankenstein*. Universal, 1931.

Whannel, Garry. *Fields of Vision: Television Sport and Cultural Transformation*. London: Routledge, 1992.

Whitfield, Charles L. *Memory and Abuse: Remembering and Healing the Effects of Trauma.* Deerfield Beach, Fla.: Health Communications, 1995.

Whitmer, Barbara. *The Violence Mythos.* Albany: State University of New York Press, 1987.

Wieczorek, Marek. "The Ridiculous, Sublime Art of Slavoj Žižek." Introduction to Žižek's *The Art of the Ridiculous Sublime: On David Lynch's* Lost Highway. Seattle: University of Washington Press, 2000. Viii–xiii.

Wiles, David. *The Masks of Menander: Sign and Meaning in Greek and Roman Performance.* Cambridge: Cambridge University Press, 1991.

———. *Tragedy in Athens: Performance Space and Theatrical Meaning.* Cambridge: Cambridge University Press, 1997.

Wilkerson, S. Jeffrey K. "And Then They Were Sacrificed: The Ritual Ballgame of Northeastern Mesoamerica Through Time and Space." Scarborough and Wilcox 45–72.

———. "In Search of the Mountain of Foam: Human Sacrifice in Eastern Mesoamerica." *Ritual Human Sacrifice in Mesoamerica.* Ed. Elizabeth H. Boone. Washington, D.C.: Dumbarton Oaks Research Library and Collection, 1984. 101–132.

Williams, Linda. "Film Bodies: Gender, Genre, and Excess." *Film Genre Reader II.* Ed. Barry Keith Grant. Austin: University of Texas Press, 1995. 140–158.

———. "Melodrama Revised." *Refiguring American Film Genres: History and Theory.* Ed. Nick Browne. Berkeley: University of California Press, 1998. 42–88.

———. *Playing the Race Card: Melodramas of Black and White From Uncle Tom to O.J. Simpson.* Princeton: Princeton University Press, 2001.

———, ed. *Viewing Positions: Ways of Seeing Film.* New Brunswick: Rutgers University Press, 1994.

Winkler, John J. "The Ephebes' Song: *Tragoidia* and *Polis.*" *Nothing to Do with Dionysos?: Athenian Drama in Its Social Context.* Ed. John J. Winkler and Froma I. Zeitlin. Princeton: Princeton University Press, 1990. 20–62.

Winnicott, D. W. *Playing and Reality.* London: Routledge, 1990.

Wise, Jennifer. *Dionysus Writes: The Invention of Theatre in Ancient Greece.* Ithaca: Cornell, University Press, 1998.

Wistrand, Magnus. *Entertainment and Violence in Ancient Rome.* Göteborg: University of Göteborg Press, 1992.

Worthen, W. B. "Staging América: The Subject of History in Chicano/a Theatre." *Theatre Journal* 49.2 (May 1997): 101–120.

Yarbro-Bejarano, Yvonne. "The Female Subject in Chicano Theatre: Sexuality, 'Race,' and Class." *Performing Feminisms: Feminist Critical Theory and Theatre.* Ed. Sue-Ellen Case. Baltimore: Johns Hopkins University Press, 1990. 131–149.

Zakharieva, Bouriana. "Frankenstein of the Nineties: The Composite Body." *Canadian Review of Comparative Literature* 23.3 (Sept. 1996): 739–752.

Zillmann, Dolf. "The Psychology of the Appeal of Portrayals of Violence." *Why We Watch: The Attractions of Violent Entertainment*. Ed. Jeffrey Goldstein. Oxford: Oxford University Press, 1998. 179–211.

Žižek, Slavoj. *The Art of the Ridiculous Sublime: On David Lynch's* Lost Highway. Seattle: University of Washington Press, 2000.

———. "Cyberspace, or the Unbearable Closure of Being." *Endless Night: Cinema and Psychoanalysis, Parallel Histories*. Ed. Janet Bergstrom. Berkeley: University of California Press, 1999. 96–125.

———. *Enjoy Your Symptom!: Jacques Lacan in Hollywood and Out*. New York: Routledge, 1992.

———. *For They Know Not What They Do: Enjoyment as a Political Factor*. London: Verso, 1991.

———. *The Fragile Absolute—or, Why is the Christian legacy worth fighting for?* London: Verso, 2000.

———. *On Belief*. London: Routledge, 2001.

———. *The Plague of Fantasies*. London: Verso, 1997.

———. "The Thing from Inner Space." *Sexuation*. Ed. Renata Salecl. Durham: Duke University Press, 2000. 216–259.

———. *The Sublime Object of Ideology*. London: Verso, 1989.

Zupančič, Alenka. *Ethics of the Real: Kant, Lacan*. London: Verso, 2000.

Index

253